THE
FOIE GRAS WARS

HOW A 5,000-YEAR-OLD DELICACY INSPIRED
THE WORLD'S FIERCEST FOOD FIGHT

MARK CARO

Simon & Schuster
New York   London   Toronto   Sydney

Simon & Schuster
1230 Avenue of the Americas
New York, NY 10020

First Simon & Schuster hardcover edition March 2009

SIMON & SCHUSTER and colophon are registered trademarks
of Simon & Schuster, Inc.

For information about special discounts for bulk purchases,
please contact Simon & Schuster Special Sales at
1-800-456-6798 or business@simonandschuster.com.

The Simon & Schuster Speakers Bureau can bring authors to
your live event. For more information or to book an event contact
the Simon & Schuster Speakers Bureau at 866-248-3049
or visit our website at www.simonspeakers.com.

Designed by C. Linda Dingler

Manufactured in the United States of America

10 9 8 7 6 5 4 3 2 1

Library of Congress Cataloging-in-Publication Data

Caro, Mark.
The foie gras wars : how a 5,000-year-old delicacy inspired the world's fiercest food
fight / Mark Caro.
  p. cm.
Includes bibliographical references and index.
1. Foie gras. 2. Food preferences. 3. Food of animal origin. I. Title.
TX750.C27 2009
641.6'92—dc22   2008032077

ISBN-13: 978-1-4165-5668-8
ISBN-10:   1-4165-5668-0

For Mary, Ruthie, and Maddie

CONTENTS

THE FOIE GRAS WARS

1.

The Shot Heard Round the Culinary World

"Maybe we ought to have Rick's liver for a little treat. It's certainly fat enough."

Charlie Trotter is notoriously prickly, but even for him, threatening to eat a rival chef's liver was a bit much. True, Rick Tramonto had called him "a little hypocritical," yet there are some things that four-star chefs just don't do. They don't trash one another's cooking publicly. They don't gloat upon winning *Iron Chef*. And they don't suggest snacking upon one another's possibly fatty internal organs.

What happens when you cross this line? In Trotter's case you trigger an often-surreal chain reaction that leads to actress Loretta "Hot Lips" Swit taking to the Chicago City Council floor to compare the treatment of force-fed birds to that of Iraqi war prisoners at Abu Ghraib. You see yourself excoriated by internationally renowned chefs who are your peers—and celebrated by animal-rights activists whom you consider to be "idiots." You look on as you're credited with placing a 5,000-year-old delicacy in the city's crosshairs, even as the fatty livers of force-fed ducks suddenly are showing up on pizzas, hot dogs and soul food. Now that you've shot your mouth off, people who'd never heard of foie gras are making special trips to chow down on the stuff. Meanwhile, Roger "007" Moore is solemnly narrating over grisly footage of a rat burrowing up an enfeebled duck's bloody butt.

1

What the hell.

Well, Charlie Trotter didn't become Chicago's most celebrated chef with an international reputation and a national TV show (PBS's *The Kitchen Sessions with Charlie Trotter*) by following convention—or being nice. When his elegant, self-named restaurant opened in 1987 in a converted townhouse in upscale Lincoln Park, it almost instantly was hailed as a flag bearer in a national haute cuisine revolution. Charlie Trotter's discarded heavy sauces and "classic" preparations in favor of more spontaneous, surprising combinations of bold, clean flavors and textures that emphasized the purity and freshness of an exotic array of ingredients. The young chef's approach was exacting, his results stunning. Each bite would offer a different taste experience depending on where the fork traveled on the plate. Each day the menu would change—he claimed never to repeat the same dish twice. Trotter didn't try to polish a dish into fixed perfection the way the French Laundry's Thomas Keller would. He saw himself more like a jazz musician, a John Coltrane of the food world, and you had to be there to catch the magic of his improvisations.

That he was hell on his staff just came with the package. He was a brilliant artist, after all, and brilliant artists are difficult. When he speaks, most of his rectangular face doesn't move; it's as if all of his energy is concentrated into his piercing, deep-set eyes and tart tongue. When Trotter is in a room, there's no question of who's giving the orders. He preaches excellence, excellence, excellence until his underlings want to plug their ears with their spatulas. He's been known to give cooks reading assignments (Ayn Rand, for instance) and spontaneously to screen movies that end an hour before service, thus sending the kitchen into a mad scramble. In his early days especially, he has yelled, smashed plates and fostered an atmosphere of constant anxiety. He has eviscerated aspiring chefs for the tiniest of infractions and jettisoned them to the sidewalk if they resisted buying into his program of constant, complete commitment. For a while Trotter instructed his wait staff to wear double-sided tape on their shoe soles so they could de-lint the new carpet as they delivered the food. If a guest complimented a server's tie, former employees recalled, Trotter required the server to place it into a box and offer it as a gift—even though Trotter might reimburse the server only a fraction of the tie's actual cost. When *Chicago* magazine listed the city's 10 meanest people in 1996, Trotter placed second, after Michael Jordan, and he characteristically complained publicly about not being number 1. Trotter frequently cites his sense of humor without cracking a smile. In the 1997 Julia Roberts romantic comedy *My Best Friend's Wedding*, he barks at a cook: "I will kill your whole family if you don't get this right! I need this perfect!" Trotter alumni often say they appreciated what he taught them—and they'd never, ever choose to relive the experience.

If animals knew such things, they might have feared Trotter as well. He serves up just about anything that once drew breath. Although he also was ahead of the curve in offering a vegetarian tasting menu, his restaurant became known for exquisite preparations of specialty meats such as antelope, bison, rabbit loin, pork belly, pig shoulder, wild boar, duck gizzards, chicken "oysters," grouse, squab, partridge, pheasant, oxtail, venison, beef cheeks and veal heart, brains, sweetbreads and tongue. "Raising a goat or a calf or a chicken or anything, to raise it and kill it and eat it—I'm all into that," he told me. "That's life."

Of his great array of specialty animal products, Trotter showed the most enthusiasm and verve for foie gras (pronounced "fwah grah"), the fatty liver of a force-fed goose or—in almost all cases in the United States—duck. This delicate delectable has long been a staple of French cuisine, but Trotter applied it to his distinctly American brand of cooking. One night he would sear a slice and layer it with soy-dressed tuna, preserved ginger slices and fried carrot threads atop a bed of puréed parsnip. On another he would extract the foie gras essence to accompany sweet halibut and a red-wine-and-wild-mushroom sauce. If he really wanted to impress someone, he would roast a foie gras lobe whole and slice it tableside. The chef's affinity for this pricey product led *Chicago Tribune* food writer William Rice to refer to Charlie Trotter's as a "foie gras and truffle emporium" in a 1998 story that also reported that *Wine Spectator* readers had named Trotter's "the best restaurant in the world for wine and food" for the second straight year. Charlie Trotter's was going through more foie gras than any restaurant in the area—50 to 60 lobes a week from Hudson Valley Foie Gras and sometimes additional ones from

Sonoma Foie Gras. Hudson Valley co-founder Michael Ginor said Trotter's was among his top 10 customers.

Nowhere was Trotter's foie gras passion more apparent than his 2001 cookbook, *Charlie Trotter's Meat & Game*. In one photo that spans two glossy, oversized pages, Trotter is seen crouching on the barn floor of a Canadian foie gras farm amid a cluster of fuzzy yellow ducklings that will grow up to donate their unnaturally enlarged livers to the cause of sublime dining. Another full-page photo depicts the compact Trotter in a white lab jacket standing stoically under the hanging shackles that, when in use, carry the ducks by their feet around the slaughter room. The book also offers 14 foie gras recipes, including Seared Foie Gras; Cured Foie Gras; Foie Gras Terrine; Foie Gras Custard; Foie Gras Ice Cream; Foie Gras Beignet; Bleeding Heart Radish Terrine with Star Anise and Thyme-Flavored Foie Gras and Seckel Pear; Sweet-and-Sour Braised Lettuce Soup with Foie Gras and Radishes; and Roasted Chestnut Soup with Foie Gras, Cipolline Onions and Ginger.

The influence of Charlie Trotter's was felt far and wide. Just as Alice Waters's Chez Panisse in Berkeley spawned countless restaurants that emphasized greens and meats with local/organic origins, Trotter's provided the template for a wave of high-end eateries, many helmed by graduates of his kitchen, that combined an affinity for natural, small-farm products with robust flavor combinations meant to tantalize your palate without weighing down your stomach. With Trotter and some like-minded colleagues spreading the foie gras gospel—all while Hudson Valley's Ginor aggressively marketed his product to chefs nationwide—the dish's popularity soared. By the early 2000s, it wasn't unusual to find seared foie gras, often with a fruit garnish, on the menu of your everyday upscale restaurant.

Yet sometime after he'd posed with those cute little duckies, Trotter underwent a dramatic conversion. In 2002, with his *Meat & Game* book relatively fresh on the shelves, Trotter quit serving foie gras. He didn't make an announcement. He issued no press release. The product just ceased showing up on the restaurant's ever-rotating tasting menus. Few patrons noticed or complained. A year passed, then another. Finally, in early 2005, Trotter mentioned his personal foie gras ban to *Chicago Tribune* restaurant critic Phil Vettel, who happened to be working on what would prove to be a particularly loaded article: a head-to-head comparison between Trotter's and Tru, Rick Tramonto and Gale Gand's younger competitor for Chicago's top dining dollar.

This was where I came in.

Knowing of my interest in the food scene (despite my primary job as *Tribune* entertainment reporter), Vettel mentioned Trotter's revelation to me and suggested I write a story. Why not? I liked foie gras. I didn't like cruelty to animals. This could be interesting.

I phoned Trotter, who told me he'd simply seen enough of how foie gras was produced. "I've had the chance to visit three different farms, and the circumstances are less than pleasant," he said in his raspy rat-a-tat. "I just felt that we don't really need to do this. We don't need to serve this product." The problem wasn't just what he saw at these particular farms, which he refused to name. The problem was inherent in foie gras production anywhere. "It's the same thing all over the world. This is the process. This is how it's done. We have these romantic visions of 50, 70 years ago when a single large and fatted goose would be in a box and a person would kind of hold the neck up and caress the animal and hold the food up and let them eat as much as they wanted, and subsequently they'd have an enlarged, engorged liver, and it would be delightful when the animal was slaughtered. But we don't do it that way now. It's done in a mass-produced farming style where literally there's tubes being jammed down their throats. We have cases of ripped esophaguses, chipped and broken beaks and ripped feet. Here's an animal that's just being pumped up as quickly as possible. If they were just eating as much as they could eat and that happened, that would be one thing. But when you're jamming something down their throat and they're clearly suffering . . ." His voice trailed off.

The rub with foie gras is that the qualities that people find irresistible are inescapably linked to the way it is produced. Unlike conventional duck, goose, chicken or calf's liver, foie gras is velvety and rich, like a mild, gamey flan. Eat it seared, and the crispy surface contrasts seductively with the melt-in-your-mouth interior, the flavor pronounced but not harsh, as if all of the edges have been rounded off. Eat it cold in a traditional French preparation such as a whole liver prepared in a terrine (a covered dish) or torchon (a rolled towel), and it's like butter you can enjoy in large savory hunks. (A foie gras pâté, which might also be prepared in a terrine, is typically mixed with ingredients such as meats or fat.) The decadent silky texture comes from the liver itself, which has grown full of fat. The dish is a guilty pleasure if only for the damage it might inflict upon your arteries. A foie gras liver balloons to six to 10 times the size of the organ in a normal duck or goose, and the reason it grows so fatty is a process known as *gavage*.

For hundreds of years, foie gras was made primarily from geese, but France has converted the bulk of its production to ducks, which are sturdier and easier to raise on a mass scale. North American foie gras production almost exclusively uses ducks in part because there's little appetite for goose in the United States, and the farms make their money selling whole birds, not just the livers. Gavage, a.k.a. force-feeding, generally begins when a duck is 12 weeks old, a goose often somewhat older. Having spent the previous several weeks free-ranging outdoors or hanging out in a relatively spacious barn, the bird is moved into a group pen (as on all three sizable U.S. foie gras farms) or a cramped individual cage (as on most Canadian and French farms for ducks) for the feedings. These involve a metal tube or pipe being lowered down the bird's throat two or three (or, with some geese, four) times daily over a period of two to four weeks. For about two to 10 seconds each time, the feeder delivers a corn-based meal down the bird's esophagus either by way of a funnel and gravity or via a pneumatic or hydraulic machine. The gullet fills up with food, and the bird digests it before the next feeding. The process is said to mimic—and exaggerate—the way birds gorge themselves before taking migratory flight, even if the made-for-foie-gras duck hybrid doesn't migrate. When the liver has approached its maximum size—and the bird's digestive system can no longer process such large quantities of food—it's slaughter time.

To foie gras farmers, the process is nothing more than standard agricultural practice, certainly no worse than how chickens, cows and pigs are routinely treated on conventional farms—and on a far smaller scale. To animal-rights activists, it amounts to torture. Despite declaring himself to be "the furthest thing in the world from that sort of left-leaning activist," Trotter was making the latter argument.

Among his fellow top Chicago-area chefs, however, he held the minority opinion. Roland Liccioni, then chef of the venerated French outpost Le Français, complained that Americans are ignorant of farm life, but he had grown up in southwestern France, the traditional home of foie gras, and found nothing wrong with the process. "The liver gets bigger, but he doesn't suffer," he said, adding that if foie gras becomes unavailable, "the customer will be the one to suffer." Jean Joho, chef of the city's four-star Alsatian restaurant Everest, said he had quit serving Chilean sea bass because it was overfished, but "I'm not banning the foie gras. I think it has to be used in moderation." Innovative young chef Grant Achatz, then preparing to open his new restaurant, Alinea (which *Gourmet* would name America's best in late 2006), said he also would continue to serve foie gras. "Can somebody say pulling a lobster out of the ocean and shipping it across the country not in water so it's slowly suffocating and then dropping it into a pot of boiling water is humane?" Still, Achatz, who briefly worked at Trotter's years earlier, had no problem with his former employer's decision. "He has a very visible stature, both in the gastronomic community and in public awareness, and he knows if he takes this stance, it's going to get a lot of press and maybe he can use his celebrity to make a statement. I respect that."

But Tramonto, himself a nationally recognized chef and cookbook author, was less approving of Trotter's position. Tru is a sleek haute cuisine destination that favors more of a greatest-hits approach than Trotter's constantly changing preparations—and it had become a chief competitor of Trotter's. The rivalry is anything but easygoing, especially given that Tramonto and his ex-wife and pastry chef Gale Gand had worked in Trotter's kitchen before striking out on their own in a less-than-amicable separation. In a deep-timbred voice made for talk radio, Tramonto told me that he too had quit serving Chilean sea bass as well as swordfish and beluga caviar so the species could replenish themselves, but foie gras just didn't seem like a problem. Given that Trotter continued to serve veal and other animals, Tramonto had no use for his former boss's new stance.

"It's a little hypocritical because animals are raised to be slaughtered and eaten every day," he said. "I think certain farms treat animals better than others. Either you eat animals or you don't eat animals. Either you believe in eating animals for sustenance or you don't."

When I repeated Tramonto's comments to Trotter, he paused momentarily, then matter-of-factly fired the shot heard round the culinary world:

"Rick Tramonto's not the smartest guy on the block. Yes, animals are raised to be slaughtered, but are they raised in a way where they need to suffer? To then be slaughtered for the pure enjoyment? He can't be that dumb, is he? You should quote me on that. What's up with that? It's like an idiot comment: 'All animals are raised to be slaughtered.' Oh, OK. Maybe we ought to have Rick's liver for a little treat. It's certainly fat enough."

I called back Tramonto to relay Trotter's response before it went into print. Tramonto laughed and asked what ol' Charlie had to say. I read him the quote.

Dead silence.

In a voice like ashes, Tramonto, a born-again Christian, responded: "I got no comment to that. Charlie's in my prayers—that's what you can put for my comment."

This celebrity-chef smackdown was catnip not just for foodies but anyone who enjoys a colorful spectacle. The *Tribune*'s editors certainly sensed the clash's public appeal, running the story at the top of the front page on March 29, 2005, with the headline "Liver and Let Live" and subhead "Charlie Trotter now says force-feeding ducks to create foie gras is a cruel, bird-brained idea. Rick Tramonto says he is a hypocrite." (The article, which also recounted foie gras's long, controversial history, was withheld for almost a week due to the ongoing drama of the comatose Terri Schiavo. Some editors feared that readers might connect one feeding-tube story to the other and thus find the *Tribune* insensitive.) Placing a 60-inch article about fatty duck livers on page 1 was far from standard daily newspaper practice, but the editors guessed right and then some. The foie gras controversy exploded nationwide, in the media as well as around the proverbial water cooler.

Trotter drew much fire, more for his hostility toward Tramonto than his position on force-feeding. On the *New York Times* editorial page, Lawrence Downes was one of the few to spring to Trotter's defense, writing—with Timesian condescension—that the chef "should feel free to use whatever materials he likes. He says foie gras is cruel, but he could have just called it boring—a cliché slurped by too many diners who, we suspect, would swoon just as easily over the velvety succulence of Spam or schmaltz on rye, if they were prohibitively priced and listed on the menus in French." *Newsweek* repeated Trotter's liver-eating threat while noting that the chef "continues to serve every other kind of cuddly creature in creation." *Tribune* political columnist John Kass got four quick columns out of the controversy, ridiculing the chef as "Hannibal Trotter" in honor of the liver-and-fava-beans-eating cannibal of *The Silence of the Lambs*. The feud even received a faux hip-hop tribute from Barrett Buss on his foodie-oriented Too Many Chefs Web site ("Charlie Trotter says . . . 'Maybe we should serve some of your liver up as a snack since you so damn fat!' and Rick Tramonto's like 'I know you didn't just go there!'").

Fevered debate over the ethics of foie gras raged on food-related Web sites such as eGullet, and letters to the editor poured in to the *Tribune* and other publications. Some deemed Trotter a traitor to the gourmet food world. Others proclaimed him a hero for condemning a vile product. The *New York Post* cranked up the temperature further by reporting in its *Page Six* column that chefs gathered at *Food & Wine*'s annual Best New Chefs party were "buzzing" about a recent dinner where Trotter had served three courses of foie gras. "What a hypocrite!" one of the anonymous attendees carped in the column. "He talks the talk but can't walk the walk. What—he can't serve foie gras to the masses but will to his snooty friends?"

As often is the case, though, *Page Six* didn't get the full story. Trotter hadn't actually served foie gras; the event's menu was assembled and presented by two of the world's most acclaimed chefs, who were featured guests in Trotter's kitchen: Tetsuya Wakuda of Tetsuya's in Sydney and Heston Blumenthal of London's aptly named The Fat Duck. Tetsuya served a salad of langoustine with foie gras and eschalot tarragon vinaigrette. Blumenthal offered one dish featuring quail jelly, pea purée, cream of langoustine and parfait of foie gras and another highlighting roast foie gras with cherry, amaretto, chamomile and almond fluid gel. In allowing them to prepare dishes featuring foie gras, Trotter told me, he was just trying to be consistent in not imposing his personal preferences on other chefs. "Yeah, it was served," he said. "I didn't serve it. They wanted to have it represent what their cuisine was, and I said, 'Fine, you can do it.'"

Anthony Bourdain, the streetwise New-York-chef-turned-bestselling-author (*Kitchen Confidential*) and TV personality (Travel Channel's *No Reservations*), was at the *Food & Wine* soiree and told me afterward that Trotter's attacks on foie gras and Tramonto were "the talk of the party." That Trotter didn't actually prepare the foie gras at his restaurant's special dinner was, to Bourdain, "a hair-thin distinction," though he added, "I applaud him for choosing friendship over principle, especially this principle." Bourdain thought that Trotter's thorny personality helped fuel the angry backlash against him. "He's easy to pick on. He's a stuffy guy. He's not exactly famous for his sense of humor. There is an element of schoolyard pile-on in this case, vicarious enjoyment of his embarrassment."

But resentment of Trotter went deeper than personality issues. As the chefs saw it, the gasoline in this battle already had been poured, and Trotter, of all people, shouldn't have been the one striking a match. California chefs and Sonoma Foie Gras (the state's sole producer) had been contending with vandalism, threats and the likelihood of the product being legislated out of existence, and activists had been conducting an aggressive campaign against Los Angeles celebrity restaurateur and foie aficionado Wolfgang Puck. New York State, where the country's two other major foie gras farms are located, also was weighing a ban.

Back in Trotter's home state, representatives from Farm Sanctuary, one of the leading anti-foie forces, had been lobbying legislators to move against foie gras, and one of them bit. Illinois state senator Kathleen L. "Kay" Wojcik, a Republican from the mall-heavy Chicago suburb of Schaumburg, introduced the Force Fed Birds Act just weeks before Trotter's statements went public. The legislation initially was intended to ban the force-feeding of birds and the sale of resultant products, but restaurateurs quickly managed to have the bill watered down to apply only to the production of foie gras, not the sale. Of course, no foie gras was being produced in Illinois in the first place, but Wojcik said the activists had convinced her that

the state should never even *potentially* become host to such a horrific practice. Getting the Land of Lincoln to ban foie gras in any way
certainly would have been a feather in the cap of the animal-rights
advocates. Wojcik had never actually witnessed foie gras production
firsthand, but the Farm Sanctuary folks had shown her pictures and
video clips, and she didn't like what she saw. "I do fine dining and I
do pâtés, but we do the pâté where the duck is killed naturally or the
goose or whatever," she explained to me. "It's not being brutalized.
I just have compassion for animals." (Somewhere, a duck was keel-
ing over from a heart attack, then being shipped to Wojcik's house to
become pâté.)

Part of what made this conflict so compelling was that as you
watched Trotter's and Tramonto's arguments crash into each other
like high-speed trains on the same track, you still could reasonably
think: They're both right. If you're seeking a symbol of culinary decadence, it's hard to top the image of unnaturally obese ducks being
sacrificed so rich folks could spend $16 for delectable nibbles of the
fatty livers. At the same time, if you think animals suffer too greatly
in food production, why go after a tiny niche item such as foie gras?

The delicacy's producers were worried. Unlike beef, pork, chicken
and veal, foie gras didn't constitute a full-fledged U.S. industry, and
it lacked any corresponding legislative muscle. Tens of thousands of
U.S. farms were dedicated to broiler chickens and layer hens. Three
were producing foie gras on any scale. The foie gras farmers viewed
this disparity as the driving force behind the campaign against their
product—that and the fact that foie gras (a) has a funny French name,
(b) is enjoyed by the relatively affluent, (c) remains unknown to your
average Tyson chicken eater, (d) is *liver*, and (e) is made from ducks.
We like ducks. What politician would see any advantage in defending
a gross-sounding practice toward little quackers so that a minority
of rich gourmands could feast on their bloated livers? Sonoma Foie
Gras owner Guillermo Gonzalez argued that Trotter and his supporters were serving the purposes of "animalists" using foie gras as a
wedge issue. "They may not realize that they are being instrumental
in the ultimate agenda of the movement," Gonzalez said, "which is
to terminate the consumption of animals for food altogether." Farm
Sanctuary president/cofounder Gene Baur didn't completely deny the

point, acknowledging that foie gras *does* offer a fatter bull's-eye than the much larger meat industries. "The foie gras industry is smaller and does not have the resources of those other agribusiness industries, so change is likely to occur sooner," he told me.

True to his libertarian views, Trotter argued against any government action on foie gras, preferring the free market to take its course. (He also opposes laws against drugs and prostitution.) He declined to support Illinois's anti-foie-gras bill, and when Farm Sanctuary representatives requested that he sign a pledge not to serve the product, he turned them away. "How dumb could they be?" Trotter said. "Here's like the only major chef in the country that's basically not using the product. Why would I be a guy who would need to sign a pledge? Even if I wanted to. Which I wouldn't . . . These people are idiots. Understand my position: I have nothing to do with a group like that. I think they're pathetic. The best thing you can do in any case is just to try to educate people, and some of their tactics are pretty crude and uncivilized even."

But if Trotter didn't want foie gras to be outlawed, what did he want? Merely, he said, for chefs and consumers to know what he knew so they could draw their own conclusions, which presumably wouldn't stray far from his. "I'm not out there trying to preach. I'm not out there trying to tell other chefs and restaurateurs what they should and shouldn't do. I'm just telling you what I've seen, and it's not cool; it's not a good thing."

Yet behind Trotter's words lay a mystery: What did he see, and when did he see it? He wouldn't say, but others were determined to find out. "OK, who's the last person who saw Charlie Trotter on their farm?" Ariane Daguin, whose Newark-based company, D'Artagnan, is the country's biggest foie gras distributor, asked a gathering of domestic foie gras producers. "In fact," she told me, "only one person ever saw him on the farm, and that was Guillermo [Gonzalez], and it was in 1993." A former Trotter's chef confirmed to me that Trotter had visited Sonoma Foie Gras around then. Michael Ginor said Trotter had declined every invitation to see Hudson Valley Foie Gras despite its being Trotter's key supplier for years, as well as North America's largest foie gras farm. The photos in *Charlie Trotter's Meat & Game* were taken at one of three major Canadian foie gras farms.

So . . . if Trotter had visited Sonoma Foie Gras in the early 1990s, why wasn't he appalled back then instead of continuing to be one of foie gras's biggest boosters for almost another decade? What had changed between 1993 and 2002? And was he judging the American farms by the conditions at farms elsewhere?

When I initially spoke with Trotter, he refused to get into the specifics regarding his change of heart, but others were less shy about speculating. One of his former cooks theorized that in the 1990s Trotter was still trying to earn the respect of his haute cuisine peers and might have been considered "a wack job" if he'd trashed such a classic fixture of French cooking—but once Trotter had risen to almost iconic status, he had the liberty to take his stand. Ginor, who had known Trotter for years, saw the chef's public statements as cynical in intent and ill informed in regard to the ducks' treatment. (Trotter had contributed a recipe for Cumin-Crusted Foie Gras with Crispy Sweetbreads, Napa Cabbage, Ramps, Morels, and Red Wine Emulsion to Ginor's 1999 book *Foie Gras: A Passion*.) Calling Trotter "first and foremost a marketer, a really smart marketer," Ginor complained: "You would think if he visited the farm and felt that the ducks were being abused, he would not have included that in his book. But back then foie gras was fine. Now . . . there's this massive animal-rights activity against foie gras, and he's smart enough to recognize that that is where the wind is blowing, and that's something he ought to endorse."

Trotter retorted that if he had intended on promoting his position, he would have announced it back when he initially quit serving foie gras. As for this issue of why he made his decision when he made it, Trotter finally told me that his *Meat & Game* book already was in production when he visited another foie gras farm and the balance tipped. "This was my fourth farm, and I thought: This isn't happening. I can't support this personally." Trotter still wouldn't say which farm he'd visited, but he did confirm that it was one that kept the ducks in the tiny individual cages, which means he most likely was in Canada or France.

Some thought Trotter was having his liver and eating it too, which he literally had done, as he admitted to having sampled foie gras when it was served to him elsewhere even after his restaurant's ban. Bourdain, who calls foie gras one of the world's 10 great flavors, argued that although Trotter might not see himself as an advocate, he nonetheless was a highly influential chef giving "comfort and succor to the forces of evil . . . Deep inside, most of us believe that the people who agree with Charlie and PETA will win the day. The bad guys will win."

"But maybe they're the good guys," Trotter shot back. "I know it's not making it easier for chefs, but is that a bad thing? Would chefs suddenly feel like they were less of a chef if they were no longer able to serve foie gras? I would hope not."

At least in the short term, both Charlie Trotter's and Tru reaped the benefits of their public spat. Trotter's fans rallied around him and his ethical stand, and the restaurant seemed newly relevant at a time when younger chefs (and Trotter's alumni) such as Achatz, Moto's Homaro Cantu and Avenues' Graham Elliot Bowles (who served the Foie-lipop, a foie gras lollipop coated with Pop Rocks) were being lauded for their creative applications of so-called "molecular gastronomy." Tramonto, meanwhile, kept wondering to himself, What just happened? Who would've figured that two brief conversations with a reporter could alter his life so drastically? His e-mail inbox was constantly overflowing, and his phone rang almost nonstop for months with calls of support and interview requests from, among others, *Entertainment Tonight* and *Newsweek*. The feedback he received was overwhelmingly positive, though eventually PETA briefly camped out on Tru's sidewalk.

Still, Tramonto said he was bothered about how ugly his relationship with Trotter had turned, so he wrote his former boss a letter apologizing if there had been any misunderstanding. Trotter called him back in the kitchen, and Tramonto reiterated his apology. Trotter's response, according to Tramonto: "OK." As Tramonto later recalled, "It wasn't like, 'Hey, bud, I'm sorry for calling you names in the newspaper.' It wasn't like, 'Let's shake hands and hug and forget about it and come to my next dinner.'" A couple of years later, Tramonto had an assistant reach out to Trotter to offer to help out with the restaurant's 20th anniversary celebration, which invited back many veterans of Trotter's kitchen. He said he received neither a return call nor an invitation to any of the festivities.

Trotter did tell me after the fact that he respects Tramonto and that the language he chose in slamming him was uncharacteristic. "Sometimes you say what's in your head, and that's the way it is. I'm not trying to hurt anybody, whether it's Chef Tramonto or a foie gras farm or anybody else. That's not my MO. That's never been my MO." But with almost the next breath, he stressed that he wasn't backing off the gist of his statements. "You know what? If I hear something that I don't like, I will say whatever it takes, and I'll send a message. If I have to use some sarcasm or open a can of whup-ass or do whatever, I'll do what I have to do."

One reader followed Trotter's adventures in the headlines with particular interest. Chicago alderman Joe Moore was a left-leaning fringe player in a city council dominated by Mayor Richard M. Daley's supporters. Moore had a reputation for proposing bills that sounded populist, progressive notes that rarely reached an audience beyond those in microphone range. But as he put down the newspaper upon first reading of Trotter's foie gras stand, he sensed that he had found a winner of an issue, one that not only would appeal to his North Side working-class ward (which featured zero upscale restaurants) but also might have a shot of gaining approval from his fellow council members.

The foie gras wars were about to escalate.

2.

Animals vs. Appetites

"God made ducks to have that liver—and He made it incredibly delicious!"

This was a lot of firepower being expended on duck livers. Many found the whole debate laughable, a tempest in a Crock-Pot. Take a dish with a funny French name, add ducks, top it all off with celebrity chefs eating each other's livers, and that's entertainment. Yet beyond the jokes lay a serious, lingering aftertaste. Trotter thrust foie gras into our consciousness at a pivotal moment in our ever-evolving relationship with food and how it's produced. Most people may never have sampled foie gras, but everyone must come to terms with the notion of living things becoming meals. For some, this process leads to vegetarianism or veganism (the latter eschews all animal products), but the vast majority has been more likely to adopt a don't-ask/ don't-tell policy. We don't associate chicken with an animal kept in an overcrowded barn; we think of it as a pink slab lying on cellophane-wrapped Styrofoam or as something molded into a "nugget." Collective denial has been our modus operandi.

But for many of us that dynamic has changed. More consumers are asking questions about the journey that food takes to our plates. We look for the organic label, inquire about grass-fed beef, ask whether salmon has been line caught and feel better if a chicken is "free range." We've turned specialty outlets such as Whole Foods into full-fledged, albeit pricey, supermarkets to benefit our health and to salve our consciences. Of course, many of us don't know how "organic" or "free range" actually translates to an animal's quality of life; we take the label on faith and move on. And most people can't afford to pay Whole Foods prices anyway; the food industry remains driven by consumers who buy factory-farmed products because they are cheaper and more widely available. Still, when Burger King is committing to cage-free eggs (though a small percentage) and McDonald's is enforcing supposedly humane slaughterhouse guidelines, a significant mainstream shift has occurred.

At the same time, the so-called foodie culture has been in ascent, spurring the popularity of the Food Network and Bravo's *Top Chef,* countless food blogs and the phenomenon known as "food porn." (If you've seen the fetish-like photos and overheated prose dedicated to capturing every delectable detail of a superlative meal, you've seen food porn.) Celebrity chefs and their ever-growing platforms have opened up new culinary vistas for the rest of us who wish to experience more unusual flavor, texture and temperature combinations and to bring into our kitchens such techniques as heat-resistant gelling agents and *sous vide* poaching. We want to sample more gourmet products, whether vegetables and fruits such as salsify and yuzu or animal products such as pork belly (as opposed to bacon) and foie gras.

So while the move toward animal-treatment consciousness tugs us in one direction (foie gras *bad*), increased awareness of gourmet food's sheer pleasures and artistic possibilities yanks us in another (foie gras *good*). Meanwhile, the ethical issues regarding foie gras are far from clear-cut as there is sharp disagreement over whether the ducks' suffering is worse than that of, say, your everyday broiler chicken—or whether the ducks even suffer at all. Sure, the image of a tube down the throat nauseates many of us, but our biology doesn't allow us to swallow whole, spiny fish. We also don't routinely store fat in our livers. But even before we try to pinpoint how much foie gras ducks actually may suffer, we can wrestle with other philosophically vexing issues.

For instance, before the two-to-four-week gavage period begins, your average American foie gras duck lives 12 weeks either free-ranging outdoors or dwelling in long, spacious barns. Meanwhile, a non-force-fed duck that you'd order in a nice restaurant—from Indiana's Maple Leaf Farms, say—has been slaughtered somewhere closer to five and a half weeks. Commercial broiler chickens now are processed at six to seven weeks of age. (A 2003 study from North Carolina State poultry science researchers found that thanks to genetic advancements, a 2001 broiler required about one third as much time as a 1957 broiler—32 vs. 101 days—to reach four pounds.) Modern-day chickens have been bred to gain weight that fast.

Which would you rather be, a duck that experiences 12 relatively comfortable weeks before the start of force-feeding sessions or a chicken who never sees natural daylight, is packed in a barn feather to feather with tens of thousands of other birds, grows to Pamela Anderson–sized proportions so quickly that its legs can't necessarily support its weight, and gets whacked in the middle of its second month on earth? I know I'd also rather live twice as long even with the prospect of eventual suffering—though just by answering that question, I'm guilty of anthropomorphizing. The other obvious fallacies in my argument are (1) You can't ethically judge the treatment of ducks based on the treatment of chickens and (2) I'm placing a value on the length of life, a matter that's seen as almost beside the point in the current debate.

In his 1975 book *Animal Liberation,* as close as you can get to a bible of the animal-rights movement, Australian philosopher Peter Singer laid out the terms in which animal welfare continues to be measured. Although he promotes veganism as the most ethical choice in a world dominated by "speciesism," he is not an absolutist. Singer allows that there are reasons a human life might be valued more highly than a nonhuman animal life—and even that there are justifications for killing animals for food, though he disagrees with them. His key distinction is that treating animals well before they are slaughtered is ethically superior to causing them to feel pain before, and during, their deaths. That is, he takes the question of killing animals off the table, writing that his arguments "flow from the principle of minimizing suffering alone." He quotes English utilitarian philosopher Jeremy Bentham's influential assertion of animals' rights in the late 1700s: "The question is not, Can they *reason?* nor Can they *talk?* but, Can they *suffer?*" Singer concludes: "There can be no moral justification for regarding the pain (or pleasure) that animals feel as less important than the same amount of pain (or pleasure) felt by humans." In other words, even if animals' and people's lives aren't necessarily equal, the value of their suffering is.

Suffering remains *the* accepted yardstick for assessing the welfare of any "sentient being" (to use another preferred term of the animal-rights movement). You don't hear many protests about the sheer numbers of animal lives taken (close to 10 billion a year, almost 9 billion of those being broiler chickens) or the fact that veal calves and lambs are far from the only young creatures going to slaughter. Not only do broiler chickens last a matter of weeks, but do you know what happens to the male version of layer chickens? The females, of course, are bred to lay eggs, but the males can't lay eggs for obvious reasons, and they also won't be grown for eating because layer chickens now are a completely different genetic strain from those über-meaty broilers. Given that industrial-sized farmers have no economic incentive to raise these male chicks, once the birds are out of their eggs and sexed, they're snuffed out "humanely," usually by being gassed with CO_2.

This is standard agricultural practice, and until recently I had no idea. Wouldn't you think the mass killing of day-old boychicks would be common knowledge? Protests of the egg industry invariably focus on the use of battery cages for hens, which are crammed together so tightly that they can't even flap their wings; all they can do is lay eggs for about a year starting when they're close to four months old. That, to animal-welfare advocates, is the epitome of suffering, and public railing against these conditions has led to increasingly common "cage-free" labels. Such steps may be a positive development, but meanwhile, the instant euthanasia of the newly hatched male chickens—which happens at nurseries that supply chicks to organic, cage-free farms as well as big factory operations—goes almost unmentioned. In the view of the animal-rights movement, suffering is a fate worse than death.

I asked Farm Sanctuary president Gene Baur why animal groups don't make a big stink about all of those euthanized chicks. After all, this country isn't too approving of the killing of babies—especially, I would think, when they're fuzzy and cute and say things like *Cheep! Cheep! Cheep!* "We look to address issues that can be resolved relatively easily, and in terms of battery cages, that's a clear abuse, and these animals could be given more space," Baur said. "In the case of the unwanted male chicks, they're going to be killed. From a legislative standpoint, all you can do is say that they have to be killed in as painless a way as possible, and everybody already agrees on that." The practical problem, he continued, is "there's millions of them, and they're roosters. Roosters are hard to place. So practically speaking, there's not very much we can do except to raise awareness and let people know that with egg production, there are inherent problems." Besides, eggs feed an awful lot of people who would rather not measure their hunger or appetite against the fates of day-old chickens. Likewise, the industries contend that their methods of mass production are what enable them to keep meats and other staples affordable for those non-elites who don't shop at Whole Foods—i.e., most people. The animals' and humans' interests are far from aligned.

So as animal-rights advocates take up the cause of foie gras ducks, the issue isn't *whether* the ducklings should be killed, because these ducks are far outliving male layer chicks as well as those ducks that wind up hanging in a Chinatown window or roasting *à l'orange* at a fancy restaurant. The passionate objections are based on the birds' perceived suffering (or "torture") from having tubes dropped (or "jammed") down their throats for the purpose of expanding their livers well beyond their normal size. This is where Trotter drew his ethical line. One key reason this controversy has had legs is that it challenges us to consider where *we* draw our own lines regarding how much suffering we find tolerable before an animal winds up at the dinner table.

Let me just note that I'd wrestled with great inexactitude over such matters prior to my engagement in the foie gras wars. Well before my exposure to the terms "humanocarnivore" in Michael Pollan's *The Omnivore's Dilemma* and "conscientious omnivore" in Peter Singer and Jim Mason's *The Ethics of What We Eat,* I'd struggled to balance my desire to enjoy whatever tastes good with nagging feelings of discomfort over complex animals being processed like conveyor-belt widgets—not that I'd actually seen how this was done, but that's the image I had in mind. Many animal-rights campaigners discuss how their connections to other species were forged through their relationships with their pets, and I'll proudly admit: I've been a cat person since the age of eight and, yes, felt a spiritual connection to that warm ball of fur that would crouch on my chest and purr in my face. So eating kitties was out of the question. And although I lacked regular contact with farm animals, I developed an affinity for cows, in part because I produced an excellent *Moooo!*

I didn't immediately abolish beef from my diet, but after college I quit eating veal and never looked back. The propaganda had worked, and I didn't like the idea of baby cows being forcibly made anemic while confined in tiny crates. (Here's the part I didn't know: Veal calves are the boy versions of dairy cows. You can't milk them, and they're not bred to make great steaks, so if they're allowed to live at all, they become veal—thus when I buy milk or cheese, I'm indirectly supporting the veal industry.) Several years later I redrew my personal line at eating mammals, figuring that the higher-evolved the animal, the worse it was to mistreat and to consume it—though I basically equated mistreatment with forced death rather than any specific living conditions. At any rate I found myself eating lots of chicken. Of course, a friend argued that I now was responsible for many more deaths given that one chicken feeds a fraction as many people as one cow. But still, I figured, birds were lower on the evolutionary scale than mammals, and given that I lacked the proper conversion tools to calculate just how many chicken lives equaled to a cow life (I would willingly see thousands of mosquitoes killed before I would harm a kitten, after all), I just let it go and stuck with my initial rule: Killing mammals—wrong. Killing birds—not so bad.

This, of course, was a very unscientific conclusion, and I've since heard several animal advocates, including Singer and top PETA and Humane Society of the United States officials, argue that on a purely ethical level—that is, not getting into human health or environmental concerns springing from hormones, antibiotics, irradiation or global warming—beef poses fewer problems than chicken, pork or even fish. "If people only ate cattle, I'd probably do something else," Bruce Friedrich, PETA's vice president of international grassroots campaigns, told me. "We eat 200 times as many chickens as cattle. The intensification, the vertical integration of the chicken industry, is total, whereas cattle, unless hit by a snowstorm or heat wave, spend half their time doing what they'd like to be doing." In other words, by roaming in pasture for significant chunks of their lives, they get to experience their true *cowness*—even if they eventually must fatten up on corn despite their natural diet being grass. (They're not literally being force-fed, but they're certainly being forced to eat something that is not natural to them.) Chickens and pigs have no such luck. But I didn't know any of that at the time I began my personal mammal-eating ban. I did know that inconsistency lay at the heart of my position, but given that I wasn't willing to take what I saw as the most consistent position and become a vegan, I had to live with my compromise.

I didn't discover foie gras until I was several years beyond college. It's an expensive dish, and as a journalist, I wasn't eating out much in the kinds of places that would serve it anyway. When I finally tried it—seared, with a jelly-like interior—I knew that it involved the force-feeding of ducks, but that was about it. What I learned immediately was that it was delicious. Sorry, duck. That's not to say that I began seeking out foie gras with any regularity, but when I did eat out somewhere special for a birthday or some other big occasion, I sometimes ordered it, and it invariably was a meal highlight. As for the possible guilt factor, well, ducks fall into the bird category, don't they? Sorry, duck.

It actually was at haute cuisine destinations such as Trotter's (where I was taken by my wife in my 30s) that my birds-mammals line began to erode. When I dined at restaurants that operated on a higher culinary plane, I felt that imposing "dietary restrictions" on the chef was akin to removing paint colors from his or her palette. I must let the artist work without inhibitions! Plus, these restaurants tend to support small-scale, eco-friendly farmers and suppliers, so no matter the animal being eaten, it most likely had been treated better than any creature on a factory farm. But if it was ethically preferable to eat a happy pig than a miserable chicken, where did that leave me with my no-mammals rule?

Obsession over such matters might have been considered odd

in some ages past. Yes, vegetarianism dates back centuries, and now many restaurants have followed the lead of Berkeley's Chez Panisse in stressing the sources of their meat and produce; the farms' names appear on the menu as if the chef is vouching: I know these guys, and they are providing me with humanely raised, yummy product. In fact, the contemporary culinary world increasingly equates better animal treatment with better flavor; a free-range chicken simply tastes more chickeny than one of those big, bland supermarket roasters. But historically, the preparation of food has not taken into account how the animal might feel about its participation in this process. Even in 1981 there was little hand-wringing when Commonwealth became the United States' first sizable foie gras farm. The new production of fattened ducks' livers—and the appearance, at long last, of fresh foie gras on local restaurants' menus—sparked no public outcry. Discussion focused on what was on the plate, not how the animal lived and died.

That said, the controversy over foie gras is far from a modern phenomenon. Over its long history, sometimes the delicacy has been rhapsodized as God's gift to discerning palates, sometimes it has been excoriated as the taste of damnation. Often both have happened simultaneously.

I was talking foie gras with Martina Navratilova at an animal-rights benefit when she asked *the* basic question about this strange delicacy: "I can't figure out how we even figured out that that's how you make the livers enlarged. I mean, how did it get to that? We're force-feeding geese and ducks, and then we figure out that the liver enlarges five to 10 times and it's delicious? Oh, my goodness, it's crazy."

"Well, Martina," I began (no, I didn't—sorry, I'm still carried away from writing, "I was talking foie gras with Martina Navratilova . . ."), and proceeded to note that the delicacy is actually thought to date back 5,000 years to the time of the Egyptian pharaohs.

"Back then human life wasn't worth much," she volleyed back. "We had slaves, and all kinds of things were OK, but now we know better." No, the nine-time Wimbledon singles champ is not a foie gras fan.

It's certainly odd to consider that something requiring such specific labor and animal manipulation to create so rarefied an end product would have lasted so long. Yet fatty waterfowl livers have endured while other dishes (stuffed dormouse, anyone?) have become long-forgotten curiosities. The five-millennium history of foie gras is like a connect-the-dots picture where you have the option of drawing straight lines or loops between the widely separated points. Ancient artifacts, literary citations and records of cookery and farming provide the reference points, but how this delicacy got from one place to the next is often anyone's guess. What *is* known is that foie gras has been around for a long, long time and has spurred ethical arguments for much of that duration.

The story begins with ancient Egypt's domestication of wild geese that landed along the Nile during migration. To store energy for these long flights, the birds ate voraciously and grew fat, but they didn't get plump where people do. Waterfowl store fat under their skin and in their livers. For most of history, animal fat has been a valued commodity, for its calories and nutrients as well as its usefulness in cooking and baking; squeamishness about eating fat is a relatively modern phenomenon among the Western well-to-do. So it probably was the fat that the ancient Egyptians were after when they force-fed these birds, evidence of which can be seen in bas reliefs such as one on display in the Louvre that dates from 2350 BC.

Skip ahead a couple of thousand years, and goose-fattening had been established in ancient Greece, with Homer alluding to the practice in *The Odyssey* and the poet Epigenes writing in the fourth century BC about someone getting stuffed "like a fattened goose." "Those sumptuous goose livers" finally get a shout-out in *The Deipnosophistae* (*The Learned Banquet*), the written record of a third-century AD Roman symposium that looked back on Greek gastronomy. The art of fattening geese was refined and codified in Rome, the place where foie gras apparently first was produced specifically as a delicacy. In *De Agri Cultura* (*On Agriculture*), a Roman farming manual of the second century BC, Cato the Elder offers these instructions:

> To cram hens or geese: Shut up young hens which are beginning to lay; make pellets of moist flour or barley meal, soak in water, and push into the mouth. Increase the amount daily, judging from the

appetite the amount that is sufficient. Cram twice a day, and give water at noon, but do not place water before them for more than one hour.

Pliny the Elder's *Naturalis Historia,* an exhaustive encyclopedia from about AD 77, contains what is thought to be the first direct mention of foie gras preparation, noting: "Stuffing the bird with food makes the liver grow to a great size, and also when it has been re- moved, it is made larger by being soaked in milk sweetened with honey." He also writes of a Roman gourmand, Marcus Gavius Api- cius, who devised a method of "stuffing" geese with dried figs. Those figs gave foie gras its name. The fattened liver originally was called *iecur ficatum, iecur* being Latin for "animal liver" and *ficatum* referring to the figs with which the geese were force-fed. For some reason the fig half of the name is what stuck: *Ficatum* became the root for *foie, higado* and *fegato,* the French, Spanish and Italian words for "liver," respectively. (*Gras* is French for "fat.") *The Art of Cooking,* the only surviving ancient Roman cookbook, includes two foie gras recipes, one for a marinade and the other for some sort of grilled sausage.

Even in Roman times, some viewed foie gras as a symbol of deca- dence and moral decay. The poet Horace mentions it disapprovingly in his depiction of excessive aristocratic banquets in one of his *Sat- ires*. When the Roman Empire fell in 476, foie gras and the culture of gourmet feasting went along with it. As the monastery became central to early Christian society, the human body was viewed with suspicion, and food was seen as mere fuel for a useful, faithful life. This, after all, is when gluttony got billing as one of the seven deadly sins. However, the era's monks did the culinary world a favor by stu- diously copying down Roman texts, thus providing a historical record that would come in handy centuries later.

At this juncture, with documentation scarce, the foie gras roads diverge depending on who's doing the telling. One school of thought has foie gras pretty much disappearing for almost a millennium until French Renaissance chefs rediscovered it via those monk-copied Roman texts. Another theory is that scattered European farmers per- petuated the fattening and foie gras production techniques, and, in a popular French variation on this theme, carried their know-how directly to farmers in southwestern France, who kept the tradition alive until the French court's chefs caught up with it. But the most-repeated theory is that foie gras survived thanks to Jews who had learned of force-feeding practices while under Roman rule and carried the tradition around Europe as they kept getting kicked out of countries. Some speculate that Jewish slaves were the ones doing the force-feeding all the way back in ancient Egypt, though there's scant evidence to back that claim. Silvano Serventi, whose *Le Foie Gras* (2005) is one of the best-regarded French histories, downplays the Jewish influence, writing that their reputation as foie gras producers was not fully established until the 16th century. But documentation does connect European Jews to foie gras as of the 11th century. That's when a venerated French rabbi known as Rashi wrote an extensive Talmudic commentary about a third-century parable from Babylonian mystic Rabbah bar-bar Hannah. Here's the parable's relevant passage:

> Once upon a time we were traveling in the desert, and we saw those geese whose feathers had fallen out on account of their fatness and under whom flowed rivers of oil. I ventured to ask them: May we expect to have a share of you in the world to come? One of them lifted its wing and one lifted its thigh (leg) as one might lift a standard. And when I related this incident before Rabbi Eleazar, he remarked: The Israelites will eventually have to account for their conduct before Justice.

Rashi interpreted this tale to mean that Jews would have to face the music "for having made the beasts [geese] suffer while fattening them." Judaic law prohibits *tza'ar ba'alei chayim*, suffering to animals, though this principle has long been debated as scholars weigh the animals' interests against those of humans seeking, for instance, sustenance or medical care. In any case, this earliest-known reference to Jews and goose fattening is a negative one, as is what Michael Ginor writes in his 1999 book *Foie Gras: A Passion* is the earliest direct reference to Jews eating fat liver (though of what animal isn't specified). In a 14th-century ethical will, a dying man, Eleazar of Mainz, instructs: "Now, my sons and daughters, eat and drink only what is necessary, as our good parents did, refraining from heavy meals, and holding the gross liver in detestation."

Gross livers aside, Jewish people had a practical reason for raising geese and perpetuating force-feeding. In the Mediterranean they were able to cook with olive oil, in Babylonia with sesame oil, but as they were pushed farther north and west, those substances disappeared. Meanwhile, the Jews had to adhere to the laws of *kashrut*, and pork fat, the main cooking fat of European Christians throughout this time period, isn't kosher. Nor is most beef fat, and butter was problematic due to the prohibition on mixing meat and dairy products. Hence their best option became poultry fat, known in Yiddish as *schmaltz*, of which geese were prodigious, portable producers; for good reason were they referred to as "walking larders." So Jews fattened the geese, ate their meat, used their fat, made *gribenes* (cracklings) out of the skin and enjoyed their livers. Some speculate that chopped liver originally was made with foie gras—and that some foie gras preparations were directly spun off from this traditional Jewish dish.

By the time of the Renaissance (roughly the 14th to 17th centuries), fattened goose livers were being rediscovered in Europe. The Church had cast off its ascetic streak to embrace gourmet foods (and other riches), and classical preparations were once again in vogue. In his 1570 cookbook *Opera*, Bartolomeo Scappi, Pope Pius V's chef, writes of the huge goose livers being produced by Jewish farmers, and he offers such recipes as dipping the liver in flour, frying it in lard, squeezing Seville orange juice on it and sprinkling it with sugar— the first known sweet-sour foie gras preparation, writes Ginor. For the next couple of centuries, the Jews of such places as Bohemia, Hungary, Metz and Strasbourg were celebrated for obtaining what naturalist René-Antoine de Réaumur called "goose livers renowned for their enormous fatness and for their excellence."

As of the 16th century, these fattened livers, yet to be dubbed "foie gras," remained more a regional novelty than a staple of fine dining in France. To put things in perspective, haute cuisine had yet to emerge, and flavor was less the rage than theatrical presentations. Giambattista della Porta's mid-16th-century book series compiled as *Magia Naturalis* offers several outrageous recipes that play on the sense of spectacle, such as one titled "That flesh may look bloody and full of Worms, and so be rejected" (it's basically a practical joke in which you cook harp strings in meat so they look like they're squirming around) and "A boiled Peacock may seem to be alive" (this involves propping up the roasted bird with small iron wires and putting camphor in its mouth to ignite at the table for a fire-breathing effect). *The Vivendier,* a 15th-century French cookery book, offers another fun one called "To Make that Chicken Sing when it is dead and roasted": The cook fills the neck with mercury and ground sulfur (don't try this at home, folks), ties it off and heats the bird so that "the air that is trying to escape will make the chicken's sound." Good lord.

At least in those recipes, the animals endured such indignities after they already were dead. In contrast, there's della Porta's "A Goose roasted alive." No, this one does not turn out well for the bird. The author explains that he'd heard of this dish being presented to the king of Aragon. "And when I went to try it, my company were so hasty, that we ate him up before he was quite roasted. He was alive, and the upper part of him, on the outside, was excellent well roasted." Della Porta proceeds to give vivid, grisly instructions on how to get to that point, and trust me, it's a horror movie.

"A Goose roasted alive" must have been extreme even in its time (no?), but the Middle Ages, Renaissance and early modern era weren't exactly grand times to be an animal regardless. European countries offered all sorts of public spectacles revolving around cruelties such as the French Midsummer Day tradition of torturing cats and throwing them onto a big bonfire. "Baiting" was another charming practice. As Keith Thomas writes in *Man and the Natural World,* in late-18th-century England, a bull or a bear would be tethered to a stake, then set upon by dogs. If the tethered animal broke free, all the better for the excitement of the dogs' swarming attack. Such "entertainment" crossed class lines, serving up amusement for royal guests and country-fair attendees alike.

Yet bullbaiting had a culinary application as well. Thomas writes that this violent exercise was thought to "help to thin the animal's blood and make its flesh tender." Louis Eustache Ude, a famed French chef working in London in the early 19th century, recommended throwing live eels onto a fire before skinning them to improve their digestibility. Writes Stephen Mennell in *All Manners of Food: Eating and Taste in England and France from the Middle Ages to the Present*, Ude also "defended such practices as whipping pigs to death and nailing geese by their feet to boards in front of roaring fires to be force fed for foie gras."

Charles Estienne's *L'Agriculture et la maison rustique* (1564) gives what apparently is the first detailed account of French goose fattening, which involves keeping the birds in a warm, dark place for a month or two, feeding them barley flour and wheat soaked in water and honey three times daily, and in some cases blinding them and plucking their stomach and thigh feathers. The historical accounts from this time are sketchy, but the 16th and 17th centuries also are thought to be when some farmers felt the need to nail geese's feet to the floor. The reason was to reduce their mobility, also apparently the point of digging out the birds' eyes, though Ginor notes that modern farmers are baffled by the blinding because geese are "extremely sensitive to stress." Ginor also writes that an update of Olivier de Serres's *Le Théâtre d'agriculture* (1600) featured an 1805 appendix that contends that by then farmers pretty much had abandoned foot nailing, while as far as the blinding was concerned: "Of a hundred fatteners, it is now difficult to find two who still do it, and even they only put out the eyes two or three days before killing." Well, OK then.

Animals, in other words, often were expected to suffer for the culinary arts, or as a 17th-century preacher is quoted by Thomas: "We kill and eat them, and regard not their cries and strugglings when the knife is thrust to their very hearts." That attitude was echoed in the mid-1800s when English essayist Abraham Hayward wrote in *The Art of Dining: or, Gastronomy and Gastronomers:* "A true gastronome is as insensible to suffering as is a conqueror."

In contrast, force-feeding birds never caught on in Britain, where 19th-century society showed signs of discomfort with certain aspects of animal treatment. As Mennell writes, slaughterhouses, which had been out in the open throughout Europe for generations, gradually disappeared from view in Victorian England. The Society (later Royal Society) for the Prevention of Cruelty to Animals (SPCA) was founded in 1824, and Parliament enacted laws against cruelty to horses, cattle and dogs plus baiting and cockfighting. Novelist Thomas Hardy captured the conflict between accepted food preparation and humane animal treatment in *Jude the Obscure* (1895), in which Arabella chides husband Jude about his reluctance to slaughter a pig that is crying with despair:

> "Don't be such a tender-hearted fool! There's the sticking-knife— the one with the point. Now whatever you do, don't stick un too deep."
>
> "I'll stick un effectually, so as to make short work of it. That's the chief thing."
>
> "You must not!" she cried. "The meat must be well bled, and to do that he must die slow. We shall lose a shilling a score if the meat is red and bloody! Just touch the vein, that's all. I was brought up to it, and I know. Every butcher keeps un bleeding long. He ought to be eight or ten minutes dying, at least."

Jude defies her and kills the pig quickly.

François Pierre de La Varenne, considered the founding father of French cuisine, is thought to be the first to have offered recipes of "foyes gras" by name in *Le Cuisinier françois* (1651), a landmark in codifying French cooking techniques. La Varenne's book—which also introduced bisque, béchamel sauce and a roux—helped push forward a revolution in French gastronomy as chefs cast off their predominant Italian influences to create their own cuisine. While foie gras was rising in status, with a variety of preparations popular among the country's top chefs by the end of the 17th century, culinary indulgence was hitting a new peak. Louis XIV, who ruled France from 1661 to 1715, was a notorious gourmand whose banquets were huge choreographed affairs. The morally challenged Louis XV, whose reign lasted till 1774, continued the tradition of wildly ostentatious dinners. A 1953 *Time* magazine article detailed the discovery of Louis XV's secret hideaway for his mistress, where "Louis sometimes fainted at dinner, after stuffing himself to the gills. Sample menu: four soups, three terrines of foie gras, countless hors d'oeuvres, 16 meat courses, partridge, chicken, song birds, pheasant, turkey, squab, 14 desserts, creams and cakes." Foie gras's biggest boost to date came when Strasbourg chef Jean-Pierre Clause baked a whole liver in a crust with veal and lard forcemeat to create *Pâté de foie gras de Strasbourg*, an immensely popular dish of the 1780s that gained an international reputation.

The first Paris restaurants opened shortly before the French Revolution brought decadent royal dining to a crashing halt. In a major shift of culinary energies, chefs now sought to impress a bourgeois clientele—as well as the first restaurant critics, most famously Alexandre Grimod de La Reynière (from the late 18th century) and Jean Anthelme Brillat-Savarin (early 19th century). Both Grimod de la Reynière and Brillat-Savarin were major foie gras flag-wavers; the latter described a dinner in which "a Gibraltar rock of Strasbourg foie gras" was presented, thus thrilling and silencing guests:

> All conversation ceased, for hearts were full to overflowing; the skillful movements of the carvers held every eye; and when the loaded plates had been handed round, I saw successively imprinted on every face the glow of desire, the ecstasy of enjoyment, and the perfect calm of utter bliss.

A progression of France's most celebrated chefs continued to elevate this delicacy, among them Marie-Antoine Carême, Urbain Dubois (whose *Pain de foie gras à la régence* was a sculptural creation, constructed mostly of cold fat, that depicted a Roman goddess of war, a cannon, flags, eagles and a base of puréed foie gras meant to resemble parquet flooring), and the guiding light of 20th-century haute cuisine, Auguste Escoffier, whose massive milestone *Le Guide culinaire* (1903) detailed many foie gras preparations. Regional foie gras dishes also began gaining in popularity as the advent of the automobile prompted Europeans to explore the countryside and the specialties of southwestern France, though such excursions didn't truly become commonplace until after World War II.

In the United States, German and Austrian farmers were fattening geese in the 1830s and 1840s (Ginor writes that German-American butcher shops actually sold fattened goose livers until the 1970s). By the end of the 19th century, enough rich Americans had traveled to Europe that there was some demand for foie gras in restaurants

such as New York's Delmonico's. Meanwhile, the Industrial Revolution had kick-started the notion of animals as commodities to be
mass-produced. The one-two-three punch of Prohibition, the Great
Depression and World War II sucked the life out of the American
and European fine-dining scenes, and the Holocaust wiped out most
European Jewish culinary traditions where they'd been practiced for
centuries. However, as Ginor writes, a Holocaust survivor and third-
generation Hungarian goose farmer named Moshe Friedman moved
to the new state of Israel in 1948, convinced the government to support him in a trial run of producing fat goose livers on a kibbutz, and
wound up selling his product to an Alsatian pâté manufacturer, thus
making foie gras one of Israel's first exports. The young country's
foie gras industry grew so much over the years that by the end of the
century, it was among the world's top exporters of the delicacy.

The biggest, by far, was France. Through the middle of the 20th
century, foie gras had remained something traditionally produced on
small family farms—usually by the mother or grandmother—and either eaten at the holidays or sold at local markets. By this point the
figs and soaked grain balls had been replaced by corn, which was
introduced in southwest France in the 16th century. Now granny was
scooping the kernels into a funnel with a long pipe at the bottom to
go down the bird's throat. Sometimes she also had a kind of wooden
stick to jam the food down the pipe. Almost all foie gras, certainly
what was stocked in stores, was preserved in cans rather than sold
fresh. André Daguin, the French chef perhaps most strongly associated with the delicacy, told me that when he was growing up in
the southwest of France during World War II, obtaining consistently
high-quality foie gras was a challenge. "When I was 10 years old, my
mother used to buy geese and ducks whole. In the kitchen we opened
them, and out of 10, we had two or three nice livers, two or three medium and two or three pffffft! [that was a raspberry sound]. Now 80
percent are good. That's because animals are healthy. An animal who
is sick or ill cannot make foie gras." (We'll get to the "Are force-fed
ducks sick?" question later.)

Starting in the 1960s, French foie gras production grew increasingly industrialized, with the big companies and cooperatives organizing farms to force-feed birds that eventually were processed in a

central location. The most dramatic shift was from geese to ducks, as farmers discovered that cross-bred Mulard (as in "MULE-ard") ducks—the sterile offspring of male Muscovies and female Pekins— were easier and faster to raise than geese and were heartier and less temperamental than previously used duck breeds, such as the Muscovies. Around the same time came the advent of pneumatic feeding machines and tiny individual duck cages—which together sped up the feedings—and the booming of an industry in which prices dropped, consumption skyrocketed and foie gras no longer was just for Christmas and New Year's. By 2007, 35 million Mulard ducks were raised in France compared to 800,000 geese.

Some European countries were also producing foie gras (Hungary, Bulgaria, Spain); others were not. Acting on animal-rights concerns, several of those nonproducing countries took the extra step of banning force-feeding for food production, including Denmark, Germany, Poland, Italy, Luxembourg, Croatia, Norway, the Czech Republic and much of Austria. The Netherlands, Switzerland, Sweden, Turkey and the United Kingdom also enacted measures designed to curb the practice. Thanks to European Union trade rules, however, foie gras still could be bought and sold in any of the member countries. In 2003 Israel banned foie gras production, too, but not through a legislative act but rather a two-to-one Supreme Court decision that applied existing anticruelty laws to the force-feeding of birds. This was the one instance where an active industry had to be dismantled.

Foie gras wasn't an issue in the United States for most of the 20th century because you couldn't get it. Jean Banchet of the superlative Chicago-area restaurant Le Français was one of the few chefs serving the fresh stuff in the 1970s, thanks to the importation ban. He would return from trips to France smuggling foie gras packed beneath an iced order of Dover sole or even in the belly of monkfish. "You can put it inside the fish," he told me. "I'm not the only one to do this." He halted this practice after the security folks finally flagged him, and he had to watch helplessly as they tossed all of his pricey livers into a garbage can.

Soon enough, that lack of fresh supply would cease to be a problem—though, of course, other problems would ensue.

• • •

The uneasy marriage of rarefied cuisine and questionable animal treatment may be most dramatically illustrated by a controversial French tradition that involves the force-feeding and eating of a certain bird.

I'm talking, of course, about the ortolan.

This little bunting (a kind of sparrow) would be captured, blinded and/or placed in a dark box where all it could do was to get fat on millet seed (and perhaps oats or figs) before it finally was drowned in Armagnac. Then it would be roasted and popped into your mouth—bones in, feathers off, head optional—while you draped a linen napkin over your head to preserve the aromas and, as legend has it, to hide what you're doing from God. "It's delicious, an extraordinary taste," fabled southwestern French chef Michel Guérard told me. "It's similar to the way that Chinese people eat fish eyes. The French and the Chinese, from my point of view, are the only two cuisines of civilization." Former French president François Mitterrand was so enamored of ortolan that when he was close to death from cancer, he reportedly chose to eat this songbird in a last supper that also included oysters and—you guessed it—foie gras. As the story goes, after this meal he never ate another bite and died eight days later.

Such an indulgence was viewed as so unexceptional that Vincente Minnelli's 1958 Best Picture Oscar winner *Gigi* includes a scene in which Leslie Caron's title courtesan-in-training is schooled in the art of ortolan eating. But France banned hunting the ortolan in 1998, and in late 2007 government officials pledged to enforce an older law outlawing its sale—not for reasons of cruelty but because the migratory bird was considered endangered. Still, *eating* ortolans isn't technically illegal, so English TV personality Jeremy Clarkson ventured to Gascony in 2002 to sample what he called "the ultimate French delicacy, the highest of haute cuisine." On *Jeremy Clarkson Meets the Neighbours,* a Gascon chef demonstrates how to prepare these yellow birds, which are about as tall as the widths of his fingers together, by sprinkling them with salt and pepper and sticking them into the oven for eight minutes. At the dinner table, Clarkson is joined by none other than André and Ariane Daguin, who later told me that ortolan

•

actually is superior to the delicacy that launched her company: "It's incredible, a mixture of game and foie gras literally."

On his TV show, Clarkson asks André Daguin: "Do you think it's cruel to do this to these birds?"

"Animals usually are killed by other birds, other animals," he replies. "Well, when they are ortolan, they are killed by being thrown in some Armagnac, which is not a bad way to die."

As they all slowly chew these tiny birds under their napkin veils, Clarkson coos, "Mmm, mmm . . . This could be my absolute record in terms of complaints. Really good."

Olivier Desaintmartin, chef of the Philadelphia bistros Caribou Café and Zinc, told me about a traditional breakfast he used to prepare at his former girlfriend's parents' southwest France farm. The requirements: a very hot pan in which shallots and garlic are sautéing in duck fat; a knife; and a duck hanging upside-down in a funnel (as used in slaughter). Make a slight incision in the duck's neck, Desaintmartin said, and "the tradition is to put a hot pan right underneath the blood coming out, with the shallots and the garlic. When the blood starts to coagulate, you put a lot of parsley in there, and you go to the big farm table with a lot of coffee waiting for you, and there's your breakfast."

The root of the tension here is the never-ending dispute over non-human animals' place in our world. One popular school of thought is that people top the food chain for a reason and thus have the right to do as we please with those animals beneath us. The flip-side position is that as the planet's most enlightened creatures, we have a responsibility to care for other animals instead of eating or otherwise abusing them. Most people occupy the slippery middle ground, opposing the mistreatment of animals but not the eating of them—all while declining to look critically at food production. Ariane Daguin *does* know about how food is produced, and she eschews the mass processing of factory-farmed animals, but in *New York* magazine she defended foie gras thusly: "Animals have no soul. God made ducks to have that liver—and He made it incredibly delicious! Why would it exist if not for us to enjoy it?" Her sentiment echoes that of Charles Gérard, who in 1862's *L'Ancienne Alsace à table* wrote: "The goose is nothing, but man has made of it an instrument for the output of a marvelous product, a kind of living hothouse in which there grows the supreme fruit of gastronomy."

Continuing the prolonged cage match between lovers of food and animals, critic B. R. Myers turned his *Atlantic Monthly* review of *The Omnivore's Dilemma* into a withering critique of foodie culture. "For centuries civilized society took a dim view of food lovers, calling them 'gourmands' and 'gluttons' and placing them on a moral par with lechers," he begins. "They were even assigned their own place in hell, and I don't mean a table near the kitchen: They were to be force-fed for eternity. Not until halfway through the Industrial Revolution did the word *gourmet* come into use. Those who have since applied it to themselves have done a fine job of converting the world's scorn to respect." Soon Myers is contending that "the idolatry of food . . . can be seen in the public's toleration of a level of cruelty in meat production that it would tolerate nowhere else."

Michael Pollan's book isn't exactly an ode to culinary self-indulgence. Huge chunks are devoted to our food supply's industrialization, and the title refers to trying to cut a clear ethical path through a myriad of confusing choices presented by food producers large and small. Nevertheless, Pollan places a high value on the quality of the eating experience—the pleasures of a rib-eye steak, for instance— and ultimately dismisses vegetarianism after briefly trying it on. He also recounts hunting and killing his own pig with more enthusiasm than shame. The whole thing rankles Myers, who writes: "A record of the gourmet's ongoing failure to think in moral terms, *The Omnivore's Dilemma* helps one to understand why no reformer ever gave a damn about fine dining—or the family dinner table either."

Or as PETA founder Ingrid Newkirk told me, the pro-meat argument "basically boils down to the same argument that is used for fur, which is 'Yes, but I like it, and I want it'; 'I really like my steak'; or 'I like steak too much to give it up.' It's reduced to a totally selfish argument. Everybody knows they should be vegetarian or they shouldn't eat as many animals or as much meat." Everybody, of course, does *not* know this; most people consider eating (and wearing) at least some animal products to be perfectly natural. If Charlie Trotter had condemned hamburger, he'd just as likely have been attacked as an elitist know-nothing by many of the same people who shared his disdain for foie gras.

Suffice it to say that an exploration of fatty duck and goose livers isn't likely to resolve the ages-old question of whether people should eat animals. A common argument against foie gras is that it's unnecessary, but an extension of this argument is that culinary pleasure in itself is unnecessary. That plenty of vegetarians and vegans defend the tastiness of their diets is beside the point. Their guiding principle is first, we must do no harm; then we can figure out what to eat. Our ethical and moral choices should be made with no regard to how something tastes or how much enjoyment it brings, because torture is torture.

Someone who wholeheartedly would agree with that last statement happens to be the farmer who cofounded and runs Hudson Valley Foie Gras.

3.

Building the Team

"They didn't save one goddamn duck or goose!"

Izzy Yanay was making a point emphatically, which is a redundant thing to say if you know the guy. In this case, the Hudson Valley Foie Gras co-owner was gesticulating dramatically with his hands while his Israeli-accented voice swooped up and down like a jet-powered yo-yo. That he was driving a rental car 70 miles an hour en route to Kohler, Wisconsin, was of little concern—to him at least. To his three passengers, well, the other two had spent a lot more time with him than I had, and I figured he's probably had a fair amount of practice driving with one hand stabbing the air and thumping the steering wheel. My seat belt, of course, remained buckled.

Izzy (everyone calls him Izzy) was railing against the Israeli Supreme Court's ruling that led to the country's ban against the production, though not sale, of foie gras. Izzy comes from Israel. He moved to the United States in 1980, but he's still in touch with many people from his native land, particularly given that he learned foie gras farming there. Now all of those farmers were out of jobs, an estimated 500 families, and the biggest producers had moved to Hungary. Meanwhile, Israeli restaurants still carried foie gras, and diners still were enjoying it. "Who is benefiting from the sale?" Izzy roared. "The same operators that were benefiting from that before—and labor from Hungary. *They didn't save one goddamn duck or goose!"*

His main complaint was that instead of investigating the matter themselves, the Israeli justices took it as a given that force-feeding harms ducks. "These are people that are supposed to be smart, and I really tip my hat to them on the other decisions that they have made. But in this case *they're utterly wrong!"* To Izzy the entire foie gras issue is a matter of right and wrong. Some people on either side may hedge their statements—perhaps the ducks *do* suffer somewhat, perhaps other food animals *are* treated as least as badly—but that gray area doesn't exist for Izzy. He has been with those ducks for more than 25 years, accompanying them on their 16-week journeys from the hatchery to the slaughterhouse. He sees when they're stressed and when they're not. He knows the difference between humane and inhumane treatment. He recognizes suffering. And these ducks *do not suffer.*

Now Izzy was on a mission to spread this gospel. Accompanied by veterinarian Lawrence W. Bartholf, Hudson Valley's point person in defending and explaining its treatment of ducks, and Rick Bishop, the company's newly hired national sales manager, Izzy had flown to Chicago to convince chefs and other food-service professionals to keep the foie gras faith, though he mostly was preaching to the converted. The day after their visits to several Chicago-area restaurants, I hitched a ride with them as they headed up to the American Club, a Five Diamond resort about an hour north of Milwaukee in Kohler, the town that toilets built. There they would speak to the kitchen and service staff of the resort's various dining facilities, including the Immigrant Room, the fine-dining restaurant that features Pan-Seared Hudson Valley Foie Gras by name. "You're going to hear in the lecture today we're not trying to hide behind bogus excuses," Izzy said as he drove. "We're not trying to say bullshit just to save our asses. Everything we say is true, and we believe in what we say, and we believe that the other people are not saying the truth."

But before he got there, Izzy had to find a Starbucks, which he did just off the highway over the Wisconsin state line. He ordered a Frappuccino ("That is just for the sweetness") that he chased with a triple espresso ("This is a little bit of coffee"), into which he emptied four sugar packets. He also got a piece of chocolate. No wonder he's so animated.

If James Caan had a younger cousin who could kick James Caan's ass, he might resemble Izzy Yanay. The late-fiftysomething foie gras farmer has close-cropped curly dark hair, bright blue eyes and the barrel chest of a 1950s movie hunk, along with biceps that bulge from beneath the T-shirts he's usually wearing. However, he sounds more like Jackie Mason than Burt Lancaster, and he's got a playful streak, even when he's raising his voice for effect. At one point in the car, we were discussing conditions for animals in and out of captivity, and Izzy said all he wants is solid objective information, not just the activists' point of view. "Because I know what a jungle is," he said. "It's not Disney World. A jungle is eat or be eaten. And stress. And worms and parasites. You can't pee for one second in the Amazon because they're going to go into your pee-pee and crawl in. Then they're going to have to cut your pee-pee off. That's what I heard."

Um . . . *say what?*

"There is some fish in the Amazon that you cannot pee in the water, because if this fish feels the pee that you pee in the water, he goes up through your trunks and goes into your pee-pee."

"He'll swim up your urethra, and he has spines and barbs," Dr. Bartholf added helpfully.

"And he gets embedded inside," Izzy said.

"You can't pull him out," the doc said.

"You can't pull him out. And the only way to get it out is in about 24 hours you've got to get to a hospital or they're going to *whack* your pee-pee off!"

Well, that certainly clears up the whole animal-welfare issue.

(For the record, Izzy was referring to the notorious candiru fish, which is reported to have swum just where he said it swims—though not terribly often and not necessarily resulting in the amputation of one's "pee-pee.")

As we pulled out of the Starbucks, Izzy related a conversation he'd had that morning with Hudson Valley Foie Gras operations manager Marcus Henley about an undercover video posted on the Internet by Farm Sanctuary and Global Action Network allegedly showing abuses at one of the farms that supplies Canada's biggest foie gras company, Elevages Périgord. Purportedly shot by a temporary worker with a hidden camera, the footage shows employees kicking ducks, wringing their necks and swinging them like baseball bats to smash their heads against hard surfaces. (It also depicts just-sexed female ducklings being gassed, but not always killed, in garbage bags.) If you sought evidence of duck torture, here it was. Henley had told Izzy of speculation that the footage was staged, but Izzy wasn't having it. "I cannot stand over there in front of these people [in Kohler] and say with a straight face that this was staged," he said as he sped down the entrance ramp. "It doesn't look staged, and I don't believe it. However, these pictures showed a very, very badly managed farm. It didn't tell you that foie gras production as a principle is detrimental to ducks' health. In my farm, you will see ducks that are not hurt at all." After the video was released, Elevages Périgord president Emmanuel Nassans, while not confirming that all of the footage had been shot on one of his farms, announced that his company had suspended an employee for abusing ducks, and he stated: "All other employees caught committing similar actions will be suspended or fined."

There's an interesting conflict here. One of the ideas behind the animal-rights campaign is that foie gras production inescapably leads to tangential forms of cruelty to ducks and geese. It's kind of a trickle-down theory: The force-feeding is torturous; therefore other torturous behavior naturally follows. Izzy's contention was that foie gras production is like any other kind of farming, and a malcontented worker could abuse animals anywhere. In other words, don't judge foie gras by the worst-run farms; judge it by the best, because that's the only way you can assess foie gras as a principle. That may be reasonable given that opponents find foie gras production to be torturous even under the best of circumstances as long as that pipe is entering the esophagus.

We arrived in Kohler with a little time to kill, which turned into a *lot* of time to kill as the organizers pushed back the presentation by a couple of hours. So we walked up the block to the Kohler Design Center, a spacious showcase of fabulous new kitchen and bathroom set-ups with a basement museum detailing the company's 135-year history. (The company created the town as a planned community in

1912.) Izzy was transfixed by this shiny monument to luxury. "This bathroom is as big as my apartment," he marveled inside one such model. Downstairs, he was struck by the story of John Michael Kohler, who had added an enamel coating and four decorative feet to a cast-iron basin that he'd been selling to farmers as a hog scalder, thus giving birth to the modern household bathtub. From that innovation, everything else in this building had followed. "This guy really did something," Izzy said.

The visit to the Design Center put Izzy in a wistful mood. Everywhere you looked were signs of an entrepreneurial success story being celebrated unambiguously. Yet pioneering the domestic production and distribution of a sublime culinary delicacy had earned Izzy a mountain of hate mail and lawsuits. "If we didn't have all this *shit,* if we didn't have to fight all the time, we could do something beautiful like this," he said, taking in the nicely groomed grounds as we walked back toward the American Club. "A museum for foie gras."

Back inside the resort, one of the managers told Izzy how much the American Club's customers and employees enjoy his product. "We don't care if they like it or not," Izzy shot back. "We just want them to know we don't make it by torturing animals." About 15 chefs and servers took seats at the maroon booths and matching high chairs in the Winery Bar, an Old Money–feeling tavern accented with velvet curtains and dark wood. Standing at the end of the bar, Izzy announced that he was there "to tell you what we do and why what you hear is not true. What you hear about foie gras production is not true. About 10 years ago, when I said to somebody in the street 'foie gras,' they would not know what it is 100 percent of the time. They couldn't pronounce it; they had never heard of it. Most people now also don't know what it is, but when you stop somebody in the street today, they know one thing: that something bad is going on over there, that foie gras is something to do with torturing of animals, something that should be banned." The animal-rights crowd had succeeded in defining his product in a very negative way. Now Izzy faced the uphill battle of changing that perception.

His approach was to try to raise every standard objection to foie gras production and then to knock it down. He described Hudson

Valley's feeding method—three times a day over four weeks via a metal tube inserted 12 to 14 inches down the birds' esophagi—and acknowledged that it sounded "torturous." How could he defend that? "I say: Look, don't listen to me. I'm probably lying. I have something to protect. Let's go to the farm and see the ducks and see how it's being done."

Thus began Izzy's verbal tour of Hudson Valley Foie Gras. He described how the ducks show far more stress upon being moved from their spacious barns to the feeding pens than they do days later when they've grown used to their new environment and feeding schedule. Izzy discussed the farm tours he leads multiple times a week and invited everyone to join one. He asserted that when students visit, "100 percent of them are completely satisfied with what we do, with the conditions of the ducks." Pretty much the only person who had gone away dissatisfied, he said, was veterinarian Holly Cheever, a Farm Sanctuary consultant who accused him of not showing her representative ducks near the end of the feeding period. "That's not true," Izzy said. "She lied. She saw everything." In contrast, the American Veterinary Medical Association had struck down a proposed condemnation of foie gras several years running.

To underscore the difference between ducks and mammals, Izzy repeated one of his favorite stories about taking visitors into Hudson Valley Foie Gras's nursery and handing them adorably fuzzy, newly hatched ducklings: "Right away they start petting them. And then I say, 'You know something? Ducks, birds do not like to be pet. That's not the way you show affection to ducks. Dogs, yes. Cats, yes. Boyfriends, girlfriends, yes. But not ducks. You want to show affection to a duck? Puke in his mouth!'" Laughter and an "Eew!" erupted in the room while Izzy, a stickler for details, clarified that he realizes such a feeding method actually is for birds other than waterfowl. "But my point is they do not like to be pet like that."

What Izzy knows is that the Hudson Valley ducks lead relatively comfortable lives. He also knows that the animal-rights people know this. In fact, they know that everything he says is true, yet they keep coming after him. They want to put him out of business. Why? "Because there is another agenda," Izzy said. "Because we are very, very easy to attack. We are the key in the door . . . After doing away with us, well, it's going to be veal, chickens and some other things. We are a godsend for them."

Meanwhile, foie gras continued to be defended on grounds that, in Izzy's mind, weren't constructive. In *Saveur* magazine, Peter Sagal, host of the National Public Radio quiz show *Wait Wait . . . Don't Tell Me!,* recently had rhapsodized about the Chicago restaurant Sweets & Savories' decadent burger topped with foie gras pâté and truffle mayonnaise before concluding that, yes, force-feeding birds is "harsh," but please don't take away his foie gras burger. "This article doesn't help me," Izzy complained to the group. "Those points are not to the point. The foie gras could be delicious, but if it's being produced with the torture of animals, it should not be produced. It should be banned, and I'll be the first one to close the farm if the duck would not be comfortable. The fact that my neighbor is a child molester doesn't give me the right to do the same thing. People that have tried to help me, they always say, 'What about the lobsters? What about how chickens—' *I don't care about the lobster or about the chicken! I do not torture the animals!*"

This, then, was the message that the American Club staffers needed to convey to guests who complain about foie gras. The servers may not be able to persuade them, but they needed to plant the seed: Maybe what you hear about foie gras isn't true. Maybe you should talk to Hudson Valley Foie Gras or even visit the farm. "You need to put some doubt into their minds," Izzy said.

He yielded the floor to Dr. Bartholf, and the New York–based veterinarian expounded at length about how ducks' specific biology lends itself to foie gras production without harming them. He also debunked the notions that the livers explode ("The liver is not a balloon") and are diseased ("That's hogwash"). "I'd just like to leave you with the thought that this is humane," the doctor said, "that these birds are not suffering and that you can enjoy this and serve it with a clear conscience because these birds are very well cared for."

As Izzy and Dr. Bartholf fielded nonconfrontational questions from the staff (Do they sell the rest of the duck? Yes), servers emerged from the kitchen bearing plates of seared foie gras slices atop toast points with an orange garnish. Everyone sampled one except a blond server seated to my left who looked to be in her 30s and obviously found this offering less than appetizing. "Please, any other questions before you have to go?" Izzy asked. "Nothing? Good. So everybody's invited to the farm, whenever you can. Come to New York; give me a call."

Everyone applauded. Well, almost everyone. The woman to my left looked distraught. Her eyes were red, watery.

"I take it you're not a foie gras fan," I said to her quietly.

"No," she responded. "It's very upsetting. I disagree with it. I don't believe in it. In the Midwest you grow up with chickens; you grow up with beef. That's what you're used to. Not every family goes out and hunts. Duck is not something normally that children grow up eating. And the whole procedure of it, I don't agree with it."

"You object to the manipulation?" I asked.

"Yes," she said. "It does seem torturous."

"What do you do when a customer asks you about it?"

"Nothing. I don't say it's bad. I don't say it's my favorite. We have certain dishes that we say are our favorite. But I don't put it down."

"So this presentation didn't convince you?"

"No," she said. "I'm not going to go out and eat it. But I will serve it because it's my job."

Eventually we made our exit and hit the road back to Chicago, stopping at a strip-mall restaurant for a quick dinner. As we sat down, I was planning to mention the server's response to Izzy, but he beat me to the punch, saying he noticed that one woman was not buying what he was selling. "The way she looked at me was, You are lying to me, son of a bitch," he said, his eyes twinkling a bit. "I tried to talk to her, like straight to her, but I saw complete antagonism with her."

I relayed that she still thought he was torturing ducks.

"Yeah," he returned, pretending to address her, "but I was just talking to you about the fact that it's not, so why do you say it is?"

"Because she doesn't believe you," I replied.

"Well, come to the farm and see."

"You can't convince everyone."

"No, I can. If she would open her mind, I can. Because I am talking the truth."

Michael Ginor lacks Izzy Yanay's certitude regarding the welfare of force-fed ducks, which is interesting given that he is Izzy's partner and, as Hudson Valley Foie Gras's most public face, is routinely cred-ited with having made foie gras a staple of high-end U.S. restaurants. "I don't have the conviction in our righteousness the way my partner does," Ginor, a fellow Israeli, said over coffee a few days after Izzy's trip up to Kohler. (Ginor happened to be in Chicago for—believe it or not—Charlie Trotter's 20th anniversary weekend. Trotter had invit-ed him personally, despite their public sparring.) So while Izzy took umbrage at Peter Sagal's defense of foie gras, Ginor sided with the writer: "I have to agree with the *Saveur* thing. I couldn't tell that any animal that's meant for slaughter is not suffering. I don't quite know how that's possible. I would think that any animal that's economi-cally grown suffers some. There's no question that the duck on day 28 of feeding is not as happy as a duck that hasn't been fed. But the question then does become: How does that duck feel compared to, let's say, a woman in her ninth month of pregnancy? I don't think that there's ever a woman in her ninth month of pregnancy who's really psyched about that day."

Right, though having a baby is a happier and more voluntary out-come than what happens to the duck.

"To tell you that it's a 100-percent altruistic business that I have no issues with, no, I can't say that," Ginor continued. "It's funny, though, when I started, I never had a problem with it. When I came into foie gras, it was purely as a culinarian, not as a farmer. I had no knowledge of agriculture really. I just thought it was a great product that I would love to have and that others would love to have, and I came into it very, very excited. I knew there were issues or could be issues, and when Izzy showed me the process and explained to me, I felt like I was never 100-percent wholesome with it in the sense that I think you *can't* be 100-percent wholesome with it. But then I was convinced, I guess, that it's not different or worse than any-thing else out there that goes to feed human beings. That I kind of believed. But nevertheless, I see the issues. I understand the issues. I partially agree with the issues."

Told later of Ginor's comments, Izzy said, "Michael is a promoter, I am a farmer. No, they're not suffering."

As you may have guessed, Ginor runs cool the way Izzy runs hot. Ginor's Israeli accent is softer, his volume lower, his tone far less strident. "Michael is a people person," Izzy told me. "He's not like me. Everybody he meets, he becomes friends. For some reason I always evoke animosity"—Izzy laughed—"after a while." If Izzy is foie gras's vigorous defense attorney, Ginor is the philosophical judge, laying out all the facts on the table—even those that run counter to his interests—before rendering a verdict. His ruling, mind you, is that foie gras ultimately is justified, that the attacks upon his small industry have been inaccurate and unfair. But his nature is to try to find the middle ground that accommodates everybody, even though he knows in this case that's an impossibility.

"My philosophy in life is to piss off as few people as possible," he said. "If some people feel that we don't do the right thing, if there were a way to resolve it, I would. It's not a money thing; it's not 'so you go away.' Why not make a sector of people happy if it's possible to? So if I could've sat down with them, and they would've said, 'You know what? If you took a million dollars and did a, b, c, d, e, and we would be happy, we would feel better,' I would do it in a heartbeat. In a heartbeat. The problem is that there is no financial resolution to this, certainly not as far as they're concerned. It starts and dies with the actual feeding process. Obviously."

In his mid-40s, Ginor is about 15 years younger than his partner. Like Izzy, Ginor is a T-shirt wearer (usually black), and he's a former marathoner who has added some bulk, he said, thanks to his almost nonstop spearheading of gourmet culinary events around the world. Ginor is the one who gave Hudson Valley Foie Gras its name, which took some creativity given that the farm isn't located in New York State's Hudson Valley but rather more than 70 miles southwest in Sullivan County at the base of the Catskill Mountains. What, no Catskill Foie Gras? "Although we are a little off geographically," Ginor said, "it was a more attractive name."

At its peak Hudson Valley Foie Gras controlled the American market, and the brand name was so strong that Izzy caught at least one restaurant touting "Hudson Valley A-Grade Foie Gras" on its menu despite serving a competitor's livers. "At a certain time, not now, you could sell a telephone pole with this name, like Louis Vuitton," Izzy said. But for Izzy, the creation of Hudson Valley comes midway through his foie gras rollercoaster ride in the United States.

He'd already been in upstate New York for 10 years farming ducks and trying desperately to create a market for this 5,000-year-old, relatively unknown product with a funny French name.

Izzy didn't get into foie gras because it was his calling or some other romantic notion. "Not all of us decided at seven years old what we want to do in life," he scoffed. "Just things happen." What happened was that Izzy did his standard three years' service in the Israeli Army, and after traveling around Europe a bit, he returned to Israel to get an agriculture degree. He took a job as a field instructor for a foie gras farm's slaughterhouse, and after gaining experience in the industry, he and a fellow worker named Yossi Nishri looked into starting their own vertically integrated farm. Eventually they connected with a New York State–based sports promoter/real-estate magnate named Rubin Josephs, who wanted any new farm to be located nearby. Izzy said he repeatedly asked Josephs to find out how many farms were producing foie gras and how many restaurants were serving it, but Josephs kept coming up blank.

"I said, 'Look, Rubin, you gotta go to a French restaurant,'" Izzy recalled. "'You know how you know it's a French restaurant? It starts with a "La" or with a "Le." Ask them if they have foie gras, and if they say yes, you ask them where they got it.'"

Josephs called him back again: No dice. Izzy wondered: Could force-feeding birds be illegal in the United States? A call to the U.S. Department of Agriculture revealed that no laws prohibited the practice. The market was wide open. "We started jumping up and down in his office: 'We have to start now, now, now,'" Izzy recalled. Rubin's son Howard had a plane, and they flew around upstate New York scouting for farms, and when they touched down in Sullivan County to grab a cup of coffee, they saw what looked like the perfect location. They visited the farmer, Rubin pitched him on the concept of raising foie gras ducks, and they made him an offer that he accepted. Izzy said the farmer was so convinced they'd fail that he took off on a world cruise after telling his employees "to stay put because he's coming back."

"I don't think that's true," Howard Josephs later told me, "but Izzy says a lot of things."

One of Rubin's companies was called Commonwealth Enterprises, so that became the farm's name. Foie gras production there started in 1981, and everything was going great except for one minor matter: They still had to get someone to buy this product for which there was no established market. At the end of a two-day stretch of getting turned away from New York's finest restaurants, a grouchy Izzy visited a charcuterie/pâté store called Les Trois Petits Cochons (Three Little Pigs) in Greenwich Village. "It was five o'clock in the afternoon," he recalled. "I already called my wife, my ex, and I told her that we probably gonna have to go back [to Israel] because it's not working." He showed the livers and *magrets* (breasts) to some representatives there, "and then some tall women came, and she said, 'Oh, foie gras.'"

At this point, as Izzy's recollection goes, this French woman introduced herself as Ariane Daguin and told him that her father is André Daguin.

"My father is Shmuel Yanay, so?" Izzy replied.

"How long have you been making foie gras?"

"Many years. I've been in Israel and all that."

"And you don't know the name of my father?"

Now, Izzy said, he started to get interested. "She said, 'Look, asshole, my father is the prophet of foie gras in the world. He wrote the book. Now let's see what you can do.'"

Ariane's memory of this exchange differed from Izzy's in that she doubted she would have invoked her famous dad. "I think part of the reason I went so far, to America, was not to talk about my father."

Ariane Daguin grew up around foie gras and the Hôtel de France in Auch, the southwestern France town where André took the culinary torch from *his* father (who also had led the Hôtel de France kitchen) and grandfather (who had cooked there) and carried it to greater heights. André Daguin changed the way people ate foie gras and the rest of the duck; aside from pioneering many liver preparations, he's the one who discovered that if you cook the breast, the *magret,* rare, you can serve it like steak. A chef with an oversized, authoritative personality, his legend looms large in France; even farmers in the middle of nowhere invoke his name.

Ariane is no wallflower either. You can't miss her when she walks into a room: She's about six feet tall, dusty haired and purposeful. Convinced that her brother would be chosen over her to take the reins from her father, she left behind rural France for New York City to study political science at Barnard College, and her plan was to attend journalism school after she graduated. But she never got that far; two years into her undergraduate experience, she ran out of money and dropped out. She drifted toward what she knew and wound up working full time at Les Trois Petits Cochons. When Izzy showed up with that perfectly shaped foie gras, her past came crashing back. She had not seen a liver like that since she left France, and she couldn't believe that it was being produced nearby. Until then she'd assumed that she hadn't encountered fresh foie gras in the United States because its production was illegal.

She realized she had an expertise that no one locally shared. She knew how to prepare foie gras and how to market it—as well as the *magret*, confit and other duck products—so she and George Faison, a strong-willed fellow worker from Texas, pitched their two Trois Petits Cochons bosses on becoming Commonwealth's distributor. When the shop owners finally said no, Ariane and George decided to start their own company, D'Artagnan, named after the heroic figure of Ariane's native Gascony.

Commonwealth, which by then was working with other distributors, signed up D'Artagnan on a cash-on-delivery basis, and Ariane had to drive the 90 minutes to the farm from D'Artagnan's home base in Newark to pick up the products herself. This arrangement worked to her advantage because she could select the best livers before the other distributors got there, delivering the softer ones to chefs preparing terrines and the harder ones to those into pan searing. With Izzy and his partners producing fresh foie gras, George running the business side of D'Artagnan and Ariane passionately promoting the farm's products (including *magrets* and legs) to high-end restaurants in New York City and beyond, Commonwealth and D'Artagnan took off. D'Artagnan would grow into a $50 million business (as of 2007) that sells many game and gourmet products in addition to foie gras. (George Faison left in 2006 after a falling out with Ariane.) And Izzy would be the country's reigning foie gras farmer. "I owe her everything," Izzy said, "and she owes me everything."

Although by any measure Commonwealth was a successful start-up company, the good feelings didn't last. Yossi returned to Israel after a few years, and Izzy wound up working one-on-one with Howard Josephs, Rubin's son, but it was an uneasy relationship. In the late 1980s, after Izzy said Commonwealth was reprimanded because "we were disposing of the manure not in a very savory way," friction between Izzy and Howard grew to the point that Rubin fired Izzy in January 1989. Commonwealth kept going, and Izzy desperately needed a new job, driving tractor-trailers while he sought out investors.

Meanwhile, Ariane said, "I had a couple of crazy phone calls, voice messages, from a guy, Michael Ginor, who said he had just come back from Israel, and he had a taste of this thing called foie gras, and he saw that we were doing things with foie gras, and he's really, really interested, and he has money, and he wants to do something with foie gras." She was intrigued enough that she put him in touch with Izzy.

Michael Ginor was a "food guy" from as far back as he could remember. He was born in Seattle to two Israeli-born parents—his father worked for Boeing at the time—and spent much of his early life in Israel before attending Brandeis University, cashing in on Wall Street and joining the Israeli Army to become a patrol commander and information officer. When he first encountered foie gras grilled at an Israeli kebab restaurant, he thought it was "the greatest food I've ever eaten." What made it so? "That's always the eternal question. I think it's a combination of the flavor and the texture. I don't know that I've ever heard anyone give a great definition."

In early 1990 he and his wife went to Thomas Keller's New York restaurant, Rakel, to celebrate the birth of their son, and Ginor got excited when he looked at the menu and saw foie gras—this was a first for him in an American restaurant. It was . . . ehhh. "The preparation was fine, but it wasn't what I thought, what I remembered in Israel months earlier." He talked to Keller, whom he'd never met, and the chef told him that fresh foie gras was hard to come by because there was just one farm in upstate New York, and the quality was inconsis-

tent. "I went home, and I had one of those classic movie-like sleep-
less nights where I was like, there's a business here."

Michael, with his Wall Street riches, and his father, Amos, anted
up to start the new venture with Izzy, whose first impression of Michael was that he was a kid whose father was buying him a pony.
(Izzy was the pony.) Still, they needed a farm and a strategy. Although
he considered launching a more modest operation in Lancaster
County in Pennsylvania, Izzy's preference was to purchase an available chicken farm in New York's Sullivan County not far from Commonwealth. "It's got nice big buildings," Izzy told his new partners,
"but they have to be demolished because they're all junk." So they
bought the farm, and, Izzy said, "We never demolished the buildings,
and we're still using them. Eighteen years we're living with this junk,
and the farm looks like shit."

The farm's conditions would come back to haunt them soon
enough. They took over in July 1990, and a year later they produced
their first Hudson Valley foie gras, with D'Artagnan the primary distributor. In November 1992, as the fledgling company was gearing up
for the holiday season's heavy demands—while also trying to show
that it could top Commonwealth in terms of quality—disaster struck:
One of the coops collapsed, killing about 6,000 ducks. "All of a sudden, *boom*," Izzy said. "I called Michael. We started crying, because
all our money that we spent and everything, the whole thing is going
to go down to hell." Izzy suggested that the farm send D'Artagnan
its remaining supply for loyalty's sake while telling the rest of the
distributors they'd have to wait another year for any product. Essentially Hudson Valley Foie Gras would be starting all over. Michael
rejected this idea and, in a move that surprised Izzy, announced he
was headed to Commonwealth to make them an offer they wouldn't
refuse. Izzy thought no way, it's not going to happen, the Josephses
are too busy celebrating Hudson Valley's misfortune. Plus, Hudson
Valley, still in the red, was hardly in expansion mode. Yet Michael
went anyway, and after an all-night haggling session with Howard
Josephs, he returned home with Commonwealth in his pocket and
the holiday season saved. Soon Izzy was triumphantly reclaiming his
old desk at Commonwealth. He realized Michael wasn't such a kid
after all.

For a while, Izzy and Michael tried to maintain Hudson Valley and Commonwealth as two separate companies, but that made little sense given that expenses for doing so were higher—they had to maintain two on-site USDA offices, for one—and most customers knew that the same management was overseeing both labels. So Hudson Valley officially swallowed its rival, and the name "Commonwealth" went away, except in one case: Izzy had to fill an order for a Chicago customer who each week specifically requested 30 Hudson Valley livers and 30 Commonwealth ones. A Hudson Valley worker would glue 30 pink-and-purple Commonwealth labels over the gold-and-green Hudson Valley ones already on the packages before shipping them off to the Chicago-based distributor making the request. Finally, Izzy decided this was silly and called the distributor, who told him the livers were for Charlie Trotter. Izzy dropped the matter for the time being.

A few months later, Izzy ran into Trotter at a culinary event in Manhattan, and, Izzy recalled, the chef told him, "I like your foie gras very much, but I also buy from your previous farm, Commonwealth." Izzy explained that Hudson Valley now owned both companies, so the livers were coming from the same place, with the Commonwealth labels slapped over the Hudson Valley ones exclusively for him. "He starts laughing," Izzy recalled. "He said, 'Really? I can't believe that. And all this time they didn't tell me nothing? OK, let's stop this *mishegas*.' So the next day I come back to the farm, and I told the secretary about that. So the secretary says, 'But we are sending today 30 livers with the Commonwealth labels.' I said, 'No, you can stop that. I spoke with Charlie yesterday, it's OK.'" The secretary told him the distributor had made the request that very morning. Izzy called the distributor: "I said, 'You don't know yet, but I met Charlie in New York, and everything is OK, we don't do this anymore. We don't need to.' He said, 'No, no, I spoke with Charlie this morning, and he told me he wanted 30 Commonwealth and 30 Hudson Valley.' *After he saw me*." Izzy started laughing.

When I asked Trotter about this later, the chef said, "I like to tease. You may have noticed, I have a sense of humor."

4.

Lights, Cameras, Rat

"I personally have never seen a duck bleeding from the rear."

In recent years the legal system has been Bryan Pease's friend, lawsuits his weapon of choice against the evils of animal mistreatment. Having passed the California Bar Exam, the lanky young activist practices in San Diego, thus entering the profession of his father, an assistant U.S. attorney based in Syracuse, New York. Yet for someone who was raised in and reveres the law, Pease certainly has done his share of breaking it, albeit for the same animal-related purposes.

Pease was a high-schooler in Liverpool, New York, when he found his calling in biology class. "I refused to dissect," explained Pease. "I started learning about animal rights and started not using products that were tested on animals." He drew further inspiration from PETA's high-profile, ultimately successful anti-animal-testing campaign against Gillette, and he became a vegetarian shortly thereafter. "And then I learned about factory farming and went vegan." His first arrest came at age 16, in 1994, when he and five other protesters refused to quit demonstrating in front of a mall fur store.

As a Cornell University undergraduate, Pease agitated for animal rights and at one point helped burn a biomedical professor in effigy in front of the university administration building; the protesters felt the guy had been misinforming students about whether they were required to dissect animals, so the theme of this media stunt was "Liar, liar, pants on fire," literally. Pease was arrested and charged with conspiracy, criminal nuisance and criminal mischief before pleading guilty to reckless endangerment of property. The university also barred Pease from having contact with this professor, though Pease told me later with a laugh, "If we're burning effigies of someone, communication has probably broken down at that point anyway."

Post-college, Pease was arrested twice in early 2002, first in January during an anti-animal-testing protest at an Arkansas investment firm; he received felony charges—"trumped up," he said—of commercial burglary, battery and criminal mischief before the jury found him guilty only of such lesser offenses as criminal trespass and refusing to submit to arrest. His 45-day jail term was reduced to 30 after he rescued a female guard from being pummeled by a fellow inmate. Before that jail stint began, he was arrested again for trespassing on an upstate New York farm that raised lab animals. That misdemeanor resulted in a fine.

Pease's most recent arrest came in the fall of 2004 at a San Diego beach where harbor seals were pupping. The city recently had taken down a rope that prevented beachgoers from impinging on the seals' territory, so Pease and other activists drew a seaweed line in the sand to keep beachgoers away from the animals. A female protester called him one day to say a drunken beachgoer was harassing her and throwing the seaweed back into the ocean, so, he said, he picked up a $20 "zapping device" that he'd bought at a swap meet and went to her aid. When the unruly dude threw seaweed in his face, "I knocked him down and used the stun gun defensively," Pease said. "I took out the little zapping toy and tried to zap him." Police arrested Pease for assault with a stun gun. By then Pease had passed the bar exam and was awaiting approval from the character and fitness committee, but the bar isn't keen on admitting members with charges pending against them. As the legal resolution of Pease's case dragged on, his ascendancy to lawyerhood was delayed for more than a year. To prove self-defense, Pease would have had to show that he feared death or serious bodily injury, so he ultimately pled guilty to misdemeanor assault with a stun gun, he was fined and put on probation, and he had to take an anger management class. After his plea was accepted and he offered his explanation to the bar committee, he officially became a lawyer in December 2005. Thus closed the door—at least most of the way—on his use of lawbreaking as a tactic. "Now I'm not interested in doing anything that could even have the risk of arrest so that I can be much more effective as a lawyer," Pease told me.

His journey from fighting the law to utilizing it has parallels in the greater animal-rights movement. When he was young and angry, he viewed civil disobedience as his best and only outlet for expressing outrage over animal mistreatment; he considered his actions a small contribution to the "mass uprising" taking shape around him. The grassroots animal-rights movement of the 1980s and early 1990s was pissed off, with protesters taking inspiration from Peter Singer's *Animal Liberation* and moving aggressively to shut down animal-testing labs and other exploiters of living creatures. There were food campaigns as well, mostly visibly against veal, but it wasn't until the late 1990s that the movement dramatically redirected its energies toward farm animals. A large part of this move was sheer numbers: Almost 10 billion animals a year are killed for food in the United States, compared to about 20 million estimated by the animal-rights movement to be used in animal testing. More than 95 percent of all of the country's animals are thought to be involved in food production.

The other major shift was that as the mainstream increasingly latched on to animal issues, the movement viewed getting arrested more critically. Some protesters still crossed lines and were jailed, but groups such as the Humane Society of the United States, which became far more active in fighting factory-farming practices after vegan Wayne Pacelle took over in 2004, and Farm Sanctuary, which grew steadily after its 1986 launch as a farm animal shelter in a Delaware house, became more focused on pushing for animal-friendly laws and suing those they considered abusers. "In reality when activists are getting arrested, then the focus is on the activists and not the issue," Pease said. "Why would I do that when I can file lawsuits and do things that are more effective?"

Nevertheless, he still drew distinctions among certain types of illegality: "There is a difference between just breaking the law and engaging in civil disobedience, which is where you are open about what you are doing and you are willing to accept the consequences," he said. For instance, trespassing onto foie gras farms, making secret videotapes, "liberating" ducks and eventually making public the edited footage may be against the law, but to him those activities were justified in exposing the greater crimes of the foie gras industry.

Foie gras came on to Pease's radar early in his activist career. PETA had produced a 1991 anti-foie-gras video, *Victims of Indulgence,* in which Sir John Gielgud narrates over footage secretly obtained from Commonwealth Foie Gras. The video has its whimsical moments ("This goose has chosen a dog as a dear friend, and the two spend most waking hours together") but mostly shows the process of force-feeding, something with very little previous public exposure. After experts attest to the practice's cruelty and Gielgud describes the delicacy as "a disease being peddled as a gourmet food," the narrator makes an on-camera appeal: "Please never buy foie gras or order it in restaurants, and be certain to tell others why." At this point, of course, YouTube and other forms of viral Internet video weren't around, and the PETA effort was relatively low-key. Pease considered it a noble effort; he just didn't understand why activists hadn't followed up more aggressively. "I couldn't believe that the animal movement had allowed foie gras to take root and exist," he said. "It wasn't even on menus 20 years ago. There was nothing being domestically produced that was served in restaurants. Nobody really knew about it. It was only through the efforts of Hudson Valley promoting it to Manhattan restaurants and through their marketing angle that they were able to make it into this big thing. Obviously it's a lot harder to stop it now that it's so entrenched."

Pease argued that while other meat animals theoretically could be raised and killed humanely, foie gras duck production was inherently cruel. Mind you, when I asked Pease to name one food animal that he thought *was* humanely killed, he couldn't—"There's no humane way to slaughter an animal"—so this was all a matter of degree. Nonetheless, in foie gras Pease saw a deserving opponent—as well as an opportunity.

He moved to Oakland in 2002 and founded a small grassroots organization, the American Coalition for Animal Defense, which eventually morphed into the Animal Protection and Rescue League, which he still runs out of San Diego with his wife, Kath Rogers, whom he met in 2003 as they tried to disrupt a crow-shooting contest in upstate New York. The nascent group set up an office to spread the word about duck force-feeding and to raise money to buy cameras and other pieces of equipment to be used in an undercover operation. He had heard that California's only foie gras farm was operating in Sonoma, so he and his fellow activists—and their new cameras— headed that way.

Guillermo Gonzalez ultimately went from one war zone to another. In 1984, guerrilla fighting was tearing apart his country of El Salvador when he took a meeting with an Israeli company looking to establish a turnkey goose foie gras business there. Israel had been successfully producing and exporting goose foie gras to France, and now El Salvador could get into the mix by creating a vertically integrated business in which geese would be bred, hatched, raised, force-fed, slaughtered and processed for export. That was the idea at least. It sounded good to the 32-year-old Gonzalez, a tall, strapping man with an easygoing demeanor. He quit his family business as an engineering/arts supplier to become the proposed project's executive director and one of five partners. To get started, he imported some geese from Iowa for breeding purposes. Let the foie gras begin.

But wait. The arrangement with the Israelis didn't last long, as Guillermo realized that the parent company was dictating terms that would be impossible to meet. Plus—and this was a biggie—Gonzalez had no inkling of how to make foie gras. El Salvador wasn't exactly steeped in the artisan tradition; even raising geese was a novelty there. Guillermo had a gaggle of Iowan geese but didn't know how to plump their livers or whether this breed was even particularly plumpable. But the idea still excited him, so he and his Salvadoran partners forged ahead, Guillermo's travels taking him to South Dakota, home of U.S. goose producer Schiltz Goose Farm. Guillermo hoped to obtain some breeding stock and foie gras know-how, but although company president Marlin Schiltz knew plenty about the former, he was in the dark regarding the latter. What Schiltz did have in his desk drawer was a recent *New York Times* article about France's Weekend at the Farm program, in which tourists could spend a few days and nights being lodged, fed and treated to pastoral life on a small operational farm. The story spotlighted the southwestern France spread of Danie and Guy Dubois, who raised geese and produced foie gras in the long tradition of their ancestors. Guillermo didn't speak a word of French, but, he said, "This is where I need to go." Soon he was on a plane to France.

What he found in Ladornac, the Duboises' tiny town in the Périgord region, was a modest family farm. Danie and Guy, then in their early 40s, and their son Gilles, in his early 20s, did pretty much everything: raising and caring for the geese, force-feeding them and slaughtering and processing them at the end. Their output was 2,000 to 3,000 birds a year. In contrast, the Israelis' proposal had been for Guillermo and his partners to turn out 45,000 geese in year one. Guillermo liked the Duboises so much that he wanted to involve them in the Salvadoran project, so Danie flew back home with him. She took a look at the geese, the land and the plan before offering her professional opinion: They shouldn't take on any more geese than she and her family did, at least at first; she just wasn't comfortable with those big numbers.

Guillermo's partners were disappointed. They had envisioned the kind of large-scale operation that could handle 45,000 geese and would turn a proportionate profit. With Danie Dubois recommending just 5 to 10 percent of this anticipated volume, suddenly the business was looking mighty small. The partners outvoted Guillermo four to one, but instead of bidding *au revoir* to Madame Dubois, Guillermo split from his co-investors, who kept the geese. Impressed by his commitment and his apparent willingness to change his lifestyle, Danie told him, "I offer you the chance to come to France, and we'll teach you, we'll lodge you, we'll feed you—in exchange for you always being able to help us with our chores." Guillermo and his wife, Junny, had two daughters, then ages eight and two and a half, and, yes, of course, they were welcome, too. "That's how our new life started," he said.

The setting was rustic, the facilities far from modern as everyone worked and lived in ages-old stone buildings. At this point the Dubois farm was considered strictly an artisanal enterprise, selling

its foie gras and other products to visitors. That was how Danie's
mother and grandmother had done it, after all.

During the birds' first six months of life, before the start of the
three-week gavage period, the Gonzalezes spread straw in the barns
and poured feed into hanging containers. They collected hay in the
summertime and loaded the heavy bales onto trucks. Guillermo assisted with the pigs and cows being raised on the farm, and Junny
worked with such crops as grapes, potatoes and walnuts. Guillermo
and Junny also helped out in the slaughterhouse—toweling down the
newly plucked carcasses, removing the remaining feather fragments
with a blowtorch—as well as in the processing room, where they deveined the goose livers and prepared various products for canning.
Danie, who handled the force-feeding and slaughter herself, offered
a nonstop tutorial on the methods that her mother and grandmother
had taught her. The Gonzalezes were busy all the time, but they also
were in one of the world's more beautiful settings, the kind of rolling
countryside you see in movies that romanticize rolling countrysides.
In the Duboises, they had found a family that instantly made them
feel at home despite the language barrier and the fact that they'd
known one another for just a few months. Danie and Guy were
warm, laid-back, supportive and nonintrusive, and when mealtime
came, she served up feasts derived almost solely from the farm.

This was not a bad way to live, but after seven months, Guillermo
thought he'd better return to his own project, so he took off, though
Junny and the girls remained on the farm for an entire year. Danie
thought he still should pursue launching a farm in El Salvador, but
Guillermo was wary of competing with his now ex-partners (who
never did produce foie gras, though they were one of the country's
first goose meat suppliers)—and the country remained embroiled in
civil war. So Danie referred him to a friend living in San Francisco,
and for a month and a half he lived in this woman's home and got
assistance from the University of California Cooperative Extension
as he researched how to establish the state's first foie gras farm. He
soon struck up a partnership with a duck/goose farm that also was
interested in entering the foie gras business. The idea was that this
company would provide the birds and facilities while Guillermo and
Danie Dubois would oversee the foie gras production. Danie trav-

eled to California to test whether the company's breeds of ducks and geese would make a worthy foie gras. The verdict: no for the geese, yes for the Muscovy ducks. When a local chef sampled the product and committed to ordering it, everyone agreed to move forward—or so Guillermo thought. The following day, he said, he got a call from the other company: They were pulling out. Guillermo had his suspicions, but there was nothing he could do but go ahead on his own.

Eventually, he located a vacant licensed processing plant in Sonoma, which would enable him not only to raise and to force-feed the birds but also to slaughter them. He bought the farm and prepared to get going with Muscovy ducks (as opposed to the industry-standard cross-bred Mulards, which are considered heartier but, in Gonzalez's mind, less flavorful) when he received another blow: Danie told him that her family couldn't be full-time partners after all. Initially Gilles was supposed to join the Gonzalezes in California, but the Duboises had begun building their own processing plant, and the son was needed at home. So Gilles was able to join Guillermo for just a month to help set up the ducks' feeding routine before he returned to France. "That was a scary moment," Guillermo recalled, "because Junny and I were on our own."

California Foie Gras, as he dubbed the company, opened for business as a literal ma-and-pa operation in 1986, with the first product becoming available that September. Guillermo did all of the feedings, in which he scooped whole cooked corn kernels into a funnel equipped with a motorized auger, as well as the slaughter. Junny helped out in preparing the carcasses and processing the livers and other duck parts. In the beginning they were producing 30 to 40 ducks per week, a lower output than even the Duboises'. The first sale was a single liver to the restaurant at Napa Valley's sparkling wine producer Domaine Chandon. When Guillermo tried to solicit business from Jordan Winery in Sonoma County, a representative there informed him, "We're already buying from you." Jordan Winery indeed was buying product from California Foie Gras—that was the name being used by the company that had split from the Gonzalezes and Duboises at the last minute. (A Hungarian family-run goose foie gras company also was in operation, further foiling Guillermo's plans to become California's first foie gras producer.) So Guillermo redubbed his company Wine Country Foie Gras, a name that lasted a year and a half until, he said, a man approached him claiming he owned exclusive rights to the name "Wine Country" and threatened litigation. Rather than fight, Guillermo renamed his company and product line once again: Sonoma Foie Gras. "It hasn't been an easy road," he sighed.

As it turned out, California Foie Gras and the Hungarian operation eventually folded, all while Sonoma Foie Gras grew so steadily that by 1997 it was ready for a new home. The farm already had become increasingly at odds with its quiet rural surroundings. This was, after all, an idyllic area meant for relaxing and getting quietly buzzed on one of the popular vintages produced nearby. People in Sonoma County wished to escape the Bay Area bustle, not to deal with livestock smells and the noise and traffic from 20 employees and various delivery trucks driving in and out of a farm. Neighbors complained, and Guillermo wanted a bigger facility anyway, one where he could install modern feeding machines that would enable the operation to increase its speed and volume. It made sense to do so in an area devoted to farming.

So while Guillermo and Junny kept their home and office in Sonoma, they relocated the farm to the agricultural town of Ripon, about 80 miles east of San Francisco. On a larger scale, the farm kept doing what it had been doing: feeding Muscovy ducks that had been raised by Grimaud Farms in nearby Stockton. But after Guillermo hired Eric Delmas (Danie Dubois's nephew) as the full-time production manager, Delmas persuaded his boss to seek a bigger property where he could raise his own ducks. In 1999 the Sonoma Foie Gras farm moved again, to Farmington, where Guillermo leased buildings from a farmer maintaining a layer-hen operation on the grounds. The new location, less than 20 miles east of Stockton, was convenient because Sonoma Foie Gras was boosting its relationship with Grimaud. Not only did he contract the Stockton company to slaughter and to process his ducks, thus cutting down his need for a larger workforce and even more expanded facilities, but he also hired Grimaud as Sonoma Foie Gras's national distributor.

In addition, Grimaud continued to provide Sonoma Foie Gras with ready-for-gavage Muscovy ducks while also supplying Mulard duck hatchlings to be raised in barns and on the new farm's sizable fields. Guillermo preferred Muscovy foie gras to Mulard; he found its texture finer, the flavor more intense. But his business was selling to chefs, and most chefs favored Mulards, in part because the Muscovy livers render more fat in the hot pan. (In another couple of years he would phase out the Muscovies altogether and eventually add another product line: Artisan Foie Gras, a higher-end alternative to the Sonoma label that he distributed himself.) The interdependence between Sonoma and Grimaud would grow so strong that Guillermo ultimately came to feel his business couldn't survive without the other.

By the early 2000s, Guillermo's farm was turning out more than 50,000 ducks a year, and business kept growing. The volume still didn't approach the hundreds of thousands of ducks processed each year by Hudson Valley Foie Gras, but life was good. The old cliché applied: The Gonzalez family was living the American dream—arriving as immigrants, learning a new trade, working hard and creating a business that kept them comfortable and others employed while making people happy with their product.

Cue the cellos and dark clouds.

Guillermo didn't notice the first time that Pease and his fellow twentysomething activists snuck onto his farm in 2002. He didn't notice the second or third time either. Pease and his companions hadn't found Sonoma Foie Gras when they looked for it in Sonoma, but they did eventually locate the Grimaud slaughterhouse in Stockton that was doing the company's breeding and processing, and they followed a truck back to the farm in Farmington. When they arrived, they saw no indication that this was a foie gras farm. The barns closest to the road were populated by layer hens packed into battery cages, and only as the intruders traveled toward the back of the property did they find the duck barns. They had an easier go of it the next time. And the next time.

Pease and crew must have ventured onto the Sonoma Foie Gras farm about a dozen times that summer, almost always at night. They would park about a mile away and hoof it over the fields to the barns, which invariably were unlocked. The activists weren't wearing ski masks or any other disguise. Sometimes they entered the barns late at night after all of the employees had taken off. Other times they walked in before the 10 p.m. feeding and watched the Mexican workers going from pen to pen lowering the tubes down the ducks' throats. One night a worker even let them videotape him feeding the birds. The activists returned the following night to shoot more footage, but this time the worker said, "*Un momento,*" excused himself and walked outside. When Pease went out to check what was going on, he saw several of the workers huddled around a cell phone. If Guillermo hadn't known about the activists' excursions before, he did now. The worker told Pease et al. that they weren't allowed to be there and should leave pronto. They did, with the workers trailing them through the fields to the getaway car to copy down their license plate number.

By then Pease already had accumulated hours of footage. He'd dedicated several previous visits to trying to capture the force-feeding process by way of a pinhole spy camera that he duct-taped to the barn's ceiling, with the images relayed to a car-battery-powered VCR stashed in the bushes. Despite his best efforts, though, either the timing or camera angle was off, or the battery lost power. "Finally when we got the exact right shot, it was too dim," he said. Pease also visited the Grimaud plant to videotape the slaughter. The shackled ducks were visible through the window, so he just stood on the sidewalk and aimed the camera at the carcasses passing down the line before their immersion in the scalding tank. A manager came out and told him to leave, but Pease returned the next day. "I thought the ducks were being scalded alive. We went back, and I just ran in, and within seconds there were six Mexican guys on me, and they jumped on me. I tried to throw them off of me, and my glasses fell off and disappeared somewhere, and then we just started going back to the car." He never did determine whether the ducks were still breathing as they descended into the scalding water.

Back at the farm, the activists got their money shot. While he was trying to set up that spy camera, another volunteer was walking from pen to pen videotaping the ducks. Farmhands often place sick or injured birds into a separate pen for safekeeping, and that apparently was the case with two ducks sporting nasty-looking wounds on their rear ends. As Pease tells it, his companion that night was video-taping this pair of ducks when a rat came up and started burrowing into one's bloody butt, then the other's. *Chew, chew, chew*—yummy rat snack. On the video the lethargic ducks are seen flapping their wings ineffectually and trying fruitlessly to step out of the way, but the damn rat keeps digging in, even as light floods the pen with the camera rolling. "We were using a battery-powered halogen light that was dying down, so that might have facilitated the rat not caring," Pease said. "It just seemed like the rat wasn't aware of our presence. I had a flashlight that I thought might scare it, but it didn't." Here was your classic wartime photographer's dilemma, albeit on a crit-ter scale: Do you keep filming the abuse you're witnessing or do you shut off the camera and intervene? In this case they filmed, then in-tervened, picking up the ducks, carrying them back to their car and taking them to a veterinarian.

This clip, we'll call it "Rat Munching on Ducks' Bloody Ass Wounds," would become the number-one shock moment in anti-foie-gras horror montages to be prepared by animal rights groups. Rats aren't an uncommon farm problem, but they certainly did much damage to Guillermo Gonzalez, who remained perplexed by that video scene when I spoke with him about it well after the fact.

"I personally have never seen a duck bleeding from the rear," Gonzalez told me. "I cannot say this is impossible, but I personally have never seen it. When I see that image of the rat, I have a very hard time believing first of all that the duck is going to be bleeding in that part of the body like it is, and then in the second that a rat is going to be so completely comfortable doing what the rat is doing when it has a floodlight in front and someone filming at a very short distance. I very seriously believe, I'm almost convinced, that this was staged. It's very easy for someone in the middle of the night to put some chicken wire around the pen, to put some substance in the rear of the duck that may be attractive for a rat to come and nibble or come after. In a natural way I don't see that as a possibility." Guillermo's specula-tion that this footage might have been staged, which I subsequently printed in the *Chicago Tribune,* prompted Pease to sue him for libel. Guillermo eventually countersued in reference to Pease's response, as printed in the story: "Guillermo Gonzalez's accusation about us staging that footage is one of the craziest, stupidest things I've ever heard this psychotic animal torturer to say."

In the fall of 2002, Pease left California behind for a while; it was time to return to law school at the State University of New York at Buffalo. The location would prove convenient for the next step of his budding campaign: rounding up some East Coast activists and raiding the nation's largest foie gras farm, Hudson Valley Foie Gras.

5.

Gourmet Cruelty and the Battle of California

*"Would the duck die from the speed-feeding
process?"*
"Yes."

By the time Bryan Pease enlisted them in the still-covert war on foie gras, Sarahjane Blum and Ryan Shapiro already were seeking more effective tactics to wipe out animal mistreatment. Ryan, in particular, had grown weary of the protest method that he and his younger brother Paul had employed with some regularity: locking themselves to things. Their favorite object was a large concrete-filled oil drum that had a wide steel tube running through its center so one person on either side could stick his arm all the way inside and lock it at the center. They would do this once the oil drum was massively in the way of a business that protesters found objectionable. "Emergency services has to come in and jackhammer you out, and the store shuts for the day," Ryan explained. The New York City Animal Defense League, which Ryan and then-girlfriend Sarahjane ran for a while, used this tactic in front of fur stores. The group that Paul founded in high school, Compassion over Killing (COK), stuck one of these big drums on the elephants' entrance ramp at Ringling Bros. and Barnum & Bailey Circus, thus delaying the show for hours. Ryan and Paul ended the day locked to something else: a pair of police handcuffs.

But turning themselves into immovable objects and getting arrested soon grew old, and the tactic didn't seem to be saving many animals either. "It wasn't the most effective strategy that we could've employed," Ryan admitted in retrospect. So Ryan and Sarahjane went their way, Paul went his, and the three of them managed to make themselves into a bigger nuisance for the foie gras industry than any of them might have imagined.

All three of them were vegans. As a teenager growing up in New York City, Sarahjane couldn't eat fish because "they smelled like their home, and it freaked me out," but her epiphany came one summer when she was riding bikes with a friend in the country, and she saw roadkill for the first time. "That was when I decided to stop eating meat," Sarahjane said. "Nobody ever talked to me about what animal death was. Nobody tried to preordain in my mind what place the death of animals should have in the consciousness." In the Shapiros' Washington, D.C., area household, when 13-year-old Paul saw a video depicting ill-treated factory farm animals, "I saw my dogs in those animals. I recognized that I would do anything to prevent my dogs from enduring that type of terror, and I didn't think my dogs had any more moral value so to speak than other animals." Ryan became a vegan by way of learning that during the Holocaust, concentration camps were located within functioning towns where people shopped beyond the camp walls. One day when Ryan was driving to a mall, he passed a truck carrying cows to slaughter, their eyes peeking through the slats, and he felt like one of those insensible World War II villagers. "The cows have been so abandoned that literally people are driving to the mall while they are being taken to be killed. I decided that I could not be party to that anymore."

Sarahjane met Paul at Vassar College before she dropped out to become more involved in animal activism, and he put her in touch with Ryan, then a New York University film undergraduate heavily involved in the animal-rights movement. Soon Sarahjane and Ryan were living and protesting together. The couple met Bryan Pease at a New York City anti-fur demonstration in the late 1990s, and over the ensuing years the three of them continued to see each other at assorted animal gatherings. Knowing that Ryan had studied film and that Sarahjane remained a dedicated activist, Pease called them upon his return to the East Coast and proposed that they collaborate on a new project: collecting undercover footage of Hudson Valley Foie Gras to incorporate into a videotape.

Targeting foie gras struck Ryan as a fine idea given that he'd recently decided to redirect his efforts toward factory farming. "So many billions more are suffering on factory farms than they are in any other animal industry," Ryan said. Also, convincing someone to quit buying fur was nice, but getting someone to stop consuming factory farm products—i.e., meat—represented a building block toward a radically different society.

Still, if Ryan was driven by numbers, why would he dedicate himself to fighting foie gras? U.S. foie gras producers kill about as many ducks a year—500,000—as some factories kill broiler chickens in a *day*. Plus, it's tough to argue that you're effecting major lifestyle changes by convincing people not to eat something that most of them had never heard of. Ryan acknowledged the contradiction, as well as the calculated pragmatism underlying this campaign, as he told me he considered foie gras to be "a tremendous stepping-stone to broader issues of factory farming. It's not that far of a leap to show that while this is so clearly and egregiously cruel and needless, it really isn't significantly different from any of the other billions of animals who are suffering currently on factory farms." Also, any changes in the poultry industry would, almost by definition, have to be on a massive scale, but with foie gras, "discrete victories were possible": convincing legislatures to ban it, convincing restaurants to quit serving it, convincing people not to eat it.

Sarahjane, who had never been on a farm before her activism career began, knew little about foie gras and didn't realize it was being produced in the United States. When she found out it was being farmed less than two hours from New York City—"really in my backyard"—she was appalled, so she agreed to check it out, with Bryan leading her and another volunteer up to Hudson Valley Foie Gras on a cold, crisp night. "The first thing that hit me both literally and conceptually was the smell," she said. "It was the most awful, stenchy smell ever. Now, in my mind, that is the smell of death. It's the mix of the smell of a chemical and the smell of a bog is the best way to put it." They passed through an unlocked door and entered a room lined with ducks confined in individual cages. "They were weak, and they were just kind of panting, and the ones who had a lot of strength, you'd see them just trying to push, trying to open their wings, which they couldn't do, against the wires of the cage. And then you'd see them trying to lift their heads up as far as they could, just trying to get out."

Ryan's first impression of the farm was similar. "I was immediately overcome by the sense of feces and death. It was tremendously overpowering. Staring down rows and rows and rows and rows of birds trapped in isolation cages so small they couldn't spread their wings, much less turn around, I was overcome by a completely overwhelming sense of grief."

Sarahjane, Ryan and Bryan hit Hudson Valley Foie Gras at an odd point in the farm's history. Since it had produced its first foie gras in 1991, its methods hadn't changed much: Once the ducks transitioned into the gavage period, groups of 10 or so resided in relatively spacious pens and were fed individually with auger-equipped funnels. But in 2001 the farm hired poultry veteran Marcus Henley as its general manager, and Izzy took him to France to show him the modern facilities over there. Most of the French farms were using individual cages and pneumatic feeding machines, which speed up the actual feedings as well as the overall period over which the ducks are force-fed; the French gavage was down to less than two weeks, compared to four weeks at Hudson Valley and 14 to 17 days at Sonoma. Henley estimated that Hudson Valley's feeding method cost four times that of the French, so if the other way was that much more efficient and profitable, why not have Hudson Valley try it out?

So, Izzy said, Hudson Valley imported the French cages and machinery and installed them in one of the barns on a trial basis. He deemed the results disastrous: The ducks didn't respond well, and the livers were no good. "It was disgusting. So we junked it!" Izzy said, noting that the individual cages were used for three cycles of ducks—three months—before the plug was pulled.

Ryan and Sarahjane said Izzy is lying and that those cages were in use for more than a year. "From the first time I went there to the last time I went there must have been a period of at least 15 months," Sarahjane said. "They had them the whole time."

"That is not true," Izzy insisted, seated in his office with Henley. "But let me ask you this: So what? Let's assume that we are lying. They're not here now. What's the difference with what happened seven years ago? Let's assume I'm an evil person, and I don't care about nothing. But I didn't get the stuff I needed. It was not good economically for us. Forget about animal rights."

"The small cages, we were uncomfortable with that," Henley interjected.

"Everybody in the world is doing it," Izzy said of the individual cages. "We are too stupid. We don't know how to do it. So we took them out."

"*Before* those pictures ever hit the Internet," Henley added.

Ultimately the activists and Hudson Valley folks agreed on this point: Individual cages are bad. And as far as anyone knows, they're not in use anywhere in the United States. Even when Sarahjane, Ryan and Bryan were sneaking into Hudson Valley, the majority of birds in gavage remained in group pens, and Sarahjane admitted that these ducks "seemed better in such a relative way. Certainly there were not as many just really severe, physical injuries. You didn't see as many abscesses." The individually caged ducks were the ones with "horrific feather loss and broken wings" as well as skin and foot problems. "It just was what the confinement did to their bodies, nothing else— even without the force-feeding," she said, though she noted that the penned ducks did show some feather loss and "really goopy eye infections," and some of the weak ones got "trampled" by the strong ones (which is one of the French justifications for using the individual cages). What was constant for both groups of ducks, she said, was "the part where they can't walk or they can't sustain their own body weight, or they can't swallow right on their own or they can't breathe right on their own."

Sarahjane and Ryan said they snuck on the farm between 12 and 24 times, though Izzy and Marcus argued that the number actually was one or two. Most of the times, Sarahjane said, they went so late at night—well past midnight—that no one saw them. Sarahjane visited the most often, sometimes not even taking a video camera with her. She tried to figure out when the ducks were fed, where they were slaughtered, where the ducklings were being raised, how conditions differed depending on the season, when the birds would start to show symptoms of the force-feedings. Sometimes she just entered a barn alone and contemplated the ducks, looking them in the eyes and musing about her responsibility to them. She believed the way she could help them the most was to show their conditions to the world, but "I couldn't help but feel like I also had to at least try to let some of them actually swim in a lake, actually eat on their own, actually socialize with other animals in the sun."

A key element of Sarahjane and Ryan's efforts was "open rescue"—videotaping themselves and other volunteers removing ducks from their cages and getting them veterinary help. Such work was popularized by an American-born activist living in Australia named Patty Mark, and Compassion over Killing, Paul Shapiro's group, followed her lead by having members videotape themselves rescuing caged layer hens, releasing the footage to the press and hosting news conferences. Pease said he always planned on incorporating open rescue when he recruited Sarahjane and Ryan, though he personally didn't want to be filmed removing ducks because he didn't want to derail his law degree. At the same time, Pease wanted to get the footage out quickly, including the Sonoma Foie Gras material that he'd given to Ryan and Sarahjane for inclusion in the final product. In the summer of 2003, Bryan moved to San Francisco to incorporate the Animal Protection and Rescue League (APRL) and to open a new branch office, and he rounded up volunteers to lobby the California legislature against foie gras upon the videotape's release. But Ryan and Sarahjane weren't ready.

"Our intentions kind of just evolved from it being, 'Hey, let's take a camcorder in and take some pictures and see what we get' to 'Let's really figure out how to create a cornerstone piece that groups nationwide can take to restaurateurs, can take to their representatives in government, can take to the media and can use again and again to really educate about something nobody knows anything about,'" Sarahjane said. "Bryan really wanted to just throw rough-cut footage together and get it on the news, and we realized that if he did that, there was no way to build a movement behind it." Countered Pease: "The news is designed to be able to take footage and put it on the air. It doesn't have to be a slick video with a glossy cover." At one point Ryan and Sarahjane envisioned releasing an hour-long documentary before heeding warnings of how difficult it would be to find an audience for something so lengthy and grim.

Sarahjane and Ryan kept shooting and editing and working with volunteers to compile anti-foie-gras literature all while Bryan grew increasingly impatient. He felt like he was being stalled by Ryan's filmmaking ambitions and promises of a *New York Times* exclusive that never materialized. Finally, Ryan and Sarahjane officially split from Bryan and formed their own group, GourmetCruelty.com. People often called it Gourmet Cruelty, but to Ryan the ".com" was crucial because any reference to the organization would advertise the Web site. "GourmetCruelty.com was supposed to just be a campaign Web site for APRL, but then they split off," Bryan said. "I think Ryan just wanted his own group for some reason. I don't know why." Calling the rupture "a little messy," Ryan chalked it up to "some mix of practical and personal. Coordinating that many different people on two coasts who had so many different agendas and trying to balance all of that, it just ended up being the most viable way to do it."

Sarahjane and Ryan finally called their movie *Delicacy of Despair*. There were two versions: The shorter one, aimed at politicians and restaurants, ends after 11 minutes and focuses exclusively on foie gras. The other, more generally targeted one includes an additional five minutes showing Sarahjane, Ryan and others removing ducks from their Hudson Valley cages and taking them to veterinarians for rehabilitation, and it ends with an appeal for viewers to become vegans. Over the course of their farm visits, Ryan said, they took a total of 15 ducks, almost all of whom were placed with the waterfowl equivalent of foster families. "These animals cannot fly, so they can't be released into the wild."

In an intriguing sidelight, although the activists were rescuing the sickest-looking ducks near the end of the force-feeding process, Ryan said only one of them could not be rehabilitated. Yes, the recovery for some took longer than others, particularly the two ducks that had difficulty walking, but "as they lived normal lives, the ones who could walk, their livers just naturally shrank back down almost all of the way." The notion that the fat livers eventually would return to normal if the feedings ended has been a key argument of foie gras supporters, who say such recoveries demonstrate that the livers aren't actually diseased. Ryan, though, still considered the disease label to be fair, noting, "I think obesity is now called a disease." (Anti-foie veterinarian Holly Cheever's take on this debate was that if you break someone's leg, it also will heal, but that's still not a nice thing to do.)

Even in its shorter version, Pease found *Delicacy of Despair* to be overlong given a chef's or legislator's attention span. "It had to be this big fancy video that Ryan could wave around," Bryan said. "He's a film student. It was his masterpiece." No one would confuse *Delicacy of Despair* with a Steven Spielberg production, but it does make its points vividly. It begins by showing ducks swimming outdoors as a high-pitched female narrator, Sarahjane, describes their grace, their ability to form relationships, their formidable diving and flying abilities (though the made-for-foie Mulard crossbreed can't actually fly) and their lifespan of up to 18 years. (Some ducks are thought to live that long, though it's tough to pinpoint a natural lifespan for a bird that's been crossbred specifically to be eaten rather than to exist in the wild.) Then the ducks lift off, leaving the pond empty and making way for ominous strings and images of canned foie gras. "Medically known as hepatic lipidosis," she narrates, "foie gras is a disease marketed as a delicacy."

The film proceeds to show force-feeding in the Hudson Valley individual cages ("They must endure this trauma three times a day every day"), frozen water troughs, an assortment of sick-looking birds and a dead duck montage culminating in a yellow bin full of *canard* corpses. The discomfort of the "tiny isolation cages" is stressed, with Sarahjane noting, "These ducks know only hard wire for a bed and steel wires for a home." (For what it's worth, the flooring of a Hudson Valley duck pen is plastic-wrapped wire mesh.) Then comes that Sonoma horror highlight, "Rat Munching on Ducks' Bloody Ass Wounds"—three separate shots of the rat burrowing into the ducks' backsides accompanied by the narration: "Here two ducks are literally being eaten alive by a rat. They have been rendered so weak by life on the factory farm that they are barely even able to struggle."

The video was ready for prime time—or at least the evening news.

Before *Delicacy of Despair* was unveiled to the world, the public campaign against foie gras in northern California already was off to a violent start. In late July 2003, vandals attacked the Santa Rosa home of Didier Jaubert, an investor in a soon-to-open specialty shop/restaurant called Sonoma Saveurs, in which Guillermo and Junny Gonzalez and renowned San Francisco chef Laurent Manrique also were partners. Sonoma Saveurs, located on the historic Sonoma Plaza, was slated to carry foie gras and other products from Sonoma Foie Gras. The vandals covered Jaubert's house with red paint, Super Glued his locks and garage doors and left graffiti messages such as "Foie gras is animal torture" and "Stop or be stopped." "We cannot let this restaurant open," read an anonymous dispatch on Bite Back, a Web site (and magazine) promoting the violence-prone Animal Liberation Front. "Jaubert needs to hear immediately that people will not tolerate this atrocity."

Two nights later, "concerned citizens" (as Bite Back called them) assaulted Manrique's Marin County home in similar fashion, splashing red paint all over the house, dumping paint thinner on his car and leaving painted messages that the Gascony-born chef was a "torturer" and "murderer" who should "go home." Manrique, who runs the kitchen at the San Francisco restaurant Aqua, was upset, but he was even more disturbed the next day to receive a videocassette showing him playing in his garden with his young son. The tape was accompanied by a simple slip of paper that read: "Stop the foie gras, or you will be stopped."

In mid-August the attacks escalated further when vandals broke into the classic adobe building that housed the under-construction Sonoma Saveurs. They covered the walls, fixtures and new appliances with red paint and anti-foie-gras graffiti ("Go home," "Shame," "Misery," "End Animal Torture," "Foie Gras = Death"), poured concrete down the drains where sinks and toilets were to be installed and turned on the water taps, thus flooding the place and neighboring businesses. A Bite Back message characterized the poured concrete as "symbolizing the forcing of high density feed down the throats of ducks. The damage this will do to the plumbing symbolizes the damage done to the ducks' digestive systems by force feeding them." The flood, it continued, was to punish Gonzalez for not providing his ducks with ponds in which to bathe. "Now Guillermo will be sure to have a swim when he opens the door, symbolizing his blatant neglect for the birds' desperate need of water."

Police characterized the attack as "domestic terrorism," as well as felony vandalism and burglary. Damage to Sonoma Saveurs alone was estimated at about $50,000, and the adjoining jewelry store and women's clothing shop also faced significant repairs. No one claimed responsibility for these acts, and no arrests ever were made.

Meanwhile, the GourmetCruelty.com folks still were trying to find a landing place for their footage. Although the *New York Times* didn't bite on Sarahjane's pitches, Viva!USA director Lauren Ornelas, whose now-defunct American wing of the British animal-rights group had been campaigning against Sonoma Foie Gras and Grimaud, got *Delicacy of Despair* to reporter Dan Noyes at San Francisco ABC-TV affiliate KGO. The September 16, 2003, newscast led with an extended "I-Team Investigation" that relied largely on the video's clips and used the movement's terminology. "Workers force-feed the ducks so they develop a disease called hepatic lipidosis," Noyes states before cutting to an avian veterinarian, Laurie Siperstein-Cook, who says, "A friend of mine refers to pâté as hepatic lipidosis on toast." Noyes asserts that "the tube sometimes perforates the side of the duck's throat," and he gives "Rat Munching on Ducks' Bloody Ass Wounds" its public debut as he notes, "Rats were eating these two ducks alive."

The report also discusses the Sonoma Saveurs vandalism and features an interview with Laurent Manrique that mostly consists of Noyes showing him ghastly farm footage and prompting the chef to respond. Sarahjane receives much camera time and comes off as earnest and sympathetic in a straitlaced, blond Tina Fey sort of way. When she states, "There is no question that if people knew what foie gras really was, they would not be eating it," you're inclined to believe her. Noyes apparently did, giving the less-than-legal aspects of her undercover work a positive spin: "Sarahjane Blum and her crew may have broken some laws. They ignored the no-trespassing signs at the ranch and took 15 ducks from Sonoma Foie Gras and Hudson Valley, including the ones you saw being eaten by rats. They nursed the ducks back to health, taught them to eat on their own and even gave them workouts on a water treadmill."

"They're living a great and happy life now," Sarahjane says on camera, smiling at last. "I haven't done anything wrong. The people who are torturing animals day in and day out and then selling their corpses on the market, they're the criminals."

Speaking of whom . . . heeeere's Guillermo. Noyes reports that the Sonoma Foie Gras owner didn't agree to speak with him until earlier that day. As a result, the report features a tacked-on coda in which Gonzalez says of the videotape: "As in any other animal husbandry operation, there are things that can go wrong. I think it's a very partial and very negative representation of the truth."

Pease considered the report effective, though he remained annoyed that Ryan and Sarahjane hadn't launched the activists' many months of work on a larger stage. "It was a really good piece, but it was not worth waiting almost a year just to get it on a local news show," he groused. Still, the report did its damage. *Los Angeles Times* freelance reporter Marcelo Rodriguez contacted Pease, who invited the reporter to tag along the night after the KGO broadcast as he, Kath Rogers and two other Animal Protection and Rescue League members headed out to Farmington to sneak back into Sonoma Foie Gras. The barn doors now had locks, so instead they slipped through a gap where the plastic cooling system was located. (Rodriguez reported that Rogers squeezed in first and "let out a mild yelp as her wet skin made contact with electrified chicken wire used to keep rats out of the building." So, hey, at least that rat problem was being dealt with.) The reporter noted that the group surveyed the 1,500 or so ducks in the building, selected the four "in most need" and carried them away in plastic bins, making sure not to leave behind any damage or traces of their visit. The group arrived at a "safe house" at 5 a.m., and an avian veterinarian inspected the ducks. One that had been marked for slaughter died on the spot, corn kernels having fallen out of its beak. By afternoon, the other three "were waddling around and drinking water."

When contacted by Rodriguez, Gonzalez said he wasn't aware that anyone had entered the farm or removed four ducks, but he thought the thieves should be prosecuted. "It's not about four ducks," Gonzalez was quoted as saying. "It's that they are abusing my rights as both a businessman and a human being." As he told me later, he also was livid that someone representing a legitimate newspaper would participate in trespassing and burglary. Ryan, meanwhile, was chagrined that Pease was basking in the spotlight of an open rescue after having avoided such on-camera work earlier. Pease justified the move thusly: "It was just an incredible opportunity to be able to expose what was going on. Even though there was a possibility of criminal charges for taking those ducks, it was definitely a risk I was willing to take because we believed we had a pretty good justification defense: that these ducks were being tortured in violation of the animal cruelty law and we were taking them to be treated by a veterinarian." Plus, Pease figured that prosecutors were less likely to act with the *Los Angeles Times* involved. He gambled right: No criminal charges against Pease or the others were filed, though Gonzalez sued him in civil court for trespassing and theft, and Pease and the Marin County–based In Defense of Animals, which had been actively opposing Guillermo's company, sued Sonoma Foie Gras for violating anticruelty laws.

Rodriguez's *Los Angeles Times* story ran September 18, and the next day Noyes included some of Pease's newly shot video in a follow-up KGO report that also detailed the TV reporter's own visit to Sonoma Foie Gras and interview with Gonzalez. The farm owner told Noyes that he had fired a worker shown on the GourmetCruelty .com video to be force-feeding the birds too roughly. Gonzalez also did himself some major, long-lasting PR damage when discussing what would have happened if the so-called speed-feeding went on indefinitely.

NOYES: Would the duck die from the speed-feeding process?
GONZALEZ: Yes.
NOYES: Does that tell you something about the effect on the duck, then?
GONZALEZ: Well, imagine a human who doesn't stop eating.

The implication that only slaughter was preventing these ducks from being stuffed to death became a major talking point in the war on foie gras. When I was later at the farm, Gonzalez complained about Noyes's juxtaposition of his statement with the activists' footage of distressed ducks. His simple point was that slaughter took place when the duck essentially was done and the liver could grow no larger. "At one time they are going to stop digesting, so there is no point," farm production manager Eric Delmas told me.

The national media took notice. *Time* reported on the righteous duck thievery and gave Sarahjane the last word: "If this were being done to dogs or cats, the producers would without a doubt be in prison for animal cruelty." (Of course, the same might be true of anyone who tried eating those pets.) The *New York Times* finally weighed in, though Patricia Leigh Brown's September 24 story focused less on the birds' plight than the attacks on Sonoma Saveurs and Manrique, the thefts at Sonoma Foie Gras and the overall escalation of animal activist violence. Fox News's *The Big Story with John Gibson* was more protester-friendly as it recounted APRL's rescue mission to Sonoma Foie Gras—"They call themselves duck freedom fighters . . ."—and showed Kath Rogers describing one bird's poor condition while a helpful caption announced: "BIG FACT: FOIE GRAS IS OFTEN BAKED IN A CRUST."

By the following spring, the Animal Planet cable network already had shown a touchy-feely documentary about Sarahjane and Ryan's duck-rescuing and -rehabilitating exploits. On April 23, 2004, Sarahjane was exiting a Syracuse, New York, auditorium where she had just presented *Delicacy of Despair* at an animal conference when police officers placed her in handcuffs and drove her to the police station. She eventually crossed multiple counties, being handed from squad car to squad car, to wind up in Liberty, New York, where charges against her had been filed on behalf of nearby Hudson Valley Foie Gras. By the time she was booked and processed, two conference organizers had arrived to bail her out and drive her back to the event. She was thought to be the first person in the United States ever arrested for open rescue.

Ryan's arrest came a few months later in less dramatic fashion: His lawyers were notified the day beforehand, and he turned himself in. The main charge against Sarahjane and Ryan was felony burglary, punishable by up to seven years in prison. At first the pair was determined to have their case go to trial for all to see, but the more they thought about it, the less appealing that prospect became. The two of them feared that the case might distract people from the core duck-treatment issues, they worried that a conviction might limit their film's circulation, and they realized they might wind up behind bars for a year or three. Ryan figured prolonged incarceration was a distinct possibility given his prior arrests and the facts of the case. "Here's the thing: We committed the crime; we made a movie about committing the crime; we talked to everyone who would listen to us about committing the crime," he said. "There was no defense as to us not having committed the crime." Sarahjane tried to be philosophical: "These are the days and nights of my life that I have done the things I am most proud of, and nothing was going to change that no matter what the outcome of the case was." Still, when the prosecutors offered a deal that dropped all felony charges and required Ryan and Sarahjane to plead to a misdemeanor and to do 50 hours of community service, they signed on. (Henley said Hudson Valley didn't push the issue further because they were "first-time offenders.")

Sarahjane and Ryan fulfilled their community service requirements by working for the Humane Society of the United States. That showed 'em.

While Pease has remained out front in the foie gras fight—as has Paul Shapiro—Sarahjane and Ryan receded from the scene. She took extended time off to care for her ailing mother, and he eventually enrolled in the Massachusetts Institute of Technology to work toward a Ph.D. in the history of science technology and medicine, focusing on animal experimentation from Nazi Germany to the Cold War–era United States. They were no longer a couple. The GourmetCruelty .com Web site remained active, however, and the footage collected by them and Pease continued to be the foie gras debate's dominant imagery. "People take pictures of terrible things all the time, and they don't become international campaigns," Ryan Shapiro said. "I think the way this has borne out vindicates the approach we took."

• • •

Three days after Sarahjane's arrest, California's Senate Business and Professions Committee met to hear a bill—SB 1520—authored by Democratic senator John Burton of San Francisco and co-sponsored by Viva! USA, the Association of Veterinarians for Animal Rights, Farm Sanctuary and Lawyers for Animals. The senate's president pro tempore, a man with round glasses, white hair and a bushy mustache, Burton had opposed foie gras before; he touted his role 30 years earlier as a House of Representatives member in banning the product's importation. Now he was pushing California to pass a prohibition on foie gras's production as well as its sale, though that's not how he characterized it. "This bill has nothing to do, despite the mail that many of us get from restaurants, with banning foie gras," he said at the hearing's outset. "What it does is prohibit a process of which most people consider to be inhumane: of force-feeding ducks and geese for the purpose of unnaturally enlarging their livers beyond the normal size." The mechanism for prohibiting that process, though, not only was banning the production but also the sale of any product that was "the result of force-feeding a bird for the purpose of enlarging the bird's liver beyond its normal size"—so despite confusion expressed at this and subsequent hearings, Burton's bill effectively *was* banning the sale of foie gras.

Burton was one of the state's most powerful lawmakers, and by this point his bill seemed to face a relatively clear road. The hearing began with him accepting another senator's suggested compromise of sorts: that any ban be put off for five years to give the state's only producer, Sonoma Foie Gras, time to make whatever transition it needed to make. An oft-repeated notion was that this delay would give Guillermo Gonzalez time to discover a new "humane" way of producing foie gras—that is, without force feeding—despite hundreds of prior years with no such breakthroughs.

This being California, the celebrities testified first: a frail-looking Bea Arthur (from TV's *The Golden Girls* and *Maude*), whose voice cracked as she described the birds' "torture" before concluding, "There is no room in our wonderful state for such a nightmarish industry that thrives on violently force-feeding helpless animals"; and fashion-oriented red-carpet interviewer Melissa Rivers, who contended that if society could prohibit the eating of cats and horses, banning bird livers wasn't such a leap. (Committee chairwoman Liz Figueroa joked with Rivers, "I guess I'm supposed to ask you who you're wearing, but it would be more appropriate to ask you what you are eating." "I am not eating foie gras," Rivers replied with a laugh.)

In the battle of the expert witnesses, New York–based veterinarian Holly Cheever and two other animal specialists detailed the ducks' "terror" and variety of injuries and infirmities caused by the feedings. The bill's opponents included Francine Bradley, a poultry scientist at the University of California, Davis, who had consulted with and continued to advise Gonzalez in his operation; she complained that "portions of the current bill reflect poor understanding of avian anatomy, physiology and foie gras production." Another avian specialist who was impressed by a visit to Sonoma Foie Gras and a couple of chefs also testified against the bill.

Dozens of the bill's supporters lined up and, due to time constraints, simply offered their names and identifications for the record. The bill's opponents later did the same, though there weren't nearly as many. Guillermo Gonzalez, looking dapper in a tan jacket, yellow tie and glasses, gave more extensive testimony, telling of the support he'd received from the state through the California Department of Food and Agriculture as well as the UC Davis Extension to launch his successful agribusiness. "Without the approval of these two authorities, I would have never risked moving my family from El Salvador to California," he said. He complained that the bill was "based on misinformation promoted by animal-rights groups acting together and exercising every means possible to weaken our will and compromise our ability to conduct business, including the use of threats, intimidation, violence and the public scrutiny of our morality and our integrity." He finally implored the committee to rely upon scientific evidence, not emotional arguments, and to understand that "treating the birds well is the best way to produce the highest quality products. May God bless America."

Figueroa asked whether Gonzalez would accept the bill's amendment that would give him a five-year grace period to figure out how to produce foie gras humanely. "Does that neutralize you?" she asked.

He replied that he was not a researcher and wasn't at a stage of his life where he could "decide to do something else in a hurry."

"I think he was very generous in offering the five years, but that's up to you," Figueroa said.

The biggest twist of the hearing came when Senator Michael J. Machado (D-Linden), himself a farmer, told his colleagues that he recently had spent several hours at Sonoma Foie Gras and found that the witnesses' negative descriptions "were not borne out in practice." For instance, the ducks didn't show resistance to the feedings as described, and their handlers didn't have to struggle with them to insert the tubes. Machado concluded that of the poultry operations he had seen, Gonzalez's could be considered "exceptional" in the animals' treatment and environment.

Senator Gilbert Cedillo (D-Los Angeles) found it notable that the only two witnesses who had been to Sonoma Foie Gras opposed the bill and that Senator Machado had raised serious questions about the animal-rights complaints. Their testimony, Cedillo said, "seemed to refute all of the allegations." Senator Kevin Murray (D-Culver City) summed up a common frustration of many when he said, "The hardest thing for me is coming to a conclusion about the facts, let alone the policy. Both sides say everything the other side said is not true." The committee narrowly passed the bill.

For Gonzalez, the legislation wasn't going away, and neither were the lawsuits. He said the anticruelty suit from In Defense of Animals and Pease already had cost him $400,000, and the case hadn't even gone to court yet. He had no foie gras association or other industry group to turn to for help. D'Artagnan and Hudson Valley weren't hosting legal-defense fundraisers for him or getting involved in the battle. Big poultry wasn't about to help a little guy like him. Gonzalez had arrived in the United States from a war-torn country and started a successful business that employed 25 people and provided fresh, local, high-end product to California restaurants. Now his farm was repeatedly burglarized, his shop had been almost destroyed and his methods of production were about to be legislated out of existence. Sonoma Saveurs already was in trouble; it didn't help that Manrique bailed out not long after his house was attacked and he received that creepy videotape. "I said, 'Let me run my business as a restaurateur, and let Guillermo be a farmer of foie gras,'" Manrique told me. "I don't want to take risks anymore." (The shop wound up closing after barely a year in business.)

So although Senator Machado's testimony hadn't turned the tide, it at least gave Gonzalez some new leverage. A five-year stay of execution was too short, but seven and a half years? Maybe. But if the idea was for him to come up with a new way to produce foie gras, he'd need research funds that he just didn't have. Could the state give him a grant to cover such expenses? Sure . . . well . . . no, actually. Sending chunks of public money to a foie gras farm wasn't going to fly. So instead, Guillermo asked: Could the state immunize him from any lawsuits regarding his farm practices? As it turned out, *that* could be done. If Guillermo agreed to let California force him out of the foie gras business as of July 1, 2012, the state would take that IDA lawsuit and other possible future ones off the table. True, Guillermo would have to run his company while a time bomb slowly ticked toward its destruction, which wouldn't be fun, but for the near future the headaches would go away—at least in theory. Maybe he could find an alternative method for producing foie gras over the next seven and a half years or prove to the legislature that what he was doing wasn't cruel and therefore didn't really need to be outlawed. At the very worst, Guillermo would be turning 60 in 2012 and might be ready to do something less controversial by then.

So it was that at a hearing of the California State Assembly's Standing Committee on Business and Professions, Burton touted his bill again, dozens of citizens again lined up to take turns stating their names in support of the ban, and toward the end, a man arrived at the microphone and said: "Guillermo Gonzalez, owner of Sonoma Foie Gras, foie gras producer. I want to take the opportunity to express my appreciation to the author of the bill for granting us the extension and allowing us to continue in operation. We are very appreciative in the name of my family, my employees and myself. We are committed for the next seven and a half years to adhere to the best and the newest animal-welfare practices and animal husbandry, and we have withdrawn our opposition and we have adopted a neutral position."

Governor Arnold Schwarzenegger signed SB 1520 into law on September 29, 2004.

Years later I asked Ariane Daguin whether she thought Gonzalez had screwed up. "Yep," she said. "On the other side, I can't blame him. He was alone. Nobody was helping him. He cried for help, but we weren't organized. He was seen as a competitor to everybody. We had no idea what was happening and the scope of the thing, and he had to fend for himself. He had all those lawsuits piling up. I can't blame the guy. But yes, he messed up."

Said Gonzalez: "I didn't have an option."

DISPATCHES

January 1, 1994:
Responding to pressure from People for the Ethical Treatment of Animals (PETA), Air Canada agrees to stop serving pâté de foie gras to first-class passengers.

August 23, 1999:
The Smithsonian Institution cancels a foie gras tasting and panel discussion following complaints by actors Sir John Gielgud and Bea Arthur and animal-rights groups.

2002:
Cardinal Joseph Ratzinger, the future Pope Benedict XVI, says of the industrial fattening of geese: "This degrading of living creatures to a commodity seems to me in fact to contradict the relationship of mutuality that comes across in the Bible."

April 19, 2005:
Geoff Latham, owner of the Portland-based game meats distributor Nicky USA, launches In Defense of Foie Gras to combat legislation being pushed by In Defense of Animals.

April 2006:
A member of a Chinese delegation visiting southwest France says his company plans to ramp up foie gras production in China. "Our aim is to reach 1,000 tons over the next five years with 2 million geese."

September 29, 2006:
New Jersey Democratic assemblyman Michael Panter, a vegan, introduces a bill to ban the sale of foie gras in the state.

6.

Down on the Farms

"I'll show you suffering! I'll show you suffering!"

When we initially spoke about his decision to quit serving foie gras, Charlie Trotter repeatedly urged me to check out the farms myself. I should see what he had seen. Then I would know.

When I called Hudson Valley Foie Gras and Sonoma Foie Gras, I didn't get shunted off to publicists or subjected to a fog of corporate doublespeak. Michael Ginor, Izzy Yanay and Guillermo Gonzalez not only were happy to present their points of view directly, but they also welcomed the opportunity to have me visit their farms. Regardless of how you ultimately come down on this issue, I find it telling that the producers of a product as controversial as foie gras would invite me (and others) to witness the process in full, but the companies that produce the food we eat every day say no, you can't see it. Sometime before Thanksgiving I called Butterball asking whether I could observe how its turkeys are raised for that most American of meals. Sorry, I was told, but I was welcome to get basic information from the National Turkey Federation. I also called some of the top U.S. chicken producers requesting to visit their farms. Forget it. Shouldn't the food we eat most often be the most transparent?

I also didn't get to see LaBelle, the third U.S. foie gras producer, which sits less than a mile up the road from Hudson Valley Foie Gras.

LaBelle was (and is) part of a larger chicken farm, Bella; at some point a former Hudson Valley worker defected to Bella and helped the company enter the foie gras business in 1999. LaBelle produces foie gras on a smaller scale than Hudson Valley—it's been more in the range of Sonoma Foie Gras—and chefs generally consider its product to be similar to that of Hudson Valley. (I know some top Chicago chefs who favor LaBelle.) D'Artagnan has distributed Hudson Valley and Sonoma Foie Gras—as well as some Canadian companies' product— but not LaBelle. "I prefer the way Hudson Valley functions," Ariane Daguin, who had visited LaBelle, told me. She would say no more. I arranged with LaBelle owner Herman Lee to see for myself, but when I got out there, Lee had a young lawyer in his office who grilled me on my intentions, expressed concern that I might be an undercover animal-rights activist (despite my having given them my business card and sent them clips weeks earlier), and ultimately told me I'd wasted the trip. Instead, the lawyer said, Herman would speak to me on the phone at a later date. Herman, who said next to nothing during this exchange, didn't return subsequent calls.

The first foie gras farm I visited was Sonoma in May 2005, about eight months after California passed its 2012 ban and just weeks after my initial *Tribune* story about Trotter and foie gras had been published. As it happened, I was covering the junket for George Lucas's *Star Wars: Episode III—Revenge of the Sith* at the Skywalker Ranch in Marin County, and I tacked an extra day onto the trip to see Sonoma Foie Gras—though I was disappointed to learn, as Bryan Pease had earlier, that the farm wasn't actually in Sonoma. Before I set out on my trip, Trotter told me, "The couple that owns the farm, Guillermo and Junny Gonzalez, couldn't be sweeter, nicer people. They're sweethearts, and I love them to death. This is the irony of all this stuff. If people work hard and they're trying to make a living, you certainly don't want any bad repercussions based on what ultimately may happen with this whole foie gras thing. But that said, it'll be good to see what's going on."

The drive covered miles of unpaved road past rows of livestock farms. Signs near the entry gate read, "*Alto,*" "*¡No entre!*" "Stop" and "Keep out! Biosecure Area." The words "Sonoma Foie Gras" appeared nowhere, but from the road and the long driveway leading up to the main buildings, you could see large clusters of ducks huddled beneath shade trees on the lawn. These ducks were living the presumably happy free-range weeks of their existence. As Guillermo would tell me, "If not for the last 14 to 17 days, they are in paradise."

The on-site office is a desk and seating area in the modest trailer home where Eric Delmas, who runs the farm day to day, works and lives. Behind the trailer lie the long, low barns, where every two weeks 4,000 to 5,000 male Mulard ducklings are delivered from Grimaud. (Female ducks are considered more temperamental, and their livers have more veins running through them, so they generally aren't used for foie gras.) The day I visited, about 2,000 four-day-old bright yellow ducklings were gathered along the far long wall of one such barn. The room was warm, the air thick and musky. One dead duckling lay near one of the several water stations. Another duckling stood apart from the rest of the group *cheep-cheeping*. "He's probably blind," Delmas said. "He'll have to be euthanized." Pease's cameras had lingered over images of dead ducks, including corpses filling large plastic garbage bins. These fatalities, the activist charged, were evidence of the farm's cruelty, but Gonzalez said such deaths are typical of farm life and that Sonoma's mortality rate was lower than your average poultry farm's. On my tour the garbage bins were empty.

An adjacent barn held about 4,000 18-day-old ducks that ate and drank at stations set up around the cavernous space. This barn was less hot than the previous one, but the air still felt dense, buzzing with flies and scented with gaminess and the wood shavings that covered the floor. At this point each duck weighed about 0.75 kilos, or 1.65 pounds, Gonzalez said, noting that each was capable of eating up to 15 percent of his own body weight daily. You could tell the ones that had just eaten by the bulges in their necks; such gorging was often referred to as "pre-gavage" because the ducks were increasing their capacity for ingesting large amounts of food.

"They just eat, sleep," Delmas said.

"Play," Gonzalez added.

Still yellow, these ducks tended to sit and move en masse. A few would start heading toward the water reservoir and—*they're off!*—duck convoy. Mirroring one another's movements in ways that appeared vaguely programmed, they resembled an avian variation on the computer-generated masses of some Hollywood spectacle like *Troy*. They sure didn't come across as individuals, so . . . um . . . turning them into delicious food products wasn't so bad, right? Then again, they *were* awfully cute.

After five or six weeks during which they develop their feathers, the ducks are let outside to roam. Those carefree days of waddling on the grass and seeking shade under trees would last until they were 12 weeks old. Some activists complained about the area's summer heat and the grounds' lack of ponds, thus preventing ducks from engaging in their natural swimming behavior. To Guillermo, the latter complaint illustrated the activists' lack of understanding of animal agriculture. "Ponds are a source of disease of animal husbandry," he said. "To have ducks with access to ponds, it's creating a bank of bacteria, and you don't want to do that."

Then came the process known as gavage.

The final two to three weeks of these ducks' lives took place in two adjacent long barns that were darker and danker than the others. The air was suffused with the pungent aroma of duck feathers and droppings. Single exposed 40-watt bulbs hung from the rafters offering dim light. At the barn's far end, large fans blew cool air through the building. The three-and-a-half-foot-by-10-foot pens were lined up in four long rows, their slatted floors raised about three feet from the ground to let the manure fall through. The ducks, usually about 10 per pen, had a fair amount of room to maneuver, though they tended to cluster toward the back when anyone unfamiliar walked by. Near the barn's entrance sat a large wheelbarrow filled with corn kernels that had been cleaned, cooked and mixed with corn oil to make the ducks' feed.

At the time of my visit, the ducks in each of the two barns had different diets. The ducks in this one were being raised to make Artisan Foie Gras, the business's premium line, so a machine cooked whole corn kernels and fed them to the ducks via a copper tube inserted down the esophagus. These gravity-driven feedings took five to eight seconds apiece. The other barn's ducks were producing the standard Sonoma Foie Gras line and thus were fed a slushy combination of ground and whole corn plus water and minerals. These feedings, also through a copper tube but powered by a hydraulic machine, lasted just a few seconds apiece, and the food was cheaper to make than the whole cooked kernels, though Guillermo said it also was harder for the birds to digest. The Sonoma-brand ducks also appeared to be damp because, Gonzalez said, their feed included grain salt that impelled them to drink more water. The more expensive, more labor-intensive Artisan process led to a sweeter, more refined liver as well as a five-dollar-per-pound markup from Sonoma Foie Gras's wholesale price.

Three workers in each barn fed the ducks twice daily. On this late morning, a thick-mustached employee named Jorge Vargas was stepping from one pen into another, plopping a milk crate onto the raised floor, squatting down and wielding a long copper feeding tube suspended from above like an oversized dentist's drill. The ducks huddled in a corner of the pen. "They know what's going to happen," Delmas said, "and they don't like to be grabbed."

Did they look happy about the force-feeding that was about to take place?

No.

Did they look particularly fearful or agitated?

No.

They looked like ducks, big ducks.

Vargas took the first one by the neck, pointed the beak straight up and dropped the copper tube down the throat. The machine whizzed and, over several seconds, spat the corn into the bird's esophagus. Vargas hoisted the copper tube and placed the duck to his left, his body separating it from those still to be fed. The just-fed duck flapped its wings and looked around, much as ducks in the other pens were doing. It didn't appear to be traumatized or even particularly bothered. "You can feel the corn," Delmas said, placing his extended fingers at the base of the duck's bulging throat. "He is full here"—he moved his fingers up to just below the chin—"to here."

Vargas continued the feedings with the rest of that pen's ducks, then moved on to the next one. These birds were nine days into gavage, just more than halfway through the process. Farther into the barn resided fatter ducks a day or two from processing. A few labored to walk, falling over as they tried to move away from us as we passed. "Here's an example of a lame duck," Gonzalez said of one that couldn't get up.

"He is weak, and he is going to go into processing tomorrow," Delmas said.

The activists complain about lack of veterinary care for these farm animals, to which some might respond: But they're about to die anyway, so what would be the point? On the flip side, here was a suffering animal with nothing being done to relieve its pain, aside from slaughtering it the next day. To Guillermo, the most relevant point was that lame animals are a reality of agriculture, and on his farm they were the exception, not the rule, despite claims to the contrary. "As you can see," he said, "it's one in about 100."

Some of these ducks also were breathing heavily. "They are panting," Delmas said. "They're like dogs."

"The panting is a thermal regulation mechanism," Gonzalez said. "They are so fat, so they are hot."

Panting is another point of contention in the foie gras fight. Although farmers and various researchers contend that it's a natural way for these down-covered birds to process heat, foie gras opponents say the problem is that the liver grows so big that it crowds out the air sacs, thus causing breathing difficulties. "The primary reason for the panting is because of respiratory compromise, not due to heat processing," said Holly Cheever, the U.S. veterinarian most outspoken against foie gras. But Francine Bradley, the UC Davis animal scientist who advised Gonzalez, testified before the California Senate committee that this common animal-rights argument is misinformation. "The liver is not at any close proximity to the lungs nor the air sacs," she said. Daniel Guémené, France's most prominent foie gras researcher—whose work has been assailed in the animal-rights community because of its partial funding by the French foie gras industry—described the panting as "a metabolic response" to the ever-rising number of calories that the ducks must process during the feedings. "It's the only way for them to export energy," Guéméne told me.

"When they are panting, is that uncomfortable for them?" I asked.

"That I don't know," was Guéméne's response, and he added:

"We don't have any measure that can provide an indication for that."

Guillermo didn't deny that his ducks were experiencing some stress. Any species raised for food is being manipulated to some degree, and many animals are transported, housed and fed in ways contrary to how they would live in the wild, which isn't necessarily a picnic to begin with. The key, Guillermo said, was the animals' capacity to adapt to that stress. "When they are fat, when they are heavy, obviously the animal is not moving around like it would in the orchard when it weighs five less pounds. No, we are aware that we are demanding an effort from the animal. But that is not exclusive to us doing foie gras, and we are demanding of the animal only in the last three or four days of that two-week period. This is simply about raising ducks for food and giving them the very best care possible in order to obtain from them the very most economically—and all this within a frame of respect and animal welfare that we feel honestly committed to."

I left Sonoma Foie Gras more confused than when I had arrived. I'd expected to see something more dramatic and disturbing. The ducks at the end of the process were large but not Orson Welles obese. I didn't feel great about the limping, lame ones, and I wasn't sure what to make of all that panting, but still, most of the birds appeared to be relatively unaffected by those eight-second-long feedings. The word that came to mind was "mundane." When I later spoke with Elliot Katz, the veterinarian who founded the Mill Valley, California–based In Defense of Animals that sued Sonoma Foie Gras, he contended that as prey animals, ducks are conditioned to mask any feelings of pain. "The birds can't talk," he said. "All they can do is waddle and suffer. They don't scream like other animals." In other words, I couldn't necessarily draw conclusions from what I saw.

Still, Trotter didn't have a veterinary degree when he concluded that the birds' treatment was cruel. When I caught up with him after my trip, he asked me whether I now knew exactly what he was talking about. I told him I wasn't sure. He let out an impatient breath. "Hey," I said, "it's not like you immediately made your decision about foie gras the first time you visited a farm." He moved on to the next subject.

In a later conversation, he said, "If you and I saw the same thing,

I can't believe you'd come out thinking that this is something that people should consume." But everyone processes information differently, and given that he made his decision after visiting individual-cage farms, perhaps we didn't see the same thing.

When I finally visited Hudson Valley Foie Gras a couple of years later, I set up the trip as an exercise in moral whiplash. On Monday I'd meet Ariane Daguin at D'Artagnan in Newark. On Tuesday Izzy Yanay would give me an extensive tour of Hudson Valley Foie Gras, a bit more than 100 miles to the northwest in Ferndale, New York. And on Wednesday I'd spend the day with Gene Baur and friends at Farm Sanctuary in Watkins Glen, New York, another 160 miles west. The cultural clash between Farm Sanctuary and the other two was both obvious and subtle. When I mentioned Farm Sanctuary to Daguin in her D'Artagnan office, the point she couldn't shake was that in a recent *New York Times* profile, Baur, the organization's president, was photographed wearing sandals in a pigpen. "My cousins were in farming, and I saw pigs all my life, and I will never, ever enter a pen of a pig with sandals," she said in her husky, French-accented voice. "This guy is not a farmer. He's there to take care of animals until the end of their lives and to bury them when they die of old age. To me, it's natural; cows, beef, quail, chicken would not exist if man was not on earth to exploit them. 'Exploit' is a bad word; maybe I should say to 'take care of them but also enjoy them.'"

"So you wouldn't wear sandals in there for sanitary reasons?" I asked.

"Yeah, it's . . ." She laughed and shook her head. "He's leaning on the pig, and he has sandals. I don't know. To me, it's like heresy. It's like, which world is this? I cannot understand."

In Daguin's world, the current arrangement between animals and the people who eat them is as it should be. "If you see all those TV series with wild animals and how the lion goes after the wildebeest and stuff like that, talk about stress!" she said. "But this is life. It's the predator that is above the prey that is below, and man is a predator, and duck is a prey. I believe God made that arrangement because it works like that, and I believe He made the duck delicious so that we would enjoy the whole process. So to deny that is not right. It cannot be right. But that's where we're going, that's for sure."

Located in an industrial area of Newark, D'Artagnan occupies a nondescript low-rise building with attached warehouses, and as you walk from the parking lot to the entrance, you pass a big window revealing Daguin behind her desk in her office cluttered with products, papers and knickknacks, often duck related. "The Duck Stops Here," reads a sign as you enter. A yellow wooden duck stands atop her desk alongside stacks of letters. Atop a bookcase shelf is a mask of California governor Arnold Schwarzenegger with a corn-filled foil feeding tube stuck in his mouth alongside the message, "Eat this, Arnold." Daguin explained that the mask was part of a hat that an employee made for a party contest. (He placed second after the guy who wore a whole goose on his head.) On the wall there's a color photo of Daguin and an all-star cast of chefs—Daniel Boulud, Alain Ducasse, Eric Ripert, Jean-Georges Vongerichten and Drew Nieporent—in their chef's whites running on some lush lawn toward a white duck waddling toward the camera. Ariane is closest to the duck, her arms outstretched. The photo was shot in New York's Central Park to illustrate a *Talk* magazine story, and Ariane said her pose was spontaneous. "They never told me to go and grab the duck."

"It looks like you're about to take the duck down and make foie gras on the spot," I said.

"I took that duck." She laughed. "Look, look. I caught that duck."

Ariane is prone to joking in a way that would not amuse the Gene Baurs of the world, but she gets serious when discussing her sense of food and business ethics. D'Artagnan works primarily with small farmers—and, yes, she considers Hudson Valley among them, despite activists' charges to the contrary—to procure its array of foie gras, wild game and other gourmet items. "I think something good has to be coming from a farm that you recognize, with farming practices that you recognize," she said. The equation is simple: Good farming practices lead to good products. "This is what D'Artagnan is all about. Gourmet has to be linked to sustainable farming."

This attitude carries over to her home life. She credited activists with raising awareness of something she'd already known: that eggs from free-ranging hens are superior to those from caged birds. She said her college-age daughter, from the time she was born, "never had an egg that was not organic or at least came from a free-range hen. Not because I feel for the hen. I do feel somewhat—like everybody, when I see animals, I prefer that they are comfortable—but because I know and I taste the difference. An egg from a happier, free-ranging hen is better than an egg factory-made."

Given this mindset, Ariane found herself in "a big dilemma" when it came to fighting on foie gras's behalf. The producers she patronizes have very little money compared to the nation's large meat industries or, more relevantly, the Humane Society of the United States. But although foie gras farms were being attacked through lawsuits and costly lobbying efforts, she felt she could not turn to, say, big poultry for support. "Those guys are totally the antithesis of what I am all about here," she said. "I don't see how I can get their help because getting their help means compromising what we're going to be saying. And you can see that the priority of the big agriculture lobby in America has nothing to do with foie gras, nothing to do with small farmers, nothing." (Gonzelez would have welcomed support from the larger agricultural interests.)

Restaurateurs posed another frustration. Although many independent chefs had spoken out for foie gras, others connected to bigger operations had grown squeamish. "Anybody who has two or three restaurants or more, they just shut up, and they try to stay under the radar," she said. She even had learned of instances when, knowing that *New York Times* critic Frank Bruni was in the house, restaurants removed foie gras from the menu so "the review will be about other dishes but not foie gras. And as soon as the review is out, boom, they put foie gras on again. This is not a healthy situation. This is wrong. This is hypocritical. Then again, these people are my friends. They are my clients. I do business with them. What can I say?"

She reserved her biggest disappointment for Wolfgang Puck, one of her most enthusiastic foie gras customers. She handed me a copy of Puck's book *Adventures in the Kitchen,* which he had inscribed, "To Ariane: In friendship with truffles and foie gras." She recalled that months earlier Puck had embarrassed Charlie Trotter at a charity event by tempting him with foie gras. "In front of a couple of people, he told Charlie, 'Come on, eat this. You know it's good. You know it's good. Come on.'" But in March 2007, three years into an aggressive campaign waged against him by Farm Sanctuary, which organized protesters to picket his Spago in Beverly Hills and hammered him on its wolfgangpuckcruelty.org Web site for serving foie gras, Puck announced that he, too, would banish the fat liver—and any other inhumanely raised food—from his many restaurants nationwide. "Our guests . . . want to know where the food comes from and how the animals were raised," Puck said in a statement. He insisted the decision had nothing to do with Farm Sanctuary's efforts, though the group thought otherwise, splashing "Wolfgang Puck Victory" across the top of its formerly Puck-bashing site. His about-face prompted chef/TV host Anthony Bourdain to tell the *Wall Street Journal:* "He got squeezed and pressured and phone-called from all angles, and like a good German shopkeeper he folded and sold out the people hiding in the cellar next door. I got no respect." Daguin didn't put it quite so harshly: "To me it's the saddest thing. The guy loves foie gras. He's a bon vivant. He knows what's good. And he's trying to tell me, 'Please, I'll help you try to create a noncruel way of making foie gras.' 'You're kidding, Wolf. You know you're kidding.' And he knew he was kidding. When we went along in the conversation, he basically told me that it was all PR stuff." (Puck declined to be interviewed for this book.)

Eventually, Ariane handed me a heavy red D'Artagnan jacket and took me into the large chilly warehouse. She pointed out the great variety of meat items—including such duck products as confit legs, raw *magret,* smoked breasts and tubs of fat—and when we arrived at the shelves holding boxes of whole fresh foie gras lobes (marked "A," "B" and "C" depending on their quality), she pulled out some vacuum-packed Hudson Valley livers that exceeded two pounds each and a few somewhat smaller, yellower ones from a couple of Canadian farms. The Canadian ones were almost perfectly shaped, the Hudson Valley ones a bit more irregular, with a horizontal ridge cutting across each one. The Hudson Valley livers are bigger because the ducks are fed more gradually over twice as long (28 days versus 14 days). The shape discrepancy, she explained, was due to the difference between hot and cold evisceration.

And now you're thinking: *Finally, I'm going to learn about hot and cold duck evisceration.*

The French style, also practiced in Canada, is hot evisceration, which, as Daguin described it, means: "You hang the duck, you stun the duck, you kill the duck, you pluck the duck, you open the duck, you take the liver out. So at that point the duck is still at body temperature, and so because of that, the liver is hot and slippery, like a calf liver, and doesn't take a shape." Producers often place these livers into molds so they become nicely rounded and symmetrical as they cool.

The Israeli style, which was also the older French style, is cold evisceration, the method used by Hudson Valley as well as Sonoma. "The duck is stunned, it's killed, then it's plucked, and then it goes like that intact, hanged by the neck in a refrigerator overnight," Daguin said. "Then the temperature is going to go down very fast, the inside, the outside, everything. The next day it's opened, so when you take the liver out, it already has the nice shape, and it's cold already." The horizontal ridge comes from the liver cooling and solidifying while resting against the duck's breastbone.

Mind you, the reasons for choosing hot or cold evisceration have nothing to do with the resultant shapes. Each method imparts specific chemical properties to the liver, thus causing them to react differently depending on the cooking method of choice. Hot evisceration is preferable for the slow cooking involved in making a terrine or other cold preparations, as are most popular in France. "It keeps the properties of the lipids and the protein cells bound together, so when you do slow cooking, it is not going to melt," Daguin said. The more the liver melts, the more fat you lose, and the fat, of course, is the point (as is the volume of food). Yet when you cook a hot-eviscerated liver over a *high* heat, such as in searing, it renders a lot of fat—not a desired outcome.

Which brings us back to cold evisceration, which acts in the opposite way. Lots of fat melts away when you heat the liver at a low temperature, but with grilling or pan searing, the foie gras "holds very, very well," she said. Hudson Valley adds a bit of soy to its corn feed, thus making the foie gras melt even less, though the flavor isn't quite as sweet. "It really holds a flan-like texture. It's incredible." The disadvantage, she continued, is that the veins in the liver are bloodier this way, though the veins are far less noticeable when the liver is served hot than cold. In the United States, where foie gras is enjoyed almost exclusively at restaurants, the hot preparations dominate, particularly pan searing. Customers love the contrast of the crisp crust and wobbly inside, and chefs appreciate that the cooking takes about 30 seconds per side, as opposed to the days that might go into making a terrine. Plus, when restaurants are paying more than $40 a pound for something, they prefer to lose as little as possible to its preparation. No wonder American restaurants buy more Hudson Valley Foie Gras than any other. "When you have a restaurant with 200 covers a night, you need the foolproof thing that's going to work every time," Daguin said.

Back in her office, Ariane admitted she's far from certain that she'll be able to continue selling foie gras over the long run. "If you ask my brain today, I'm pretty pessimistic. If you ask my heart, because it's my legacy I guess, I have this hope that somewhere there's going to be a high-profile restaurateur or somebody who's going to take it for what it is, which is it's not any more cruel than anything else . . . I'll fight to the end because I believe the cause is just. The treatment of ducks is as humane as the treatment of free-range chicken. There is not any more stress in ducks being force-fed than there is with free-range chickens. So if you want to stop all cruelty, that means you want to stop all slaughterhouse activity. Then stop everything. Then, OK, let's all be vegetarians. But otherwise don't single out those ducks. That's wrong."

Izzy Yanay has a lot of ideas that he figures will never come to fruition. He had a brainstorm that he could sell foie gras with toast crisps in little convenience store packages like cheese and crackers. "You know the creamers in a diner, those white things?" he asked. "I wanted to make foie gras tubs like that." He went to a packaging show in Chicago to explore the idea, "but it never flew off the ground." Eventually, Izzy saw such a product in France. They can do a lot of things over there that he can't do in the United States.

Izzy's blue eyes light up when he discusses France's gleaming foie gras facilities. Even the slaughterhouses inspire him to wax poetic. "They stick them with a knife through the beak, and then they go into the bleeding and the rest of the stuff," he said, "Everything is clean. Everything is beautiful. I mean, the blood's going in a trough, going to the other side. It's collected. Ah! It's a fantastic place. You want to cry from envy, but you can't have the tears on the floor because it's contaminating. You have to collect your tears, it's so clean over there."

That's not to say that Izzy finds his own operation wanting. Sure, he routinely uses the words "junk" and "shit" to describe the buildings he has yet to raze and rebuild after almost 20 years, but as far as taking care of his animals and producing a fine product goes, he yields to no one. The contrast between the somewhat shabby surroundings and upscale output is apparent along the Hudson Valley Foie Gras office's corridor walls, which are lined with framed menus from restaurants that offer the product by name. I asked Izzy whether I would find a Charlie Trotter's menu there, and he replied, "There was one, but I took it down." The menus and vintage French foie gras posters bespeak a refinement that the setting—a rudimentary one-story building with fake wood paneling inside—otherwise didn't match. This was a no-frills farm building, and Izzy is a farmer whose job is dealing with animals, not menus. "The question is not whether we produce any kind of a luxury item that goes to very fancy restaurants," he said. "The question is one thing and one thing only: Are these ducks suffering? With your lay eyes, you tell me what you think after you look around for any length of time that you want. I'm not hiding anything."

Izzy was giving me what he called the full tour, from birth (or close to it—we didn't actually visit the two hatcheries) to slaughter, with in-between stops in various barns that use a variety of feeding methods. After the eggs are hatched, the ducks are sexed, and, Izzy said, the female ones are shipped to a buyer near Venezuela who raises them for meat. (At some other farms they're euthanized like those male layer chicks.) The males eventually move to the farm's nurseries, one of which was our tour's first stop. This was a spacious barn with plenty of floor room for 3,000 to 4,000 fuzzy yellow ducklings to move around. They sipped water from a long pipe with nipples on the left wall and pecked at food stored in feeders on the right. Hudson Valley uses four different feed formulas for the birds over the course of their lives, with the protein level the highest (about 21 percent) when the ducks are the youngest. Infrared heat lamps in the nursery were programmed to switch on when the ducklings approached, though on this August day, they weren't needed. As Izzy walked through the barn, the little birds paid little mind and didn't actively avoid him. "At that stage of their life, they will come to you because they don't know that you stink," he said with a laugh.

The ducklings grow in the nursery for four weeks, then move to another barn that is better equipped to handle their waste because by this point, Izzy said, "they are eating machines, and whatever they eat, they shit." Unlike the Sonoma Foie Gras ducks, these were never kept outside. Izzy said fear of avian flu moved them inside full-time in 2006, on the New York Department of Environmental Conservation's recommendation, although another significant concern was dealing with the runoff from that many birds and their waste on the grass. As it was, Hudson Valley had installed a new $600,000 system—a lagoon the size of a hockey rink—to treat and neutralize the birds' manure before it eventually is spread over nearby fields.

Izzy drove me to a row of white barns where we would see the birds in the growing stage. "I'm just a farmer," Izzy said in his car, "but you know how the ducks are feeling just by looking at them. You don't need to be a big scientist for that. You just walk in. You open the door. You see how they behave. And if you hear a lot of screaming, and you can see all kinds of struggling, you don't need to look in the books. It's so simple."

I mentioned what Dr. Katz, the In Defense of Animals veterinarian, had told me: that the ducks are conditioned not to display signs of suffering, including screaming, because they're prey animals.

"So I'll show you suffering! I'll show you suffering!" Izzy said.

"He's saying they could be suffering, but you wouldn't know it because they're not showing you," I reiterated.

"But I will show you suffering," Izzy said, now getting impatient. "Right now! I'll show you the next place. Let's go."

"All right," I said, "let's go see some suffering."

We got out of the car and approached the entrance of another barn where the ducks, now black and white, were about 10 weeks old. "Now stand here and look at them suffer," Izzy said and proceeded to walk into the barn and through the cluster of ducks, who scrambled to get away, leaving him at the center of a circle with a radius of 10 to 12 feet between him and the nearest bird. "You see how they suffer? They ran away from me."

"Is avoiding you suffering?" I asked.

"Well, they are afraid of me," he said. "Look at this big area that they created when I was walking over there. Why are they running here? Because they don't know me. And look at how they're screaming. They're talking now." The ducks indeed were quacking up a storm, and they maintained that security zone between themselves and Izzy. They appeared to fear him. His presence made them stressed. In the language of animal welfare, they were suffering. Izzy implored me to keep this behavior in mind as we moved on to a barn in which force-feedings—or "hand feedings," as he called them—were taking place.

Hudson Valley's feedings differed from those at Sonoma Foie Gras and just about anywhere else in that they were stretched over 28 days and took place three times a day instead of two. The idea is that by giving the ducks less food per serving over a longer period, the farm will produce healthier birds with larger livers. The feeding barns themselves didn't look much different from those at Sonoma. Groups of 10 or so ducks reside in elevated four-foot-by-six-foot pens, their waste dropping through the plastic-covered wire mesh flooring. Hanging 40-watt bulbs kept the light level dim (veterinarian Lawrence Bartholf said prey animals prefer low light), and large fans loomed above every six or seven pens to blow cool, moist air through the room. The smell was gamey but not offensive, with little detectable ammonia.

As we walked down the long aisles between the rows of pens, some of the ducks moved away, but most of them barely reacted, either standing or sitting. They just went about their duck business. We were a lot closer to them than Izzy had been to those younger ducks in the previous barn, and they appeared not to mind. "Pay attention to their behavior," Izzy said. "That's the important issue here. See if they look to be in panic with your lay eyes."

They did not.

The Hudson Valley feeders are primarily Mexican workers who

live on the farm's grounds, and each one is assigned 300 to 350 ducks to oversee for the 28 days of gavage. (Michael Ginor says most farms have closer to a 900 to 1 duck-feeder ratio.) This means that the employees work with the same ducks for four straight weeks so the birds can become familiar and comfortable with their exclusive human contacts. The workers are paid bonuses based on the ducks' health and the quality of their livers at the end of the process.

A cord runs suspended over each row of pens so the feeder can pull the hanging feeding apparatus down the line. A man wearing red pants and big black boots seated himself on a milk crate in a pen with all of the ducks off to one side. These ducks were 22 days into the feeding schedule. He took each bird, positioned it between his legs and lowered the metal pipe down its throat, just like at Sonoma. Here, though, the machine was little more than a funnel at the top of the tube with an auger rotating slowly inside. Into this the feeder deposited a measuring cup scoop of gerbil-food-resembling nuggets, and he massaged the duck's throat as the auger whirred and gravity carried the food downward. The massaging was not only to help the food descend but also to make sure that no undigested food remained from the previous feeding. If the duck hadn't completely digested its last meal, this one would be skipped—and the bird might be ready for processing. The ducks tended to bunch up in the corner before being taken by the feeder, but afterward they appeared unfazed. When you stepped back and observed the row of pens, there was no perceptible difference between the ducks that already had been fed and those still awaiting the feeder. Some of them were panting. I didn't notice any lame ones.

For contrast's sake, Izzy took me to another area where the birds were on their first day of gavage; they'd been moved from the "growing" barn the previous day. These ducks were much more skittish and moved away from us as we walked by. "It is so obvious to you when you look at them yourself," Izzy said. "Obviously they are afraid here, and they are not afraid over there [in the first area]. So the conclusion is the process of feeding made them accustomed to the human being, but it did not make them *afraid* of the human being that is coming to 'torture' them three times a day. That's the major point here." What I saw was the opposite of what Cheever told the

California Senate committee that she had observed at Hudson Valley regarding the ducks' "terror": "This avoidance behavior increased the longer the ducks were involved in the force-feeding procedure, meaning that the first two or three days they were not as terrified as they became as the procedure went on into the next two or three weeks." Somewhat contradictorily, other animal activists have charged that the ducks' growing calmer as the feedings progress is a sign that they're experiencing "Stockholm syndrome" (i.e., the hostage embracing his kidnapper).

Next stop was the slaughterhouse, for which we had to don white lab coats and hairnets. The ducks arrived on carts, two in each small cage that was stacked one atop the other. One of the lower ducks was spattered with feces from one of the upper ducks, though that wasn't the worst of its problems. It also was DOA. Izzy said birds in transit simply don't make it sometimes. "When you take chickens to the slaughterhouse, you know how many die on the way? A lot."

As for the rest of the ducks, a worker removed each one and hung it by the feet from shackles that moved slowly along a U-shaped conveyor belt. At the base of the U, the duck's dangling head was dragged into a shallow pool of electrically charged water, instantly stunning it so it would not feel what happened a second later: A guy wearing a yellow apron that looked like it had been splashed with red paint slit the duck's throat. Still suspended from the shackles, the upside-down duck continued traveling slowly, its blood draining into a metal trough, its body occasionally twitching.

"Some of them jerk around a bit afterward, like that one there," observed your faithful slaughterhouse novice, pointing to a bleeding bird that had flapped its wings.

"They should," Izzy said. "You never saw a chicken being killed?"

He mused that he'd been advised never to bring guests into the slaughter room because people don't know what they're seeing. "I lived with this for 35 years, 40 years, and I don't feel nothing about that, but people that are not aware that the hot dog that they eat in a baseball game actually came from a dead animal, they are getting a little bit squeamish," he said, turning his attention to the birds at the end of the line. "They're going in the scalder now, see?"

After bleeding in the trough for 12 minutes, each duck was plunged into hot water—142 degrees Fahrenheit, for those of you playing along at home—for two minutes to loosen the feathers. Then a worker wearing a purple soccer shirt under his yellow apron ran the wet carcass back and forth and up and down over a pair of tabletop rollers spinning inward to defeather it. That pretty much stripped the belly and back before the worker ran the duck's head and various nooks and crannies over another table equipped with rollers sporting little rubber fingers to finish the job. The feathers subsequently would be cleaned, dried and sold to a down company in Chicago. A couple of other workers did some cutting, trimming and scraping— bye-bye, head and feet; so long, remnant feather fragments—and pretty soon the duck looked like something you'd buy in a supermarket, albeit with its exposed neck still hanging out.

The ducks' (and our) next destination was a walk-in refrigerator where a cart full of hanging, plucked ducks already was planted. "They will stay here for the night," Izzy said. "We will open them tomorrow morning."

"Because you do cold evisceration," I said knowingly. (I'm sorry, but my chances of showing off my newfound evisceration knowledge seemed otherwise limited.)

"By tomorrow the liver inside will become very hard," Izzy continued. "If the liver has a large amount of fat in it, it will become harder. If it doesn't, it will not. That will determine the quality of the liver. Most times the restaurant would not want the hardest one, because the hardest one is all fat and nothing else but fat and would melt more in the frying pan."

The newly removed livers are weighed, cleaned and placed in white plastic tubs layered with shaved ice and paper. They're kept like this for three days so the blood in the veins will drain to the ice, because the less bloody the liver is, the more likely it will be classified as an "A" to be sold at the top price. Izzy said 55 to 57 percent of the livers wind up as A's, 30 percent are B's (which may be a bit smaller, bloodier or just less aesthetically appealing) and the remainder are C's (more likely to be used in sauces than prepared as is).

We walked through another room where a worker was trimming the *magrets*. Tomorrow morning, Izzy said, this room would be filled with activity as a male worker performed "a cesarean section" on the duck before his wife pulled out the livers and viscera, all while a USDA inspector made sure everything passed muster. Once the USDA inspector deems a duck OK, the bird is chopped into pieces to be sold separately, such as the breast and legs. Izzy worked up one of his characteristic heads of steam as he pondered this inspector, not because he resented the USDA presence, which is required at all such licensed processing plants, but because the Humane Society of the United States was suing New York State for allowing the sale of "an adulterated and diseased product," i.e., HSUS had petitioned the USDA with the same complaint even though the agency is charged with not allowing tainted food to hit the marketplace.

"So you're saying the USDA is not doing their job then," Izzy complained. "I mean, what are you talking about? I went to the lawyer, and I was sure that this is going to be completely frivolous. He looked at the paper and said, 'You know what? This is very serious. Very good lawyers arranged that lawsuit. It's not simple.' And I said, 'Why would they go and sue us for wholesomeness while they know that we are USDA?' He said, 'Because they want to bury you with the discovery.'" Proving that the ducks were not diseased, Izzy continued, would cost so much money that the farm could go out of business. "And they know that. So we have to attack them with something on the legality of the lawsuit."

When Wayne Pacelle created a new HSUS Factory Farming Campaign in early 2005, he hired as its leader a bright young recruit who'd been fighting this fight with Compassion over Killing: Paul Shapiro, Ryan's younger brother. In August 2006 HSUS sued the state of New York to block a development grant of more than $400,000 to the farm. The following month it sued Hudson Valley, charging that it was violating the Clean Water Act through its discharge of chlorine and other chemicals into the Middle Mongaup River. The New York State Department of Environmental Conservation had cited the farm for hundreds of violations, almost every one referring to the daily readings of the discharge. Hudson Valley operations manager Marcus Henley said a contracted company had taken the readings in the wrong place over and over, thus causing the multiplication of the same irregularity, but the farm denied actually polluting the water. The state apparently took a lenient view, fining Hudson Valley $30,000, a figure that HSUS complained was way too low given that the facility could have been penalized up to $37,500 per violation. The state considered the matter settled. The Humane Society did not.

In November 2006, HSUS led a coalition of groups, including Farm Sanctuary, in filing the "adulterated and diseased product" lawsuit, which was expanded and resubmitted in July 2007 to add that foie gras also can trigger "a multitude of human health problems, including extensive organ damage, kidney failure and even death." Those additional claims were based on a University of Tennessee study that found links between foie gras and amyloids (a fibrous protein) found in people suffering from such afflictions as rheumatoid arthritis, tuberculosis and Alzheimer's disease. The researchers had injected large amounts of amyloids extracted from raw foie gras into mice that were genetically predisposed to develop high amyloid levels. And guess what? These mice developed high amyloid levels.

"It is not known if there is an increase of Alzheimer's disease, diabetes or other amyloid-related disease in people who have eaten foie gras," professor/researcher Alan Solomon said in the university's June 2007 announcement of his findings. He noted that his study merely showed that the amyloids in foie gras "could accelerate the development of AA amyloidosis in susceptible mice. Perhaps people with a family history of Alzheimer's disease, diabetes, rheumatoid arthritis or other amyloid-associated diseases should avoid consuming foie gras and other foods that may be contaminated with fibrils." The mainstream press reacted to this news with characteristic restraint and nuance. "Foie gras could be tasty way to get Alzheimer's," read a headline in the *Times of London*.

HSUS submitted a deposition from a University of Pennsylvania pharmacology professor backing the notion that foie gras amyloids could cause human health problems. Still, there was a certain irony to HSUS and its fellow petitioners using an animal-testing experiment to reinforce the case against inhumane animal treatment.

At one point I asked Paul Shapiro whether HSUS's overall strategy was to use litigation to drive Hudson Valley—as well as LaBelle, but not the lawsuit-immune Sonoma Foie Gras—out of business.

"I would say that we are committed to reducing animal suffering in whatever legitimate means we are able to do so," he responded.

Back in his office, Izzy vented his frustration at having to spend so much time and money fighting lawsuits. "We created a business that was not here before. This is now the foie gras area of this country. It could be a tourist attraction! We own a piece of land 20 feet by 20 feet over by the road. We could make a store over there, like in France, and when people go to the mountains, they can stop over there and have some foie gras. We are afraid to do that because they're going to vandalize it, you understand? Everything that we think, all these ideas that we came up with, we always say no."

He sighed. "They are wearing me out. I'm not so happy-go-lucky like I used to be. I can't just do this all my life."

7.

Where the Animals Have Names

"The fact that these animals are our friends, not our food, is a very strong message."

Although Hudson Valley Foie Gras may not represent anyone's notion of an idyllic farm, Farm Sanctuary in Watkins Glen fits the bill. Covering about 180 acres of lush, rolling countryside, with big red barns that could have leapt from the pages of a children's book, the home base of Gene Baur's animal-welfare organization is a monument to harmony between human and nonhuman creatures, a pastoral wonderland located just a few miles from one of the key racetracks on the NASCAR circuit. The day I visited Farm Sanctuary, it had 745 animals on the premises, including 52 cows, 35 pigs, 39 goats, 70 sheep, 27 rabbits, 30 turkeys, 35 ducks, 29 geese and more than 400 chickens, most of which had been dumped on a field and left to die in Mississippi following Hurricane Katrina; staffers and volunteers rescued as many as they could and delivered them to Farm Sanctuary. Three of the farm's ducks apparently were foie gras Mulards that someone had dropped off in a box. All of Farm Sanctuary's animals are given names, even all those chickens.

Of course, a key distinction between Farm Sanctuary and almost any other farm is that this one doesn't actually produce anything—aside from compassion and healthy, long-living animals. The people who work here view themselves as the animals' caretakers and friends. They're vegans who no sooner would eat or exploit one of these creatures than a pet owner would dine on a dog. From May through October each year, about 7,000 visitors tour the barns, mingle with the animals, learn about the evils of factory farming and the benefits of a vegan lifestyle, and pick up books, toys and vegan munchies in the gift shop.

As Gene Baur and I sat at a red picnic table nestled into the edge of the woods near the main house-turned-office building, I told him about Ariane Daguin's reaction to his wearing sandals in a pigpen. He laughed and recalled how a visiting pig farmer had expressed shock at seeing a pair of young female interns in a barn among 500-pound sows, and the farmer warned the women that the animals were violent: "One will knock you down; the other will have your guts in a second." To support his point, the farmer told of how dangerous the sows get when you take their babies away. The moral of the story to Baur? Don't take animals' babies away. "A whole different approach is that the animals could be seen as friends, as they are here, and the animals are not afraid of people, and they don't need to be," he said. "It's a whole different environment, so, yeah, you can wear sandals with pigs." In fact, he was wearing them now, along with navy blue shorts.

Baur has become one of the animal movement's most public faces and with good reason. He's a fit, camera-friendly man in his mid-40s with bright blue eyes, neatly trimmed pepper-and-salt hair and a gentle demeanor. He's well spoken, rational minded and boasts an expert politician's ability to articulate broad values. He's also not a flamethrower. In most fields that last disclaimer wouldn't be necessary, but the popular image of animal-rights activists is radicals who splash red paint on fur-clad women and otherwise would rather provoke than persuade. In some cases the shoe fits, but other times that association becomes a convenient crutch for the unconverted. We want animal-rights activists to be crazy because we don't want them to be right.

While PETA remains fond of grabbing headlines through outrageous stunts and statements—founder Ingrid Newkirk announced that she'd willed her liver to French activists to use in anti-foie-gras demonstrations—the Humane Society of the United States and Farm Sanctuary have changed the dynamic with their middle-of-the-road appeal. HSUS retains much popular goodwill (and generated more than $120 million in 2007 revenues) as a mainstream organization widely associated with saving lost puppies, even though Wayne Pacelle has pushed the group in a more activist direction. Paul Shapiro's Factory Farming Campaign spurred the largest beef recall in U.S. history through its 2007 release of secretly shot "downer" cow footage at a California slaughterhouse, and it also landed an initiative on California's November 2008 ballot to ban factory-farm veal crates, sow gestation crates and layer-hen battery cages.

Farm Sanctuary lacks the huge HSUS war chest—it took in $5.4 million in fiscal 2007—but it has made inroads in other ways. It harnessed the power of the Internet to spread the anti-foie gospel on nofoiegras.org (launched in 2004) and led the successful campaign to get Wolfgang Puck to quit serving the fat livers at any of his restaurants. Baur and his cohorts also have enlisted more than 1,000 restaurants to sign a pledge that they would never serve foie gras, though the group's overture to Charlie Trotter is what prompted him to deem them "idiots." Farm Sanctuary made celebrity recruitment a significant priority as well. A wall in the visitors' center offers photos and testimonials from such notables as Paul and Linda McCartney, Alicia Silverstone, Joaquin Phoenix and members of the band R.E.M., and among the many stars to have participated in Farm Sanctuary events or public-service messages are k. d. Lang, Ellen DeGeneres, Forest Whitaker, David Duchovny, Chevy Chase, Mary Tyler Moore and Kim Basinger.

When I attended a spring 2007 Farm Sanctuary fundraiser at the Jivamukti Yoga School in Greenwich Village, the eclectic roster included event chairman and Def Jam founder Russell Simmons, feminist icon Gloria Steinem, innovative music maker Moby and Martina Navratilova. I asked Simmons what made foie gras such a hot issue, and he responded: "We do so much greedy and selfish shit to animals, but this is somewhere near the top." Moby, a 20-year vegan who also works closely with HSUS, didn't consider foie gras the movement's most pressing issue because of the low numbers involved, but he viewed it as an excellent educational tool.

"Like insofar as pot is a gateway drug to harder drugs, banning foie gras to me is like a gateway issue to get people to evaluate their eating habits, kind of like the way veal was," he told me. "The means of production are so repulsive and so profoundly unethical that once your general consumer becomes aware of it, they'll never eat foie gras again."

Back at the farm, Farm Sanctuary communications director Tricia Barry acknowledged: "To us foie gras is low-hanging fruit." Getting people to oppose it certainly hadn't been difficult: Just describe how it's produced, and they're repulsed. But she echoed Moby (and Ryan Shapiro) about making those larger connections. "I guess part of it is also awakening people to the hypocrisy of it," she said. "When people find out about foie gras, they're like, 'I couldn't possibly eat foie gras.' It's like, well, do you know how chickens are raised too? And do you know how all these other animals are raised as well?" Foie gras, after all, is far from Farm Sanctuary's only food-related campaign; the group also had been working against veal, pig gestation crates and even the Thanksgiving turkey. But those efforts never got widespread public attention; nor could Barry entice anyone in the media to bite on a video about dairy industry abuses—and a lot more people drink milk than eat foie gras. "For some reason, foie gras took off, so we just kind of went with it," she said. Baur theorized that your average citizen appreciates being able to judge this dish from the comfort of the sidelines. "Many people can look at that and agree with us because they're not complicit in the problem," he said. "The abuse of other animals is also egregious, but because most people are complicit in the other abuses, they're less likely to want to address them."

I told Gene Baur that I had just come from Hudson Valley Foie Gras, and he was curious about what I'd seen. I summarized how the ducks looked and reacted, and Baur immediately speculated that I'd received the "white glove" tour. "I don't imagine they showed you every single barn, and what I would guess is they showed you the barns where the ducks were in better shape," he said.

I said I'd seen several barns, including two different ones for force-feeding. Baur countered that I'd probably been shown ducks that weren't that far along in the process and thus weren't yet exhibiting ill symptoms. "Did you get a chance to see the birds before they were getting slaughtered?"

"Not only that, I saw them *while* they were getting slaughtered," I said, relating that I'd also spent time observing ducks on their 22nd day of the feedings and that Izzy had shown me ones on day 28 destined for the slaughterhouse that afternoon. The two pens on either side of those birds had been cleared out earlier that day.

"And it's possible that those ones were going to be processed that day," Baur said, "and it's also likely, I think, that he cherry-picked the healthiest ones and the other two pens were the sicker ones that went earlier."

"I don't think you would have seen what I saw and thought, Oh, this is great," I responded. "I felt like I was seeing what goes on there."

"My guess is that Hudson Valley is just very good at choreographing the tour," Baur said, citing Holly Cheever's complaints that the farm had done just that when she had visited years earlier. "I think they're trying to show you things in the best light. I do believe also— and I have seen this on various other occasions—that certain potential problems are removed from sight before the tour begins."

"Have you ever been on a foie gras farm?" I asked him.

"I have not," he said. "I've talked to a lot of people who have worked at these places and experts who have visited them, but I have never been on one myself. And I would love to visit it if they would let me."

"Have you asked Hudson Valley?"

"Izzy has just been so combative that I didn't even think it was worth asking him."

I noted that if he thought Hudson Valley was giving the "white glove" tour, then Farm Sanctuary and other animal groups could be accused of giving the "black glove" tour through their videos and rhetoric. Farm Sanctuary had produced a few of its own videos to supplement those from GourmetCruelty.com and PETA: a relatively sober one called *Foie Gras: Culinary Cruelty,* which intersperses interviews with straightforward force-feeding footage, and two more graphic ones that detail workers' duck abuse at Canadian farms. Did he think the widely distributed horrific images accurately represented what goes on at these farms day to day?

"The conditions that are on the videos may not be happening at every moment in every part of the farm, but they are representative of the attitude that allows animals to be exploited and mistreated the way they are on foie gras farms," he said. "So some of the abuses may be more acute than others, but they're all representative of the same callous attitude toward other animals."

"What about the use of phrases like 'exploding livers'? From what I understand, the liver doesn't explode if you keep feeding the duck."

"Now in terms of the exploding livers, that wouldn't be done by actually being force-fed to the point where they explode," Baur said. "They would more likely rupture when the liver is in such a weak state that when they're held a certain way or squeezed a certain way, it could pop." (When I later mentioned this to Izzy, he said, "I never heard of such a thing.")

"I also hear a lot about duck vomit. I have yet to see any duck vomit."

"I think that's actually pretty common, because they're pushed to eat so much or they're shaking their heads to try to get rid of the feed," Baur said. "They even admit at the foie gras places that some of the food doesn't go down and doesn't get digested; it's in their throat and could come out. I think that those are common problems."

"So duck vomit is common?"

"Well, undigested food coming out is common. How much they vomit, I don't know."

"From the pictures you'd think that ducks were vomiting all over the place and wallowing in their own puke." (Reader, I apologize. This line of inquiry is almost over.)

"Yeah, well, it depends on the definition of vomit in a sense," Baur said. "Does it go down and get partially digested and come back up? I think if it's undigested food coming up, I'd call that vomit." He laughed.

(For the record, I think what the photos and videos show is the corn slush that some farms feed the ducks. I eventually saw geese and ducks being fed this stuff in France, and some of them did shake their heads after the feeding, thus spraying their neighbors and pens or cages with whatever yellow goop remained in their mouths.

It wasn't the most appetizing sight ever, but I'm not sure I'd call it vomit. That's not to say that no ducks are overfed.)

The bottom line for Baur was that the campaign was trying to address how awful foie gras production is, and anyway, "it's hard to say there's anything good about it." The public, he noted, agreed. Campaigns in various cities and states routinely mentioned that polls showed 75- to 80-percent support for a foie gras ban. These were polls that Farm Sanctuary commissioned from Zogby International, which phoned voters in New York State, Illinois, Pennsylvania and other places. How meaningful are these numbers? You be the judge.

The survey, conducted in 2005, also asked: "How often do you eat foie gras?" In New York, 40 percent answered "Never" and 51 percent answered "Never heard of it." In Illinois, "Never" got 36 percent, and "Never heard of it" got 52 percent. So basically about 90 percent of those surveyed had no exposure to foie gras. Another 4 to 5 percent answered "Less than once a year." Zogby thus felt the need to describe how foie gras is produced before requesting an opinion. Here's how the question reads in full:

> Foie gras is an expensive food item served in some upscale restaurants. It is produced by force-feeding geese and ducks large quantities of food, causing the animals' livers to swell up to ten times their normal size. A long metal pipe is inserted into the animal's esophagus several times a day. This process can cause the animals' internal organs to rupture. Several European countries and the state of California have outlawed this practice as cruel. Do you agree or disagree that force-feeding geese and ducks to produce foie gras should be banned by law in [your state here]?

Hmmm . . . "expensive" . . . "upscale" . . . massively swelling livers . . . "long metal pipe" down the esophagus "several times a day" . . . rupturing organs . . . unnamed European countries and California outlawing it as "cruel." Go figure—78 percent answered "Agree" in New York, 79 percent answered "Agree" in Illinois, and similar results were found elsewhere.

I asked Zogby communications director Fritz Wenzel: Who came up with the poll's wording? He said Farm Sanctuary approached his company with the idea, but Zogby was responsible for making the language "defensible from a research standpoint." The challenge with this poll, he noted, was how few people were familiar with the subject. "The only way you can get people to respond to a topic of which they know nothing is to give them some information," Wenzel said. "I don't think the industry likes the wording of this question, but we feel comfortable about it because it objectively identifies the steps in this process, even though it's not a pretty process, and it objectively states facts about actions taken by states or countries to deal with it. We're simply laying out a menu of facts for respondents and gauging their response."

Playing devil's advocate, I noted that the question also could have read:

> Foie gras is a delicious food item prepared by many of the world's greatest chefs and enjoyed in many of this country's finest restaurants. It is a delicacy produced according to a tradition that dates back thousands of years. Scientific studies have shown that ducks and geese raised for this product do not experience elevated stress levels. Foie gras has become increasingly popular in the United States as American farms have made the product more freshly available. Do you agree or disagree that the production of foie gras should be banned?

"There is some subjectivity to this," Wenzel said. "The clients wanted to measure what people thought of the process, and that's why we came up with the question we came up with." He acknowledged: "Food production is a tough field because if Americans knew what happened to this food on the way to its plate, people would be eating a lot less."

Baur certainly thought the Zogby poll was meaningful. "Zogby is a professional polling firm so they do craft questions to measure public opinion, and when they're talking about something like foie gras, it's hard to describe it in a kind way. I think the way the questions were asked reflect what is done to the birds."

My Farm Sanctuary visit took place not long after Atlanta Falcons star quarterback Michael Vick had been arrested for operating a dogfighting ring. Baur saw a connection: "The same argument that would be made to defend foie gras production could be made to defend dogfighting: 'It's our choice, it's our culture, we've been doing it for years, we enjoy this, people make a living doing this, it's part of the community.'"

"Although there might be more agreement over whether the dogs suffer in dogfighting," I said.

"Well, that's an interesting point," Baur said. "In the case of farm animals, there's a greater level of denial. I guess some people might argue that the dogs like it. They're doing this willingly. I mean, a person could make the argument that the dogs are less abused than the foie gras ducks because foie gras ducks have this done to them." Besides, the suggestion that the foie gras ducks don't suffer struck Baur as "astounding. Some of the callousness that exists on these farms is unbelievable. In the case of ducks raised for foie gras, I would say they are treated like machines. They're being abused for their livers, for this organ, and to say that those ducks don't suffer is, in my opinion, just a complete denial of reality."

This notion of treating animals like machines leads to another of the ongoing semantics debates: over the term "factory farm." Activists insist that Hudson Valley and the other North American foie gras farms fit the definition, with Baur noting that the 500,000 foie gras ducks produced annually in the United States is "still a sizable number." But to him factory farming is as much about approach as the physical setup. "It's an attitude that commodifies sentient life," he said. "If you see an animal as a commodity, then you're not going to recognize that they have feelings, and if you don't think that they have feelings, then you'll do a lot of bad things to them, and you'll justify them and say, 'Well, they don't really feel it anyway,' or 'We really need to do this,' or 'They're going to die anyway.'" In Baur's mind the fundamental questions about the animals are "Do they need to die?" and "Do they need to be mass-produced like they are?" His answers to both are no. So Farm Sanctuary was set up as an alternative to that mindset, a shelter where animals from factory farms could live instead of die.

Baur grew up the oldest of six kids in a conservative Catholic family in Hollywood and, believe it or not, was an extra in McDonald's

commercials as well as the movie *WarGames* and TV's *Happy Days*.
("I hung out in Arnold's," he said.) He first became a vegetarian one
night as a high schooler when his mom served chicken and all he
could see was the live bird on the plate. He went back to eating meat
in college before committing to veganism in his early 20s as a conscious political statement "against cruelty" and "for health and for
compassion." While working at Greenpeace in Chicago, he met Lorri
Houston, and the couple founded Farm Sanctuary in 1986, starting in a house in Wilmington, Delaware. (When they got married,
they merged their last names and Gene Baur became Gene Bauston.
When they split years later, he went back to being Baur.) Their first
rescued animal was a sheep named Hilda, whom they'd found atop a
pile of dead animals in a Lancaster County, Pennsylvania, stockyard.
There would be many more. The group expanded to a rural Pennsylvania farm (a former dairy that produced tofu) in 1987, then moved
to the current Watkins Glen spread in 1990. In 1993, Farm Sanctuary
opened a second, larger shelter in the small city of Orland, California.
The members have made it their mission to remove animals from
the horrors of factory farms, even if that act sometimes involves trespassing. "The fact that these animals are our friends, not our food, is
a very strong message," Baur said. "And although we can only rescue
a relative handful compared to the billions that are slaughtered, sym-
bolically the message is very powerful."

By the time I visited the Watkins Glen farm, Farm Sanctuary employed about 60 people nationwide (mostly at the New York site).
Susie Coston, the animated, nurturing shelter director, had 16 people
on her staff—people who would feed the animals, give them medicine, clean the barns and more. Susie credited animals with heal-
ing and rejuvenating her after a painful divorce, and she felt like she
owed them. As she gave me a tour of the animals under her care, she
not only could tell me each one's name but also his or her disposition. "This is Symphony. Symphony is really sweet. She's very shy
with people." Symphony was a layer hen who had been on the farm
since 2000. Nearby was Diana, a chicken whom a Farm Sanctuary
volunteer negotiated away from a New York City toughie about to use
her to bait pit bulls.

In the turkey area, a large white male was kept separate from a group of females because "if he jumps on any one of those girls, he'll split them wide open," Susie said. Barry, who was tagging along on the tour, called these birds "Frankenturkeys" because of their genetic manipulation; they could reproduce only through artificial insemination (as is also true of Mulard ducks). "They are also bred so they have really tender, thin skin so it's crispy," Susie said. She had to limit the diet of this big white fella because otherwise he would grow to a weight that would be fine for Thanksgiving dinner, not so fine for farm life. "If I was to let him just eat as much as he wanted, he would be about 60 to 80 pounds. We keep him at 35 pounds because his legs will give out. The number one problem we have with the birds from the factory is their legs. They have outrageous chest muscles, and that's for breast meat."

Susie took me to a group of Muscovy ducks with a particularly strange backstory: "There was a guy that was a renderer"—that is, he renders dead animals into products—"and his wife used to dress as a clown, and she would take a child with her, say that the child was her baby and he had leukemia and they were raising money. It was a scam: (a) It was not her child, and (b) he did not have leukemia; she shaved his head. They got caught and put in jail for fraud. So the clown's in jail, and then the husband has no money, he has a rendering facility. He leaves, and leaves all the animals that they had in a barrel. There was a barrel that was sealed. It was full of ducks. And on the top there were 10 of them still alive, and we took all 10, and that's them." The fenced-off area included other breeds, too, including Mallards, Rouens and combinations. One was brown with a Mohawk, another black with purplish wings and a dark green head. Nothing was wrong with these guys, who were cohabitating with a group of chickens.

I asked Susie to compare the ducks' and chickens' behavior. "Ducks are not as curious as chickens," she said. "Chickens are very curious, and so are turkeys. Chickens are foragers: They go through, and they pick at everything. The ducks love to swim. The ducks filter feed, so anytime you spill a bucket of water, they'll drill holes in the ground to get bugs and stuff. It's really cool. Ducks are very comical. They like to play. They run around a lot. They'll chase a bug for a mile, which cracks me up. Chickens run to you. If you notice, the ducks are not running to me. Ducks are more standoffish with people unless they know you, whereas these chickens didn't have to necessarily get to know me; that's just who they are."

We moved on to the farm's three foie gras ducks kept in a separate outdoor area next to their own barn; they weren't thought to be capable of defending themselves against the other ducks. Here, a wooden ramp propped up on a cinder block led to an oval watering tub in which the birds could bathe. "We're going to build them an in-ground pool," Tricia said. Susie had found them (plus one that didn't make it) a few months earlier in a box left on the porch. Her theory was that maybe a farmworker had noticed these birds' precarious health and rescued them—though it was a good three-hour drive from the nearest foie gras farm to Farm Sanctuary. "We get a lot of boxes of factory birds on the porch," she said. "We don't get cows on the porch." The ducks' names were Burton (for California ban sponsor Senator John Burton), Harper (for veg-friendly actress Valerie Harper) and Kohl (for Chicago-based activist Jana Kohl).

These ducks' arrival posed a challenge to Susie, who was far more used to working with chickens because ducks "don't have as many health issues. They're not genetically modified like the other birds. Chickens, like the turkeys, constantly have health issues because they've been genetically manipulated. Broiler hens and broiler roosters have leg problems and heart problems. They're constantly full of parasites when we get them from factory farms. That is the first group of ducks that I've seen unhealthy that have come to this farm except for starvation cases."

Working with Cornell University veterinarians, Susie got to work on the three Mulards' recuperation. Initially the birds wouldn't eat on their own, so Susie had to feed them by dropping a tube down their throats into their crops. "So you actually had to force-feed them to keep them alive?" I asked.

"Yeah, but not the same way," Susie said. "It was a very small tube, very skinny that they hardly even feel. The stress of it was that you have to put it into their throat; they don't like it."

Burton was the healthiest, and Susie said it was unclear whether he actually ever had been force-fed; he came in solely with respiratory problems that had been cleared up. Harper was missing his left eye,

Kohl had deformed feet, and both had fatty livers, Susie said. As the Farm Sanctuary Web site explained: "Kohl and Harper endured the trauma of daily torture together. Today, now at our shelter, they are never found apart. They literally huddle together, seeming to feel safe only in each other's company. Kohl follows Harper everywhere, with his deformed feet limping all the way. And if he ever lags behind, Harper goes right back to get him."

"These two love each other completely," Susie said of Kohl and Harper. "When they sleep, they cross their necks."

Kohl and Harper were interacting with each other more than the more robust Burton. The three talked in their faint Mulard squawks and pecked at food from two round tins. Occasionally, one took a dip in the water. "They're chatting all the time," Susie said. "They play with each other. They swim. They are happy birds. They are so thrilled. The thing that I like most is they spread those wings, and they flap. Because they can't even spread their wings in foie gras facilities; they just can't. It almost looks like a torture device because their heads are sticking out." (It's unlikely that these ducks actually had been confined in the kind of isolation cages she described, unless they had arrived from a Canadian farm.)

After being shown around the rest of the grounds—and, yes, spending time in a barn with some absolutely enormous pigs without them knocking me down and having my guts—I returned to Baur. I asked him about the common notion, certainly among the producers, that those seeking to abolish foie gras were merely pursuing a greater vegan agenda.

"That is the world that we dream about," he said. "But we also recognize that laws codify societal values and that we cannot dictate to people how they must live." So naturally he felt a force-feeding ban should be added to the many anticruelty laws already on the books, but he also freely acknowledged the practical benefits of fighting this particular battle. "When you have a much bigger system that is much more embedded in the culture, as we do in the case of chickens or other farm animals, the change happens more slowly."

I asked: "If you were president and had legislative omnipotence for a day, what laws would you pass?"

"I think you'd start with transparency," he said. "People need to know what happens on the farm, and they need to know what type of practices they are supporting. I would love for the world to be vegan, but passing a law to do that, I'd have to think about that. People need to be able to make informed choices. And that is a problem right now. People are not making informed choices. Most people don't know what goes into food production, and most people also assume that they have to eat a certain way. People assume that they have to eat meat when they don't."

8.

How Duck Sausage Gets Made

"Nobody cared. Including myself."

Here are some of the ordinances included in the omnibus vote that passed the Chicago City Council meeting of April 26, 2006:

The Committee on Transportation and Public Way allowed Uncle John's Bar-B-Que "to maintain and use one (1) existing sign over the public right-of-way adjacent to its premises known as 9025 S. Commercial Avenue." The committee report packaged hundreds more such ordinances.

The Committee on Traffic Control and Safety approved the "removal of disabled parking permit 13816" (and many more like it), the amendment of loading zones, the installation of traffic warning signs and/or signals, street weight limitations and other matters that also numbered in the hundreds.

The Committee on Historical Landmark Preservation moved forward three permit-fee waivers and two ordinances.

The Committee on Buildings approved ordinances allowing the sale and purchase of various buildings.

The Committee on License and Consumer Protection waived fees for the Ravenswood Community Day Care Fair.

The Committee on Finance approved payments of hospital and medical expenses to police officers and firefighters injured in the line of duty, payments to senior citizens eligible for some sort of rebate, and settlements in lawsuits against the city.

The Committee on Energy, Environmental Protection and Public Utilities . . .

OK, I'll stop. I don't mean to put you to sleep, but I wouldn't blame you. Controversial issues may inspire the impassioned floor speeches and grab the headlines, but ordinances like these are what make the city run, and they've all got to go through the city council. So the 19 committee chairmen report the matters being passed out of their committees, and almost all of these measures are lumped into one big omnibus that is approved in a single perfunctory roll-call vote. While these reports are being presented on the floor— often after a couple of hours of special resolutions honoring public servants or private citizens who have made major contributions to city life—the aldermen typically mill about, entering and exiting the chamber floor, kibitzing with reporters and lobbyists and rolling their eyes when the speeches seem more endless than usual. They're all in their seats when a particularly important item is up for debate, but the rest of the time they're just waiting for the sausage to finish being ground.

The initial printed list of committees presenting reports at the April 26 meeting did not include the Committee on Health, but at some point a single sheet of paper was added to the stacks of committee reports on the aldermen's desks in the chamber. Here, in its entirety, is what it said:

> **Health Committee Agenda.** An ordinance introduced by 49th Ward Alderman Joe Moore calling for a ban on the sale of "Foie Gras."

There was no mention that it had been six months since this ordinance had been approved by the Health Committee. There certainly was no indication that this was a matter worthy of discussion or debate by the full council. The city immortalized as "hog butcher for the world" by poet Carl Sandburg and made notorious by Upton Sinclair's 1906 novel/meatpacking exposé *The Jungle*, was about to grapple with fattened duck livers, and it would do so the Chicago way.

• • •

Some of Chicago's 50 aldermen have earned reputations as tough dealmakers, powerbrokers, arm twisters, clout flouters or just enforcers of Mayor Richard M. Daley's firm rule. Joe Moore was not among them. Tall, beefy and baby faced, Moore had spent seven years working as an attorney in the city's Department of Law when in 1991 he ran for the 49th Ward city council seat vacated by David Orr, a progressive politician who had just become Cook County clerk. Daley backed another candidate whom he'd appointed to Orr's seat in the interim. Orr supported Moore. Moore won, in a runoff. He would never become one of Daley's men.

You might say Moore became a thorn in Mayor Daley's side, except that most thorns need to be removed, and the alderman hadn't previously caused the mayor that much pain. If anything, he was most widely known for championing progressive causes that had little practical impact. In January 2003, Moore sponsored an ordinance opposing a U.S. preemptive strike against Iraq. The council passed it, and Moore wound up on CNN, not that President Bush paid any attention. A few years later, Moore showed up at a White House gate attempting to present more than 300 end-the-Iraq-War resolutions that he had collected from various towns, cities and states. He was turned away, though he made a speech outside the locked gate that was captured for posterity on YouTube. The mayor, a die-hard Democrat (like almost all of the aldermen), had little use for what he viewed as symbolic lefty gestures.

Moore's ward covers the northernmost stretch of the city's lakefront and much of the neighborhood known as Rogers Park. Most of its residents are working class or less well off; the area's northeast corner along the lake, which should be prime real estate, has continued to be marred by drug dealing, gang bangers and a high crime rate. The 49th Ward's southern portion, which stretches up to Loyola University, is home to the campus crowd and an earthy-crunchy contingent that patronizes various coffee shops and homey eateries. Upscale restaurants have been pretty much nonexistent in Rogers Park. Certainly you wouldn't find foie gras there.

To the north, Rogers Park borders Evanston, a racially and socioeconomically diverse suburb of about 74,000. That's where Joe Moore grew up and in 1976 graduated from Evanston Township High

School, where he was an editor on the student newspaper, the *Evan-stonian*. I mention this last fact just because I was six years behind Moore at ETHS and became the *Evanstonian*'s editor in chief. I found this coincidence funny because Moore's introduction to the foie gras issue came with my *Tribune* story about Charlie Trotter removing the product from his menus. Moore hadn't previously known about the controversy surrounding the delicacy or even how it was produced. He did realize he'd eaten foie gras before—at Rick Tramonto's Tru— though it made little impression on him. He didn't initially contact any animal-rights groups, foie gras producers or restaurateurs to gain more information, and they didn't contact him. The week after my story ran, he simply took action and proposed a ban on the sale of foie gras in Chicago.

"So it was a gut reaction to reading the article?" I asked him months later over lunch at Leona's, a family-friendly staple of Rogers Park. Frankly, I was incredulous that the proposed ban was in some way my doing, particularly given that Trotter had stated his opposition to any legislation in that article.

"Yeah, and that's why I did it," the alderman said, eating a chicken sandwich. "I thought this is something that would appeal to a number of people who live in my ward. A lot of folks who are concerned about the treatment of animals live in my ward, so I knew that would have some appeal to those folks."

Moore introduced his ordinance on April 6, 2005. Typical of the language of these things, it lists a whole bunch of "WHEREAS" clauses before getting to the point, such as:

> WHEREAS, The City of Chicago is home to many famous restau-rants offering the finest cuisine and dining experiences to their customers; and . . .
> WHEREAS, Recently the media has shed light on the unethical practices of the care and preparation of the livers of birds; and
> WHEREAS, Birds, in particular geese and ducks, are inhumanely force fed, via a pipe inserted through their throats several times a day, in order to produce a rare delicacy, foie gras, for restaurant patrons; and
> WHEREAS, Arguably our City's most renowned chef, Charlie

Trotter, has stopped serving the delicacy, foie gras, in his restaurants; and . . .

WHEREAS, By ensuring the ethical treatment of animals, who are the source of the food offered in our restaurants, the City of Chicago is able to continue to offer the best in dining experiences . . .

Finally came the "THEREFORE" part, which dictated that the city of Chicago add the following rule to its Municipal Code: "All food dispensing establishments . . . shall prohibit the sale of foie gras." The penalty would be "no less than $250 and no more than $500 for each offense," though it was unclear whether "each offense" meant each violating restaurant or each dish of foie gras sold. If the latter, those fines could add up quickly.

Moore's proposed ordinance wasn't seen as big news. The *Tribune* included it as almost a footnote in a city council roundup story that first mentioned a taxi fare hike, a proposed ban on hand-held cell phones in moving vehicles, approval of a plan to expand Wrigley Field, a new strategy for catching city vehicle sticker scofflaws and a possible sales-tax increase to bail out the city's public transportation system. Illinois's proposed foie gras ban wasn't a high priority in the state legislature, and many assumed Moore's ordinance wouldn't gain any more traction in Chicago.

But if the city establishment didn't take Moore's proposal seriously, the animal-rights community did, springing into action once word got around about a possible Chicago ban. The various groups— including Farm Sanctuary, the Humane Society of the United States and Bryan Pease and Kath Rogers's Animal Protection and Rescue League—engaged in a coordinated dance, working closely with Moore and seeking support among the rest of the city's aldermen as well as its citizens. HSUS took out full-page ads in the *Tribune* and *Sun-Times*. Farm Sanctuary hired a lobbying firm in Chicago in addition to the statewide lobbyist it already had pushing the state bill to ban foie gras production. (That bill will wound up passing the Illinois Senate but died in the House.) Farm Sanctuary's Gene Baur contacted Jana Kohl (of the Kohl's department store family), a Chicago-based clinical psychologist who had become an active member of Farm Sanctuary and HSUS. Her main fight was against puppy mills, the subject of her 2008 book *A Rare Breed of Love,* but when activists told her how foie gras was made, she was outraged. She compiled literature against foie gras and presented it to as many aldermen as she could, sometimes accompanied by Alderman Moore, sometimes alone. She told the aldermen about the countries that had banned foie gras, and she showed them hideous photographs.

"There wasn't one alderman who wasn't horrified, appalled, distressed to see the reality of foie gras," Kohl said. "How can you not be? I had photos of ducks and geese with their throats torn, lying in a box of their own vomit 24 hours a day, who couldn't walk, whose beaks were broken from the process." Bernard Stone, a veteran alderman then in his late 70s, remembered Kohl's visit. "How many people even knew what foie gras was?" he said, pronouncing it "foh grah." "I really wasn't familiar with this. When they started telling me how the poor ducks suffer and all that, I was feeling sorry for the poor ducks."

Moore's ordinance was directed into the council's Health Committee, chaired by Alderman Ed Smith, who had maintained a reputation as a corruption-free reformer since he took office alongside Mayor Harold Washington in 1983. *Sun-Times* columnist Mark Brown wrote that over Smith's 20-plus years on the council, he had "pretty firmly established himself as one of the good guys." Also, Smith had been a vegetarian since he was a toddler, though he told me the reason was simply that he couldn't digest meat. A solidly built African American with a professorial beard, the alderman grew up on a Mississippi farm and maintains a soft southern twang in his voice.

Smith held the first Health Committee hearing on the ordinance in July and invited only its supporters to testify. This was not unusual; separate hearings often featured a measure's proponents and opponents, so it was assumed that those against the ban would get their own exclusive say down the line. The ordinance's second Health Committee hearing wasn't scheduled until late October, and when restaurant and foie gras industry representatives showed up to testify against it, they were surprised to see the supporters of the ban signing in on the witness list. Farm Sanctuary had flown in veterinarian Holly Cheever (who also had testified in July) plus the inevitable star witness, Loretta Swit, who played "Hot Lips" Houlihan on the popular 1970s

TV series *M*A*S*H*. Granted, the general public hadn't seen much of Swit over the past couple of decades (though she'd done some theater work in Chicago), but in the world of Chicago City Council committee meetings, she qualified as an honest-to-goodness celebrity.

One person who was not testifying: Charlie Trotter, although Moore had invoked his name in the ordinance and although both sides had urged him to back their cause. He was pointedly staying out of it.

The October 25 Health Committee hearing was a testament to how coordinated the animal-rights side was in its message, strategy and execution. Although Farm Sanctuary and HSUS had done the heavy lifting, PETA also had become involved by this point; it mobilized its considerable network of grassroots volunteers to press for the ban, and it also prepared a new videotape to be debuted at the hearing, with Sir Roger Moore narrating as Sir John Gielgud had done on the group's 1991 exposé. A PETA representative asked Bryan Pease for some updated foie gras farm footage, and Pease sent them clips that he and the GourmetCruelty.com team had shot for *Delicacy of Despair*.

Included was the infamous "Rat Munching on Ducks' Bloody Ass Wounds," a clip that sparked intense debate among those creating the new video. "I didn't want it in there," PETA vice president Bruce Friedrich said. "I like rats. I think it makes the rats seem unsympathetic. We have a bumper sticker that says, 'Rats have rights.' Rats are the most experimented-on animals. A lot of these rats are GMO [genetically modified organism] rats who are being induced with various chemicals. They are actually interesting, groovy, smart little animals." Pease agreed that the footage "did make the rat look pretty bad," but he didn't care. "Rats are mean. I'm not a rat guy. I was looking after someone's rat who was on vacation, and it bit my cat. They are not nice animals." The clip made the cut, with Roger Moore solemnly narrating over it: "Sick, diseased and unable to move under the extreme weight of their livers, many birds are unable to defend themselves from rats gnawing on their open wounds."

If the ban's opponents thought they'd get to dominate the October hearing, they were mistaken. The ban's advocates got to testify at the beginning and end, with the pro-foie chefs, producers and experts sandwiched in the middle trying to dispel the image of ducks being treated worse than Jim Caviezel in *The Passion of the Christ*. This was no easy task. Alderman Moore started things off by responding to criticism he'd received for proposing a law in Chicago to protect ducks hundreds of miles away. "We as a society believe all God's creatures should be treated humanely, and accordingly our laws should reflect those beliefs, which is why I introduced this law in the city council, so that the city of Chicago is on record as denouncing this cruel and inhumane practice . . . Of course, no foie gras farms exist within the city limits of Chicago, but we in the Chicago City Council can do our part to discourage this brutal agricultural practice by outlawing its sale within our city. The fewer restaurants that serve this product of animal torture, the fewer animals that will be subject to this unspeakable cruelty."

That was a mild prelude to Cheever's gut-punch testimony in which she shared her disgust with this "absolutely outrageous" practice. "The birds are raised in a fairly normal fashion till they're a few weeks of age, at which point they're brought into the production system" of force-feeding. This was not accurate, by the way, unless you believe that "a few" means "12." ("I misdefined 'few,' apparently," she admitted to me later.) She went on to detail the ducks' shabby treatment as they are "grabbed" and have "a rough inflexible metal tube . . . jammed down their esophagus three times a day while they are being forcibly restrained . . . Once they can no longer walk, because they are so crippled by their swollen abdomens, they are seen pathetically dragging themselves on their wings to try to escape the humans who are feeding them."

This was one vivid, awful picture that Cheever was painting. It got worse. In graphic detail, she described the ducks' other hideous maladies: fungal infections, bacterial infections, fractures, arthritis, severe esophageal trauma, "horrendous scar tissue," various ruptures. "Some of them have choked to death," she reported. "There is food in their esophagus spilling out of their mouth and spilling out of their nostrils. I apologize. As I read this, I realize how grim this is, and I'm sorry if I'm unsettling anyone's breakfast here." However, she couldn't have been *that* concerned with her listeners' breakfasts given that she continued: "We all know what liver color looks like. This is a swollen, dripping, butter-yellow organ that I could never with all my years of veterinary medicine identify as a liver if I hadn't been prewarned that that's what it is. While they're alive they pass abnormal stool. It's a bright green liquid diarrhea." Later, she told the committee: "I would just as soon eat out of a cat box as eat a liver from one of these diseased animals."

"I want to thank you for coming down," Smith said at the end of her testimony, "but I guarantee you Donald Duck today wishes he were Foghorn Leghorn." He laughed.

Next up was Swit, by then in her late 60s but nonetheless carrying that bleached-blonde Hollywood aura. She certainly still knew a thing or two about drama. "I'm Loretta Swit," she began softly. "I'm an actress. God, that doesn't sound like much . . . If I'm sounding a little breathless, I am always overwhelmed by listening to descriptions of torture and abuse." Her voice was growing shakier by the second. "My heart is pounding, and I'm very close to tears. And I'm only saying this so you understand why I'm speaking slowly and trying to get a grip, not because I'm ashamed of feeling this way. And if some people lost their breakfast over it, this is a good thing. It shows that you're feeling, and feeling is *good*."

Swit said she didn't know how to discuss this torture until the previous evening when she read a newspaper column (by the *Sun-Times*'s Laura Washington). "She wrote: Creating the delicacy may not be pretty, but it pales in comparison to problems like Abu Ghraib, police brutality and racial profiling. . . . She misses the point. This is all related. Are we ever going to forget the memory of that girl smiling, holding a tortured prisoner on a leash and enjoying it? . . . She grew up with the acceptance of this kind of behavior in whatever form it was, whether it was torturing a cat or a dog or seeing somebody doing it and looking the other way. So if we're still losing our cookies over the description of torture, that's good!" Later, Swit addressed the committee members: "We look to you for your vision, your wisdom and your vote against anything that allows cruelty and torture to be pervasive and to exist toward any life form. I would fight just as hard for you as I would for this duck or a goat or"—her voice lowered to a whisper—"a mouse."

Moore offered Swit "a big thank-you" for using her celebrity "to draw attention to a very important issue." South Side alderman Shirley

Coleman paraphrased a Gandhi quote about the interrelationship of society's treatment of animals and humans before she concluded rather bizarrely, "Thank you for showing us the human humanness of what we sometimes reflect as Hot Lips."

"Thank you," the actress responded softly and intensely. "It was lovely getting to know you. I know you'll do the right thing."

Next came Pease and Rogers, who showed the new five-minute Roger Moore–narrated PETA video to the room. "As revolting as it is to eat an animal's diseased organ," Moore intones over an image of a dead duck split open down the middle, "the cruel treatment of the birds is even more disturbing." When Pease and Rogers had finished their testimony, Alderman Moore nudged them along: "Given that this is your one chance at the microphone, are there any arguments that you've heard [from the foie gras industry] that you would like to refute in advance?" Pease mostly deferred to Cheever's previous testimony, though he added: "We're volunteers, unlike the industry representatives who are paid to be here . . . When you listen to the testimony from the other side, keep in mind they're making a lot of money from selling these livers."

Finally, almost an hour into the hearing, the pro-foie side had its first witness, and Moore and Smith couldn't have chosen a better figure to represent the opposition. No disrespect to Didier Durand, chef/owner of Cyrano's Bistrot, but he is French, speaks with a thick accent and is an idiosyncratic fellow. He told the aldermen about having force-fed ducks alongside his mother in his native southwest France, but his primary defense of foie gras was its health benefits: "Today in Périgord region, we have the least heart attacks and the lower cholesterol in the world as a result of our diet, which consists of significant duck, duck fat and duck foie gras consumption."

The aldermen were dubious. "Are you implying that the consumption of this delicacy is the reason the people of your region are healthy?" Alderman Danny Solis asked him.

"One hundred percent right," Durand said. "Yes."

"I'm no doctor," Solis said, "but I don't think you can state that. Because you eat this liver of a goose and a duck, that's why your cholesterol is low and you're healthier?"

"And heart attack low. In that specific area of France."

This exchange didn't exactly refute the lingering cruelty issues.

Carrie Nahabedian, chef of downtown's acclaimed Naha, implored the council members to get more information, because she trusted her foie gras providers' product and integrity. "A number of people that sit in this chamber on a weekly basis have stated that they don't know enough about it," she said. "So how can you intelligently vote for something if you don't know enough about it?"

"This is the second hearing we have had and hearing this testimony with regard to the cruelty, and I think that's ultimately our decision as a body to make," Moore replied. Nahabedian subsequently admitted that Cheever's testimony had put her in "the gray area." Michael Altenberg of the North Side's Bistro Campagne testified in support of the ban, saying he'd been swayed by the GourmetCruelty .com video. A letter from Rick Tramonto opposing the ban was submitted as evidence but never read.

The hearing's main showdown came when Marcus Henley, Hudson Valley's operations manager, took the microphone. Admitting to nervousness at the outset (Henley is as soft-spoken as Izzy Yanay is boisterous), he methodically described Hudson Valley's feeding process and drew careful distinctions between what the aldermen had heard from Cheever and seen on the video and what actually takes place on the farm. He pointed out that although Hudson Valley long ago had briefly experimented with the cramped, individual cages shown on the tape, his farm and the others in the United States exclusively had been using more spacious group pens for years. Henley cited studies (such as those of French researcher Daniel Guéméne) showing that foie gras birds don't experience heightened stress, he described how Hudson Valley ducks don't avoid the feeders, and he reiterated Hudson Valley's invitation to the lawmakers to visit the farm. "The decision that you're making, it does set precedents," he said. "It is important outside the city of Chicago."

What they would see if they visited, he continued, was 100,000 ducks residing in 17 football fields' worth of barns. If you took 100,000 people, you'd no doubt find some who were sick or in otherwise hideous shape, but you wouldn't videotape those unfortunates and hold them up as representative of the entire population, he said, and that was what the animal-rights folks were doing. "I believe that

I'm a good person," he said. "I was an army officer. I have children and grandchildren, and I've spent 1,400 days taking care of these animals, every day, for economic reasons but also responsibility. We go out there and try to do a better job." Henley had arrived at Hudson Valley in September 2001, he said, "and for 1,400 days I'm not seeing what was described to you."

After Henley had finished detailing how the video misrepresents what actually occurs on the farm, Smith still tried to get Henley to defend what's on the tape. "How do you say that there's no avoidance?" he asked.

"I watch this process every day," Henley said. "They don't like to be touched, but that level of avoidance behavior is not there."

"I don't think my eyes fooled me," Smith insisted. "When this person was holding on to the beak of the bird, the bird has been traumatized. You can see him shaking and going on when he's pushing this thing down in his throat. I don't see how you could say that there's no avoidance here. I don't understand it."

"I watch it every day, sir," Henley said and cited the scientific studies about avoidance behavior that he had just submitted to the committee members.

Moore jumped in: "Clearly there's a lack of desire on the part of the duck to have the food. Otherwise you wouldn't have to grab it by the neck and force a tube down . . . They are being forced to consume more food than nature intended them to consume. Isn't that correct?"

"Yes," Henley responded. "Agriculture takes advantage of the characteristics that animals have. Do you think that cows are producing milk at the same level that they were 300 years ago? Chickens now are so genetically 'improved' that you could almost see them grow. They go to slaughter in six weeks, six days, at a live weight of six pounds. That's our business, agriculture."

"I understand," Moore said, "but I've never seen a cow being forced to eat or a chicken being forced to eat."

"No," Henley said. "They get their BST [bovine somatotropin, a growth hormone] shots every day, though."

Moore then mentioned the European countries' and California's foie gras bans and asked, "Why are they all wrong and you're right?"

The animal advocates' campaigns had been very effective, Henley replied. "We're an easy target, and that appearance of the tube in the throat, it's an easy sell."

"*I'll* say," Moore harrumphed, breaking into snickers.

"The documentation's here, sir," Henley said evenly, referring again to the studies he had submitted. "The only thing that we have is to present our information, to open our doors to people who really are open-minded, and hope that the people who have been elected to make correct decisions will look at both sides of the information and not be overwhelmed by that weight of money and influence and talent."

Moore shot back, "I'm inclined to listen to my fellow legislators, whether they're state legislators or members of parliament in another country, rather than someone who has an obvious financial interest in the continued sale of a product of animal torture."

Gong!

Kay Wheeler, a retired Department of Agriculture inspector who had been working with Hudson Valley Foie Gras on biosecurity practices, testified that the farm's ducks were not being mistreated, that their stress was "minimal," that postmortems on 600 ducks found no lesions on their esophagi, that the notion of the tube inflicting damage was "a myth" and that the livers aren't diseased because storing fat is one of their natural properties. Instead of addressing the substance of his testimony, Smith hammered him for being a general veterinarian rather than an animal husbandry specialist, and Moore tried to demonstrate an ulterior motive for the veterinarian's testimony.

MOORE: You say you have a business relationship with Hudson Valley?

WHEELER: Yes sir, I do.

MOORE: So you receive compensation from them for your business relationship with them?

WHEELER: Yes sir.

MOORE: Did they compensate you for your travel here to Chicago today to testify?

WHEELER: Yes sir. As you well know, no professional should ever have to apologize for accepting a just fee for the services they provide.

MOORE: I'm not asking you to apologize. I'm just asking you a question. Thank you very much.

Dismissed.

That Farm Sanctuary had flown in its own consultant, Cheever, went unmentioned. Anyone with a financial interest in supporting foie gras was portrayed as having an agenda. Anyone with an ideological interest in obliterating the product was given hearty thanks. Can *anyone* who volunteers to testify before a governmental committee be said to lack some sort of agenda? The final two witnesses certainly were there to promote a desired outcome: Kohl, who identified herself as a Chicago resident without noting her role in lobbying the aldermen, and Baur, whose position as Farm Sanctuary president was not mentioned.

Once the testimony was over, one might have expected the aldermen to discuss what they had just seen and heard or to take time to examine the materials presented to them during the almost two-and-a-half-hour meeting. Unlike in the California Senate committee hearing, there had been no back-and-forth among the legislators up to this point. Instead, Moore immediately said: "Mr. Chairman, I move that this committee recommend to the full council passage of this ordinance."

This motion surprised Illinois Restaurant Association representatives who had been led to believe that no vote would be taken at this meeting.

"Alderman Moore has moved the passage of this ordinance," Smith said. "All in favor say 'aye.'"

Some "ayes" rang out.

"Opposes?" Smith asked and after a silent beat he declared, "'Ayes' have it, and so ordered."

Applause burst out in the room. Moore's motion and the committee vote—officially seven to nothing—had taken 15 seconds.

Later, I asked Smith about the speed of the vote and the lack of discussion and examination of the submitted materials, and he assured me that this was standard practice and that everyone had ample opportunity to make their opinions known. "As a general rule, the debate is held while the hearing is going on, and once we take the last person, there's a motion, a move to pass, all in favor 'aye,' opposes 'nay,' that's the way it's done . . . We do it right. We believe in good government and participation. We believe that government is of the people, by the people, and for the people, so we do it right."

The morning after the hearing, a Cyrano's Bistrot employee showed up at the restaurant to find a smashed window, destroyed flowerboxes and lattices, and a red blood-like liquid splashed on the door and sidewalk. Didier Durand charged that the timing couldn't have been coincidental. "I would like these people to come forward and give me a chance to explain how foie gras is done in a humane way," he told the *Sun-Times*. Pointing out rooster figurines inside his restaurant, he added, "You see, I love animals."

Joe Moore expressed remorse over the incident, telling the *Tribune*, "Obviously we don't know who did it, but if it was related to this issue, it would be a very, very extreme element. We want to end one form of violence, so I'm very sorry it happened." No suspects were identified, though Gene Baur had an idea of the culprit: "I believe that when Didier Durand's restaurant was vandalized, it was likely self-inflicted, whether from him or somebody else in the foie gras industry," he told me. "I don't know who did it, but I do know that those kinds of incidents are routinely used against the animal community, and I also know that we have been unfairly labeled as terrorists and violent."

Baur based his accusation on the incident's timing and nature. After all, the animal activists had just won a big victory, so why would they feel the need to strike out like that? "Usually these acts occur at a time of desperation, when somebody feels like there's nothing else they can do," Baur said. "And at that point I believe Didier Durand perhaps felt that this thing is moving forward, they put on a good argument and they weren't able to stop it, so now they needed to tarnish the animal movement."

Durand dismissed Baur's accusation as ridiculous.

The day after the Health Committee's vote, Mayor Daley was causing some damage himself, amplifying his disdain for the council's intrusion into restaurant menus. "What is the next issue? Chicken?

Beef? Fish?" he asked. He predicted that if the ban passed, restaurants would just call the foie gras something else because city inspectors wouldn't be testing what actually was on customers' plates.

The next city council meeting was scheduled for the following week. The aldermen rarely push through ordinances that the mayor actively opposes, so it came as no surprise when Alderman Ed Burke, the council's senior member and chairman of the powerful Finance Committee, announced before the meeting that if the ordinance were introduced, he'd use a parliamentary maneuver to delay a vote because he "wanted to take another look at it." Joe Moore OK'd the delay, and the measure was not moved forward.

But on the eve of a mid-December council meeting, Moore not only was saying that he intended to call for a vote on foie gras, but he also predicted that the mayor would do nothing to stop it. These were tricky times for Mayor Daley. City Hall had become enveloped in a scandal over the city's Hired Truck Program, in which private trucks were collecting taxpayer money for doing, in many cases, next to nothing. That the truck operators often were linked to city employees (and/or the mob) deepened the sense of corruption, and members of Daley's administration, as well as his brother's brother-in-law, were ensnared by a federal investigation into bribery, job rigging and mail fraud. At the same time, charges of patronage and worse were flying over the city's hiring and minority-contracting practices.

For a rare moment in his then-16-year tenure in office, the mayor was considered vulnerable, and the council had grown a bit combative. One of their fights was over an ordinance to ban public indoor smoking: Ed Smith's Health Committee had passed it, but the mayor and the Illinois Restaurant Association were opposed because of the negative impact they claimed it would have on restaurants. Finally a compromise was struck, and in early December, the council voted 46 to one for the ban but with a two-and-a-half-year grace period before stand-alone bars and restaurants with bars had to implement the law. (The state of Illinois subsequently banned all indoor public smoking, thus wiping out this delay.) A week later Moore was saying he was ready to submit his foie gras ordinance to the full council. "The political reality is that the mayor has to husband his political capital for issues he really cares about," Moore told the *Sun-Times.* "The mayor has taken a lighter hand in the council of late. Democracy in Chicago, it's wonderful. Let a thousand flowers bloom behind the Iron Curtain."

Activists had been calling the aldermen's offices. The PETA video was deposited into every alderman's mailbox. The Humane Society had bought more full-page ads pushing the ban. The simple question now was whether Moore had the votes. Everyone figured that if he could count on a council majority, he and Smith would move the ordinance forward.

They did not.

The year ended with no foie gras vote. So did the following January. And February. And March. By the April 26 city council meeting, it had been a full six months since Moore's ban had moved out of the Health Committee. The Illinois Restaurant Association expected no action that month and hadn't been actively lobbying the issue. Unlike in November and December, Moore hadn't told any reporters of his intention to push for a vote, and the lead-up coverage to that meeting never mentioned that the ban might finally come before the full council. All was quiet. Mayor Daley wasn't even chairing the meeting by the time the Health Committee report came up; he had left, replaced by the president pro tempore.

From his seat on the chamber floor, Smith announced, "The Committee on Health met on Tuesday October 25, 2005, at 10 a.m. in the city council chambers to hear an ordinance introduced by Alderman Joe Moore of the 49th Ward calling for a ban on the sale of foie gras in the city of Chicago. The measure was passed with no dissenting votes. In omnibus, if no objection."

After a pause of literally one second, a clerk said, "Hearing no objection."

"Hearing no objection, so ordered," announced the chair, and he rapped his gavel. "Alderman Ed Burke?"

Burke stood and said into his microphone: "I don't think we should let this pass without noting that the champion of animal rights in the city council has been successful in getting Chicago to be the very first legislative body in the nation to ban this product from restaurants. So Alderman Moore deserves a good deal of credit for being the leader of this movement not only locally but nationwide. It's quite an accomplishment." There was a smattering of applause, no doubt from Gene Baur, Jana Kohl and other activists in the audience who had been tipped off about the vote.

That was it. A turbulent year after Joe Moore had introduced his foie gras ban, it had become law over the course of 20 seconds. (In his book *Farm Sanctuary,* Baur's recollection of the ordinance's passage differs a bit from what actually is on a tape of the meeting. Baur's version goes like this: "'Is there any discussion?' the chairman of the council asked. We waited. Silence. There was no further discussion. The facts had spoken for themselves.") By moving the ordinance into the omnibus, Smith had placed the measure under the safe umbrella of a roll-call vote that was the equivalent of taking attendance. Voting down the omnibus would be like moving to erase a month's worth of city business; it's something that simply isn't done.

But the omnibus almost by definition is a way to deal quickly with undisputed matters. Given how heated the foie gras squabbling had been, most followers of the Chicago battle expected a full council debate on the proposed ban or at least a separate vote. That's generally how controversial issues, such as the smoking ban, were treated. Joe Moore would give a speech. He *always* gave a speech. Folks would argue. The council would vote. *Fin.*

Instead, Moore stayed silent while Smith took care of business. Even when you count Burke's subsequent congratulations to Moore, the foie gras ban occupied less than a minute of the full council's attention—and it didn't even have that. Moore had told Alderman Tom Tunney—a restaurant owner, the Illinois Restaurant Association's former chairman and, in Moore's words, "the man who expressed the most concern about this ordinance"—that the ban was headed to the council floor, and Tunney told his colleague he would vote against it. Yet hours into a typically drawn-out council meeting, Tunney realized he had missed his opportunity. "I didn't know it was even on the Health Committee report that day," Tunney said. "It went so quickly, and there was no discussion on the floor." Tunney said he didn't hear Smith say the words "foie gras," and thus didn't object in the two seconds between Smith's request and the chairman's "so ordered."

Alderman Richard Mell said he also wasn't aware of the ordinance being moved into the omnibus. "I didn't even see it come in," said Mell, one of the more senior aldermen (and father-in-law to Illinois governor Rod Blagojevich). "That's the time when you're walking around, and you're talking. Omnibus? Fine . . . It should've come out and had an actual roll-call vote on it. I think then you might have had people thinking what they were voting for. It was a *boom bang bing bong!*—it's gone."

When I spoke with Smith, he bristled at the suggestion that he had done anything out of the ordinary or that anyone who actually cared about this issue lacked opportunity to speak up. "I got up, made the presentation. No one called for any questions, no one had anything to say, and it was passed in the omnibus." Also, no one had moved to defer the vote to the next meeting, as any two aldermen can do. "When you report out your committee, your agenda is on everybody's desk, so there's no excuse for people saying, 'I didn't see it.' It was there." Moore said he wasn't about to get up and make a speech about foie gras if no one else was going to raise the issue; he'd certainly said much on the subject already. Even when Alderman Burke was congratulating him, Moore said, an alderman could have moved to pull the ordinance from the omnibus. "It didn't happen," Moore said, "because you know what? I had worked, I had talked to every single individual alderman, everybody was aware of the issue, and nobody thought it was a big deal at the time. It was only after the fact that it became a big deal."

"It wasn't a big deal to anyone except Joe Moore," agreed Alderman Ted Matlak, who said he disliked the ban but didn't think it was worth fighting about. "I think that most people either didn't realize it was there, or they think that Joe Moore owes them a favor. They traded a vote." Alderman Stone chalked up his own vote to indifference: "I knew it was going in there. I thought it was a stupid ordinance, but I just didn't care . . . Nobody cared. Including myself. I guess we thought we'd make Joe Moore happy."

Of course, there's a long tradition of mutual back-scratching in just about any voting body. If a legislator is passionate about a pet cause, colleagues are often inclined to lend a friendly vote, especially if they don't think the issue has much importance to their constituents—as was the case with foie gras in most of Chicago's 50 wards. Moore is so far removed from the council's power center—and he pursued the ban with such vigor—that some aldermen may have felt he deserved a rare victory. "I think that was part of it," Burke told me. "He doesn't get too many favors, so every once in a while throw him a little daisy."

Besides, Burke, who had a reputation himself for introducing ordinances that the mayor considered meddlesome (such as a trans-fat ban, which didn't pass), was intrigued by the ordinance ("It was an interesting way of drawing attention to a problem") and impressed by the work that Moore, Kohl and their allies put into it. That effort, he couldn't help but note, wasn't matched by the other side. "Had they mounted a vigorous lobbying effort at the time, it probably never would have passed," Burke said of the pro-foie forces.

Most chefs work long, grueling hours, and they're not generally inclined to attend government hearings or to get actively involved in lobbying. That's especially true when an issue goes dormant for six months, as happened after the Health Committee passed the foie ban. "The thing dies down, kind of gets quiet, and what do you do? You go back to trying to keep your restaurant afloat," said Michael Tsonton, the sharp-tongued, classically trained chef of downtown's Copperblue. Plus, many chefs simply didn't believe the city actually would ban foie gras. "When it passed, we were all like, 'You're kidding, right?'" Tsonton said.

The mayor's reaction to the ban's passage was to scoff, "We have children getting killed by gang leaders and dope dealers. We have real issues in this city. And we're dealing with foie gras? Let's get some priorities." The ordinance nettled him so much that he started to get wacky: "I have a fish tank. I don't want any aldermen coming up there, putting their hands in and start eating sushi. My little fish there. That would really bother all of us."

When the ban finally went into effect in August, the mayor offered a sound bite that would be repeated just about every time the subject came up: "I think it's the silliest law that they've ever passed."

But here's the real puzzler. If the mayor thought the ordinance was so idiotic, why didn't he put a stop to it? The going theory again was that he was weakened by scandal and thus didn't want to expend political capital on such a fringe issue. But there were any number of tacks he could have taken, like requesting that two of his loyalists move to delay the vote or simply persuading enough indifferent aldermen to vote against it. (As mayor he had yet to veto an ordinance, and he wasn't about to take that kind of stand on such a noncritical matter.) "I think if he was going to show us some leadership," Tunney said, "it should have happened in the beginning so we didn't go through this circus." Burke also laid the responsibility on Daley's doorstep: "Frankly, if the mayor had indicated that he was against it, it would have been voted down when it came up for a vote, but he chose to let it go through. Later on, of course, he criticized the members of the council for voting on it and said it was the silliest thing he had ever heard."

"But you guys didn't know that he was opposed to it?" I asked.

"I asked him," Burke said. "I said, 'Rich, do you want us to stop this?' And he said, 'No, let it go.'"

Previously, Burke had told Kohl that the ban had no chance unless the mayor backed it. Kohl met with representatives of the mayor's office, and, she told me, they assured her that he would not oppose the ordinance. Why, I asked Burke, would Daley let this ordinance pass?

"Probably because he didn't think it was going to get to be the big issue that it became."

There was yet another theory regarding the mayor's actions, or lack thereof: The aldermen had been asking for more rope, so he gave it to them—and sat back and watched as they dealt with the consequences of going off the reservation.

Local chefs and restaurateurs were outraged by the decision and soon found creative ways to vent, but the impact went far beyond the city's boundaries. The Chicago vote was a cold reality slap to the nation's handful of foie gras farms as well as to distributors such as D'Artagnan and the Chicago-based European Imports, which saw a sizeable foie gras market going *poof.* Chicago was a large domino, and if other cities and states were to follow, the tiny foie gras industry might find itself spending a lot of money traveling from hearing to hearing to fight an ultimately losing battle. They'd been outhustled, outspent and outmaneuvered in Chicago, and they'd have to step up their game.

The animal-rights activists were ecstatic. The Humane Society's Paul Shapiro heard the happy news just as he was about to take off for Arizona to push for (successful) ballot initiatives against veal crates and pig gestation crates. Baur and Kohl celebrated by sharing a champagne lunch with other activists at a restaurant across from City Hall, then taking a walk in Lincoln Park, just Baur, Kohl and her three-legged toy poodle, Baby, whom she'd rescued from a puppy mill. "Eventually," Baur wrote in *Farm Sanctuary,* "we sat on a bench near a big pond of geese and ducks swimming, diving and flying—the perfect end to a very good day."

Dismissed for so long as out-of-the-mainstream radicals, the animal advocates had achieved a striking victory in a city known both for its vibrant food scene and its meat-and-potatoes ethos. The California ban had come with the big asterisk of a seven-and-a-half-year waiting period, and the rest of the country considered California to be vaguely nuts anyway. But Chicago was a sensible heartland-values city, and if it decided that a yucky-sounding French delicacy should be banned, who could argue?

The bottom line is that after the foie gras ban was passed into the omnibus at the April 26 city council meeting, Alderman Patrick Levar approached the clerk and asked that his vote officially be recorded as a "no" ("I said, 'I'm not voting for this anonymously'"), thus making the final tally 48 to one. That margin would be repeated again and again by activists making the case that Chicago had risen up almost unanimously to reject foie gras and animal cruelty. Wrote Baur: "I believe what happened that morning in Chicago was a confirmation that we all share a deeply held revulsion against cruelty to other animals, even if we don't always give voice to our feelings."

9.

Hugs Against Chefs

"We know where you sleep at night!"

Nick Cooney has a friendly face and a demeanor that says Polite Young Man. His brown hair is parted in the middle and has a bit of fluffiness to it. His almond-shaped hazel eyes draw you in with their earnest focus, while his small mouth rests in the position of a perpetual sigh. His nose is prominent but in harmony with a long, lean face that suggests a softer Adrien Brody. He wears button-down oxford shirts that tuck easily into his slim-cut jeans or khakis. He looks like the kind of guy you'd want your college-grad daughter to bring home, though that appeal isn't limited to the twentysomething set.

"The first time I saw Nick Cooney, I wanted to fuck him," said Terry McNally, the late-fortysomething co-owner of the London Grill.

Cooney is not legally allowed to come within 50 feet of her restaurant or home.

Cooney and McNally spent much of the summer of 2007 together, and it was a tumultuous time, what with Philadelphia Police or Civil Affairs officers chaperoning almost every meeting. The 26-year-old Cooney directs a Philadelphia animal-rights group with a moniker that novelist John Irving probably wishes he'd thought up first:

Hugs for Puppies.

To the uninitiated, the name may conjure up images of cuddly

145

warm fur, but to many Philadelphia restaurateurs, it evokes bullhorns, shouting and intimidation.

The London Grill sits at the intersection of 23rd Street and Fair-
mount Avenue in a residential neighborhood a bit north of Center
City and a short walk from the Philadelphia Museum of Art, where
tourists still regularly reenact Rocky's famous jog up the steps.
Twenty-third Street, like many of Philadelphia's colonial-era byways,
is about as wide as alleys in more modern cities, so when protesters gather just across the one-way street from the London Grill, they
don't have to speak much above a whisper to be heard by patrons sitting outside. And the protesters weren't whispering.

It was a Friday afternoon in late May when Cooney and five Hugs
for Puppies followers first visited the London Grill. The outdoor seating area, where the restaurant derives much of its income over the
summer months, was open, though few folks were out there at that
time. On duty was general manager Jenny Holcomb, an 11-year London Grill veteran who, indeed, looks like a Jenny Holcomb; she's
a petite, friendly faced woman in her early 30s (though she looks
younger), her apparent sweetness belying the steeliness necessary
for someone managing a busy restaurant. A fellow worker told her,
"There's a bunch of hippies out there," and she saw a cluster of protesters across the street. Assuming Holcomb was the owner, they told
her they were there to get the restaurant to quit serving foie gras. She
told them she'd run it by the owners, but they probably wouldn't take
it off the menu because they didn't think foie gras was cruel. Out
came the bullhorns and signs. "We're here to let you know, foie gras
has got to go!" went one of the rotating set of chants. They stayed for
a bit more than an hour.

The group returned the following day, also in the afternoon when
business was slow. Holcomb thought the protest seemed "innocuous" and "kind of laughable and weird." Also taking in the scene
were co-owners Terry McNally, who oversees the restaurant's books
and service, and her ex-husband, Michael McNally, who reigns in the
kitchen. Michael read the worry in Terry's face and, after the group
left, asked her, "What do you think about all this?"

"Well, I don't know how far we can go with this," she replied.
"We might have to sit down and talk to them."

As Michael McNally recalled months later, "We were worried about how it would affect our business."

The London Grill isn't the kind of restaurant you'd normally associate with expensive French delicacies. The space originally opened back in 1843 as the Golden Lager Saloon, and in the decades leading up to the late 1960s, it was an Irish bar called P.J. McMenamins. In 1968 it was redubbed London, the name it held as a tavern until the McNallys, then married, bought the place in 1991 and added "Grill." (Terry had waitressed there since 1988; husband Michael joined the kitchen in 1989.) The front room is pure neighborhood pub, with maroon walls, a long front-to-back bar and high tables set atop the white-and-black tile floor. Sit here, and you can order burgers and other standard bar-food offerings. But walk up three steps past a stained-glass divider, and you reach the smaller dining rooms in the back and off to the side, where the look is more refined and the cuisine more adventurous. Michael McNally, a deep-voiced, towering man in his early 50s, may have begun his career as a dishwasher rather than a culinary school student, but he likes to play around—hence such appetizers as pumpkin goat cheese dumplings and duck quesadillas and such entrées as cavatelli with wild boar ragu and grilled calf's liver with foie gras custard.

The latter is one of the various foie gras preparations that the London Grill was serving after the protests began, but when Hugs for Puppies first came calling, the fat liver's sole representation on the menu was a foie gras–green peppercorn butter that complemented the hanger steak. That's why the chef was surprised that the group had decided to confront his restaurant. "We literally just had it on one dish," he said. "It wasn't even the focal point. That was what we tried to say to him: We're serving it with a steak." But Cooney wouldn't budge. At first Terry McNally had a hard time reconciling Cooney's levelheaded demeanor—and cuteness—with his hard-line stance. "He just seemed straightforward, a nice guy," said Terry, a gregarious, full-bodied woman who makes self-mocking cracks about "my fat ass" and tools around Philadelphia on a scooter. "But there's no compromise at all."

The battle lines were drawn, and as the days passed, the fusillade's intensity increased. "Stop the torture, stop the pain! The London Grill is to blame!" blared the bullhorns. "It's your menu, your fault! Your restaurant, your fault! Your money, your fault! Your choice, your fault!" There was also the call-and-response of "Boycott! London Grill! Boycott! London Grill!" To the restaurant's managers, one of the chants was particularly unnerving—with good reason, as it turned out: "For the animals, we will fight. *We know where you sleep at night!*"

Such an escalation of protests had been yielding results elsewhere, but with the London Grill, the effect was more akin to poking a bear. "As time went on, instead of worrying about the business, we decided to fight them," Michael said.

"It's just in my nature to fight," Terry said. "I like a good fight."

Philadelphia is a city made for folks with a pugnacious streak. Its sports fans boo more than any other American sports fans, and that's for the home teams. When I lived in West Philadelphia while attending the University of Pennsylvania in the mid 1980s, I appreciated the city's colonial charm and general lack of pretension but couldn't help but notice the collective chip on its shoulder. New York, less than 100 miles away, was like the magnetic older brother who seemed to excel at everything. Philly was the overlooked, scrappy sibling who played in the corner. While New York was basking in the glow of Broadway, David Letterman, what have you, Philadelphia was reeling from the mayor's bombing of a row house filled with radicals, a disaster that killed 11 people, left many more homeless and destroyed almost an entire city block. The nickname "The City of Brotherly Love" always struck me as more of an aspiration than a statement of fact.

As for the dining scene, you could find excellent Italian food in South Philly, but otherwise there's a reason the city was known primarily for cheesesteaks, hoagies, soft pretzels and scrapple (that savory mush of cornmeal, flour and pig parts formed into a loaf). It's a sign of Philadelphia's profound culinary evolution that a rarefied product such as foie gras is even part of the vocabulary now. I certainly never encountered it when I lived there; for one, I couldn't afford to go to Le Bec-Fin, by far Philadelphia's most celebrated restaurant at the time. Le Bec-Fin chef Georges Perrier is pugnacious. So is the Philadelphia councilman who thinks Perrier should shut up and quit serving tortured animals' organs.

Philadelphia's foie gras fighting, like that in other cities, was the natural follow-up to what happened in Chicago. The Chicago ban was a milestone, as no city, state or country previously had enacted a ban on this product's sale. Now that this most American of big cities had said no to foie gras, people on both sides suddenly found it much easier to envision a day in which such a prohibition applied to the rest of the country and beyond. The foie gras producers organized; the animal advocates mobilized. But what the activists soon found was that other legislatures weren't as keen on leaping into the foie fray as Chicago's had been. After the Trotter-Tramonto fireworks, Chicago's battle over fat duck livers was fought mostly in hearing rooms, but elsewhere, it was out on the streets—or at least sidewalks—of cities such as Austin, Texas; Portland, Oregon; Salt Lake City, Utah; and Philadelphia, where the clashes became characteristically nasty, bitter and out in the open after at-large councilman Jack Kelly launched the issue into the public discourse, then left it unresolved to create a vacuum for Cooney and his ilk to fill.

The almost-70-year-old Kelly, an animal advocate and one of just two Republicans in the Philadelphia City Council, first heard of the controversy over force-fed birds when a local radio reporter told him of Chicago's ban. The councilman, like many others, interpreted the 48 to one vote as the city's definitive declaration that foie gras equaled cruelty. "Once the [Chicago] aldermen and women were familiar, actually saw what was happening to those poor animals, they overwhelmingly passed the bill to ban it," Kelly rasped out while sitting behind the desk of his City Hall office. "And I thought, you know what? I'm against the torturing of any animals. I will not stand by and see any poor animal being tortured."

If you went to Central Casting to get someone to play a craggy ol' city politician, you couldn't do better than Kelly. Silver haired, broad faced, jowly and clad in a charcoal suit, the veteran councilman is a no-nonsense type with street smarts accumulated from his years in the feisty middle-class enclave of Northeast Philadelphia. He's blunt and salt tongued, yet he ties much of his image to a cause rarely associated with the meat-and-potatoes crowd: the defense of animals. A few years earlier, he spearheaded an overhaul of the city organization that oversees animal shelters and reportedly had been euthanizing

25,000 to 30,000 animals a year, including lost pets killed within an hour of being turned in. Full-page newspaper ads for his 2007 reelection campaign featured a photo of a tabby cat behind bars and the headline: "Jack saved my life." His campaign slogan was "Fighting for everyone. Two-legged and four-legged."

In May 2006, the month following Chicago's passage of its ban, Kelly proposed that his city follow suit, thrusting Philadelphia into the foie storm. And then . . . nothing. For the rest of 2006 and all of 2007, Kelly didn't push the issue for a vote or even move it to a committee. He spent the summer of 2007 defending his seat in an electoral battle that he wound up winning by 122 votes amid accusations of vote-counting irregularities. At the time, Philadelphia was reeling from its skyrocketing homicide rate, and Kelly was savvy enough to sense it would be dumb politics to push the plight of force-fed ducks on voters preoccupied with murdered humans. "This is a lower priority," he admitted to me. Nevertheless, foie gras, which he pronounces "frah grah," certainly riled him up. "The lifespan of a duck is about six years, I believe," he declared. "When they try to bloat them up and to do it in six months, that's not right. They should let these ducks live their normal lifespan, and then at that point, that's fine if they want to make foie gras. But I don't believe in torturing any animals, and these animals are tortured. I don't care what anybody says. Anybody who comes in here and says otherwise is either a damn liar or naïve."

Kelly's notion of letting ducks live for six years before killing them for food certainly would be novel in the agribusiness world. He gave little sense that he knew how long foie gras ducks actually were raised and force-fed, or that he realizes that non-foie-gras ducks and other poultry grown for food are killed even earlier. "I would think that the people who raise these animals would probably get more for their buck if they made it fatter or they made it bigger," he said. "Six months or eight months to me is not long at all. I would prefer them to live a longer life. There's no doubt about it. But my point is don't torture the animals. Period."

Had Kelly visited any foie gras farms before proposing the ban? "No, I wouldn't want to. I'd probably be sick if I ever saw that. It's bad enough they have films of it, and I've seen pictures of it, which is bad enough."

Had he watched the films then? "I couldn't even watch them."

Ah, why subject oneself to such unpleasantness just for the sake of proposing legislation for a city of 1.5 million? He already had certainty on his side. "These poor things, their livers are exploding, and they can't even walk," he said. "They can't even walk right. It's just not right. These animals shouldn't be tortured every day. They do it for weeks, for months, and it's not right." The councilman truly couldn't fathom why the foie gras industry felt force-feeding was necessary in the first place. "I don't know why they don't just feed them. Just feed them. Because it's going to cost them a few extra bucks," he scoffed.

Well, I couldn't help but note, the ducks wouldn't eat as much, their livers wouldn't expand, and foie gras, for what it's worth, wouldn't exist.

"Then that's too bad," he snapped. "If they want to feed animals the regular way, let them feed, and let them get fat if they want to, fine. I have no problem with it. But don't force them. Would you like to be force-fed every damn day for two weeks or five weeks or six weeks or two months? I don't think so. Let them feed the ducks normally. Period. And if the livers aren't that big and that fat, then forget about foie gras if that's what it takes to make it. I have no idea. I even heard that they can make it without liver ducks."

Hugs for Puppies' headquarters is a large street-level room in a rented, run-down corner row house in the poverty-ridden, African-American-dominated northern reaches of West Philadelphia. The space was a delicatessen years earlier, an irony not lost on the stridently vegan Cooney. He has four housemates, one of whom is a fellow Hugs member, though at some point everyone living there was in the group. They're the only white faces you see for blocks; thus at the height of her agitation over the protests, Terry McNally once went looking for his home by asking the neighbors, "Which house do those skinny white kids live in?" That's her version, at any rate. Cooney complained that she "went to our neighbors across the street and said we were white troublemakers and to stay away from us and things like that." As he and I spoke, street chatter and marijuana smoke drifted through the barred windows in front.

Cooney sat at a computer by the door, and on a shelf above him was a row of six bullhorns, three of which actually worked. Several cans of spray paint also lined one of the shelves. No, Cooney said, they weren't being used to spray anti-foie slogans on unsuspecting walls but rather were for painting 14 newspaper stands to be stocked with free PETA Vegetarian Starter Kits. The house cat's litter box sat off to the side, and a drum set was planted near the front windows, with Cooney's Suzuki electric guitar and a Yamaha keyboard nearby for household jam sessions. (When the guys play, they call themselves the Undercover Bastards.) Shelves filled one long wall stacked with pamphlets, leaflets, flyers, newsletters, Vegetarian Starter Kits and other pieces of literature. Two large white plastic postal bins on the floor overflowed with just the previous year's worth of legal papers generated from Cooney's protest activities. In one file, Plaintiff's Exhibit 79 was a photo of the back of someone's T-shirt depicting two assault rifles and the line, "I believe in the use of violence to achieve animal liberation."

"That was me years ago," Cooney explained. "I wore the shirt as a joke for one day, and then I gave it away to somebody." He denied that he actually did believe in violence to achieve animal liberation, saying he was a nonviolence studies major at Hofstra University on Long Island. Nonetheless, Cooney speaks softly but carries a long rap sheet.

When he was on spring break from college in 2000, he was among several hundred people arrested and jailed while protesting the World Bank in Washington, D.C. His more recent arrests have been for protests concerning Huntingdon Life Sciences, a British research company that conducts animal testing for companies such as pharmaceutical giant GlaxoSmithKline. Huntingdon's New Jersey headquarters secured an injunction against Cooney and Hugs for Puppies—along with codefendants Stop Huntingdon Animal Cruelty (SHAC), an international organization that has been likened to terrorists by the FBI and the Southern Poverty Law Center—following aggressive protests at the homes of company officials. A similar injunction against Cooney, Hugs and SHAC was enacted on behalf of a New Jersey–based accounting firm that works with Huntingdon. These injunctions prohibit, among other things, harassing or intimidating employees or their families, making threatening phone calls, sending threatening e-mails, disrupting business and conducting protests within 100 feet of the company. In late 2006, Cooney got 18 months' probation for harassment and terroristic threats allegedly made during a protest at GlaxoSmithKline's Philadelphia headquarters; an employee claimed he threatened to kill her children. Cooney told me that this woman, who was in her car yelling at him to get out of the way, misunderstood him. What he said he actually told her was "How would you like it if we came to your house and told your kids you kill puppies?"

Such tactics led FBI deputy assistant director John Lewis to declare militant animal-rights groups to be the country's top domestic terrorist threat, a characterization that Cooney finds laughable. He said the group's ridiculous name actually was intended as a wry commentary on this notion that animal-rights organizations are terrorist groups. After all, how silly would such heated rhetoric sound when applied to a group called Hugs for Puppies?

Cooney didn't launch or name the organization, and its primary initial focus was those Huntingdon demonstrations. It had been operating pretty informally for about a year when Cooney, a Northeast Philadelphia native, graduated from Hofstra and returned to the city. In college he'd become a vegan after hearing about vivisection and reading Peter Singer's *Animal Liberation,* and he learned about organizing from a campus social justice group. He also spent a couple of months interning at Farm Sanctuary in Watkins Glen before he assumed Hugs' leadership role, eventually incorporating the group as a nonprofit in 2005.

The first Philadelphia foie gras protest that Cooney attended, in fall 2004, was organized by another activist incensed by the $100 Philly cheesesteak being offered by Barclay Prime, a restaurant in Rittenhouse Square owned by the city's premier restaurateur, Stephen Starr. The triple-digit sandwich boasted slivers of Kobe beef, shaved truffles, Taleggio cheese and sautéed foie gras. Cooney was among the five protesters who showed up and quietly handed out leaflets. A week later the woman who organized the protest e-mailed everyone to say Barclay Prime was killing the dish.

Cooney took note: activists 1, foie gras 0.

Another small group, Philadelphia Advocates for Animals, organized more anti-foie protests, and Hugs soon joined the cause. In the
summer of 2005, they demonstrated outside two more Starr restaurants plus Le Bec-Fin. Cooney and his cohorts used bullhorns right
from the start, but their hold-their-feet-to-the-fire intensity wasn't yet
there. No one was e-mailing chefs and owners. No one was creating
Web sites specifically targeting each offending restaurant. No one was
visiting anyone's home or leafleting neighborhoods. And the protests
took place maybe once a month, so the restaurateurs had yet to learn
what constant pressure felt like.

At that point Hugs for Puppies had other priorities. A flyer describes the organization as "a 501(c)(3) animal advocacy non-profit
dedicated to aiding animals in the greater Philadelphia region." One
pamphlet features a cover photo of a sad-looking beagle behind the
inevitable bars with the words: "Membership has its benefits . . . Just
ask her." Among its programs were an effort to teach animal compassion to schoolkids; vegan outreach; opposition to factory farming
and animal testing; and the rescuing, rehabilitating and relocating
of abused or abandoned pets or other animals. One of the group's
newsletters reported:

> Recently, Hugs for Puppies came to the rescue of 47 beautiful white
> rats slated to be gassed to death after being used in a University
> psychology experiment. A supporter contacted us and secured the
> rats' release, and within several weeks we had adopted out every
> one of the little boys to a new home.

As Cooney's surroundings indicated, Hugs for Puppies was not
awash in money. The organization took in $14,000 in 2006 and,
Cooney said, about $35,000 in 2007, most of that last figure thanks
to a year-end gala and one particularly large donation. Funding comes
from individual donors and members—not, he said, larger groups
such as PETA, HSUS or Farm Sanctuary. The donations must cover
such expenses as producing and printing pamphlets, launching multiple Web sites, paying for gas (on those occasions when members
can't ride their bikes) and getting those bullhorns to work. Cooney
said his total personal income for 2007 was $3,500, money he made

from doing odd jobs such as designing friends' Web sites. Some Philadelphia restaurateurs have dismissed the Hugs members as "trust-fund kids," but Cooney insisted he's been supporting himself since age 18. There was a reason he was living in such a rough part of town with his thermostat set to 58 degrees in the winter and his diet dominated by Food-Stamp spaghetti.

What Cooney and Hugs for Puppies lacked in money, they made up for in volume. While the foie gras producers and distributors considered themselves overmatched by the deep pockets of the Humane Society, Cooney saw his group as the underdogs lacking the companies' advertising budgets. Hugs was armed with an even more powerful weapon: the First Amendment, which gave members the right to assemble and to raise their voices against animal cruelty. "I don't think that loud protests are a bad thing," he said. "I think they're a good thing."

Cooney said he considers battery-caged egg-laying hens to be the worst-treated factory farm animals, while he placed foie gras ducks in the second echelon along with gestation-crate pigs and veal calves. Yet from early 2007 onward, Hugs for Puppies concentrated almost exclusively on eradicating foie gras in Philadelphia. You pick your spots. The press wasn't writing about Hugs for Puppies giving out 45,000 kits and 75,000 leaflets to encourage vegetarianism, but it was all over the foie gras fireworks. Restaurants were dropping the dish, Kelly's proposed ordinance was pending, and the time had come to push harder, faster.

By now Cooney had refined his approach to restaurants. First he'd visit the chef or owner bearing an information packet and DVD detailing the evils of foie gras production. Then he'd try to set up a meeting. In several cases the personal approach worked and restaurants removed foie gras from their menus. When it didn't, Hugs for Puppies mobilized. "Like any classic protest or public pressure campaign," he told me, "we generally will use an escalating level of pressure."

Philadelphia chef David Ansill came up with a joke to sum up his feelings about the foie gras controversy:

"A chef, a duck, a foie gras protester and a foie gras producer all go to Paris together on vacation, and they take the elevator up to the top of the Eiffel Tower. And they're staring at the rooftops of Paris when all of a sudden a big gust of wind comes and blows one of them off, crashing to his death. Which one?"

He paused, then delivered the punch line:

"Who cares?"

Ansill told the joke with a pained half smile. The first time he saw the Hugs for Puppies folks gathered in front of one of his restaurants, he was amused. By the time I caught up with him, the only humor he could find in the situation was of the gallows variety.

In his late 40s, Ansill is one of the skinnier chefs you'll see; he looks like he's been stretched out from the top and bottom, an effect intensified by the pointy goatee protruding from his long face. He spoke with an air of weary, chagrined resignation as he sat at the long L-shaped bar of his two-year-old restaurant, named simply Ansill, located in the Queen Village neighborhood a block south of bustling South Street. Until midsummer 2007, he also owned a small French BYOB bistro called Pif, which was nestled amid the Italian restaurants of South Philadelphia. It was there earlier that year that Ansill first encountered Hugs for Puppies. "It was comical almost," he said. "They're pretty aggressive. I sent them out a tray of decaf coffee and went on from there."

Having trained with various French chefs in Miami and Philadelphia, Ansill didn't have to think hard about putting a foie gras torchon on his bistro's menu. It fit the restaurant and the tradition he was following. "I would marinate it in some port and mirabelle and eau-de-vie and then poach it and chill it and slice it," he said. "Serve it with some grapes cooked in port and some toasts. Very simple classic French stuff. That's the kind of cook I am." But Cooney and his cohorts weren't interested in culinary reverence. Pif, which offered a mere eight tables topped with paper, and the newer Ansill, with its full bar and a capacity of 75, were on Hugs' checklist of restaurants serving foie gras, so the group began showing up every week at Pif and, eventually, Ansill. At the larger restaurant, foie gras initially appeared only as a garnish on a baked-egg dish, and as a concession to the protesters, Ansill made it an optional add-on. "That wasn't enough for them," he said. The demonstrations continued.

"There were like seven or eight people," the chef/owner recalled. "They're young, holding signs of sickly looking ducks, screaming, 'David Ansill, it's your fault!' Some of them have megaphones sometimes, and they're just screaming—as people walk by, screaming in their faces. 'We know where you sleep at night' is one of them." Ansill came up with a nickname for one of the protesters, whom he didn't yet realize was Cooney. "We used to call him the Pointer. He would just sit there and point like this"—Ansill demonstrated a stiff-armed Uncle Sam pose—"and it made one of my waitresses a little, you know, nervous. He would just point at a server or point at me for five minutes, staring through the window." Ansill wondered: "Did he study these techniques? Is there a handbook for aggressive protest techniques? 'Number four: Pointing'?"

Later, I asked Cooney whether he'd learned this action from fellow protesters. "No, no one told me to point," he replied. "I like to think that everything I do is for practical purposes, and a lot of those practical purposes have to do with psychology. Simply the fact that people think of me as the Pointer means that it's gotten to their heads in some sense." He cracked a bit of a smile. "I think it just makes people uncomfortable. If I were to sit here and go like this and point at you"—he pointed at me—"especially if I'm surrounded by people who are yelling at you, it just makes someone feel uncomfortable."

Well, yes.

"It directs attention toward them, either in their mind or in reality. It's just a way to get under their skin and to make them realize: You're the one that's doing this that's wrong, and you're the one who needs to change."

"It's obviously a successful tactic," admitted Bridget O'Toole, the Ansill server who was bugged by the finger thrusting back when she was working at Pif. "I move around a lot, and he would often point at me with a really angry face. Sometimes they do it all together. It was just making me uncomfortable. I wasn't the one eating it, and the people who were in the restaurant found it hilarious. We sold more foie gras when they were out there. For me it was like, I'm working, and you're fuckin' pointing at me."

These protests didn't actually affect business. People kept making reservations. People showed up. "They weren't going to be intimidated by having to walk through these screaming people at the door," Ansill said. But Hugs for Puppies continued upping the ante. The chef closed Pif in June 2007 to concentrate on Ansill, and the group adjusted its efforts accordingly. It set up a Web site, AnsillPollutes.com, that linked the restaurant to the Humane Society–alleged environmental violations by Hudson Valley Foie Gras, one of Ansill's sources. Cooney and crew also printed up small AnsillPollutes.com flyers that, alongside a photo of brown sludge pouring into a scenic waterway, stated that the restaurant "serves products from a farm that illegally dumps feces, ammonia, solid waste and other pollutants into the Delaware Riverway every single day. Boycott Ansill!" These flyers were stapled to "Say 'No' to Foie Gras" leaflets that showed "sick, wounded and dying ducks" on foie gras farms. Hugs distributed about 1,500 of these packets in the restaurant's immediate vicinity. "The zoning commissioner lives across the street here," Ansill sighed. "He was a little tired of the noise and the pamphlets. I need my neighbors to support me, and it just pissed them off more than I could make them happy with my food."

Protesters also visited his former address two weeks after he had moved elsewhere—"I'm sure this poor Chinese guy who's the owner of the house had no idea what the hell's going on," Ansill said. Philadelphia Advocates for Animals also loudly protested at the home of local chef Guillermo Pernot one Saturday morning after Cooney mistakenly identified him as being involved with Pif. But the campaign against Ansill was not to be stalled. At the final protest, about 20 loud activists rounded the busy corner at Third and Bainbridge Streets, thus surrounding the restaurant early one Saturday evening. The neighbors complained about the noise, and, Ansill said, "I just got tired of it. You know, Terry McNally's London Grill, that's not her name on the front of the door. It doesn't say, 'Terry McNally pollutes,' does it? It says, 'London Grill pollutes.' But it's my name. Ansill, Ansill, Ansill, everywhere. Jesus. Just having my name, my family name, being dredged through the mud like that, who the hell needs that?"

Way back when, Ansill generated publicity for his cooking. Now it was all about his use of a single ingredient. A newspaper story featured a photo of his baked eggs topped with foie gras, and from then on "every article in the paper, there I am with my foie gras dish. So

I was the face for the forefront of it." Yet he wasn't trying to fight a cause or to be on the front lines of any movement. "I wasn't like Terry and these guys going to meetings and hiring lawyers. I was in the kitchen cooking most of the time."

So he sent Cooney an e-mail. He was folding. "Nick, foie is off my menu," he wrote. "I hope you'll be as aggressive (or maybe a little less) in letting people know, especially in Queen Village. David Ansill."

Cooney e-mailed back thanking him for his decision but continuing: "The only question I have for you is if that removal represents simply a seasonal change in menu (and that foie gras may be served in the future), or if your decision means that foie gras will not be served at Ansill in the future.

"If you can clarify that for me, and your decision does indeed mean that you do not plan on serving foie gras in the future (a decision dozens of other chefs have already made), then we will immediately remove the AnsillPollutes.com website; remove you from the 'boycott' section and endorse your restaurant on our website and on the Professionals Against Foie Gras website (www.pafg.org); submit letters to the editor of the *Inquirer* and the *South Philly Review* praising your restaurant for its ethical decision; and otherwise spread the word that Ansill has shown its concern for animal welfare (and the environment).

"Thank you, have a nice evening."

Ansill assured him that foie was gone gone gone. But if the chef thought his decision would direct the spotlight elsewhere, he was mistaken. Cooney indeed followed through in touting Ansill's new stance, so the chef found himself back in the papers as the poster boy for those who had thrown in the torchon towel. "I'm the one that caved now," he said. "I can't win."

"I was actually a little disappointed when we took the foie gras off the menu here at Ansill because of the tactics they used," said O'Toole, the pointed-at server. "I thought it would have shown more solidarity had we kept it on the menu, that you can't push us around and people can eat whatever the hell they want. But he has to pay the bills, and it's a very tight-knit community around here, and people were starting to believe the propaganda."

Two days after Ansill discontinued the ingredient, Ariane Daguin visited him to enlist him in a five-dollar-foie-gras promotion that she was organizing among Philadelphia's restaurants. He told her she was too late. He was done. The whole situation struck him as absurd. "I can't believe that she would take the time to talk me into serving duck liver," he said. "It's ridiculous."

I asked Cooney: "Does it make a difference to you whether a restaurant takes foie gras off the menu because they've seen the light morally or because they've been battered into submission by you and your bullhorns?"

"I certainly want to change their opinion about it because that's one way to make long-term change in terms of keeping it off the menu, and that might carry over into other food choices that they make," he replied in a thoughtful tone. "That's absolutely what we want. That's why we're always trying to set up meetings, give information, things like that. But when that clearly doesn't work and they're clearly not going to come around to agreeing with our opinion and the majority public opinion that foie gras is cruel, then it's perfectly acceptable for me to pressure them into taking it off the menu through protest tactics, because those animals are being saved."

So Hugs for Puppies pressures and "puts shame on" the restaurateurs, who, worried about their businesses (and emotional health), shift positions regardless of whether their hearts or minds have been swayed. That's fine with Cooney. "I shouldn't say this now, but I think history bears this out with a lot of social change struggles: Go to David Ansill in a couple years and ask him about foie gras, and he'll say, 'Yeah, I took it off the menu. We try to buy from farms that treat their animals the most humanely.' And whether that's because they've come around to thinking that way, whether it's because they try to provide a reason for what they did that makes it look like their own decision and not something they were pressured into, what exactly is going on in that person's psychology or in the social psychology that causes that, I don't know exactly. It's probably a number of factors. But that does seem to be the case."

As anyone who has taken Psychology 101 knows, this dynamic is called "cognitive dissonance." Cooney is positing that because Ansill won't want to think of himself as someone bullied into taking an action that violates his true beliefs, he'll eventually convince himself that the position he took was, in fact, correct and consistent with his worldview. But Ansill had no problem admitting that he had surrendered for purely pragmatic reasons, even as he diminished the significance of his move. "He could claim victory for me taking it off the menu if he wants, but it wasn't because of foie gras. It was just because my neighbors didn't like the noise, and if I can get rid of the noise by taking something off the menu, make my neighbors happy, then it's not that big of an issue. If it turns into something else, if they decide now, 'Oh, we got him to take off duck liver, let's see if we can get him to take off his lamb,' if they come here with pictures of sheep and stuff, then the foie gras is back on, and I'll do a five-course foie gras menu every night." He laughed ruefully. "Or not."

Dropping foie gras had no perceptible impact on Ansill's business, though some customers asked for it and expressed their disappointment in his decision. Meanwhile, the chef decided not to play that game of keeping foie gras in the back for special customers who knew the right code words. He was officially sick of fatty duck livers. Months later, he still spoke of the conflict with the bewilderment of someone who had been hit by a bus that had fallen from the sky. "You know, I'm just a cook," he said. "You open a restaurant, you're just trying to make people happy. Now I'm just trying not to make them pissed off."

DISPATCHES

July 2–3, 2007:
A vandal dubbed the "V-Gangster" spray paints obscene graffiti on seven downtown Austin, Texas, restaurants to protest their serving of foie gras and/or veal.

August 2, 2007:
Harvey Nichols announces its "commercial decision" to drop foie gras in advance of a planned Viva! nationwide action against the British department store chain.

August 11, 2007:
Members of SHARK (Showing Animals Respect and Kindness) demonstrate outside the Salt Lake City restaurant Metropolitan, one protester wearing a "body screen" that displays *Delicacy of Despair.* Metropolitan eventually eliminates foie gras from its menu.

September 6, 2007:
Through camera surveillance, Austin police identify a vandal shown defacing the foie-serving restaurant Jezebel with the words "Spit it out."

November 2007:
Glen Tanswell, proprietor of Gloucester's Bearlands restaurant, removes foie gras from his menu, claiming he was "bullied" by the group Gloucestershire Animal Action. He blames police for not stopping the "constant harassment and intimidation."

December 20, 2007:
A hooded intruder splashes paint over a Swiss specialty store to protest its stocking of foie gras. A group called "The Masked Ducks" claims responsibility.

10.

Duck!

"Maybe trying to be too consistent isn't really such a great idea."

Richard Wiseman, a psychology professor at the University of Hertfordshire in England, joined forces with the British Association for the Advancement of Science in September 2001 to launch a year-long effort to deconstruct the psychology of humor. This quirky project took place on a Web site called LaughLab (www.laughlab.co.uk), which collected more than 40,000 jokes and 1.5 million ratings as the researchers sought to determine the reasons that men and women, old folks and young folks, residents of this country or that country, and people at various times of day found certain jokes humorous. One of the study's conclusions was this: "Many of the jokes submitted contained reference to animals. We found that jokes mentioning ducks are funnier than others. Perhaps it's because of their beaks, or webbed feet, or odd shape. Regardless, the implication is clear—if you are going to tell a joke involving an animal, make it a duck."

One example (which fits in the LaughLab's genre of jokes that prompt laughter because they make us feel superior to other people): "A woman goes into a café with a duck. She puts the duck on a stool and sits next to it. The waiter comes over and says: 'Hey!

That's the ugliest pig that I have ever seen.' The woman says: 'It's a duck, not a pig.' And the waiter says: 'I was talking to the duck.'"

Cartoonist Matthew Diffee reached a similar conclusion to Wiseman: "I think ducks are the funniest bird." That's why ducks were his bird of choice in a *New Yorker* cartoon that depicts a middle-aged man on his doorstep faced with two small white ducks, one of whom is asking him: "Have you ever thought about becoming a duck?" In a December 2006 essay on the Huffington Post, Diffee explains: "It's hard to beat that bright orange bill and those webbed feet. It's like a chicken wearing Groucho glasses and snorkeling flippers." Diffee also notes that a quack is funnier than a cluck and that "waddle" sounds as silly as it looks.

The most prominent ducks in popular culture are funny: Donald, Daffy and the one that launched Aflac insurance into the household vernacular. Even in the classic 1995 kids' movie *Babe,* the one riotous character is Ferdinand, the duck who imitates a rooster and engineers the theft of the farmer's alarm clock. All of these quackers are spunky, comically irritable and prone to expert double takes when confronted with things even more absurd than their own sputtering, aspirational selves. Their voices are as fun to imitate as their walks. With whom would you rather hang out: Donald Duck or Mickey Mouse? Daffy Duck or Porky Pig? The Looney Tunes Web site explains Daffy's appeal thusly: "Despite his failures, Daffy, like the Greek hero Sisyphus, is a victim of injustice who continuously protests. And it's his refusal to surrender his will to the whims of the conspiring universe that makes him heroic. How could one not feel sorry for an ill-equipped duck with Daffy's voice that just can't seem to get a break?"

Our affection for these birds is reflected even in our language. Consider the negative associations we have with so many animals we eat. Around every Thanksgiving pundits unveil their lists of the year's biggest turkeys, and you don't want to be one (or, even worse, a jive turkey). You also don't want to be called a chicken or henpecked, and being deemed a pig, pigheaded or piggish is an insult despite pigs' considerable intelligence. It's rude to refer to someone as a cow—or the somewhat redundant "fat cow"—and few people desire to be goosed. Lamb is one anomaly because "little lamb" is a term of affection, and we think lambies are cute, but we eat them anyway. Then there's our beloved duck. Being a sitting duck makes us vulnerable, but I can't think of any duck insults. When you note someone's good fortune, you say that person's a lucky duck. When you're able to shrug off an insult, you say it's like water off a duck's back. Feeling just ducky is a happy thing.

Perhaps because these birds prompt us to laugh as well as to root for them, we're more sensitive to their treatment than that of, say, chickens. In a sense, chickens are the anti-ducks. Diffee calls them "creepy." Holly Cheever told me she considers chickens the most ill-treated of all animals in part because "they are not a charismatic species. Even if people have never known a cow, if they look at a cow and get close to her, they can really fall in love with those big brown eyes and lovely sweeping eyelashes. But no one looks at chickens and falls in love with chickens."

Our real-life associations with these birds make a difference, too. Because chickens are almost fully domesticated, we rarely encounter them in the wild. In contrast, we routinely see ducks in nature—even in large urban areas as long as there's standing water. There's a reason Robert McCloskey's classic children's tale isn't titled *Make Way for Chicks*.

When I was at Farm Sanctuary, I mentioned the theory about ducks being the funniest animal to Susie Coston, Tricia Barry and Gene Baur.

"Well, look how they walk," said Susie, the shelter director. "They've got the flappy feet."

"Duck feet are similar to clown feet, I guess," Gene added.

"They're adorable," Susie said.

"They look like they're smiling, too, the way their bills are shaped," Tricia added.

"Well, their bills are smooth," Susie said. "They're not violent looking, like an eagle."

"A softer beak, a rounder beak," Gene said.

"What did the duck say to the doctor when he got his new glasses?" Susie asked. "'Just put it on my bill.'"

Given the human attributes we project onto ducks, it's not surprising that we're particularly distressed by the notion of one of these

animals having a tube stuck down its throat so it can grow an extremely large liver. But just because we don't want to see Daffy deep-
throating a metal pipe, does that mean that real-life foie gras ducks
actually are made to suffer? Can this question be answered on a
purely scientific basis without input from our emotions?

When I set out to explore this whole controversy, I assumed
that science would offer a clarifying light. There are so many things
we now know about this infinitely complicated world; how a duck
or goose feels about tube feedings that expand its liver to 10 times
its normal size must be one of them, right? But knowledge is more
limited than one might expect, and although some scientists believe
they do know how a bird experiences the force-feedings, they often
disagree vehemently. Not only are they unable to reach a consensus
on such subjective issues as how much pain or discomfort the bird
might sense, but they also debate what might be considered objective
facets of a bird's biology. Is the duck's esophagus sturdy or fragile?
(Dr. Bartholf likens the lining to the bottom of a human foot; Dr.
Cheever says it's easily torn.) Does it have a gag reflex? Does it pant
because it's hot or because its air sacs are being crushed?

Part of the problem is that relatively little research has been done
on ducks because they *aren't* a major part of the world's food system.
There have been far more studies of cows, pigs and chickens. When
the European Union's Scientific Committee on Animal Health and
Animal Welfare convened to produce a comprehensive report released in late 1998 on "the animal welfare aspects of the production
of foie gras using ducks and geese," it raised as many questions as
it answered. The committee's 12 scientists and academics often had
to admit that adequate research hadn't been done on certain areas
they were examining. And even where research had been done, the
conclusions weren't always conclusive. Scientists may have ways to
measure stress levels in ducks, but they can't be sure how the numbers match up to the birds' actual feelings—or how stress translates
into suffering, how suffering translates into pain and what it's like to
be a duck experiencing any of that.

The committee's final report, "Welfare Aspects of the Production
of Foie Gras in Ducks and Geese," became a touchstone as one of
the only seemingly comprehensive pieces of work about the feeding

conditions' effect on the birds. Running 89 pages, the report sets out to define welfare as it relates to the birds, then to determine whether the European foie gras industry meets a reasonable standard. It acknowledges from the outset that a "problem in the evaluation of animal welfare is the lack of knowledge of how animals experience, for example, the states of disease, conflict or frustration . . . Many agree that welfare particularly concerns what an individual animal feels but think that the techniques to measure feelings are not very well developed at the present time."

One measurement of the birds' welfare is whether they're able to engage in characteristic behavior, such as swimming. Most foie gras farms, which do not provide bathing pools or ponds, immediately come up short in that department, though the same would be true of almost any farm raising ducks or geese for meat. Ducks are natural foragers, so in the force-feeding stage, they're being deprived of this behavior—though the authors can't say whether ducks actually are motivated to forage when they're no longer hungry. Eighty percent of the ducks observed for this report were being kept in individual cages during gavage (the percentage would rise in ensuing years), meaning that they could not spread their wings, move around or engage in their typically social behavior. This struck the researchers as unacceptable. Also, the report states, "a high percentage of ducks force-fed in individual cages have lesions of the sternum and bone fractures at the abattoir." (No geese are kept in individual cages; they're split between group pens, inside which the feeder sits during the feedings, and cages that tend to hold three geese each, with the feeder applying the tube from the outside.)

However, members of the committee observed that the birds in individual cages showed less avoidance of their feeders than of strangers in the barn; if the ducks felt they were being tortured, one might assume they'd be most averse to those wielding the tubes. In general, the observers noted that most of the ducks and geese appeared to avoid the force-feedings, but this material was purely anecdotal. "There is no conclusive evidence as to the aversive nature of the force-feeding process," the report states. Likewise, the authors theorized from their observations that the birds' fat abdomens caused their legs to be pushed outward, "but there is no evidence available concerning the frequency of inability to stand, or of joint damage, or of the extent of difficulty in walking."

One area where they could point to scientific data was measurement of the birds' levels of corticosterone, a hormone produced by the adrenal gland that, in theory, should be elevated when the birds are experiencing acute stress. But the studies that looked separately at how ducks responded to the tube insertion and to the filling of their esophagi with food—and compared these reactions to those of control ducks that were not force-fed—found no significant difference in the ducks' corticosterone levels. "This measure therefore gives no evidence that intensive force feeding is stressful to the male hybrid duck," the report states.

Among the other findings, the birds' "gut capacity" was deemed "sufficient for the largest amounts fed during the force-feeding period of foie gras production." The birds produced "loose feces." The birds' mortality rate was greater than that of non-force-fed ducks: 2 to 4 percent vs. 0.2 percent (though producers note that the higher rate is in line with or lower than other animal agriculture). Liver function was found to be impaired during the force-feeding period, but in many birds these problems were reversible—and pathologists disagreed over whether the birds' condition was pathological (that is, diseased). The researchers observed panting, which "might cause pain and distress, but no scientific study has been carried out on this."

All in all, it's a complex report, by turns critical, conflicted and incomplete. The authors communicate a basic discomfort with the reality of force-feeding—particularly as it was being practiced in France with the individual cages—but find little scientific backing to indicate stress or suffering felt by the birds. Nonetheless, the report's conclusion was easy to repeat, and the animal-rights community would do so: "The Scientific Committee on Animal Health and Animal Welfare concludes that force feeding, as currently practiced, is detrimental to the welfare of the birds."

In the ensuing recommendations section, the authors are most critical of the process's industrialization rather than the basic concept of force-feeding birds: "The traditional technique of force feeding has been substantially modified during the past thirty years to rationalize and industrialize the production of foie gras and increase profitability . . . These modifications have been introduced without paying attention to animal welfare considerations. There is evidence that not only animal welfare has not benefited from the change but that instead it has deteriorated." Specifically, the report recommends that the liver shouldn't be enlarged to the point of losing its functionality or causing death, that "no feeding procedure should be used that results in substantial discomfort to the animals" (despite the apparent inability to measure such discomfort definitively) and, most bluntly, that "the use of small individual cages for housing these birds should not be permitted." The French industry followed this last recommendation by banning individual cages—as of 2015. The authors did not recommend that foie gras production cease.

As the European Union report was being compiled, a French researcher named Daniel Guéméne was preparing the first of several studies of foie gras ducks; some of his then-unpublished data is cited in the report. A 2006 summary of his research, co-written with three other authors and titled "Force Feeding: An Examination of Available Scientific Evidence," argues that the foie gras debate has been driven by "much emotion" and that opponents "refer mainly to personal feelings and observations rather than from experimental approaches. Opponents generally assert that the 'cruelty' is quite obvious and there is, therefore, no need for scientific investigation." The paper goes on to cite data debunking several foie opponents' notions, such as that force-feeding causes stress. Again measuring corticosterone levels, Guéméne and his fellow researchers find that ducks in individual cages show no increased stress during feedings while penned ducks indicate increased stress only upon the first feeding, leading the authors to conclude that it "resulted from holding the ducks rather than from the actual force-feeding." (In contrast, corticosterone levels increased when control ducks experienced the stress of being constrained in a net.) The researchers also found no heart-rate increase when the tube was introduced into the esophagus, and the paper reports that the birds' brain activity shows no signs that force-feeding induces pain, in part because ducks and geese already have expandable esophagi for the purpose of swallowing large fish—and the windpipe entrance is located at the center of the tongue, enabling the birds to breathe (and not gag) even with the tube present.

As for avoidance, the paper cites one study in which force-fed and traditionally fed geese show similar patterns and another in which force-fed ducks again show more aversion to a stranger than the feeder. Also addressed is the notion of the liver being diseased; Guéméne and colleagues contend that although hepatic lipidosis is pathological (and irreversible) in humans, it isn't in waterfowl, who have the capacity to store even more fat in their livers than what is typical in foie gras without corrupting their tissue or cells. The paper winds up by challenging the European Union report's conclusion that foie feeding is detrimental to the birds' welfare. "That statement, while clearly taken for granted by opponents of foie gras, was based on the very limited amount of scientific literature available at the time and is not supported by the extensive scientific experimentation done in the intervening years."

Citing his employment by the French National Institute for Agricultural Research (commonly known as INRA) and his studies' partial funding by the Comité Interprofessionnel des Palmipédes à Foie Gras (CIFOG, the French foie gras producers' group), French and U.S. foie gras opponents dismiss Guéméne as an industry tool who studies what the producers want him to study rather than other issues, such as the ducks' mortality rates. (Guéméne said the mortality rate among ducks under observation was so low that it didn't merit further investigation.) In reference to a 2004 Guéméne-co-authored paper published in *World's Poultry Science Journal,* Gene Baur wrote a letter to the New York State Department of Agriculture and Markets charging that the article "has no objective validity because it was commissioned by" CIFOG. Guéméne responded with a letter noting that the paper was published in a legitimate, UK-based scientific journal whose independent review process should answer any questions of validity. He also noted that applying for CIFOG research grants is routine (almost all French research is sponsored in part by the state) and that the money received did not exceed 20 percent of the budget and doesn't factor in his salary.

Robert Dantzer, a University of Illinois psychoneurology professor who was one of the European Union report's co-authors (he lived in Bordeaux at the time), told me he thinks Guéméne's work is inherently flawed because it relies upon hormonal levels to measure stress. "The hormonal system is very adaptable, and it can show adaptation over time," he told me. "This doesn't mean that there is no stress. It just means that the system is adapting, that's all. It doesn't mean that the animal is not suffering any pain . . . You have to keep in mind that we have no biochemical measure of stress in any animal species, including human beings."

"So you're saying the methodology is just wrong?" I asked.

"The methodology and the interpretation are wrong, totally wrong," Dantzer said. "It's obvious that the animal is feeling discomfort. The animal is panting after the gavage because it is producing too much heat, and in addition there is discomfort related to the weight of the organ and the space it is taking in the abdomen." When told of Dantzer's criticisms, Guéméne said the EU report co-author had failed to consider his later papers that more directly showed a link between ducks' corticosterone levels and their apparent stress, and he reiterated the lack of evidence that panting or the liver's size causes the birds discomfort.

Foie gras opponents have compiled much literature as well, detailing severe problems revealed in observations and necropsies of force-fed ducks. Veterinarians with impressive credentials line up to attest to how horrifically the birds are treated. Other veterinarians with equally strong résumés accuse that first group of distorting facts and not backing up their assertions with valid statistics. Meanwhile, governments must make sense of all of this information as they decide whether to take action about birds being force-fed.

One of the most intriguing debates over the ethics of foie gras production took place in the Israeli Supreme Court. A coalition of Israeli animal-protection groups who adopted the name "Noah" petitioned the court to prohibit force-feeding in the production of foie gras. At stake was a robust agricultural industry in a small, largely arid country where farming successes aren't taken for granted. The 2002 Noah petition sought to outlaw foie gras farming by applying Israel's 1994 Protection of Animals Law, which states: "A person will not torture an animal, will not be cruel toward it, or abuse it in any way." It also sought to nullify 2001 government regulations that specified how feedings be carried out and ordered that no new foie gras farms be

established and no existing ones be expanded. Israeli foie gras production predominantly involved geese, not ducks, and, as mentioned
before, geese were not kept in individual cages.

In August 2003 the Noah petition came before the three veteran
Supreme Court justices who would decide its fate: Asher Grunis,
Tova Strasberg-Cohen and Eliezer Rivlin. Their written opinions offered the kind of intellectual heft—and fodder for arguments—that
legislatures in California and Chicago wouldn't attempt to match.

Grunis's lengthy opinion (29 pages in the court's official English
language translation) methodically analyzes the moral, legal, historical
and religious issues at play. The prohibition on *tza'ar ba'alei chayim*
("cruelty to animals" in Hebrew) is rooted in Jewish religious law and
cemented in Israeli civil law. The broader question, he writes, is how
to balance the competing interests of humans and animals.

For all of his opinion's breadth and detail, Grunis spends little
time weighing whether force-feeding geese actually constitutes cruelty, instead yielding to the 1998 European Union report: "It seems,
in light of the Scientific Committee's statement, that force-feeding
does cause suffering." To Justice Grunis the real question was
whether this suffering yields sufficient human benefits. In an earlier
case, the Israeli Supreme Court ruled against a spectacle in which a
man fought a crocodile; the decision was that the animal's suffering
was not justified by the end result: entertainment. "Clearly, in the
hierarchical ranking of purposes, production of food for human consumption will rank above entertainment," Grunis writes. A section of
Israel's anticruelty law even specifies that the minister of agriculture
must consider "agricultural needs" when determining whether animals are being treated properly. "Agricultural needs," Grunis notes,
are not the same as "farmers' interests"; they also cover food production, something that's beneficial to the general public. "Force-feeding
geese is an agricultural need. In this aspect it is no different than
raising cows for milk or meat, than raising calves, or than raising
hens for eggs or for poultry meat." Of course, one of the key arguments against foie gras is that it is nonessential; no one views fatty
goose liver as basic sustenance. The Noah filing even refers to foie
gras as "gastronomic entertainment" in an effort to link this case to

the crocodile one. But Grunis rejects such reasoning as leading to inevitable "hairsplitting distinctions" between so-called basic and luxury foods. "What would we say of veal? Clearly substitutes can be found for both foie gras and veal."

Ultimately the justice is swayed by the human impact of obliterating a healthy industry. "It is unacceptable to transform those who have been employed in force-feeding geese for decades into felons in a day," he writes, noting that "proper weight must be given to the farmers' interests, who have worked in this occupation for many years with government support and encouragement." Grunis's recommendation was that the foie gras regulations be revisited and perhaps revised when they expired in 2004. "At the end of the day, I have found that the force-feeding process does indeed cause suffering to the geese," he concludes. "And yet, in my opinion, it is unjustified to prevent the suffering of the geese by bringing suffering upon the farmers—which would be the result of their livelihood being wiped out in an instant."

Justice Strasberg-Cohen disagreed. Her 23-page opinion lays out the same tension between protecting and using animals, but to her the animals' interests pull more forcefully. She cites the *tza'ar ba'alei chayim* prohibition as well as philosophers' musings about "obligations of man's own sense of compassion." She asserts, "There is no real disagreement that the practice of force-feeding causes the geese suffering," and she writes that the process is "violent and invasive" and "causes a degenerative disease in the geese's liver."

Strasberg-Cohen also draws a line that Grunis purposefully avoided. Although she agrees that food production should be valued more highly than entertainment, she argues that it "will have greater weight the more the food item is necessary for human existence. Thus, basic foods are different from luxuries. Unlike my colleague, I do not think the distinction between foods should be completely ignored. This is particularly true when the food is a luxury and its production inflicts grave suffering on animals." Despite acknowledging the pitfalls of criminalizing what had been a government-supported practice, Strasberg-Cohen concludes that "the regulations do not stand up to the test of 'prohibition of abuse' of the law . . . The regulations should still reflect the price our society is willing to pay in order to produce the delicacy known as foie gras. The price paid at present, the harm caused to the geese, is too high."

Strasberg-Cohen's reasoning prevailed because Justice Rivlin concurred in a rather lyrical opinion that takes up all of three paragraphs. "I have no doubt that wild animals and house pets alike have feelings," he writes. "They possess a soul that experiences the feelings of happiness and grief, joy and sorrow, affection and fear. Some develop feelings of affection toward their friend-enemy, man. Not all would agree with this view. All would agree, however, that these creatures feel the pain inflicted upon them by physical injury or by violent intrusion into their bodies. Indeed, one could justify the force-feeding of geese by pointing to the livelihood of those who raise geese and the gastronomical pleasure of others. Indeed, those wishing to justify the practice might paraphrase Job 5:7: It is right that man's welfare shall soar, even at the price of troubling birds of light. Except that it has a price—and the price is degradation of man's own dignity."

Bye-bye, foie gras industry. The one concession to the farmers was that the ban wouldn't go into effect until March 31, 2005, 19 months after the court's ruling.

To David J. Wolfson, a British-born New York corporate lawyer who does pro bono work for Farm Sanctuary, the Israeli decision was a stunner. Wolfson, a vegetarian, appreciated that unlike typical American legalese, this ruling speaks of moral values and compassion. But he was particularly intrigued by Strasberg-Cohen's "fascinating distinction" between so-called luxury items and basic foods. "If you look at it close enough, I'm not sure that's a correct distinction," he said. "If you are arguing that something is a luxury item, it implies that something [else] is a necessity. Most people in the modern day will recognize that you do not need to consume animal products to survive, so nothing is a necessity."

Yet he applauded the ruling nonetheless because it places the principle of alleviating animal suffering ahead of the need for consistency. From Wolfson's perspective the consistent ruling would have been to determine that all animal farming is cruel, but the court wasn't about to do that. Wolfson felt "the genius of the decision" lay in how the justices found a way to address foie gras production apart from everything else. "Now maybe it was not logically and absolutely a correct point, but it opened a path where some regulation of some farming practices that were cruel was possible," Wolfson said.

He and attorney Mariann Sullivan argued for such an "evolutionary" approach in a paper that appeared in Duke Law School's *Law and Contemporary Problems* quarterly ("What's Good for the Goose . . . The Israeli Supreme Court, Foie Gras, and the Future of Farmed Animals in the United States"): "It is a sad fact for incremental improvements for farmed animals to occur, we will need to be inconsistent." At a Columbia Law School panel discussion hosted by Wolfson and featuring Justices Strasberg-Cohen and Rivlin, Sullivan, a vegan, told me the problem with each side's rigid approach is "it's either do nothing or do everything. And since we're probably not going to do everything and we really shouldn't do nothing, maybe trying to be too consistent isn't really such a great idea." Justice Rivlin agreed, saying, "You must be inconsistent. Because if you draw a line, you go nowhere."

I'd previously raised the consistency question over lunch with Joe Moore when I asked him whether by outlawing foie gras on the principle of preventing animal cruelty, wasn't he therefore obligated to look into other cruel farming practices brought to his attention? He said no. "The intent of this ordinance is not to tackle every animal cruelty problem in the world. It defies logic to suggest that if you address one wrong, then ipso facto you have to address the entire category of wrongs. In this particular case, it's something that I was particularly appalled by. I had no idea that this would create the firestorm that it did."

Get ready for a surprise: Such reasoning drives Izzy Yanay nuts. When I spoke with him about the Israeli decision, he said, "You've got to be consistent because if you are not consistent, then your theory does not hold water. What I read in the Israeli court [ruling] is that they do not want to go all the way. They hope to be stopped somewhere in the middle, so the world would not lose all the agriculture inventions and ingenuity that the world has gathered in the last 5,000, 10,000, whatever thousand years." Izzy continued that at the moment they cease pursuing the logic behind their arguments, "*they . . . are . . . not . . . consistent.* Therefore, all the theory is bogus."

Izzy also was incensed that the justices took the 1998 European Union report as gospel regarding the birds' welfare. "Isn't that injustice?" he asked. "Just to listen to one party and to say, 'That's it,' just like that?"

At the Columbia event, I asked Justice Rivlin and Justice Strasberg-Cohen if they'd ever visited a foie gras farm, and they both said no, though they'd seen videos.

"Do you think the force-feeding of the geese is torture?" I asked Justice Rivlin.

"That's what I thought," he said.

I asked what research he had done on the subject, but he continued to muse on how torture is defined: "Think about a goose that was born, a very young goose, that didn't have any opportunity to enjoy the pleasure of eating normally, naturally. I don't know. There was no scientific evidence, but the intuition is that that's one of the pleasures not only of humans but also of animals. They gave them the opportunity for a few days to eat, as they called 'in the green way,' which means naturally, to find their food and to eat it. And then immediately after that, when they were very young, they were force-fed."

I asked him how old the geese were when the force-feeding started, and he said, "They're very young, a few days after they were born."

"*Days* after they were born?" I asked.

"Yes," he said. "Days after they were born, they start feeding them in that way. They didn't have any opportunity to enjoy eating, the pleasure of food."

Mariann Sullivan had never heard this argument and found it fascinating. "Isn't a life without pleasure a form of suffering?" she said.

I wouldn't argue her point, but I was perplexed by the justice's statements. The pleasure-of-eating argument echoed the EU report's concerns about birds being deprived of their natural foraging behavior, though I assume most farms are indifferent to whether animals actually enjoy their food, tube or no. But did the justice really insist that the force-feedings begin *days* after the geese are hatched? Yes, he did. And that's wrong. Foie gras geese spend at least a couple of months being grown before gavage; the standard in Israel was nine to 10 weeks at least. During this period they were often outside voluntarily eating their feed, foraging when the mood struck and otherwise engaging in goosey behavior. Shouldn't the justice know this if he's providing the swing vote in a precedent-setting ruling that's shutting down an industry—and he's basing that decision in part on the notion that these geese didn't get to enjoy eating on their own?

I spoke briefly with Justice Strasberg-Cohen, and she also conveyed a shaky grasp on the life arc of a foie gras goose: "It lives only 21 days," she said, "and during 21 days every day it gets stuffed unnaturally in a form which is against all nature."

In their inconsistency, at least, these justices were consistent.

Guillermo Gonzalez had seven and a half years instead of 19 months to make the transition from foie gras and to enjoy what he was doing while he could. As 2005 drew to a close, Gonzalez thought he had survived the worst. Yes, the ban that California Governor Arnold Schwarzenegger had signed a year earlier likely would shutter Sonoma Foie Gras in 2012, but that legislation also protected him from animal-rights groups' lawsuits, so now he could concentrate again on business. And business was good, with 2005 amounting to his best year yet, as the company produced more than 80,000 foie gras ducks. With Chicago looking to hop aboard the ban wagon, Guillermo knew his little industry was troubled, but there was no point in fretting about what might happen well down the line. At present, finally, he had no complaints.

The blow took him completely by surprise, and it was a doozy.

In mid-November, Grimaud Farms president Rheal Cayer told Gonzalez that his business was cutting off Sonoma Foie Gras. A letter dated November 30, 2005, confirmed that in six months not only would Grimaud cease supplying Mulard hatchlings to Sonoma, but it also would quit processing the fattened ducks as well as handling their national distribution. Cayer assured Gonzalez that this wasn't a decision he wished to make. On the contrary, he said, his hand had been forced.

Whole Foods Market, the country's largest natural and organic supermarket chain, had notified Cayer that if Grimaud didn't dump Sonoma Foie Gras, then Whole Foods would dump Grimaud, whose

Muscovy ducks were carried by the chain. At that point Grimaud's relationship with Sonoma went back 20 years, and Gonzalez's business was providing about 25 percent of the Stockton company's revenues, according to court documents. The relationship was such that on November 4, 2005, Cayer had met with Sonoma's on-site production manager, Eric Delmas, and made arrangements for Grimaud to continue distributing the Sonoma brand through 2006. In a deposition, Cayer said that six days after this meeting, Grimaud received a letter from Whole Foods stating:

> [W]e can no longer continue to do business with any company associated with the foie gras business in any way.

> We are thereby giving notice to Grimaud Farms that the company has until March 31, 2006, to completely disengage all connection with the foie gras industry. If this timeline is not met regarding all aspects of association by the March 31, 2006, deadline; Whole Foods Market will terminate our business with Grimaud Farms.

"We were given a choice: foie gras or Whole Foods but not both," Jim Galle, a Grimaud vice president, said in a deposition. Grimaud needed Whole Foods, with its network of almost 200 stores and its devoted clientele, more than it needed Sonoma Foie Gras.

If Grimaud felt stuck in the middle, then perhaps so did Whole Foods (though executives at both companies declined to be interviewed). Whole Foods representatives stated in depositions that the chain had a policy of not carrying foie gras since 1996. Nevertheless, in September 2000, Viva!USA launched a campaign on behalf of factory-farmed ducks and soon was targeting Whole Foods over its association with Grimaud, though mostly over the conditions of its own ducks' being sold for meat. (Viva!USA complained that Grimaud's ducks had their beak tips snipped off, were kept indoors and lacked water for bathing.) Viva!USA and PETA activists protested Whole Foods' annual meeting in Santa Monica on March 31, 2003, hoisting banners that declared, "Whole Foods Supports Animal Cruelty." They also displayed papier-mâché ducks and, as court documents note, "disrupted the meeting in progress to present 'uncomfortable evidence of a connection between Grimaud Farms and Sonoma Foie Gras.'" At the time, Viva! was spreading the word that "Sonoma Foie Gras is a brand name of Grimaud Farms."

Whole Foods CEO John Mackey subsequently had a lengthy e-mail exchange with Viva!USA director Lauren Ornelas but rejected taking any action. "He finally said, 'I'm not going to talk to you anymore,'" Ornelas recalled. In the Association of Veterinarians for Animal Rights' summer 2003 newsletter, she wrote: "It has become glaringly apparent that Mr. Mackey and Whole Foods will continue to defend Grimaud and would rather use distraction tactics versus end their business with an inhumane supplier."

But months later, Ornelas said, Mackey contacted her again and said he had been doing much reading and thinking. On October 21, 2003, Whole Foods announced that it was adopting a new set of "animal compassionate standards" to ensure that it carried only products that had been humanely treated. That same day, Viva!USA issued a news release announcing a moratorium on the campaign against Whole Foods. It also included this statement from Mackey:

> "Viva! was instrumental in helping Whole Foods Market leadership come to understand the importance and necessity of making changes to animal production methods—changes that both eliminate cruelty and neglect, but also that will allow animals to do the things they would like to be doing. In addition to Whole Foods Market's corporate commitment to raise the bar, my research on animal welfare issues while in dialogue with Ms. Ornelas convinced me to personally become a vegan. I believe a vegan lifestyle is the most animal compassionate lifestyle possible."

A court filing on behalf of Sonoma Foie Gras asserts that Whole Foods met privately with Grimaud to try to convince the company to disengage from the foie gras business, specifically from Sonoma, with the promise that it would make up for Grimaud's lost revenues with additional purchases. Grimaud declined, at least until Whole Foods could implement a concrete plan to replace the lost revenues. (Ornelas also sat in on a meeting in which Whole Foods pressed Grimaud on its own duck-raising standards.) Whole Foods later claimed it had made clear to Grimaud that it had expected some movement on the foie gras issue before it finally issued its November 2005 ultimatum.

Guillermo's immediate reaction to Grimaud's decision was Game Over. His farm needed hatchlings to grow ducks. It needed distribution to sell product. True, Gonzalez already was overseeing the distribution of his higher-end Artisan Foie Gras line, but Sonoma had been the more established brand. The loss of Grimaud posed an even more immediate, significant problem: USDA-certified processing plants were not easily replaced, especially in a climate where taking on a foie gras client might result in protests and a supermarket chain boycott, and none of Guillermo's products could be nationally distributed without on-site USDA inspections. He tried "by every means" to find a new USDA plant, but "nobody wanted to do it." Finally, a small state-certified processing plant in the town of Turlock agreed to take him on, which allowed Guillermo to continue to distribute in California. So he kept raising the ducks he already had on site and researched French hatcheries that might supply him with duck eggs.

Gonzalez also put out a call for help to his fellow domestic foie gras producers, who, realizing they needed to work more cooperatively for their mutual survival, had formed the Artisan Farmers Alliance, a trade group intended "to educate the public about our centuries-old farming practices and to defend the rights of consumers to make their own decisions about food." In the spirit of solidarity, Izzy Yanay made Guillermo an offer: move Sonoma Foie Gras to the Hudson Valley grounds, where he could have his own buildings and make and distribute his own products. "He'd have complete autonomy," Izzy told me.

Although relocating a company from California to New York would be a daunting task, Guillermo was tempted. Such a move, after all, would have removed the 2012 ticking time bomb from his company's future. "We were almost ready to go there," he said.

But then a surprising other shoe dropped: in late May 2006, after Grimaud had split from Sonoma, Whole Foods terminated its relationship with Grimaud anyway. "So Grimaud ended up without Sonoma Foie Gras and without Whole Foods," Gonzalez said. "I had to bite my tongue and go back to them and say, 'Would you consider restoring our business?' and they said, 'Yes, we'll do the processing again and supply ducks again.'" Grimaud didn't, however, resume distribution of the Sonoma Foie Gras label. Once that brand was gone from the marketplace, Guillermo said, other foie gras providers quickly filled the void, so the door was pretty much closed on a return to business as usual. "Right there we lost 50 percent of our business," he said.

Gonzalez's farm thus became devoted exclusively to Artisan Foie Gras, which used whole corn kernels and more traditional feeding machines in a process that was thought to be easier on the duck and tastier for the human. Business crept back upward without reaching the 2005 levels.

Meanwhile, Sonoma Foie Gras sued Whole Foods over intentionally interfering with its contract with Grimaud Farms. It sought compensatory and punitive damages as well as various fees. Whole Foods insisted that Grimaud had made an "independent business decision" to terminate its contract with Sonoma Foie Gras to comply with the supermarket chain's known animal-treatment standards.

Whole Foods moved for the judge to issue a ruling in lieu of a jury trial. The motion was denied, and Whole Foods and Sonoma were headed toward a courtroom showdown.

11.

Raising the Philly Stakes

"You should die of cancer."

The conflict at the London Grill went from polite to nasty in a hurry. The Hugs protesters showed up every day of Memorial Day weekend, ratcheting up the rhetoric each time. As Jenny Holcomb testified at a hearing to enact an injunction against Hugs for Puppies: "They started across the street from the restaurant and screamed and chanted through bullhorns, 'We'll find out where you live!' 'How many ducks have you killed?' They called us duck rapists and terrorists, and it was pretty intimidating and scary."

Duck rapists?

"'How many ducks have you raped today?' was the chant," Holcomb told me as she and Terry McNally sat in the London Grill's tight office quarters upstairs from the kitchen.

In those initial protests, Holcomb recalled, the activists hadn't identified the restaurant personnel by name, "so they would chant and point at me, tell everyone that it was my fault . . . Every time I'd be outside working, they would be chanting and pointing and yelling at me."

"And then they started calling out for the owner," Terry McNally said, "and they found out I was the owner, so then it became personal. They found out our names, 'Little Jenny Holcomb,' my name, Terry, and I was the big, obese restaurant owner, right?"

"And greedy," Holcomb said.

"Fat and greedy," McNally said.

"Is that a quote?" I asked.

"Yeah," McNally said. "They just throw out insults."

"On any given day, if she walks by, it was, 'How many glasses of wine have you had today, Terry?'" Holcomb recalled.

"Yeah, they didn't like alcohol either," McNally said.

The general procedure for these protests was that Civil Affairs officers, having been notified of the protesters' schedule, would show up beforehand and tell the restaurateurs that a demonstration was on its way. As long as the protesters stayed on the opposite side of 23rd Street, the officers wouldn't do anything. Even when the situation got heated, they didn't necessarily get involved.

During one protest on an especially hot day in early June, Terry McNally finally went outside to speak with Cooney. The meeting was perfectly civil as he asserted the evils of foie gras and she discussed the restaurant's involvement with Fair Food, a project that connects chefs with small family farms. She thought he seemed reasonable, even as the protesters continued their angry chanting. Then a particularly irate diner came out onto the restaurant's front step, flipped a lit cigarette in the direction of the protesters across the street, and barked something to the effect of, "If I had a gun, I would shoot you all in the head." The man disappeared back into the restaurant while Cooney's hand shot up to signal that the protest was over, and he called 911 to report the death threat. "Nick just went into action," McNally recalled. "It was like David Koresh [the doomed Branch Davidian cult leader]. It's like dealing with abortion people, which I'm not supposed to say." Later, when I asked Cooney about comparisons between his group and the anti-abortion crowd, he didn't bristle. "We're an aggressive protest campaign," he said. "We're frequently active and vocal. In that sense I think the comparison is certainly valid. There's obviously significant differences. Animal-rights people have never shot anyone, for example."

After the Hugs members put down their bullhorns and said they'd ended their protest, the Civil Affairs officers left. But the confrontation was far from over. The Hugs members crossed 23rd Street to talk to several just-arrived police officers. Now directly in front of the restaurant, in close proximity to the outdoor tables, they continued their jawing about foie gras and the London Grill. A table of female diners complained that they were too close and loud, and a protester snapped back at one of them that she should get on a treadmill because she was so fat. With the situation growing increasingly volatile, a busboy approached the chef and said, "Mr. McNally, I think you should go outside." Michael McNally emerged from his hot kitchen to view a sidewalk crowded with people, including five or six police officers standing by the front door. As Holcomb gave him the update, a slight, dark-haired protester named Dezeray Rubinchik called out, "Boycott London Grill! Boycott London Grill!"

The McNallys and Holcomb agree on the following: Michael McNally responded, "No, don't boycott London Grill," and Rubinchik angrily pointed at him and shouted, "You're an asshole!"

"*I'm* an asshole?" he responded. "*You're* an asshole!"

Michael McNally recalled: "She was just like screaming in my face, and I'm like, who is this crazy girl? Then her boyfriend comes up, gets into my face. He's like this far away from me." He indicated a few inches. "I mean, they wanted me to hit them. Meanwhile the cops are standing right there." Holcomb and Terry McNally wound up pulling the angry chef away.

Rubinchik later testified that Michael McNally had "stormed out of London Grill" and started screaming at one of the protesters and lifted his fist. "And I yelled to him, 'Don't hit him,' and I called him a scumbag. He turned to me and got this close to my face . . . 10 to 12 inches away, and he raised his fist like this at me. He's much bigger than me. I was yelling for the police that he was making a violent gesture toward me to hit me, and that's when the police came over, and he ran back in the restaurant, and they went in to find him to get his information as well." Cooney also said Michael McNally raised his fist at Rubinchik. The chef and Holcomb testified that he never threatened the protester in any way. The judge didn't seem to take the accusation too seriously; it was a nonfactor in the injunction hearing. Police interviewed Michael McNally at the restaurant, and he went to the police station a couple of days later, but no charges against him had been filed, and that was that.

Amid all of that commotion in front of the restaurant, Holcomb said, the biggest of the male protesters looked her in the eye, pointed at her and whispered, "Watch your home."

By this point Hugs for Puppies' Web site claimed that 40 local restaurants had quit serving foie gras. Some had done so willingly after being contacted by the group. Others had gone down fighting. When I first spoke to Jose Garces, chef of Philadelphia's popular, highly regarded Spanish restaurants Tinto and Amada, he wasn't yet on the no-longer-serving-it list. "I'm on the I'm-figuring-out-what-to-do list," he said. "Once they come to your home, it just becomes a lot more personal. I have two little children. I have a four-and-a-half-year-old daughter and a one-year-old son. For them to be exposed to that, screaming my name, neighbors out on the front stoop, saying I'm a murderer and so forth . . . " His voice trailed off. "They had bullhorns. They were right out in front of my house, like two feet from my door." Garces called the police, and the protesters left. The chef eventually removed foie gras from his menus but kept some in the back in case a customer requested it—all to dodge aggressive, barely funded young protesters conducting a culinary inquisition.

Then there was Stephen Starr, the brash restaurateur who had taken a blah eating city and given it a vital shot of energy, glamour and creativity, beginning in 1995 with the sleek, hipster-friendly Continental Restaurant and Martini Bar. His oversized, theatrical restaurants—which span such cuisines as modern Japanese (Morimoto), funky Chinese (Buddakan) and "Mexican-American meets East L.A. in a Tijuana Taxi" (El Vez)—attracted the food-savvy and beautiful-people crowds alike, earning him *Bon Appetit*'s and Zagat's "Restaurateur of the Year" awards in 2005 and 2006, respectively. His braggadocio-filled move into the New York City market, to open lavish outposts of Morimoto and Buddakan, was one of 2006's bold-faced headlines in the food world. From the beginning of the modern anti-foie movement, Starr had been a frequent target, with that $100 Philly cheesesteak an early casualty. But surely his formidable empire could withstand the blows of a ragtag group of young loudmouth activists, no?

Douglas Rodriguez, the Miami-based executive chef of the Starr-owned Alma de Cuba in Philadelphia, explained: "His 11-year-old daughter was made fun of at school—'Your father's a murderer of ducks'—by another 11-year-old. And that's the day that we took it off the menu, restaurantwide, the whole companywide." Hugs protesters also had demonstrated outside Starr's house, and the widespread story among Philadelphia chefs was that the group not only scared his daughter but also yelled out personal insults in reference to a family matter. Cooney characterized the Starr visit as just your standard home demonstration in which 25 to 30 protesters lined up in front of his house, handed out flyers and encouraged everyone to pester Starr into removing the fat liver from his menus. Whatever actually was the trigger (and Starr wasn't talking about it), the restaurateur announced that his restaurants no longer would serve the controversial product. Starr told reporters his position shifted not because of the protesters' pressure but rather the issue itself. "Honestly, deep down when I really understood what was going on with the ducks, I think it's kind of not cool to serve it," he told *New York* magazine. (Rodriguez, meanwhile, briefly served foie gras at De La Costa, his small-plates restaurant in Chicago, despite the city's ban. "We call it 'What the Foie Gras's Going On,'" he said.)

Cooney was happy with Starr's reversal, but hey, he thought, give credit where credit is due. "I do think it was our pressure that nudged him to actually take action on that. We had been protesting him for about a year, and then we did this home protest. Shortly after that is when it got taken off of all the menus."

Le Bec-Fin chef Georges Perrier wasn't buying the purity of Starr's conversion either. "I'm not happy with Steve Starr what he has done," he told me as he sat in his chef's whites in his restaurant's elegant downstairs bar. "I like him as a restaurateur. He's a great guy. But *he's wrong!* I'm sorry. He's wrong. He's wrong on that one. But he bent over because he didn't want the people screaming in front of his doors."

Perrier, a diminutive man with a booming voice and combative personality, did not bend over. Foie gras had been a part of his life since his childhood in France. It had been a staple of his Center City haute-cuisine destination since before he even was able to obtain fresh foie in the United States. He wasn't about to change his menu at the behest of some meddling youngsters with checkered pasts. The mere mention of Cooney's name turned Perrier's face the color of his cranberry-consommé-and-beet-salad appetizer.

"Nick Cooney?" he asked, his accented, sing-song voice reaching skyward. "You mean that guy from *Upset Puppy*?"

Um, yes.

"Nick Cooney, he's the guy who runs this organization Hate for Puppy, something like this. He's a very dangerous man."

In early 2007, Hugs for Puppies began visiting Le Bec-Fin every weekend. The protesters would line up on the same side of the street as the restaurant and let loose, never mind that this was a particularly tony block of Center City or that Perrier's establishment had given the city something to brag about in its culinary dark ages. Le Bec-Fin opened in 1970, and it quickly became known as the best restaurant in the city and beyond. The *Mobil Travel Guide* routinely awards it five stars, *Esquire* called it "The Best French Restaurant in America" in 1993, and a Condé Nast readers' poll the following year named it the country's best restaurant, period. Perrier may be an ornery French cuss, but he's a legendary ornery French cuss. Who the hell were these kids to call him a duck murderer and threaten him with nasty innuendo? "He said, 'We know where you live, and we're gonna get you.' He said, 'When you go to a nightclub with another woman, we're going to take a picture, and with a prostitute, we're gonna get you.' *What is this?!?*" Perrier's voice boomed. "Nick Cooney said that to me: 'We're gonna get you with a prostitute, and then we're really going to get you.' What the hell is this all about? What is a prostitute and get me? I mean, I'm a decent man. I'm married. I have a wonderful wife. *What is all this about?* This guy's a real sick man."

"I think someone said that to him," Cooney told me later. "It wasn't me."

If anything, Cooney insisted that the Hugs members largely had been the victims in their Le Bec-Fin dealings. The dynamic was all too familiar: No matter what anyone was doing to him or his protesters, the activists always got portrayed as radical troublemakers. "He's come out, gotten in people's faces, held his fist up at them," Cooney said of Perrier. "At one of the protests, he came out, jumped in his car, which was parked across the street, and then basically veered right at us and turned at the last second, basically to give us the im-

pression that he was going to run up on the curb and run us over."
Cooney complained that the *Philadelphia Inquirer* account of this incident failed to mention Perrier's driving maneuver. What columnist
Michael Klein wrote was, "While protesting Friday night outside Le
Bec-Fin, Cooney and eight followers spotted Perrier stepping into his
black Mercedes and screamed, 'Shame! Shame! Shame!'" Cooney
also claimed that a Le Bec-Fin manager made "obscene sexual gestures" at a female protester (pointing lewdly at her buttocks) and,
eventually, at him (making the universal "small penis" pantomime).

As the demonstrations continued week after week, the bad feelings grew, at times involving customers as well as employees. Things
came to a head, so to speak, on the busy Friday night of May 11. While
four Hugs for Puppies protesters (Cooney not among them) chanted
slogans on the sidewalk, a large man who was well dressed and apparently tanked up came out of the restaurant and started harangu-
ing the group. He yelled, jumped and danced on the sidewalk, falling
down repeatedly and loudly declaring, "This is what foie gras did to
me!" The man eventually reentered the restaurant's front glass door
and . . . well, I'll just let Deanna Calderaio, one of the protesters, describe it to you as she did to me:

"He unzipped his pants and pressed his thing against the window."

In writing about the incident, *Philadelphia Daily News* columnist
Stu Bykofsky, a vocal supporter of the anti-foie movement, took the
cops to task for failing to arrest this man (who disappeared into the
restaurant and never was seen again) or at least to curb his obnoxious
behavior. Bykofsky also ripped the police for treating the protesters
rudely and for throwing a bystander, teacher Diana Eberhardt, into a
squad car for sticking up for the demonstrators. Eberhardt told me
she was just walking by when she saw the drunken man yelling and
swearing at the "Foie Gras 4" (as Bykofsky dubbed them) with no
intervention from the cops. "The protesters were not screaming or
obstructing business or using offensive language," she said. "I felt
I had a duty to speak up for somebody who was being treated unfairly." After failing to heed an officer's warning to butt out or else,
she wound up sitting in the squad car for "quite a long while" before
a Civil Affairs sergeant arrived and released her with apologies. She

later was asked to recount the experience to the police department's Internal Affairs division.

Perrier found it infuriating that the protesters were receiving any protection at all. "I understand in a free country in a free society, there are always people who protest this and protest that. But when you have criminals who are pursued by the FBI and went to jail and have done bad things and continue to do them, and the government is not stopping them and lets them do whatever they want to do, and the police—I think it's *wrong*! I think there's something wrong with our *system*!" Perrier, after all, had been serving fine food to the city for close to 40 years; shouldn't that count for something? "I put Philadelphia on the map, and you get absolutely no respect from anybody. These people have been in jail. I've never been in jail. I've been a good citizen."

Jack Kelly, no surprise, was unsympathetic to Perrier's lament. "Well, I could say, Mr. Perrier"—the councilman pronounced that last "r"—"have you been losing money every year, or are you making money every year? You're not here because of the city. You're not doing anything other than making a damn good dollar with your restaurant, so don't kid around in saying you're such a big philanthropist or you're only doing this for the good of the city. That's bullshit." For his part, Perrier wondered of politicians such as Kelly: "Are they a bunch of idiots? The schools are a mess in Philadelphia, but they want to ban the foie gras!" He slapped his hand against the bar surface, his voice rising higher and higher. "*What is wrong with our society?* It's not us. It's the political people that are wrong! And they're stupid and crazy."

Finally, the legal system put the restaurant and its tormenters out of their mutual misery. Perrier got an injunction settlement against Hugs for Puppies limiting the scope of the group's protests: They aren't allowed to stand within 10 feet of the restaurant or to use bullhorns. "I certainly don't think the injunction is valid because there is no illegal conduct that occurred, but it's fairly reasonable," Cooney admitted. "It's not a big burden on our free speech rights or our ability to do what we have the right to do." Nonetheless, the group suspended its protests of Le Bec-Fin. When I spoke with Perrier, Hugs for Puppies hadn't visited his restaurant for months. Life was peaceful again. But the chef was far from happy. Paying $45,000 in legal fees to get rid of someone who had been harassing him certainly didn't help his mood. "Something's wrong with the system!" he roared. "Something's wrong with our country!"

. . .

TERRY MCNALLY: I was in my backyard, I live next door to the restaurant, I heard the bullhorns, and my son and I both went outside, and there they were. And Michael was outside with them and another chef, they were standing up against the restaurant in front of the bar door.

ATTORNEY WILLIAM J. CLEMENTS: When you say "they," you are referring to . . . ?

MCNALLY: The protesters.

CLEMENTS: How many were there?

MCNALLY: I think four.

CLEMENTS: Can you describe their appearance?

MCNALLY: They were wearing either black hooded masks, ski masks or bandanas pulled up over the bridge of their nose with their eyes showing and black clothing.

CLEMENTS: So, if I understand this, you just saw the slit with their eyes?

MCNALLY: Yes.

CLEMENTS: Dressed up like ninjas?

MCNALLY: Ninjas, that's what some of the kids thought. Ninjas.

It was a Monday morning in June when a group of activists showed up at the London Grill wearing black hoods over their faces and began protesting directly in front of the restaurant instead of across the street. Civil Affairs officers were nowhere to be seen. "It was pretty scary," said Michael McNally, who noted that one of the protesters approached him in front of the London Grill's next-door coffee-and-ice-cream shop and blared the bullhorn in his face to try to incite him. The McNallys called the police. "That was the first time I remember Terry losing it," the chef said. "I mean crying. Finally when Civil Affairs showed up, she said, 'They showed up without you guys. What's going on? They can't be here at 11 o'clock on a Monday morning. They can't be on my sidewalk in front of my door. They can't be in front of my coffee shop.' Kids were actually eating ice cream, little kids, and they're just blaring this stuff."

Because of the masks, no one could conclusively identify these protesters. The London Grill team said they recognized at least one Hugs member, but Cooney said no, they were out-of-town activists visiting Philadelphia for a weekend of demonstrations who had gone out independently. "I would have been happy for them to be going," the Hugs director said, "but I would not have had them wearing those masks and bandanas."

Cooney, however, did take responsibility for another protest that snared kids exiting the ice-cream shop. In one of the movement's more confrontational tactics being used here and in other cities, a red-haired, bearded Hugs member wore a flat-screen TV over his chest to display foie gras horror footage while he walked among the sidewalk tables or stood near the restaurant's entrance. Terry McNally videotaped him one afternoon as he planted himself on the corner directly in front of a neighborhood girl and boy who were transfixed by the disturbing images. You can see on the tape that as they watch, tears well up in the girl's eyes, dripping down her cheeks and pooling on her chin. Finally, she wipes her face and crosses the street, prompting Cooney to blare on his bullhorn: "The way that you treat animals and the food products you serve have caused someone to walk away in tears! How do you feel about yourself, Terry?"

"Their neighborhood ice-cream parlor is torturing ducks—that's literally what they're telling 8-year-olds in the neighborhood," Holcomb said later. "These are kids that have grown up coming here. They know us. London is their neighborhood ice-cream shop. Their moms all bring them here."

"I had to pay their mothers, buy their ice cream," Terry McNally said.

Later, Cooney professed to "mixed feelings" about involving children in the protests. "The person who cried, she was pretty young, probably nine or 10," he said. "The first time I saw these cruelties, I cried too. Sometimes it's good to see these things. On the other hand, perhaps nine or 10 is too young to see these things and process them and make decisions. It's not something I would want to put in the face of young children at every turn."

Yet putting sickly duck images in the faces of adults out for a nice meal was fair game. Civil Affairs allowed the Hugs member to walk among the outside tables wearing a flat-screen TV even though the remainder of Hugs' activities had to take place across the street, the reasoning being that the footage was silent, the protester didn't chant, and he kept moving on a public sidewalk. "It brings home the cruelty and the reason why we're out there," Cooney said of the footage. "Certainly no one looked at the images and thought, This is OK by me. The people who looked at it were rightfully upset."

But some of that rightful upsetness came from customers mad that some jerk was aggressively trying to turn their stomachs while they were dining out. They bitched at him. He shot back insults. The vitriol went back and forth. Jenny Holcomb testified about these confrontations at the injunction hearing:

ATTORNEY MARY CATHERINE ROPER: What do you recall them saying to your customers that you are characterizing as threatening?
HOLCOMB: "You should die of cancer."

When he started mixing it up with a table of eight to 10 males who had been drinking, Civil Affairs police officer William Stuski finally had to step in and direct the protester back across the street, testifying later that he had to ask him four times: "Keep moving, leave . . . Stop with the confrontation with the customers."

For the London Grill regulars, the foie gras demonstrations became a kind of dinner theater. Patrons would call asking whether the protesters were expected that night; then they'd book an outdoor table for a front-row view. This proved to be a mixed blessing for the restaurant: Reservations were up, but turning the tables became tough. People wanted to stay for the show—and an interactive show it was. Forget Ed Debevic's, the restaurant chain where rude service is part of the shtick. Here you could be insulted and spew back rancor without the winking. As a bonus, some protesters made a point of writing down customers' license plate numbers as they parked in front of the restaurant.

The battle also made its way to the Web, with Hugs for Puppies applying pressure through its Web site Londongrillpollutes.com, which greeted viewers with a YouTube video that, set to a dance-beat version of the *Love Story* theme, offered GourmetCruelty.com's images of sad waterfowl, "representational footage" of the Delaware River and the charge that the London Grill was one of the only remaining local restaurants to serve "products from the notorious Hudson Valley Foie Gras farm." Alongside the video-screen window was the message:

> The London Grill Restaurant. A place to kick back outside of the bustle of Center City. A place where, unknown to you, your purchase could be funding the dumping of fecal coliform, phosphorus, chlorine and other pollutants directly into a tributary of the Delaware River . . . Eating a great meal shouldn't make you feel dirty—so BOYCOTT London Grill Restaurant!

Fed up and defiant, the London Grill folks began serving more foie gras. "Yeah, we just went crazy with it," Michael McNally said. The restaurant also printed up olive-green T-shirts with "Suck my duck" and a pair of smiling Daffy-esque duck lips on the front and "Vive le foie!" and "London Grill, Philadelphia" on the back. Terry McNally visited Hudson Valley Foie Gras, and she wasn't disturbed by anything she saw, except, she told me, some fat ducks panting. She defended the farm on the London Grill's Web site, writing: "We have researched this topic and believe that scientific evidence has concluded that this is not a product of animal cruelty. Our doors will remain open for any questions or concerns that you may have. We hope that you will continue to be proud of us and what we do!"

Hugs for Puppies returned to the London Grill every weekend, sometimes twice a night on both Fridays and Saturdays, and the rhetoric grew even more heated. "The reason we're out here today, on Father's Day," one protester announced through his bullhorn, "is that we felt it was important enough to expose the London Grill for the terrible human beings that they are!"

One call-and-response went:

"One, two, three, four!"

"Open up the cage door!"

"Five, six, seven, eight!"

"Raid the farms and liberate!"

"Nine, ten, eleven, twelve!"

"Terry McNally, go to hell!"

Other chants called out to Terry McNally and "Little Jenny" Holcomb: "How many ducks did you torture today?" They proclaimed,

"Murderers!"

"Leave town!"

"Little Jenny Holcomb!"

"Leave town!"

"Terry McNally!"

"Leave town!"

Even though she was the general manager rather than an owner or chef, Holcomb continued to be a favorite target, especially when she was checking on the diners seated outside. The bearded guy who had worn the flat-screen TV particularly reveled in taunting her:

"Stop the torture, stop the pain!

"Sweet little Jenny is to blame!"

And:

"For the animals we will fight!

"We know where Jenny Holcomb sleeps at night! Sweet little Jenny!"

Turns out they did. In early July, the London Grill obtained an emergency temporary injunction against Hugs for Puppies that, among other things, prohibited home protests. Soon thereafter, on a Saturday afternoon, Holcomb left her apartment for the restaurant when she saw several of her neighbors standing out on the sidewalk. They asked, "Jenny, have you seen this?" and handed her a small piece of paper stapled to a "Say 'No' to Foie Gras" leaflet.

Please Ask Your Neighbor Jennifer to Stop Supporting Animal Cruelty!

Your neighbor Jennifer Holcomb is a manager at the London Grill Restaurant in Philadelphia. Unfortunately, London Grill continues to sell "foie gras," a controversial dish that has been banned in several states and over a dozen countries and has been taken off the menu at over 30 Philadelphia res-

taurants in the past year . . . Please ask your neighbors to stop
supporting animal cruelty and stop serving foie gras at the
London Grill!

Also on the page, in larger type, was her home address. The
group may not have protested directly in front of her building, but
Cooney and friends had distributed several hundred of these leaflets
door to door in her neighborhood. Holcomb, a single woman living
alone, was "pissed off and shook up." She knew that when activists
had targeted pharmaceutical reps' homes, vandalism sometimes ensued. She imagined coming home to find her home trashed or her
dog killed by poison tossed into her backyard. The next day, a bang-
ing on her front door jolted Holcomb out of her chair. "It was these
two little girls who wanted to know why I was cruel to animals," she
recalled.

Cooney dismissed her fears of violence. "We've been doing demonstrations for two years, and that's never happened. I just think it's
extremely, extremely, extremely unlikely." Holcomb's problem, he
continued, was that she simply didn't want her actions exposed to
the light of day. "Certainly the intent is to get people to go up to her
and say, 'Hey, are you the person being mean to animals? You should
stop.' Social pressure. The attitude against leaflets being handed out
is 'I don't want my neighbors to know what I'm doing to animals.'"

Cooney also rang Michael McNally's doorbell one day. They had
a brief awkward conversation in which the activist asked the chef
whether he would quit serving foie gras, and McNally replied, "No
way, Nick. No way." But Cooney's main purpose was to confirm
McNally's address. Soon the group had leafleted his neighborhood
with more detailed accusations than those against Holcomb. Aside
from his address, the leaflets included a list of "things to know about
your neighbors at London Grill, owners Terry and Mike McNally,"
including that Terry was a racist (because of her alleged comments
to Cooney's neighbors when she was trying to locate his house), that
Michael was a violent criminal (because he'd supposedly cocked his
fist against Rubinchik) and that the restaurateurs were destroying
the environment thanks to their association with Hudson Valley.
Michael responded with his own letter to the 20 or so houses in his

complex: "I just wrote a personal note with some literature in there saying, 'Listen, we're not duck rapists. We're not slaughtering innocent ducks.' I never really heard anything from my neighbors."

The London Grill had had enough. The restaurant was preparing for its annual large-scale, whimsical Bastille Day celebration at the defunct Eastern State Penitentiary on the other side of 23rd Street. (On YouTube you can watch footage of Terry McNally dressed as Marie Antoinette showering onlookers with Tastykakes from atop the penitentiary walls.) Hugs for Puppies had planned a large "Veg Outreach" for the same time, same place, and the McNallys assumed the intention was to disrupt their event. So they went to court to get a permanent injunction.

The hearing took place July 12. Holcomb and both McNallys testified, as did a couple of police officers. For Hugs, who were represented by American Civil Liberties Union lawyer Mary Catherine Roper, Rubinchik testified but not Cooney, although at one point Judge Gary F. DiVito admonished him for shaking his head when Rubinchik was being asked a yes/no question. (She answered no.) The judge was the same one who presided over the GlaxoSmithKline injunction against Hugs, so Cooney felt the guy had it in for them. The judge certainly did the group no favors.

The resultant injunction prohibited Hugs for Puppies from demonstrating within 50 feet of the restaurant or the restaurateurs' homes and also barred them from using bullhorns and having more than two protesters present at a time. Terry McNally wasn't thrilled that she'd spent $20,000 on legal fees, but she was pleased that she won a far more limiting injunction against Hugs than George Perrier had gotten with his $45,000. Cooney assumed the ACLU eventually would get the London Grill injunction overturned for its restrictiveness. In the meantime he could console himself that he'd cost the restaurant $20,000. "I'm glad at least the London Grill is having to pay for taking away our free speech rights."

12.

FoiX GraX

"If any of the sugar gets wet, you have to throw it all out."

Little did Chicago's aldermen suspect that banning fatty duck livers would spark foie gras mania. Even restaurateurs who hadn't served the product and didn't attend the hearings now got involved; they'd seen the city take the unprecedented step of meddling in their menus, and they didn't like it. Foie gras was a legal product that wasn't even produced in Chicago. What right did government have to criminalize its sale? "If it's legally produced, we should not be told what we can and cannot use," said Copperblue chef Michael Tsonton, cofounder of the newly formed Chicago Chefs for Choice.

That contention became the basis of the Illinois Restaurant Association's lawsuit filed against the city the day the ordinance went into effect; it charged that the city council lacked the authority to impose such a ban. The suit wouldn't be resolved for months (and eventually would be dismissed), but in the meantime restaurants found other ways to express their displeasure. In the weeks leading up to the ban's August 22 take-effect date, several restaurants scheduled farewell-to-foie-gras dinners, be they at the highest end—such as Tramonto's Tru and the Peninsula hotel's Avenues (where a 12-course, all-foie tasting menu ran $245)—or a popular North Side hot dog storefront known as Hot Doug's, which offered the "Joe Moore": a duck, foie gras and Sauternes sausage topped with foie-gras-truffle-Dijon-mustard sauce and marinated goat cheese. Some of the organized events were fund-raisers to help Chicago Chefs for Choice combat the ban and fight for culinary freedom. Didier Durand, also a Chicago Chefs for Choice officer, reported that foie gras sales at his Cyrano's Bistrot had tripled since the council passed the ban. Other restaurants reported similar numbers.

When August 22 finally arrived, restaurants across the city staged a day of civil disobedience, with foie gras supplied at a discount by Hudson Valley. Connie's Pizza created its first-ever foie gras deep-dish pie. South Side soul food restaurant BJ's Market & Bakery made foie gras the daily special. (The manager, who'd never previously tried it, declared that it tasted like chicken.) Harry Caray's, the ca-sual downtown Italian steakhouse named after the late, colorful Cubs broadcaster, offered foie gras on a sea scallop appetizer and in a ten-derloin entrée. Rather than sending the food police out on massive raids, the city delayed the law's enforcement for another day. Chicago Department of Public Health officials no doubt took notice that the day the ban took effect, the mayor made his public pronouncement on it being the silliest law ever passed by the city council.

Thus began Foie Gras Prohibition. The Illinois Restaurant As-sociation recommended that its members not flout the law after Au-gust 22; it was counting on the courts to strike down the ordinance, so negative publicity over lawbreaking wouldn't help. Its legal staff also was discouraging restaurants from exploring possible loop-holes in the law, such as attempting to serve the foie gras for free while charging extra for the garnish. Nonetheless, when August 23 came around—and August 24 and August 25—you still could order foie gras in Chicago restaurants; you just needed to know where to look. In some places it was out in the open, like at downtown's wine-oriented Bin 36, which offered "Summer fig, apricot and honey terrine, and a foie gras torchon, on us." Similarly, the North Side's X/O Chicago (which has since closed) offered "brioche toast points with a complimentary side of foie gras." Yes, these restaurants were using the ol' "It's free!" gambit, and they weren't getting busted for it. In fact, after sales dipped on X/O Chicago's foie dish with the new description, the restaurant reverted to identifying it as it originally had, with the foie gras mentioned first. The numbers zipped up again, and no one was fined.

Some restaurants with fixed-price menus employed another tactic. Alinea occasionally sent out a small foie gras dish as part of its 24-course "Tour" menu. Given that patrons already were paying nearly $200 for the meal with or without foie, the restaurant contended that it, too, was giving the dish away. Then there was the dodge known as renaming the foie gras and daring city officials to tell the difference. At Copperblue, Tsonton cheekily invoked Chicago's foie-banning alderman with his newly redubbed appetizer "'It Isn't Foie Gras No Moore' Duck Liver Terrine."

Some chefs simply kept foie gras off their menus but in their kitchens so they could offer it to special guests at their discretion, again gratis. That was the case with Naha chef Carrie Nahabedian as well as Durand, who initially quit carrying it altogether but soon became convinced that he was losing customers, all while the law was barely being enforced. "I don't sell it, but I serve it," Durand told me. "People were asking for it and going to the suburbs to get foie gras." Inside Cyrano's Bistrot the chef registered his displeasure by displaying a photo of Alderman Moore next to the words "*Trou du cul!*"—French for "asshole."

The Health Department didn't proactively raid restaurants in search of outlawed livers; it relied upon consumers calling the city services hotline, which put the burden on foie gras opponents to keep tabs on restaurants they might otherwise never have patronized. Still, enough complaints were filed that by the end of 2006, the city had sent warning letters to nine restaurants, including X/O Chicago, Bin 36 and Copperblue, though no fines had been issued. Health Department spokesman Tim Hadac told the *Tribune:* "It is most definitely one of our lowest priorities. We do not enforce it aggressively."

Meanwhile, Hot Doug's kept openly serving its "Joe Moore" foie gras sausage plus two other wieners containing the forbidden liver: a smoked-pheasant sausage topped with foie gras cubes and another dog in a foie gras sauce. Owner Doug Sohn was willfully, cheerfully prodding the sleeping giant. A former cookbook editor in his mid-40s, Sohn opened the original, tiny version of his instantly crowded eatery in the largely residential Roscoe Village neighborhood in 2001, and when fire gutted that building, he relocated to a slightly larger space in a less residential, less traveled area and lost no business. The walls are cluttered with baseball and pop-culture memorabilia, and T-shirts for sale declare, "There are no two finer words in the English language than 'encased meats,' my friend." He closes at 4 p.m. each day, doesn't open on Sundays, takes long vacations at will and refuses to franchise or to move to a bigger location, even as knock-offs such as the suburban fRedhots and Fries try to fill the vacuum. The lunchtime lines typically snake out the door and around the corner, particularly on Fridays and Saturdays when Sohn sells fries cooked in duck fat.

As befits his blithe attitude, Sohn didn't bother with subterfuge regarding his ongoing sale of an illegal product. When the city sent him a warning letter instructing him to quit serving foie gras or else, he framed it and placed it next to his cash register. He continued to advertise the liver dogs on his in-store and online menus and waited to see what would happen next.

About six months into the ban, around 6:30 a.m. one day, Sohn posted a foie gras sausage special on his Web site. At 10 a.m., a half hour before the restaurant opened, two Health Department representatives arrived acting on complaints that he was serving the contraband ingredient. Given that they had visited him previously and had issued two warning letters by this point, they were pissed off—"understandably so," Sohn told me. "I was being a complete smart-ass seeing how far I could go. I found out exactly how far."

Although they hadn't actually caught Hot Doug's selling the banned product—because the place hadn't yet opened its doors that day—the officials discovered 150 of the naughty sausages plus 12 pounds of whole foie gras lobes in the basement freezer and gave Sohn a ticket. He didn't argue. "They took all the foie gras and put it in a garbage bag and put it in our freezer in the basement with a 'Do not remove' tag on it," Sohn said. "It was like an evidence tag. It was kept in the freezer, and I was told, 'You will be contacted as to what to do with this.'"

The following month, Sohn appeared in court and became the first Chicagoan fined for carrying foie gras. His penalty: $250. Talk about cheap advertising: Hot Doug's wound up all over the local and national media, and business got a healthy bump, particularly among out-of-towners. Health Department spokesman Hadac even offered Sohn backhanded congratulations, telling a reporter, "He has cashed in, in terms of publicity, make no mistake." The vast majority of Sohn's customers supported him, though some complained by phone or e-mail. One message began, "Dear Asswipe . . ."

About a week after the court date, the inspectors returned to detach the evidence tags from the frozen, garbage-bagged wienies. "The sausage was mine, but they said I had to remove it from the premises, which I did," Sohn said. He wound up contributing it to a friend's wedding party, where "it was quite a hit." After that, he quit serving foie gras under or over the counter. "One of my points is what a waste of time and effort and energy and resources it is on the part of the anti-foie-gras people, so why would I do the same? I made my point. It's not the core of our business. I don't need the headache."

Meanwhile, the crowds kept lining up for Hot Doug's delicious duck-fat fries. Where did that duck fat come from, anyway?

Hudson Valley Foie Gras and LaBelle.

In fact, one of the least logical yet least-commented-upon aspects of the Chicago law was that it banned the sale of a force-fed duck's liver *but not the rest of the bird.* The main suppliers to local upscale restaurants reported the inevitable dips in city sales of foie gras, yet demand for the breasts, legs and fat of these very same ducks remained high. If you were serving *magret,* you were buying force-fed duck. If you were making a confit, the same probably was true. You didn't have to request that it be shipped in an unmarked box, as some restaurants had done with foie gras. You didn't have to call it by a different name. You were free to serve all of that bird except the most delicious, desired organ.

On a few occasions, even Charlie Trotter's ordered parts of those force-fed ducks (breasts, legs, fat), though the chef told me later that those must have been oversights by someone his kitchen. "We were pretty diligent," he said. "We don't just stop using something and then say the rest of the bird is OK for us."

If you didn't want to drive to the suburbs or to decipher which Chicago restaurants would serve you forbidden foie, another option to satisfy your liver jones was to go the outlaw route. You're seeking illegal product, after all, so you might as well feel like a danger-courting, authority-defying, organ-munching rebel as you covertly slip into one of the growing number of secret roaming supper clubs cropping up around town. The culinary underground had embraced foie gras, thus spawning the phenomenon referred to as "quackeasys." Through my *Tribune* food-writing colleague/friend Monica Eng, I heard about one such dinner, a BYOB "FoiX GraX Feast" that would highlight the banned liver in all four courses, including dessert. I signed up and paid my $75 online and waited for the e-mail telling me where it would take place. (Gotta prevent The Man from finding out, after all.)

The chef was a 30-year-old named Efrain Cuevas, a Mexican-American who grew up in Aurora (Illinois's second-largest city, most famous as the setting for *Wayne's World*). He'd recently moved back to Chicago after living for two years in Oakland, California, where he prepared underground dinners with a "wandering supper club" called the Ghetto Gourmet. He'd hosted some of the group's dinners in Chicago, too, but, he said, when they balked at his plan to produce a Ghetto Gourmet foie gras meal in defiance of the ban, he broke ranks to launch his own new supper club, 24Below. (Foie gras's illegality sorta-kinda should be beside the point given that these dinners were being hosted without proper licenses, hence their "underground" status.)

Cuevas was no foie gras veteran. He'd tasted it for the first time in 2006 at an Oakland underground dinner, and at that point he knew nothing of how it was produced or of the controversy surrounding it. All he knew was that he found it delicious, even though he'd tried it in a form that sounds, let's say, unconventional. "This guy made buckwheat waffles and melted the foie gras into the waffles, cut them up, put it inside quail and roasted the quail," he recalled. "It was really good." The meal prompted Cuevas to do a little research. He watched horrific animal-rights videos ("I was like, Wow, this is pretty bad") and a sunnier one from the pro side ("The ducks were so happy: 'Oh, yes, stick a pipe down my throat. I love it.'") and finally decided to explore the issue in the way he knew best: by cooking.

"To Foie Gras or Not to Foie Gras??" read the headline on his 24Below blog as he announced the October 14, 2007, "FoiX GraX" dinner. "I consider myself a very responsible, sensitive, and socially conscious individual," he wrote. "I'm the guy that brings canvas bags to the market, gets on everybody's case about recycling, and saves up for a biodiesel car. I eat cage-free egg omelets, and I even like cats, a lot. But I also like the Foie Gras, and I appreciate the right to eat it and especially to serve it." His hope was that by serving up a lavish meal featuring the yummy livers, he would inspire his guests to weigh the pros and cons of force-feeding birds. "I've bought all this foie gras," he told me a few days before the event. "I've prepared the menu. I'm going to cook it. The question I have to ask myself next week is was it worth it?"

Accompanying me into the culinary underground was Michaela DeSoucey, a 29-year-old Northwestern University Ph.D. student writing her sociology dissertation on the contentious moral and cultural politics surrounding foie gras in the United States and France. (Michaela and I had met at a local food conference, and each of us was amazed to find a kindred foie gras obsessive.) After arriving in a warehousey area of Chicago wedged among Chinatown, the white working-class Bridgeport and the Mexican Pilsen, we entered a large art-filled loft apartment. The kitchen wasn't particularly updated, but it offered plenty of room for Cuevas and several volunteer assistants, whom he'd found on Craigslist, to roll out gnocchi and to grill tomato slices. The chef, an easygoing guy with a soul patch, was happy to chat as he pulled out a pan of foie gras slices for searing, and I was curious to learn how preparing a four-course meal might possibly affect how he weighs the underlying ethical issues.

"Does how it tastes make a difference to you as to whether it's OK?" I asked him.

"Yeah," he replied. "That's actually the biggest reason, because where is there a substitute if I want that kind of flavor, if I want that kind of ingredient?"

"So," I continued, "you think a certain amount of suffering is justified if something tastes really good?"

"Yes. Yes. But it's not like a big yes or 100 percent yes. It's like 60/40. It's hard to say. But then again it's either all or nothing."

Clearly, this chef was joining the ranks of those who have stumbled down this slippery slope. I gave him another nudge:

"So if you had the most delicious food in the world, but the only way to get it would be to take kitty cats and hang them on hooks until they bled to death, would that be OK?"

"See, that's different," he said. "That's different."

"The most delicious food in the world," I persisted.

"Another thing is the tradition, the history of the ingredient," Cuevas said. "If it's something they were doing for a long, long time—like you're saying, oh, a kitten and hanging and suffering. Well, that's just something you just threw at me. But if it was something that had been done for such a long time, I'm not that sensitive to it because it's accepted by some culture."

"Slavery was accepted for a long time," I said, employing a common animal-rights argument.

"That's true."

"There could be some secret society where they discovered that the secretions of the kittens turned the cat into the most delicious meat ever." I was officially getting carried away. "And say that in Mongolia they have this 5,000-year-old tradition of torturing cats and eating their kidneys, and it's the most delicious food anyone's ever had."

"I guess I would have to try it in that case," Cuevas admitted, finally hitting the base of the slippery slope. "I would be curious about it. I was in China last summer, and there was a dog restaurant. My co-worker was like, 'Look, there's a dog restaurant. Let's go try it.' So I'll try stuff like that."

"How was the dog?"

"It tasted a little beefy, a little porkish."

"But if it had tasted really great, would you want to go down to the Anti-Cruelty Society and pick up an unwanted dog?"

"And kill it and cook it? No."

"So there's no level of deliciousness that would have you kill a dog to eat it?"

"There is. I think there is." *Ding!* "It's like an equation: The degree of suffering plus the historic nature, the tradition of it, you sum it all up, and you have to really factor those things if you want to keep serving it. That's kind of how I am."

For this meal, Cuevas had gotten his livers from Sonoma Foie Gras, some that were shipped and some that he'd carried onto a plane from the Bay Area. "They asked what was in the box, and I just said it was chocolate. I didn't want to take any chances because I spent a lot of money on it." Most of the 20 or so people at the dinner were the chef's friends (or friends' friends), and it was a laid-back crowd without many strict foodie expectations. Before service began, Cuevas offered his quick take on the controversy and encouraged everyone to check out an animal-rights video that he'd posted on his Web site. As for the foie itself, "we're going to try it out tonight," he said as the Bee Gees' "How Can You Mend a Broken Heart?" played in the background. "I want you guys to talk about it, see what you think."

Aside from the ethical/taste issue, another question mark was hanging over this dinner, one not acknowledged or perhaps even realized by our host. Foie gras tends to be the domain of chefs who have received some classical French training or at least have engaged in a long, careful courtship of this precious product. Foie gras is a roll-out-the-red-carpet delicacy; you wouldn't use it in the kitchen like an everyday ingredient any more than you would toss white truffles into a vat of chili.

But Cuevas had no practical history with foie gras. He'd cooked with it for the first time the previous week as a practice round and was surprised that his foie gras slices had reduced to half their size when he seared them for, he realized, too long over too low heat. For the dessert, he planned to adapt a foie gras mousse recipe that he'd seen executed on the Bravo TV show *Top Chef*. With other courses he was more or less playing Iron Chef, winging it in a calculated way. His pasta course would be a gnocchi in which he substituted a whole lobe of foie gras for the ricotta cheese that his recipe originally called for. As a dessert garnish, he planned to serve a foie gras cotton candy even though he'd never made any kind of cotton candy before; in fact, the machine was still sealed in the box as dinner got under way. Cuevas may have intended this meal as a sort of referendum on whether the experience of cooking and eating foie gras transcends the accompanying ethical issues, but it also served as a culinary test of foie gras's being cooked in a way that's pretty much divorced from tradition or widely accepted ways of handling the ingredient.

The first course was a seared foie gras slice laid atop a bed of red lentils, flash-sautéed zucchini and grilled tomato. This was an unusual accompaniment, especially given that the lentils were flavored with an aggressive, Middle Eastern spice mixture that led with cumin and crushed red pepper. Seared foie gras usually is paired with some sort of fruit preparation to get that mouth-tingling sweet-savory contrast going on, the fruit gently caressing the liver and bringing out its deep yet delicate flavor. The spiced lentils here simply overpowered the foie; you could barely taste the liver for all of that cumin-and-pepper zing. Plus, Cuevas had cooked the slices on an electric skillet, and the sear didn't create any kind of crust; the foie just came out with an almost-uniform gray color. Without the dark, hard sear, you lost that sublime contrast of the crispy outside and gelatinous inside. Greg Christian, a Cuevas friend as well as a chef who specializes in working with local, organic ingredients, termed this preparation "flaccid foie."

"And when it's flaccid foie—which is mostly what people serve, even people that know how to cook—it's not that good," he told a veteran local TV producer sitting next to him. "There's really only one way to cook foie gras, and that's in a hot pan in butter, fast." (When I later mentioned this bit of wisdom to Ariane Daguin, she was appalled. "I don't know any chef, sous chef or dishwasher who would put butter in the pan," she said. "The butter is going to burn before the foie gras is going to cook. And why do you need butter? The foie gras is going to lose fat anyway. This is so not possible. He cannot be a chef saying that. The secret is hot, that's all." However, Michael Lachowicz at his three-star suburban Chicago restaurant, Michael, demonstrated to me how he places the foie slice into a freezer for a bit, dusts it with flour and then sears it at a high temperature with, yes, a bit of butter for an excellent preparation.)

Next up was the gnocchi, with the foie gras "mushed in there with the potatoes and flour," as Cuevas described it. The pasta was topped with pancetta, Manchego cheese and a variation on a traditional brown-butter sauce that actually was a half stick of melted butter combined with a cup and a half of the rendered fat that came from the seared foie gras. (Ariane Daguin also said never to use the rendered fat from searing because it's burnt—though maybe

Cuevas's was OK because the searing heat wasn't so high.) He'd cooked the pancetta in this foie gras fat as well. The result was a nice gnocchi, rich yet not heavy feeling, but I'll be damned if I could taste the foie gras. My tablemates agreed; they'd never have known that the fat liver (or liver fat) was in the dish without the advance warning.

The table conversation, no surprise, veered toward Chicago's ban of the ingredient we'd all been consuming. Christian, a leading figure in bringing organic foods to Chicago's public schools, deemed the controversy "a silly argument" given how relatively few people it affects. "In the Chicago public schools, we feed 400,000 kids dog food every day for lunch, so I wasn't willing to have much of an opinion about the foie gras controversy." He was more concerned over how many miles an average ingredient in Trotter's or Tramonto's kitchen was traveling or how many millions of chickens were being slaughtered on industrial chicken farms.

"I really think it's a function of people's unwillingness to look at their unconscious guilt around the bigger things that are happening in life," he said. "Instead of looking at things that are really overwhelming, things that are really much more serious, they'll try and change this because that's what they can get their head around. In Chicago 50 or 75 people eat foie gras in a night, right? And there's probably a million people a night eating beef that's raised really inhumanely."

"OK," I said, "but does that mean the ducks don't suffer?"

"I've actually been thinking about that," Christian said. "It's hard for me to say that's OK. I'm mostly a vegetarian. This will be the most meat I've eaten in the last four months, by far. I eat mostly vegetables, mostly vegan, almost exclusively, 99.9 percent. So it is kind of awful the way they're treated. But, I think . . . I don't know." Christian said he'd come to the dinner because Monica had invited him, and he wanted to support his friend Efrain. "This is the first time he's ever cooked foie. I said, 'What are you doing?' I offered to show him. I talked to him about it for like 20 minutes, but talking for 20 minutes is different from cooking foie gras for 25 years like me."

"So are you dubious about the foie cotton candy then?"

"Yeah," he laughed.

Cuevas came out to introduce the third course: a wild-boar roast with a rub of brown sugar, black pepper, red pepper and coriander and a red-wine reduction sauce made with carrots and a pound of foie gras that "just kind of melted and disintegrated" into it. This deeply orange sauce was a rich, complementary accompaniment to the boar, though, again, it didn't taste a lot like foie gras unless you happened to come across a stray liver niblet. So although this was a perfectly fine course, it would be hard to make the argument that the foie gras surpassed Cuevas's threshold of being absolutely necessary here.

Over in the kitchen, the chef and his volunteers were prepping dessert. "I'm getting a little nervous," Monica said with a laugh, "because Efrain's just reading the directions for the cotton candy machine right now."

Monica and I got up to take a closer look. As his helpers cut out circles of a hazelnut cake using the top of an empty organic tomatoes can, Cuevas contemplated the white cotton candy machine spinning atop the counter as he clutched a stainless steel bowl filled with a yellowish, damp sugar. "It's sugar and melted foie gras," he explained, "and then I'll just run it through the cotton candy machine."

"Will that work?" Monica asked.

The machine kept spinning. "Let's just see what happens," he finally said and dropped a bit of the sugar in there. Immediately, his black shirt looked like it was coated with dandruff. He added more of the foie sugar and waited. And waited.

A 10-year-old boy named Willie Wagner approached and peered inside. "It might be too wet," he told Cuevas. "If any of the sugar gets wet, you have to throw it all out."

The boy's father, also named Willie Wagner (and owner of Honky Tonk Barbeque in Pilsen), explained that little Willie used to make cotton candy at a circus. Cuevas grimaced. The machine kept spinning without producing any wispy threads. Cuevas took the rest of the foie sugar and stuck it in the freezer. A few minutes later he removed it and dumped it all into a sauté pan on the stove, where it began to melt. Meanwhile, he cleaned out the cotton candy machine and tried again with some regular, dry, liver-free sugar. Sure enough, the sugary threads started accumulating along the inside.

"Efrain!" cried out a female volunteer. The foie gras sugar was bubbling over the stove. Cuevas dashed over and turned down the heat. One of the volunteers poured the molten foie sugar into a plastic squirt bottle. Cuevas squirted out some of the contents onto a baking sheet to create hard, candy-like strands. They tasted like caramelized sugar, not so much like foie gras.

"Change of plans," he announced, emptying the squirt bottle back into the sauté pan. I'm going to make foie gras caramel." He added whipping cream and a balsamic vanilla reduction to the mixture and stirred. The dessert wound up being hazelnut cake and figs topped by a foie gras mousse (made with egg yolks, whipped cream, honey and melted liver) with the foie gras caramel drizzled on top and around, and a puff of white cotton candy as a "texture garnish." In this case you really could taste the foie gras in the mousse, not so much in the caramel. Foie gras and figs play well together, so the dish didn't taste as weird as it might sound. Most folks cleaned their plates.

As people finished their dinners, I asked Efrain whether he was more of a foie gras fan now than before the meal. "I am," he replied. "Yeah, everything was really good. I was a little bit put out by the dessert with the cotton candy, but it worked out fine."

His biggest surprise had been how much the foie gras slices again reduced upon searing, but he was glad that the rendered fat came in handy. "What I really liked about doing this four-course menu was I actually used everything. The fat from the first course, I used for the second course, and then whatever I had left over there, I even threw some into the sauce for the wild boar. Everything got used, the fat and the liver."

He agreed with me that the foie gras was most prominent in the first and last courses, but he wasn't bothered that it wasn't so noticeable in the gnocchi or wild boar because he liked how those courses came out. "Do you think the foie gras was indispensable for each of the dishes?" I asked.

"Yes."

The other diners were enthusiastic; certainly none of them expressed qualms about having eaten foie gras. Cuevas was intrigued enough by the experience that he tried again two months later at another underground dinner, dubbed "Fxxx Gxxx in West Town." This time he paired his seared foie gras with something sweet: seared apple slices infused with lavender honey, plus sour cherry compote. Other courses included leek and endive soup with a foie gras crouton and Gruyère; braised pork shoulder roast with purple yams and rutabaga, cognac and foie gras caramel (yes!); and Viognier-poached pears filled with fuyu persimmon custard plus pistachio ice cream with vanilla foie caramel (again!).

When I was in France weeks later, I mentioned Cuevas's foie gras gnocchi and cotton candy to André Daguin, Ariane's famous father. He gave a deep laugh and pronounced, "If he comes here and does that, he will be in the river!"

Other Chicago restaurants hosted their own secret foie gras dinners, and more new supper clubs emerged. One, organized by the local wine distributor H2Vino, was dubbed Turtle Soup, and it had a novel concept. Not only would a different restaurant present each month's multicourse foie gras dinner—which cost $99 including wine pairings, tax and tip—but at the end of the meal you'd receive two business cards with "The Turtle Soup Club" printed above the line "Saving the turtles, eat more foie" and an illustration of a happy turtle lying on its back with a bowl of something hot atop its tummy. The back of the card listed five Chicago restaurants—including Cyrano's Bistrot and Bin 36—and the instruction, "Present this card to your server at any of the restaurants below for a special turtle soup appetizer."

Yes, "turtle soup" was code, and the card was the equivalent of a secret handshake to get a foie gras appetizer delivered surreptitiously to your table. The first Turtle Soup dinner was at Copperblue in early 2008, and Tsonton's training with the ingredient was evident in his variety of cold and hot preparations, including a foie gras mousse, rice croquettes with "yummy foie gras middles," a foie gras terrine, seared foie gras in a rich risotto, and roasted foie gras with cocoa nibs alongside duck leg confit and a breast roulade. Tsonton introduced the meal to the 40 or so diners with his typical off-the-cuff enthusiasm, but he was a bit chagrined; he'd just received his second warning letter from the city for selling foie gras. (Like at Hot Doug's, his first warning letter was displayed at the restaurant's entrance, next to a basket of "Quack If You Like Foie Gras" buttons on sale for five dollars to support Chicago Chefs for Choice.) One of Tsonton's regular clients had asked him to host a private, fancy lunch for 12 staffers at the restaurant, so he offered a foie gras terrine as one of the appetizer options. Almost immediately afterward, Copperblue received the city's warning with a notation of when the complaint had been filed. "The person called at 12:10 in the afternoon," Tsonton told the group. "The lunch started at 11:45. So they were on their phone calling the city narking on me on a private lunch."

A few weeks after the Turtle Soup dinner, my curiosity about the card got the better of me. Would it really work? Did all of those listed restaurants actually keep foie gras on the premises just in case someone walked in and slipped them one of these babies? I figured Cyrano's, Bin 36 and Copperblue probably had foie gras in the kitchen, but I wasn't so sure about the other two listed restaurants: the Italian wine bar Enoteca Piattini or the French-Vietnamese restaurant Le Lan. I'd been meaning to try Le Lan anyway—in fact, I'd met its chef, Bill Kim, when he was still working in Trotter's kitchen—so Michaela and I headed out there on a Thursday night.

We perused the menu, and when our server—an appropriately refined fellow befitting the restaurant's quiet elegance—came by, I smoothly handed him the Turtle Soup card and said *sotto voce*, "I hope you'll be able to honor this."

He nodded, politely smiled and tried not to look like he'd just been handed something written in Sanskrit. Soon he and the restaurant's manager were exchanging puzzled expressions in a corner by the kitchen. When we finally ordered our meals, the server said he hadn't yet had a chance to discuss the card with the chef. But soon he returned to inform us: "We shall be able to honor your request."

Eventually, the server delivered two plates sporting lovely foie gras terrine slices. They were, as expected, tasty. "This is very similar to Michael Tsonton's preparation," Michaela noted, perceptively.

After the meal, Chef Kim visited from the kitchen, and we commended him on a wonderful meal. I told him, "I was surprised that the Turtle Soup card worked. I didn't imagine that people from that dinner had been making a run on the restaurant with those cards."

"I gotta tell you," he said with a sigh, "we don't keep foie gras in the kitchen." In fact, he explained, my request had thrown the restaurant into a tizzy. Up to that point, Kim's involvement in Turtle Soup had been to agree to host a dinner (the second one, it turned out), but he'd never seen one of those cards before and didn't know what to do. The restaurant's manager tracked down Michael Tsonton on his cell phone, and Tsonton, who was at a Chicago Bulls game that evening, informed him that he had some foie gras terrines in the Copperblue walk-in refrigerator. Le Lan's owner then drove to Copperblue, picked up one of Tsonton's terrines and delivered it to the Le Lan kitchen, where Kim plated the dish.

That was one powerful card.

13.

Foie Strikes Back

"Vegans, eat me!"

At times people's cruelty confounded Deanna Calderaio, a suburban Philadelphia postal worker moonlighting as a Hugs for Puppies protester. Sure, she'd yell anti-foie-gras slogans through a bullhorn at restaurants, but that's protected speech, and she was working to save animals. Sometimes you have to annoy customers and neighbors to make your point. But then they'd respond in such awful ways. They'd scream back in her face, stuff like, "You're stupid!" "You're wearing leather shoes!" "What about the war?" "What about homeless people?"

"They just yell anything they can," the 29-year-old protester sighed. "They probably all eat meat, and they feel some level of guilt." Calderaio is a vegan, "and all of my animals are vegan too. I have four cats and 13 different types of rodents." So as someone who loves animals, she just couldn't believe what one woman did while Hugs for Puppies members raised a ruckus outside the Philadelphia restaurant Standard Tap: This customer or neighbor (or both) tied up her dog outside the restaurant, right in front of the protesters, and went inside. "She figured if we're animal-rights activists, 'I'll tie my dog up right where they're protesting so they won't yell or use bullhorns,'" Calderaio said. "She's tying up a defenseless dog that can't untie him-

213

self in front of us. I wouldn't want to hurt the dog's ears or make the dog scared. We stopped using bullhorns. It was really horrible."

Feel free now to debate the ethics of using animals against animal-rights activists, but in the meantime we'll score this one for the anti-protest backlash. After all, the London Grill spent $20,000 to get Hugs for Puppies to shut up. This woman did the same with a single canine.

The pro-foie forces were striking back. In October 2007, Ariane Daguin spearheaded a five-dollar-foie-gras week among Philadelphia's restaurants, which had organized under the banner Philadelphia Chefs for Choice. In a statement the group wrapped this pricey French delicacy in red, white and blue, declaring, "In the city of Philadelphia, the birthplace of American liberty, we want to keep the right to serve foie gras." Almost 20 restaurants, regardless of whether they offered the dish previously, put the fattened duck livers on their menus to give everyday patrons an affordable taste of what the fuss was about. Councilman Jack Kelly responded in typically muted fashion, telling Time.com: "I could care less about those snobby French chefs. They can stick their five-dollar foie gras up their rears." A few weeks later, when I interviewed the councilman in his office, I referred to his colorful quote, and he snapped, "I meant it. I'm not backing off on it. They purposely did that five-dollar thing."

By this point Daguin already had had her own run-in with Nick Cooney and the Hugs for Puppies crew. She was making sales calls in town early in the evening on a sunny, warm Friday when Olivier Desaintmartin, the French chef at the Caribou Café and its "sister bistro" Zinc, called her to say, "Hey, now is your opportunity. Come, and I'll show you what they do." She arrived at the Caribou Café to see protesters yelling into bullhorns while the frustrated wait staff couldn't seat anyone on the terrace despite the beautiful weather. She approached the guy with the bullhorn who turned out to be Cooney, and, with all six feet of her towering over his slight frame, she told him he had his facts wrong. She said he handed the bullhorn to the young woman next to him, who began blaring away as she tried to talk to Cooney, and when Ariane asked her to stop, she handed the bullhorn back to Cooney, and the pair went back and forth this way a couple of times until Ariane lost patience. "I went very, very close to him," she said. "I think my nose was in his eye, you know? I said, 'You know, this is not nice what you are doing.' I was just talking but a little more forcefully, and I never touched him. I think he got afraid. He called the policeman who was across the street who came right away, and the policeman said, 'Do you want to get arrested?' To me. I said, 'I'm not disturbing the peace. I'm just here. I didn't touch anybody.' And they said, 'No, you're invading his privacy.' So I said, 'Yeah, but don't you think he's invading everybody else's privacy on that block and on the blocks around?' and they said, 'Yeah, but they have a permit to do it.'" Cooney said afterward he only vaguely remembered the incident, but in general, "If someone's being very obnoxious and just wants to complain and belittle us, we'll just go back to the demonstration." He didn't realize the woman with whom he'd been tangling was the famous Ariane Daguin.

The restaurants participating in Daguin's five-dollar-foie promotion were all but inviting Hugs for Puppies onto their doorsteps, but Cooney didn't mobilize so much as dismiss the whole campaign. "It's just a laughable event," he said. "I'm sure it made them feel good. They certainly got their fair share of press about it, and perhaps in the minds of D'Artagnan and London Grill, they feel like they're fighting back, but it hasn't in any way changed the direction this is going." He noted the dozens of Philadelphia restaurants that had signed the Hugs no-foie pledge, and he remained in "negotiations" with more restaurants to remove the dish. Desaintmartin, for instance, participated in the five-dollar promotion by serving sliders topped with caramelized onions and pan-seared foie gras at Caribou Café and poached foie gras with mango chutney and waffle chips at Zinc, but afterward he cut a deal with Cooney to take foie gras off his menus, though he and the Hugs leader had different interpretations of what that meant. Desaintmartin said he literally deleted the words "foie gras" but continued serving the controversial ingredient in a "duck liver mousse." "He said, 'Would you change the name to duck liver mousse?'" Desaintmartin recalled. "I said, 'Yes.' He said, 'If you do that, I will go away.' I said, 'But it's the same thing,' and he said, 'As long as there's no foie gras on the menu, I will go away.' Then I went to their Web site, and they said I took foie gras off the menu."

Cooney said no, what happened was that Desaintmartin had been serving a duck liver mousse that didn't contain foie gras in the first place, and he simply was calling it foie gras mousse for marketing purposes. Now the chef finally was being accurate. "If he was serving foie gras but calling it something else, of course we would still be out there every week," Cooney said. I relayed Cooney's reaction back to Desaintmartin, who said the truth was he was mixing foie gras with other ingredients to keep the price down (that's why a mousse is less expensive than a terrine or another undiluted form), but the dish did indeed contain foie gras.

Even if this he-said/he-said silliness stemmed from mere miscommunication, Hugs for Puppies *had* tamped down its aggressiveness at this point. The group found it easier to round up protesters in the summer than the fall, when many volunteers were back in school. More notable was that Cooney was changing tactics. After the judge handed down the London Grill's restrictive injunction, the Hugs leader booted out a few of the most aggressive members, including Dezeray Rubinchik and Mark Fonda (the bearded flat-screen TV guy), who had been sparring with restaurant patrons. "Time and time again I would go up to them and say, 'Stop, stop, shut up,' and a minute later they would do it again," Cooney said. "After the London Grill stuff came to a head, we had an important Hugs for Puppies meeting and said that sort of thing can't go on. All interaction with customers has to be positive or neutral or not at all. There was a big blowup, and that was the end of them working with us."

Part of the fallout over the London Grill injunction was that Hugs for Puppies would be sitting on the sidelines when the McNallys' restaurant hosted a $165 five-course foie gras dinner in late October being prepared by Hudson Valley Foie Gras's Michael Ginor. I flew to Philadelphia that weekend anticipating a lively scene outside the restaurant, which promoted the event as part of its occasional series pairing meals and authors. (Ginor would sign copies of *Foie Gras: A Passion*.) But the injunction dictated that no more than two Hugs members could demonstrate at a time, and they'd have to be across the street and down the block protesting in relative silence before 7 p.m. So Cooney made the call that the event just wasn't worth their while. "It's sad," he said. "With all of the London Grill's comments in the media about freedom of choice, they certainly don't want us to be able to exercise our freedom of the First Amendment in front of their restaurant."

What Cooney *really* wanted was to be invited inside the restaurant for the dinner so he could "have a nice debate with the guy from Hudson Valley. But London Grill wouldn't want that. They wouldn't want anybody educating the customers." They also might not want somebody describing bird torture, exploding stomachs and duck vomit while guests tried to enjoy a $165 meal. Still, I was intrigued by the idea of Cooney debating Ginor.

The anti-protest protests reached their pinnacle of absurdity a couple of months later when 20 or so restaurant workers and foie loyalists demonstrated outside the "No Foie Gras Gala" hosted by Hugs for Puppies and the affiliated Professionals Against Foie Gras. As the animal-welfare crowd inside the Ethical Society Building in Rittenhouse Square enjoyed vegan fare and speeches from Jack Kelly, Gene Baur, Paul Shapiro, Holly Cheever and others, the chef from the next-door Rittenhouse Hotel and servers brought out trays featuring cold foie gras torchon slices topped with cherries and little foie gras cheesecake tarts to be passed among the demonstrators and passersby. Meanwhile, a bullhorn was passed around so the demonstrators could chant, "Nick Cooney, go away! Foie gras is here to stay" and "Jack Kelly, go away! . . ." This stunt was coordinated by— surprise!—Ariane Daguin, who also made up signs such as "Save a duck, eat a vegetarian," "Tofu is the delusion of denial!" "Meat is not murder. Meat is *food*!" and a photo of a cow with the voice bubble, "Vegans, eat me!" Even Terry McNally, who otherwise enthusiastically joined in the protest payback, said of that last one: "That seemed a little harsh. I didn't like holding that one."

Funny how the London Grill was all but off limits to Hugs for Puppies, yet McNally kept finding herself in close proximity to Cooney. One night she and a friend were near the gourmet Chinese restaurant Susanna Foo when they heard the Hugs members protesting outside. McNally still had the Hugs gala signs in the back of her truck, so she and her friend started protesting the protesters. Upon seeing her, the Hugs members shot back, "Boycott Susanna Foo! Boycott London Grill!"

McNally tried to get her friend to take a photo of her with Cooney.

"Nick was saying, 'I don't want to be seen with you,'" she recalled, "and the officer came over, and Nick said, 'Officer, this woman is harassing me.' The officer said, 'Ma'am, you're going to have to go, or I'm going to have to arrest you.'" She left.

She had a far more civil encounter with Cooney a few weeks later, running into him as he handed out pamphlets on Rittenhouse Square. He said he'd just spoken to one of her cooks, and they had what McNally called "a little friendly banter." Yes, she still thought he was cute.

Meanwhile, Ariane Daguin had grown frustrated with Michael Ginor for what she perceived as his lack of fight. While she was organizing protests and Izzy was venturing away from the farm to meet with chefs, Michael was distancing himself from the fray. "I've done years of preaching the foie gras gospel, and I'm tired of it," he told me. "I'm fortunate to have done well, where I can get up in the morning and do exactly what I want to do, and that's not what I want to do, which is why Izzy's down a little bit now."

"But," I responded, "one could argue that an eloquent spokesman for foie gras is needed now more than ever."

"Yeah, maybe," he said. "But so be it. I love the product. It sounds like giving up, but if people want it, I'll produce it. If they don't, then I won't. I just don't have the interest to fight that war."

Ariane found this attitude infuriating. "Sometimes I resent Michael for it, for the way he is not behind his product," she said. "He's not going to war with us. He's not going in the battle with us." She said when she was discussing an upcoming legislative battle with him and her sales manager over dinner, "he said, 'OK, well, I'll go retire to Thailand.' And I found that so, so bad—that, (1) he's detaching himself like that, and (2) he's doing that in front of my sales manager, the guy who's responsible for increasing his sales, for making *him* money. I cannot stand that.

"If you believe in what you do, then you say it. You don't walk away from it at the first sign of difficulty. Or the second sign or third sign. This is the product that we believe in. Foie gras has been good to us, and we believe it is humane. We believe it is right. We believe that we are being sacrificed—you know the whole story. And it's wrong. It's wrong, so we're fighting. But to publicly say, 'OK, I'll go retire in Thailand—*ACHH!*" She laughed. "This is bad. This is bad."

"Obviously it was said as a joke," returned Ginor, who noted an ongoing "ego feud" with Ariane. "Nobody has spent more time and effort and capital on this fight than Hudson Valley. Nobody has carried the flag like Hudson Valley. Foie gras is and always has been my life."

Ginor drove from his Long Island home down to Philadelphia on the Sunday afternoon before the Monday dinner he was preparing at the London Grill, whose staff welcomed him like a visiting dignitary. In promoting the event, the restaurant had posted a menu on its Web site that included foie gras matzo ball soup and a foie gras crème brûlée for dessert, but Ginor, a skilled chef himself, had his own ideas. This would not be a series of gimmicky experiments. Ginor had some twists planned, but for the most part his dinner would spotlight foie gras standing tall in classic preparations. So bye-bye matzo ball soup and crème brûlée (and any foie dessert); hello, torchon and seared slices. Ginor said that when he prepared a foie gras dinner, something he did often at culinary events or charity fundraisers, the guest might not even be conscious of the rich ingredient linking all of the courses. That's a fine idea, but in this case, fat chance. Ginor, after all, had brought down his own sizable supply of vacuum-packed lobes, so he wasn't going to be one of those chefs wincing at the dollar signs represented by each slice. There was a lot of foie gras in that crowded kitchen, and there would be a lot of foie gras on each plate.

But first Ginor, in his usual uniform of a black T-shirt and blue jeans, had a radio interview to do on a local public station's food show. The host was a foodie, so the questions were soft and culinary. Ginor told her that cooking foie gras is "almost easier than cooking an egg."

At the dinner that night, Ginor, still in his black T-shirt, shuttled between the kitchen, where Michael McNally and the other cooks deferred to his specific instructions (remaking a flan at one point), and the dining room, where he signed copies of his book for some of the 40 guests who arrived at varying times over the evening. One reason Terry McNally had planned the dinner for a Monday night was so other chefs could attend, among them Desaintmartin, Tinto's Jose Garces and Alma de Cuba's Douglas Rodriguez. The event also drew fellow pub owners, the restaurant's lawyer, its local D'Artagnan distributor and various patrons keen to indulge in expertly prepared foie gras. Ginor often carried out the plates himself, giving himself the opportunity to schmooze with Rodriguez and other food industry folks with whom he already enjoyed professional friendships. The McNallys and Holcomb, meanwhile, were on their feet nonstop to keep the event moving smoothly, but this was not a stressful kind of busyness. They were surrounded by friends and supporters, they were serving what they'd been told not to serve and no one was yelling at them. Toward the end of the evening all three of them joined a large table of colleagues and let themselves be treated to the same dishes that Ginor had prepared for everyone else.

Kicking off the meal was a traditional foie gras torchon with hibiscus gelatin. Next came a Japanese-accented dish: small cubes of nori-cured foie gras and raw tuna prepared as a tartare with a truffle soy glaze and wasabi oil. The third course raised the richness ante as Ginor's truffled foie gras flan complemented lobster poached in orange butter. This was followed by a plate containing seared foie gras, duck *magret,* duck prosciutto plus pumpkin risotto. Everything was impeccably made; I especially liked the lighter tartare coming between the silky torchon and the there-go-the-arteries flan. By the time I had tasted the large seared slice, with its nicely caramelized crust, alongside the *magret* and prosciutto, I was thoroughly stuffed. Too bad I'd forgotten that another entrée was still to come: an even heftier slice of a foie gras lobe that had been roasted whole and accompanied an ample serving of rare venison loin. The roasted foie offered an interesting contrast to the seared slice—the edges had a more smoky, charred quality even as the center remained melt-in-your-mouth gelatinous—but at this point I felt like I was going to be the one with an exploding stomach. I half expected John Cleese to come out with a final foie gras chip, promising, "It's wafer thin!"

At some point I told Ginor of Cooney's desire to debate him and asked whether Ginor would want to do such a thing. Sure, he said, let's all meet for coffee in the morning. I called Cooney, and he was game as well. We were on. So at 9 a.m. the three of us convened at a local-food, fair trade, veg-friendly coffeehouse just up the street from the London Grill called, appropriately enough (in Cooney's case at least), Mugshots. Cooney arrived first and was eating a bagel with vegan cream cheese when I arrived. He wasn't sure exactly what he was going to get from this meeting—unlike the restaurants, Hudson Valley Foie Gras wasn't about to ban foie gras—but he was intrigued. Ginor arrived shortly thereafter and got himself a coffee. Polite introductions were made, and we took our seats around a small table. To my right was the rail-thin vegan with his green button-down shirt tucked into his khakis; to my left, the relatively beefy liver producer in his usual black T-shirt and blue jeans plus a silver chain hanging around his neck.

Ginor preemptively said he would not be one of those people who criticize Cooney for targeting foie gras. "You have the right to have concerns about whatever issue," he said. "People say why would people care about foie gras when women are being raped and killed in Darfur? We can't all care about one subject."

I asked Cooney if there was anything Ginor could do to alleviate his concerns about his business. Cooney suggested the company switch to a non-force-feeding process like that used by Spain's Patería de Sousa, which allowed the geese to feed themselves outdoors. Cooney complained that Hudson Valley no longer allowed its ducks outside, and Ginor reiterated the farm's avian flu and runoff concerns before calling discussion of the birds' housing "inappropriate window dressing" on an issue that begins and ends with the force-feedings. He dismissed the Patería de Sousa claims of producing non-force-fed foie gras as "nonsense."

Cooney countered that even if the de Sousa model didn't create pure foie gras, wouldn't it be better to switch to such an approximation rather than to continue a practice seen as cruel worldwide?

"It's not for us," Ginor said. "There wouldn't be a company."

"There wouldn't be a company of 200 employees and 300,000 birds a year," Cooney said.

No, Ginor said, there wouldn't be a company, period, because you can't just scale back from a company that takes in $14 million annually and has 200 employees to one that nets $1 million and employs five or 10 people. When Cooney concluded that the reason for continuing the force-feeding was financial, Ginor started to get exasperated. "I hate to put it this way, but it's a silly discussion in the sense that there wouldn't be a company at the end of the day. It's not a solution."

"Maybe a smaller company," Cooney said.

"No, there wouldn't be a company," Ginor repeated. "I would walk away from it and close it down."

"Because it's not foie gras?"

"Yeah, it's not foie gras. We're in upstate New York with the real estate values and what we're paying in tax. It's a very almost sophomoric thing to suggest. It's like saying to GM, 'Why don't you stop the car industry, make razors?'"

"Probably not that dramatic a difference, but I understand your point."

"Maybe more dramatic a difference," Ginor said, arguing that one can't just write off "financial" as a dirty word. "We have 200 employees I've been taking care of for 15 years. I don't just close my eyes and say, 'Well, you guys are out of a job.' As it's important for you to take care of animals, for me it's important to take care of people."

Ginor continued that even the question of letting the ducks back outside was financial in that the company would have to restructure the land to deal with the runoff. "With you guys there, it makes it very difficult to make any capital decisions," Ginor said.

"I don't understand," Cooney replied.

"With you guys working toward our elimination, what company in their right mind is going to go ahead and spend large quantities of money on things that take seven years, 10 years to recoup when the future is so uncertain? If you only knew the kind of backward damage that you actually cause animals in a way. It prevents you from doing things that you really want to do to take care of the animals."

What had happened, he continued, was that the U.S. market for foie gras had doubled over the past several years, but almost all of the growth had benefited Canadian and French producers. Hudson Valley's share of the U.S. market, which had been 80 or 90 percent, was down to about 45 percent. "The reason you don't see seven new foie gras operations in the United States competing but rather the same three is because which financial institution is going to lend money to an industry that's under fire? What in a sense you've done is stalled the United States foie gras industry but helped grow the foie gras industry outside of the country."

• • •

Cooney continued serving the ball, and Ginor kept volleying it back. The Hugs leader wanted to know whether Ginor still would stand by his company's structure and employees if he came to think that force-feeding was "cruel and/or unnecessary."

"Um, that's a good question," Ginor replied, noting that he had read enough studies and seen enough firsthand to answer the cruelty issue in his mind. "I think that it straddles some kind of an acceptable line to me. It's not that the ducks are just not manipulated, but at the same time I don't find the cruelty that you find. So I come somewhere along that line of not thinking that it's zero and not thinking that it's 10. I see it as a five."

Cooney seized on Ginor's use of numbers: "You said that in your opinion on a cruelty scale from one to 10, it was probably around a five, so it's straddling the line."

"I never used the word 'cruelty,'" Ginor returned, saying that even the most idyllic farm would be "a four or five because at the end of the day the ducks, the animals are being killed for food, manipulated in some way by being put here and put there and moved around."

Cooney disagreed that Hudson Valley was comparable to smaller, non-foie-gras duck farms, but to him the main question was, "If Hudson Valley is somewhere in the middle of that idyllic vision and the worst-case scenario, which might be a massive, battery-cage egg facility, why not go toward the one or the two?"

"Because it wouldn't be enough," Ginor said. "If that was the discussion with animal-rights activists, that wouldn't do it. If we said we need to give them more room, at the end of the day, it's still going to begin and end with the force-feeding side."

"I'm talking about that as well," Cooney said. "To get down to a one or two, force-feeding would be out of the picture."

Ginor laughed. "Correct. There is no one or two."

Ginor touted Hudson Valley's relatively low duck-to-feeder ratio and the system of paying employees "not to hurt the ducks, which is a very weird way to say we pay our feeders to take good care of the ducks."

"I guess it shows the cruelty endemic in foie gras production,"

Cooney said. "You're doing it in an effort to perhaps alleviate it, but that's still inevitable."

"No," Ginor said. "Car producers pay for no mistakes. UPS pays for not delivering to wrong places."

"But there's a difference between no mistakes and not a ton of mistakes. I was told by Holly Cheever that she was told that there were bonuses paid to workers who had under 50 ducks' stomachs explode on them per month, or livers."

"No, there's no such thing as an exploding liver, no such thing as an exploding stomach. It's very simple. I'll tell you because I created the system. We pay the feeder on the quality of ducks at the end of the 30-day period. I don't want someone kicking a duck, slitting its throat. I don't want that. We don't abuse ducks."

"There are ducks whose stomachs literally have exploded."

"No."

"It's been documented in some of these investigations," Cooney insisted. "They've taken away birds that were then taken to pathologists who said that this is what had happened to them."

"I have never seen or heard of an exploding liver or stomach."

"OK, I could get a hold of documentation."

"OK, I'm not going to tell you that of millions and millions and millions of ducks being produced that there isn't something similar to what you're saying, but I am completely not aware of any such a thing on any kind of a scale, meaning a percent."

More than an hour into this debate, Cooney almost exclusively had been the one playing offense, so I asked Ginor: "What are you most frustrated with in terms of what Hugs for Puppies or other groups are doing?"

"I think that many of the animal-rights activists are misrepresenting a lot of facts," he said. "I think that they're taking something that to the uneducated eye is easy to bring across, and more than anything else, there's the problem of the ends-justify-the-means scenario, which is never right. There's no question that there's been intimidation, terrorist-like tactics. I'm not a person who takes well to terrorism, and I think that those are tactics that eventually will be the cause's downfall as well.

"There's no question people like Stephen Starr and others have said they felt threatened and that they felt that their kids were threatened. The ends don't always justify the means. They didn't for Hitler. They won't for a suicide bomber. They won't for blowing up an abortion clinic. I know that the American public is not tolerant of that. I think that the gains that are made using those tactics are usually very short-term gains, meaning eventually you guys go away or stop or people are sick and tired of hearing you screaming about foie gras, and they stop sending money, and you guys go on to something else, and these restaurants go back to the way they were."

"I think it's very telling," Cooney said, "the fact that the comparisons you made to us are Hitler, suicide bombers and bombing abortion clinics."

"Well, I'm not the one who sends someone a picture of his kids in his living room, right?" Ginor said. "I'm not the one who broke into places. These comparisons are often made."

"It doesn't speak to us," Cooney said.

Ginor countered that telling restaurant workers, "I know where you sleep at night," constituted a threat. "If you said to me, 'I know where you live,' then I would make sure you don't get to see the light of day."

Cooney told of canning the most aggressive Hugs members and complained that the restaurateurs, chefs and patrons often were the most hostile ones, such as when Michael McNally allegedly raised his fist at Rubinchik. "I don't think there's any excuse for it. The only reason he did it is because this female protester was telling people as they were walking by, 'Boycott London Grill.'"

"If you're sitting outside someone's place of business—and restaurants don't make a ton of money—and you're intimidating their clients and so on, you could see someone saying, 'Hey, I'm tired of this. I'm sick of it.' You could see someone losing their cool when you're every day repeatedly harassing."

"I can understand it happening," Cooney said. "But it's still not right."

Cooney and Ginor continued tangling over conflicting accounts of what happens on foie gras farms, the relative mortality rates among force-fed ducks and other poultry and the validity of those Zogby polls. After almost two hours, I asked whether either one of them had gained a different perspective or would modify his actions in any way.

"I don't think there's anything I can do to alleviate animal-rights concerns," Ginor said, addressing Cooney: "It's not like I'm going to convince you to walk around and say, 'Well, I met them and they seem like pretty good guys.' There wasn't much for me to gain. Of course, you probably knew that you weren't going to have me get up and say, 'Well, OK, we'll just shut down.'"

Cooney felt similarly. "I certainly am glad that we met. I think it was an interesting experience, and I guess the main positive thing I took away was some additional facts about the farm and also just getting a general sense for how you are, how you see the issue, the complexities of the issue."

"The fact that you yourself are not an extremist, in a sense of anything justifies the cause, is for me nice to know—that people are not at risk for their lives, that you yourself are not tolerant of people within your organization who are nuts," Ginor said.

Everyone was getting along, which was nice. Still, I had to ask: "Nick, do you think that Michael is an animal torturer?"

"Such a loaded question," Cooney said. "I feel like I'm on *Jerry Springer* here."

"You've used the term," I responded.

"Yes," Cooney said, "I think what Hudson Valley is doing to the animals, I would consider it to be torture. When it comes to issues of suffering—be it human suffering, animal suffering, any suffering—always, always, always, we should err on the side of caution. Why not just say, 'I am not certain that this is totally good for the animals, so I'm just not going to do it. I'm going to do something else instead.' We have so many possibilities of ways to make money, of ways to make meals."

"I assume at that point that to not consume any animal protein would be the only way to fulfill that," Ginor said.

"I think that, and that's the way I live," Cooney said, "but I do think that there are a lot of steps in between what Hudson Valley Foie Gras is doing to its animals and to being vegan."

"To me it's close."

"Difference of opinion."

"I know exactly where you're coming from," Ginor said, "but for me the step from not producing foie gras to being a vegan is not that far. I've had that thought in my head of should we eat animals, should we not eat animals—sort of the bigger philosophical question about it. I can't tell you how many times I walk by and—this is kind of a silly example—there's a slug on the ground, and I would make all the effort not to step on it because why take out a living animal? I wouldn't kill a fly, and I wouldn't kill a bee, even if it was sitting on my son's head."

"We human beings are odd and often contradictory," Cooney said.

"So I would spare that, but obviously with the company and foie gras, I don't have that same approach, because I see it as food."

As we prepared to leave, Ginor mentioned that his son had applied for early admission to the University of Pennsylvania, so they might be spending much more time in West Philadelphia.

"We're right up the street," Cooney said.

"He could join Hugs for Puppies," I suggested.

"You know what?" Ginor said. "If he did, that would be his right. I would never deny him that. Who knows? He's a cool kid."

On that note, the debate was over.

Afterward, Cooney expressed surprise that Ginor was more of "a Long Island Manhattan kind of guy" than "a farmer personality." When I asked what that meant, Cooney said he'd anticipated more brusqueness and bravado, more of an attitude that "anyone advocating for animal welfare is wildly misguided. His attitude was more he's thought about it, he thinks that it's acceptable and he's trying to explain why it's not as bad as you perceive." Nevertheless, Cooney sensed "a fundamental disconnect" in someone who avoids stepping on slugs yet runs a company that force-feeds birds. "He's doing some things that are clearly cruel that he would never do if there were not economic interests or the creation of a product that satisfies his hobby or passion."

Ginor found Cooney to be "a little childish or naïve—sort of in a charming way but mostly stemming from a complete lack of understanding of the positive forces of economics." He added: "I get the sense that there are two sides to him. On one hand he comes across as very levelheaded but another side . . . fanatical."

Still, as Ginor and I walked away from the coffeehouse, he said he thought Cooney seemed like "a nice enough guy." But one issue puzzled him.

"Frankly," he said, "I don't understand why Terry wanted to fuck him."

DISPATCHES

January 1, 2008:
Portland haute cuisine destination Hurley's closes its doors. Owner Thomas Hurley says the restaurant "never recovered" from the bad feelings generated by its prolonged fight with In Defense of Animals over foie gras.

January 8, 2008:
The San Diego City Council passes a resolution praising the Animal Protection and Rescue League's work against foie gras and encouraging citizens "to avoid supporting this extreme form of animal cruelty."

February 6, 2008:
Rougié announces the opening of the first school devoted to foie gras in southwest France.

February 18, 2008:
Following a brick-through-the-window incident, the Animal Liberation Front vandalizes Michelin two-star restaurant Midsummer House in Cambridge, England, spraying graffiti, gluing locks and applying paint stripper to the door and window frames. Chef Daniel Clifford drops foie gras "for the safety of my staff and customers."

February 26, 2008:
Prince Charles is revealed to have ordered a royal ban on foie gras. Royal aide Andrew Farquharson says the Gloucestershire shop House of Cheese was in danger of losing its royal warrant because it was selling the product.

April 29, 2008:
The Pew Commission on Industrial Farm Animal Production recommends an end to foie gras production as well as veal crates, sow gestation crates and hen battery cages.

14.

French Immersion

"I thank them for the good liver they give me."

Here's something you should know about foie gras in France: It's sold in gas stations. Cruise along the autoroute (the French version of an interstate tollway) and pull off at one of the roadside gas station/truck stop/convenience store/cafeterias, and there, just a gumball's throw away from the roasted-chicken-flavored potato chips, is the wall of foie. The shelves hold jars and jars of it: duck, goose, whole liver, pâtés, confits, rillettes and whatever else can be produced from one of these fattened birds. Granted, you're more likely to discover such foie gras abundance in the southwest and Alsace, just as gas stations in Champagne stock you know what. But the point is it's there. Just there. No big deal.

Foie gras, in other words, isn't an event in France. It's part of the wallpaper—or, officially, the "patrimony." That's the term that was used in 2005 when the country declared foie gras a protected national product just in case the European Union attempted to take action against the delicacy in light of its critical 1998 report. France accounts for about 80 percent of the world's production and 90 percent of its consumption, and most French people scoff at the prospect of a foie gras ban. Some, however, take it seriously. Why would the country need to "protect" the product if it weren't under some kind of threat?

I traveled to France with Michaela DeSoucey, the Northwestern University foie-gras-dissertation writer who, conveniently enough, spoke French. We flew into Paris and drove directly to the southwest, where we sought out Guillermo Gonzalez's mentor, Madame Dubois. The way he'd spoken of her, she seemed to have mythical significance. You go to Yoda to learn the ways of the Jedi. You go to Madame Dubois to learn the ways of foie gras.

As it happened the Dubois farm was open as a *table et chambres d'hôtes*—that is, you can stay there and get fed heartily three times a day for a ridiculously reasonable price. The farm sits a few small, hilly roads from the tiny town of Ladornac, at the heart of the Dordogne if you can manage not to get lost. This is prime foie gras country. The density of farms may not be as high as farther southwest in Gascony and Landes, but if you're seeking foie gras tradition, you've come to the right spot. About 20 miles south is the medieval town of Sarlat, which is foie gras tourism central thanks in part to the presence of Rougié, the world's largest producer of fatty bird livers. But the Dubois farm feels about as far from commercialism as you can imagine. You drive around narrow, unmarked, winding roads that fork off without warning, and if you don't know the proper name of the farm you're visiting—in this case Peyrenègre—good luck. The houses don't have street addresses, and the streets don't have names, just numbers that are only occasionally displayed. GPS Lady (as we affectionately dubbed our robotic car guide) might as well have said, "Flip a coin" at each intersection for all the help that she was.

The Dubois farm stretches along its narrow road, covering 38 hectares (about 94 acres) with another 75 hectares (185 acres) of woods—"a little farm," as 43-year-old son Gilles deemed it. Continue about half a mile down the road, and it ends at the ancient house and farm buildings where Guy Dubois grew up and where Gilles and his family now lived. Danie, 63, and her husband, Guy, 65, who have been married for 40-plus years and have raised geese for almost the entire time, built their current home in 1971—a large farmhouse with a wide-open floor plan where the living room, dining areas, TV-watching sitting room, library/office and kitchen are all contiguous. Between the sitting room and one of the bigger dining areas is a fireplace so big that guests who smoke sit beside the logs and hold their cigarettes under the hood. On the mantel above the fireplace is a black-and-white photo of Danie's great-grandfather taken in 1913.

Danie is a somewhat squat woman with a face smoother than her years might suggest. Her mahogany-colored hair is short and tousled; her features, sharpened by rectangular, half-rimmed glasses, grew softer the longer you looked. There is nothing formal about the Duboises. The modest, perfectly comfortable guest rooms are in a separate building steps away from the main house, where Guy watched the TV news, Danie prepared dinner and chatted in the kitchen, and visitors lounged on sofas. Two other guests were there on our first night: 33-year-old Sylvan, whose parents were among the Duboises' first clients and who thus had been visiting the farm since he was a child, and his 23-year-old girlfriend, Charlene. When dinner was served, everyone sat down at the same table, with Guy pouring the homemade aperitifs and other wines and Danie shuttling in and out of the kitchen to fetch the procession of courses.

That first night Guy was pouring two homemade aperitifs: a dark red one made with walnuts grown on the farm and a white-wine-based one made with oranges. A jar of the farm's walnuts also sat on the table waiting to be gobbled by the fistful. Out of the kitchen came goose rillettes from the farm—meat that comes off the back and other stray parts and is simmered in fat and liquid with salt and pepper to create a succulent spread for home-baked crusty French bread—plus a fresh beet salad with a kicky saltiness to it and two main-course goose preparations served over pasta. One smothered the tender meat in a mustard sauce; the other was in a thick, deep-red wine sauce that was startlingly rich and intense with flavor. Danie said this latter dish took a full week to prepare: She cut the goose into chunks; put it into salt for 48 hours; roasted it a bit to melt down the fat and marinated it for another two days in red wine, carrots, onions and spices. Then Gilles took it out of the wine, cooked it with alcohol to make a flambé, added flour and pig blood and cooked it in the autoclave, which is basically a large, cylindrical pressure cooker.

Mmmm, pig blood.

They make huge quantities of this dish, *civet d'oie,* and sell heavy cans of it out of the farm shop. Back at the dinner table, what followed were plates featuring muffin-sized discs of cheese: half of them soft and raw, coming from a neighboring farm, and the other half firm and pungent thanks to Danie's having baked the raw stuff. I was ready to burst and/or keel over by this point; we'd just landed in Paris that morning, after all, and driven six-plus hours to the Dordogne on almost no sleep. The cheese course was my coup de grâce. Then came the crème anglaise. I surrendered.

Guy is tall and lean, somewhat amazing given the volume of food that Danie serves—and, yes, she said, they eat this way every night—and the frequency with which foie gras is part of the menu, often more than twice in one meal. (That would come the following day.) Guy had graying caterpillar eyebrows, and the rest of his hair was pretty much the same; it didn't grow so much as it sprouted. He was soft-spoken and talked in a more colloquial French than Danie (so explained Michaela), but he said plenty through gentle smiles. He and Danie had been lodging and feeding people for three decades and spoke hardly a word of English between them. But they were very patient as I leaned on Michaela to translate what I was saying to them and what they were saying to me.

The Duboises run their farm in the quiet conviction that they're doing things the right way, that they treat their animals as well as possible, and what they produce is as good and traditional as you'll find anywhere. Danie told a story of being at an event in San Francisco with legendary French chef Paul Bocuse and Ariane Daguin where all three of them had to make a duck foie gras terrine, and hers lost the least fat and was proclaimed the best. "*Magnifique*," she said matter-of-factly. Later in our visit, she would prepare that very terrine from her fresh goose livers, although it wouldn't be ready to eat until after we left. As we'd walk by the porcelain containers, she'd say, "*Voilà*."

She was proud that her protégé Guillermo Gonzalez had launched such a successful business in the United States based on her techniques, yet she wasn't interested in trying to replicate such commercial success in France. Although the Dubois family had a Web site listing the farm's offerings and room rates, they wouldn't accept credit cards, and customers generally went to the farm's little shop to pick up their products, or Gilles delivered them.

In that one-room shop, located in the building where the foie gras, confits, rillettes and other goose products are prepared, white porcelain geese of various sizes lined the shelves. Back in the house, goose figurines were everywhere: on walls, shelves, water pitchers, even sprouting up three-dimensionally from plates on which cold foie gras slices were served. You couldn't miss the three large white cut-out geese standing on the front lawn. There was also a mural of a straw-hatted woman seated next to a gray goose inside the bus shelter across the street, not that we ever saw a bus. Many of Danie's figurines were white geese, which, she informed us, are considered kings in France; thus they don't undergo gavage, at least not the blue-eyed ones. They're cooked on a spit instead. Danie had collected a fair number of chicken figurines as well because, she said, she was growing bored with all of those geese. As for duck likenesses, I spotted just two. The Dubois farm has little use for ducks. Geese rule.

The live ones arrive on the farm as hatchlings. They leave in jars and cans. In between, they experience more than six months of life with Danie, Guy and Gilles. "A farm is like a whole world," Danie said. "You have everything here, birth to death." When Michaela and I arrived, 740 geese were on the premises. One hundred and fifty were in gavage. Thirty had been killed that morning, and another 24 would be meeting their maker the following day. Meanwhile, a new batch of babies had recently arrived from an incubator in central France; they're delivered six times a year, 250 to 450 each time.

For several generations Danie's and Guy's families had been raising geese for foie gras, and to Danie this activity was about more than cultural tradition or business. "It's the money of the woman of the farm," she said. "It was only the grandmother who force-fed. They sold two or three goose foie gras, and it was the only money that the woman kept at the farm. When I was married, it was Guy's father who dispensed money to everyone. I wanted to earn my own proper money. My first foie gras helped me to buy my first plates. Before, I had nothing, nothing." She started out feeding 30 geese and selling them to Bizac, a company that processed them, "And that was my first money."

Geese, she said, are smarter than ducks, and their livers are more refined and melt less. Of course, the idea of some birds being smarter than others could be seen as a plus or minus as far as raising and killing them goes. As you sit down for your Thanksgiving feast, you may be reassured by the myth that turkeys are so tiny brained that they drown themselves looking upward at raindrops. That's not true, of course, but we're perfectly happy to believe that turkeys and other animals we eat are dummies.

Walking from the Dubois house to where the animals lived, one passes a double-decker set of cages where rabbits are kept for future meals. Just beyond that is a small fenced-off area where the Duboises have raised chickens for eggs and, more recently, meat; the farm doesn't make the common American distinction between layers and broilers. Somehow a goose named Gertrude had gotten got mixed into the delivery of chicks, and she was constantly honking and bounding after the other birds. It was easy to project a personality onto this goose: bossy, gregarious. But when Guy led us to a large barn holding 340 two-month-old geese, they walked around in a big circle as if controlled by a joystick. "Large numbers of any animal are stupid when you put them together, even people," Danie said. "When you have just a few geese or a few ducks on a farm, they're pretty smart. A goose can guard the house, protect things."

These geese certainly were elegant, with silver coats, white tail feathers and bright orange beaks. They looked more regal and substantial than the many ducks I'd seen up to this point, and they appeared to be relatively at peace. Each barn had cinderblock walls with a green tarp stretched over the top, and Guy was about to replace the straw floor in the barn housing the two-month-olds, as he did daily when the birds were spending most of their time on the rolling field. (Cleanings were even more frequent when bad weather kept the geese inside.) The barn air was suffused with a slight ammonia smell and general goose gaminess. Guy opened a small square door in the barn's corner and sent in Volga, a well-behaved black-and-white border collie, to clear the room. Volga had fine-tuned her system of herding and mobilizing these birds. Running back and forth and barking, she divided the group into thirds and hustled them out the little door in scrambling clusters, feathers flying in the air. It was like a cattle-rustling scene in *Red River*, with waterfowl.

Outside, the birds again moved in sync in a big pack, a mass of silver dramatically offset by orange. Volga watched as they pecked at the grass and insects. Guy held two yellow buckets beneath one of two small silos outside the barn, filling them with cereal-based gray pellets. The grain for the cereal was grown on the farm. Inside the barn Guy poured the cereal into six blue buckets suspended from the ceiling with red rims at the bottom to hold the food. Water troughs were off to the left. Michaela asked Guy whether the geese were happy, and he responded, "They like the house because that's where they eat. They're content." The concept of goose happiness didn't quite register with him.

We moved on to a similar barn where the hatchlings lived. Gas radiators kept the air warm. These little fuzzy guys would remain in here for three weeks. They were males and females alike; unlike with ducks, both sexes of geese are thought to produce fat livers of equal quality, so there's no need to weed out the females. These geese had a longer lifespan than foie gras ducks, growing for a full six months before the force-feeding began. The gavage period lasted up to 21 days, with feedings twice a day at first, four times daily toward the end. Gilles did the feeding and, eventually, the slaughter; he took over these two jobs from Danie about 15 years back. To Danie, it was important for one person to oversee both duties. "*C'est la vie*. It's life. Morally it is better that I do it from the beginning until the end, to accompany them to the end. The satisfaction at the end of my work is that it doesn't suffer at the end of its life. I thank them for the good liver they give me."

Does she think the birds suffer in general? "No, not at all. Not at all. Of that I am persuaded."

The slaughter was staggered as Gilles, a slender man of medium height and easy disposition, took into account the geese's varying metabolisms and selected only those who, along with their livers, had grown to the right size. Starting about 17 days into the gavage, Gilles would run his hand under each goose's belly as he fed it, and when he felt that the liver was large enough, he'd take out a scissors and clip some feathers from the top of its head. This little "haircut" meant that the goose would exit the living world the following morning.

The gavage geese, in groups of 10 or so, were kept in 24 pens lined up along the room's side walls. Gilles wore the same olive-drab jumpsuit every time he entered the room and moved from pen to pen to feed the geese. When they saw him, they remained calm, but when Michaela and I poked in our heads with Gilles not around, they honked and honked. One dead goose was lying alone in the last pen on the left. Gilles said it probably had suffered a heart attack. "It doesn't happen every day, but near the end of gavage it sometimes does," he said. "It's like us; sometimes you have a heart attack."

The food was a mélange of whole corn and *farine de maïs,* corn ground into a powder and mixed with water to create a yellow paste. The machine, which Gilles said the farm acquired in 1985, was as tall as he was and moved down the center aisle on wheels. The attached tube was about the length of a goose's neck, and the paste came out with the force of someone slowly squeezing a toothpaste tube. Gilles rolled the machine up to one of the pens, stationed himself inside so the geese were between him and the back wall, and started working his way through them. The process was efficient but never felt violent. Gilles remained relaxed and nonchalant throughout, and so for the most part did the geese. They didn't flap their wings or honk. They weren't rushing, beaks open, toward the feeding machine, but they weren't resisting either. When the occasional one wriggled a bit, Gilles whispered, "*Doucement. Doucement.*" ("Calm. Calm.") The bird usually complied. The only sudden movements came when the occasional goose, after being fed, whipped its head from side to side like the Aflac duck reacting to a Yogi Berra malapropism. Often this jerky motion caused some of the corn paste to spray out of its beak and onto its neighbors' feathers. (Yes, this was what the activists had been calling vomit in various photos.)

"Do the animals actually enjoy the gavage?" I asked Gilles.

He shrugged. "I don't think so really. I don't think they especially like it, but it doesn't do them any harm."

The following morning Gilles returned to the room and, one by one, picked up each of the 24 geese that had received "haircuts" the previous evening. As the bird sat calmly in a sort of nesting squat atop his hands, he carried it out the door, took a sharp left in a tiny hallway and entered the last room this animal would ever see—not that it gave any indication that it realized as such, even with newly killed geese with red-spattered beaks hanging upside down from a conveyor belt moving slowly over a blood-drenched metal trough.

The abattoir was musty and steamy with a slightly sour odor. The walls were white, the floors tiled in gradients of yellow to brown, with bright red puddles glistening in many spots. The whole family was there: Guy in his wheat-colored wool sweater, blue jeans, green baseball cap and blue apron; Danie in a white lab jacket with a colorful striped shirt peeking out from beneath, a cream-colored rubber apron and matching rubber boots; Gilles in that same olive zippered suit and green rubber boots; and his wife Cécile and Danie's young assistant Laura in white lab jackets, aprons and blue hair nets. They each had several jobs to do as the birds entered the final leg of their journey to become artisanal farm product.

Gilles carried the goose alongside the trough until he reached two large bronze-colored cones positioned over a rubber garbage can. With one smooth motion, Gilles flipped the bird forward and upside down into the cone, its tail feathers sticking out of the top, and stunned it with an electric current. He clutched a thin, yellow-handled knife, about 3 inches long, pulled the goose's head out from a slot at the cone's bottom, inserted the knife through the front of the throat and cut outward, severing the carotid artery. The blood drained into the can, which shielded the goose's head from view, though its feet could be seen kicking and twitching a bit, some more and longer than others. Occasionally a goose managed to raise its head out of the cone as well as the rubber can, blood spraying out of its neck onto the floor before Gilles tucked the head back into the can and turned his attention to the next bird.

After a few minutes, any kicking or twitching ended, and Gilles took the bird and suspended it by the feet from a metal hanger that moved slowly along the overhead conveyor belt for a journey similar to that in the Hudson Valley slaughterhouse: bleeding into a trough, plunging into scalding water, being defeathered on tabletop machines (by Guy) and being cleaned and having remaining feather fragments blowtorched (by Cécile and Laura).

In the adjacent narrow room, Danie hung the carcass by its head on a wall hanger and sliced down its abdomen to reveal the liver. "*Voilà*," she said. She pulled out the intestines, and with a knife she separated the gizzard—a blue-and-red organ about the size of a Hacky Sack bag—from this noodley mass and placed it into a small rectangular white tray. The intestines went into a garbage can. Now it was time to remove the liver: two attached, wobbly, almond-colored lobes that filled out the goose's abdominal cavity. This was, yes, hot evisceration, meaning that the liver was being taken out of a freshly killed bird. The Duboises had switched from cold evisceration about five years earlier due to a French regulation that the liver be removed immediately to avoid contact with other organs. She tucked her hands under the rib cage and pulled gently—"*Voilà*"—and placed the yellowish blob into a larger white plastic tray next to the one holding the gizzards. Some areas had faint red tints, some had slight purplish bruises, but on the whole these livers looked creamy, smooth, almost flan-like. As she poked at one particularly firm one, she complained, "It's too big."

When the morning's work was done, two neat rows of livers sat in the tray, and 24 goose carcasses hung beaks up on a tall rolling cart near the door to the outside. On the floor beneath the cart, drops of blood had created a small puddle. The sweet-natured Volga, so well trained that she follows you to each building but respectfully remains outside, had been lingering beyond the abattoir entrance, the hanging geese in plain sight. Finally she could resist no longer, quietly stuck her head through the doorway and began lapping up that goose blood.

Inside the slaughter room, Gilles was spraying the slightly pitched floor with a hose, the blood and grime going down a hole in the center next to the defeathering machine, which had wet, gray feathers sticking out of its base. The feathers would be stored in metal containers outside the building and eventually shipped to a factory to be turned into down. "Everything is used," Danie said. She was happy to have visitors observe the whole process because "it's a really good education for people. For the older people especially, it justifies the price to see the amount of care taken with each bird."

In the afternoon the family would reconvene to finish preparing the livers and the rest of the goose products. But first came lunch. The appetizer was a foie gras conserve: portions of whole liver that had been heated in a jar with salt and pepper, then cooled, sliced and presented on a plate with a quarter moon of bright yellow goose fat clinging to the side. You ate it on Danie's crusty bread, either leaving the goose fat on the plate (as I did) or heaping it onto the bread with the foie (as Sylvan did). The main course was cassoulet, the traditional southwestern France bean stew made in this case with goose meat. It was delicious, but that didn't stop Danie from giving the leftover portion to Volga, who gobbled it up. Apparently Volga enjoys a gourmet diet even beyond goose blood drippings. Sylvan said the last time he was at the farm, Danie had given Volga a serving of foie gras. "Danie was just bored to see this piece of goose liver in the fridge waiting to be eaten, and she said, 'For the dog.'"

After lunch everyone moved into the *conserverie,* a 20-year-old antiseptic one-story building with a walk-in cold chamber plus separate rooms for cutting up the carcasses, deveining and processing the livers, cooking the confits and rillettes, and sterilizing and sealing jars and cans. The shop occupies a small room at the front of this building, with the basement stocked with shelves upon shelves of jars and cans. The cart carrying the hanging goose carcasses sat in the cold chamber while we ate lunch, but afterward it was moved directly in front of a window in a chilly white room with fluorescent lights. From outside you could see these dead birds framed by the window, a perfectly composed shot. Then a hand would reach for one of them and remove it from the picture. Inside, Laura and Cécile were cutting up the geese on metal tables, their quiet chopping punctuated by ripping and cracking sounds as they tore off what was left of the wings and separated the *magrets,* legs, backs and necks. Laura pulled the neck skin inside out over one hand like a glove and used the other hand to cut away any remaining fat. Later these skins would be stuffed with foie gras and goose meat to make a galantine (a cold French dish involving forcemeat pressed into a cylinder and poached).

In the adjacent room, Gilles and Danie wielded small knives with surgical precision to devein the livers. Gilles, now in a white apron and chef's hat, examined the bruise on one piece and excised that part to go into a product that doesn't require top-grade foie gras. Aside from deveining and cutting away the trouble spots, Gilles and Danie were deeming which livers were worthy of being preserved whole—the equivalent of grade A—and which should be used for pâté, aiguillettes, galantine or *magret* slices wrapped around foie gras. Gilles cut off the tips of each liver because they were firmer; they were pâté bound.

He tested the quality of each liver in the most basic way imagin-
able: He'd slip a piece of it from his knife into his mouth. If it was
smooth and silky, it would go into the *entier* jars or be vacuum packed
and sold whole. If it was grainy, it would be used for other products.
Gilles cut off a sliver and held it out to me on the knife tip. Yes, I was
being asked to taste raw foie gras almost straight from the goose.
Well, when in France . . .

I plopped it into my mouth and ran it over my tongue. It
tasted . . . raw. It was velvety and butter-like, if butter had sinew. I
imagined the experience wasn't drastically different from drinking
milk straight from a cow; the foie had an almost dairy-like quality and
felt directly connected to nature, no filter. The goose liver may be mild
and delicate, but the impact was strong, primal. It was powerfully flavorful, and I did not ask for another piece. But Gilles kept sampling
bits of each liver, all the better to maintain quality control. "My kids
have it, too," he said, saying they popped it into their mouths the way
other kids might sneak bites of cookie dough.

After deveining her livers, Danie cut them into various portion
sizes and weighed them before stuffing them into the appropriate
jars and adding salt and pepper The foie gras to be sold *mi-cuit* (half
cooked) would be cooked in the autoclave for 45 minutes at 70 degrees Celsius (158 degrees Fahrenheit). The conserve, which unlike
the *mi-cuit* could be stored without refrigeration, was cooked at 102
degrees Celsius (216 degrees Fahrenheit) for an hour and 15 minutes.
In another room a white plastic bucket full of goose fat was dumped
into a big metal container and heated, and the meat-caked carcasses
were added to the brim; the meat that would fall off the bone would
become the rillettes. The legs also were cooked in fat to make confit.

Some of that day's fresh liver would find its way to the dinner
table that night. As an appetizer Danie brought out a plate of toast
slices on which she had placed thin discs of *cru* (that is, raw) foie gras,
which melted into the hot toast like butter. On top she had sprinkled
salt and pepper. This was another primal eating experience. The foie
was rich and gamey, like consuming the distilled essence of farm life.
"This is the only place where you would find this," enthused Sylvan
as he ate one toast-foie slice after another. "The goose is killed in the
morning, and you eat this at night." Next came a light soup made

from garlic, potato, egg, goose fat and vinegar, followed by, yes, more foie gras. This serving was *mi-cuit,* and it was more satiny than the *cru* stuff. It was like butter, but butter melts in your mouth faster. This stayed on the tongue, then on the palate. For the main course, Danie emerged with big plate of roasted goose backs with a smattering of meat (and the small kidneys) attached. There wasn't much to eat on each one, so you wound up accumulating a healthy pile of bones on your plate after trying to get your teeth into every last nook and cranny of the carcass. Not an ounce of this bird was going to waste.

I asked our hosts to name their favorite foie gras preparations. Guy opted for the *cru* with salt and pepper. Danie preferred the *mi-cuit,* also Michaela's favorite. Danie said she's not crazy about hot preparations because she feels the foie gras's subtlety comes out only when it is served cold. Plenty of wine was poured, another cheese course was served, plus a flaky pear tart for dessert. Around this time I realized that I was going to be in France for almost exactly the same amount of time that a duck is force-fed. I was experiencing my own personal gavage, albeit of my own free will and without a tube.

We managed to put off our departure until early afternoon the following day, so Danie insisted we join them for lunch, thus giving her the opportunity to stuff us with more foie gras—this time wrapped in the *magrets*—and more of that goose in red wine/blood sauce. Funny, I was a bit queasy about the whole pig-blood element the first time round, but now I found the dish almost addictive. Before we got in the car, Danie expressed her concern that Guillermo Gonzalez might have to stop producing his "very, very good foie gras"—and that the anti-foie movement might prevail in France as well. This statement surprised Michaela and me; we were under the impression that foie gras was culturally entrenched here and that the animal-rights activists held far less sway. Did she really think the product could be banned in France?

"Yes, it's begun. Brigitte Bardot!" She laughed, referring to the actress/activist who recently had begun agitating against foie gras. "In France, the same, yes. It's possible."

What about France's protecting foie gras as part of its "patrimony"?

"I think that it is not sufficient," she said.

Other cultural forces were at work. Lifestyles were changing. Professional desires were changing. Agriculture was changing, with small French family farms subject to some similar pressures as those in the United States. Even in the Dordogne, Danie had noticed a decrease in foie gras farms and lack of new farmers to fill the gap. Few young people apparently were saying, "Hey, I want to force-feed and slaughter birds for a living." The older generations had stayed on the farm. The next generation represented a big question mark. "It's unfortunate, because it represents our good quality of life," she said. "We are going to lose good food, nature. It is for this reason that I want to keep doing this—to continue the cuisine of my mother, my grandmother. The *paysanne* [countrywoman] is happy to transmit this extraordinary life to, I hope, our grandchildren. It's for that."

15.

Foie Gras Weekend

"The animal after the feeding seems just like the animal before."

From Périgord, Michaela and I drove farther into the heart of duckness, heading southwest to the medieval town of Auch. Our purpose was to meet André Daguin, Ariane's dad, legendary for his preparations of foie gras and the *magret*. Daguin realized that if you cooked the *magret* rare, you could serve it like steak. This happened in 1959, when Daguin was running the kitchen of the Hôtel de France in Auch. As mentioned earlier, his father had been the prestigious restaurant's chef, and his grandfather had cooked there. Daguin's *magret* revelation was one of the reasons the number of ducks processed in France had risen so dramatically. The lesson he learned? "A cook could change the economy," he said.

Seventy-two years old when we spoke to him, Daguin sold the restaurant and hotel in 1997 and did not remain on good terms with the new owners. His large, impeccably decorated Auch house (he and his wife spent weekends there and weekdays in their Paris home) is just a few buildings down the hill from the Hôtel de France, but he hadn't set foot inside the hotel for years. The retired chef has a bull-like energy about him, though his balding head, white sideburns and bushy eyebrows suggest more of a fierce eagle. He has a deep, booming voice and a corresponding air of authority, and he punctuates his points with table knocking and sound effects. He has little patience for those who, in his view, know little about foie gras yet want to prohibit it from being enjoyed.

"When I was a boy, we used to receive chickens, rabbits, and we killed them," he said. "Man eats animals. And every time you see the way animals are killed by man, it's much cleaner, much faster than the way they are killed in the wild. I used to look often at animals on the television. When you see hyenas eating a buffalo alive, I prefer to be killed in an abattoir than to be killed this way." Foie gras, he noted, wasn't controversial when he was growing up. What sparked the change? "People stayed childish," he declared.

I asked whether he preferred goose or duck foie gras, and he replied: "Cold, goose. Hot, duck."

Daguin does make hot foie gras, but he's not fond of searing hot slices; he prefers to steam the whole lobe, then to slice it, add a little salt and pepper and put it in the broiler. This way, he said, "you don't burn the fat." The classic preparation of this dish, the one that introduced him to these fattened livers back when he was seven or so (and the Hôtel de France was full of German soldiers), came in a deep, round, covered dish, "and when you opened it, it had a sauce, black sauce, the liver and grapes. It was sweet, salt and acid, because the secret was to make a caramel with vinegar, and then you finish the sauce with caramel vinegar, and it made a *psheeeew*. That was my foie gras."

He ate so much that he felt sick, but still, he was hooked. He tried to sum up what makes it so special: "Because it's tender. Then the taste is long. Foie gras is like Sauternes, and foie gras is sweet by itself, and you can play with all the other tastes, except bitter."

André Daguin didn't cook for us, but after we drove west into the Landes region, Michel Guérard prepared a knockout menu for us at the gourmet restaurant at the three-Michelin-star country resort Les Prés d'Eugénie, which he and his wife Christine own. Included were two duck foie gras dishes: a cold appetizer in which the liver was wrapped in a paper cocoon and cooked in ash, accompanied by a peach wine gelée; and a hot entrée in which the foie gras was cooked in pastry along with tender pigeon in Guérard's spin on a classic baked pâté. "Foie gras, it's not easy," he told us. "There are ingredients that have an aura, a soul."

Our journey continued with a drive to the small town of Gimont for its foie gras market. From November through March, the southwest is dotted with such markets; you could go to one or more every day of the week. Gimont's weekly Wednesday market proved so popular that the town added another one on Sunday, the day we went. The Gimont market isn't the biggest one in the Gers region; the Monday one in nearby Samatan is considerably larger and frequented more by chefs, who travel many miles to stock up on ducks, geese and their livers. But Gimont is plenty big—particularly to someone who had never previously shared a room with 1,000 bird carcasses and their carefully presented fat organs—and being there is an out-of-time experience. If you took in the scene, with dozens of farmers presenting their freshly killed wares on tabletops to be inspected and purchased by neighboring villagers, you'd have no idea whether you were in the 1950s or the 2000s.

A narrow road runs through this 13th-century hilltop town, and at the center is a covered market where, on this morning, vendors sold breads, meats and, in the case of a rather unhinged, toothless woman railing loudly against the government, caged porcupines and exotic-looking birds. Take a side street down the hill, and you hit the larger, car-friendly thruway where a cavernous municipal building sits beside a parking lot shared with a small patisserie. A poster out front featured a drawing of an elegant, happy young woman waving with one hand while the other toted a basket containing a content-looking live goose and duck.

Inside the entryway was a chained-off area where market attendees clustered beforehand; the crowd swelled to the hundreds as the clock ticked toward the opening whistle. Entry was free, and patrons had come from the surrounding area and the largest nearby city, Toulouse (about 30 miles to the east), as well as from such distant cities as Marseille and Nice. Signs indicated this schedule: "9H30 carcasses. 10H30 foie." I took this to mean that vendors would sell their geese and ducks at 9:30 a.m. and then the livers at 10:30 a.m. Actually, what it meant was that everything went on sale right at 10.

So everyone stood around in this well-lit, chilly, warehouse-like space and watched as, beyond the ropes, the sellers laid out their wares on more than 20 long rows of tables that stretched down the room with an aisle running down the center.

"Can I just buy legs?" one woman asked another as they waited.

"No, you have to buy the whole thing," the other replied.

On each table 40 or more birds lay on their backs, their foie-removing surgery scars exposed (some a straight line down the center, others with a big "U" at the bottom), their heads hanging down over the side. The goose tables were located toward the front on the right; the ducks were everywhere else. One man skittering down a side aisle knocked into one of the dangling goose heads and left it swinging like a pendulum. White paper napkins had been wrapped around many of the birds' necks, with their weights in kilos scrawled in marker: 7.6, 7.5, 6.7, 7.8. Throughout the market, the ducks and geese were uniformly priced at 2.2 euros per kilo (about $1.50 per pound at the time), and the livers were 35 euros per kilo (about $23 per pound). Some of the birds leaked stray drips of blood onto the tan tile floor.

The sellers were fairly evenly split between men and women, longtime veterans of feeding and raising birds. At the first table on the left, a farmer named Sara Da Costa proudly lifted the lid from a white plastic tray to reveal rows of fresh, creamy-complexioned livers that she had harvested the previous day. Warmed by a green fleece, she was a short, rugged woman with blond hair and gray roots; she looked like the rural French version of British actress Imelda Staunton. She'd gotten up at 3:30 that morning, force-fed her ducks, then driven across many towns to the market. She'd been doing gavage for more than 30 years—just ducks because "it's easier to do"—and she was selling at three markets a week. In her thick regional accent, Da Costa said her customers were primarily everyday people loading up for the holidays and the rest of the year. Her ducks had pale blotchy skin and the standard neck wounds, which to the untrained eye meant they resembled just about all of the ducks in the room. I commented that she had a good table up front because everyone waiting to enter could see her. She shook her head and replied, "The middle is better. People come in and go right to the middle."

At a few minutes before 10, the market's manager, a twinkle-eyed, balding, gray-mustached man who had let us roam around the selling area, suggested that we get back behind the chains so we wouldn't get trampled when he blew his whistle. He was only half joking. As he stood in front of the entrance checking and double-checking his watch, the crowd grew increasingly restless, whistling and calling out (in French), "It's time!" and "Let us in already!" The manager smiled, glancing up at the wall clock. He wasn't budging until that minute hand did. Finally, he slowly lifted the whistle to his mouth and blew.

It was like *Red River*, but with people. The throngs streamed into the room and went straight to tables that, in many cases, they'd obviously targeted in advance. Some rolled wheelbarrows down the side aisles; one woman immediately piled one duck atop another atop another atop another, then wheeled away her full load. Others stuck the livers and carcasses into large plastic bags. The activity was fast and fierce, and the transactions took place with a minimum of chit-chat. As a boy of about seven carried a tray of foies into the back room to pay, a gray-haired man pretended to grab them from him, prompting the kid to cry out playfully, "They're mine! They're mine!"

Back on the main floor, buyers placed their carcasses atop a large table where three men wearing butcher whites and paper hats chopped off the birds' heads and wings with a few quick chops of their cleavers. Tall garbage cans quickly filled with duck and goose heads and other stray parts. The ducks and geese disappeared quickly from some sellers' tables while others remained cluttered with the pale carcasses. Likewise, as people prodded, poked and took close-up looks at the livers, some trays were emptied within minutes while others went relatively untouched. Some foies were larger than others. Some were peach colored; some were tan. Some had few blemishes; some were blotchy, bruised and marked with green bile spots. Those latter ones tended to remain in their trays. Sara Da Costa was having a good morning after all; within a half hour, her inventory was almost cleared out.

By 11:30, the activity had wound down, and many sellers were packing up their empty trays. Other vendors stood around forlornly, hoping for some late business to relieve them of their still-sizable inventories. It was cold enough outside that Michaela and I probably could have picked up a foie or a whole goose or duck and kept it in the trunk until we found a place to prepare it. But we didn't. We knew our quality time with duck carcasses lay ahead.

If you're keeping a list of Things That Are Different Between the United States and France, here's something to add: In France, you can go on a "Foie Gras Weekend." This wasn't just a stay-on-the-farm deal as with the Duboises. With this package you chop up your own duck and make your own foie gras that you can take home along with other bird parts that you have preserved. There's a wacky Chevy Chase movie in here somewhere.

An increasing number of farms in the southwest have begun hosting these experiences over the past decade, tapping into a market among French people desiring to regain their connections with country life. Michaela and I signed up for one at a farm run by a Madame Daubas (not to be confused with Dubois). We would arrive Monday around 9 a.m. (the "weekend" part was not to be taken literally), do our butchering and preserving, spend the night on the farm, and finish the preparations the following morning. We each would get our own duck.

After taking the scenic route among the barely marked, winding Gers roads, we walked into an old pink farmhouse labeled "Escala" and were met by the woman decidedly in charge, Myriam Daubas. "Let's get to work," she said in French, immediately handing us white lab jackets and rubber boots to protect us from stray innards.

Madame Daubas was no-nonsense in a kindly, fast-talking sort of way. With her pulled-back curlyish auburn hair, wide-set hazel eyes and dramatically sculpted face, she resembled an actress who had been considered a hot number and a bit dangerous once upon a time. Now she was a divorced mother to a 17-year-old motocross-racer of a son, and her "complicated" (her word) life could be read into her fortysomething features. She was a commanding presence at any rate, leading us from the kitchen through a small utilities room (stocked with foie products) and into a bright, narrow room with a white-tiled floor and matching counter that stretched along the back wall with a large old sink at its center. Atop this counter, two duck carcasses lay on their backs, their heads and necks hanging far over the edge.

There wasn't much yellow to them—they were more a pale tan—and they had little brown pimples where their feathers used to be. The wings were rimmed with blood, and their heads were blotchy and red purple, like they'd just gone 10 rounds and weren't boasting, "You should've seen the other guy." Their necks were marked with telltale gashes.

They also were cold. I must admit that I was disappointed about this last point. I had envisioned us getting to butcher freshly killed ducks with warm, blobby insides. I thought we might get to see our ducks slaughtered before we whacked them to bits—or even that we might get to play God, choose our own ducks and do the lethal knife work ourselves. Call me a bloodthirsty bastard, but I felt like if I was going to have the full, honest experience of dealing with the consequences of foie gras, then I should have to do the dirty work. That's not to say that this work didn't turn out to be plenty dirty—at least if duck fat, blood, bile and the bizarrely yellow, gravelly stuff you must manually scrape from the insides of duck gizzards count—but I wanted zero degrees of separation.

Plus, these weren't even our hostess's ducks. Madame Daubas is one of the few French farmers to raise Barbary (the French name for Muscovy) ducks instead of the far more popular and durable Mulards, which are crossbred from the male Muscovy and female Pekin. The Barbaries, she said, don't get as fat, and she, like Guillermo Gonzalez, finds the livers tastier. More to the point, her parents and her parents' parents fed Barbary ducks, and tradition trumps all. So she kept 48 Barbaries in gavage for about 16 days apiece, repeating this cycle six times a year. This isn't a huge output, but then she doesn't even have a license to distribute to shops. She sells half of the ducks to customers at the farm, and the other half she preserves to sell to vacationers who stay in her guest rooms—and she doesn't even have enough for them, so she winds up supplementing her supply with foie gras from another farm. So chances are that if you visit Madame Daubas's farm, you're not likely to arrive on a day when she's slaughtering her own ducks. At any rate we didn't, so she had fetched some Mulards from a neighbor's farm for us to butcher. They'd been slaughtered Saturday and kept refrigerated until Monday morning: i.e., now.

Madame Daubas pulled one of the ducks onto the white cutting

board, started speaking quickly in French, grabbed a cleaver and—
whop! whop!—the head and neck were neighbors no more. She ca-
sually flipped the head into a garbage can beneath the counter and
took a knife to the wing joints, one after the other, slicing the skin,
then cracking the joints backward until the bones separated. *Slice,
rip, slice, rip*—off came the wing pieces, tossed into a deep plastic
tray on the floor where most of the meat would go. Then she sliced
a circle around the base of the neck, dug her fingers into the thick
fat and, with the casual motion of removing a turtleneck sweater,
pulled the skin up and over the long neck and the space where the
duck's head used to be. After this procedure, what remained was a
sad, pallid carcass like you might find in a store, except that it had
something resembling a male pony's dangling appendage protruding from the top.

Next she took a knife and sliced down the center of the duck,
careful not to cut all the way through to the liver. At the bottom she
opened it up and yanked out the intestines and other innards, setting
aside the fat-encased gizzard. Using the knife precisely and quickly to
separate meat from fat, she peeled back the left breast as if opening a
dinner jacket, then said something quickly in French, handed me the
knife and gestured for me to take over. Oh, crap. Let me just mention
that there were four of us participating in this "Foie Gras Weekend":
Michaela and myself plus Isabelle Téchoueyres, an anthropologist
from Bordeaux with whom Michaela had co-authored a paper, and
a relatively burly middle-aged man with a bushy mustache named
Dany, who lived to the east in Montpellier and recently had retired
from Goodyear Tires. I was the only one who didn't speak French,
and Madame Daubas was talking way too quickly for Michaela to
translate for me. So I just took the knife, played some *Psycho* music
in my head and got to work.

I stuck the knife in and tried to peel back the duck's right breast.
No go. I sliced and scraped a bit, and Madame Daubas managed to
refrain from rolling her eyes. Instead she spoke more rapid French
to me. When I got too close to disfiguring the *magret,* she swooped
in, took the knife and demonstrated quickly the precise crevices
where I should be jabbing and whittling. I tried again and finally
got the right flank open with a vivid ripping sound. Hence I found

myself looking at a former duck, a meaty flap of breast laid out on each side, rib cage front and center. At the bottom of this rib cage was the big foie just waiting to be removed. It looked creamy, like a firm custard made from a Starbucks latte heavy on the milk, and it was tucked tightly against the bottom of the rib cage like it couldn't grow any further.

I was ready to pull that sucker out, though I wasn't sure how. Forceps? Wait, I had to cut away those *magrets* and legs first. The trick for the former was to slice as closely as possible to the rib cage, poking and scraping against the bone so the knife wouldn't come into contact with the breast meat. I applied my knife gingerly and slowly. Madame Daubas took the knife and with a quick motion sliced off one flap and returned the knife for me to finish the job. I did, eventually, and the meat went into the same bin on the floor that held the wings. As for the legs, this surgery wasn't much different than amputating the drumsticks and thighs on a broiler chicken.

Now to the foie: The idea was to stick your fingers up under the rib cage and pull out the liver without mangling it. It was kind of like delivering a baby—that is, a cool, custardy liver baby that doesn't cry or squirm. I got my hands into what I thought was the correct position and pulled, but the liver didn't want to move; it sure was jammed up in there. I reached up farther, feeling the liver give slightly beneath my fingers—I had a horrific vision of my fingertips disappearing into the liver like bananas plunged into pudding. I pulled again to no avail. Madame Daubas gave a command that I assumed to mean "Harder!" and I yanked that foie out. Its shape wasn't bad; it looked similar to the whole livers I'd seen vacuum packed at Hudson Valley, with one lobe about twice the size of the other. Madame Daubas put it on the countertop scale, and it weighed just over 550 grams (1.21 pounds). Congratulations, Mr. Caro, you are the parent of a robust foie gras.

The only part that marred the picture was the almost neon green-and-yellow stain on the side: bile. When you're dealing with livers, bile happens. Any foie cookbook warns you to cut away such bright blotches of bitterness. You don't want to eat them or anything that has come into contact with them. I certainly didn't. But preparing the foies would come later.

First it was Michaela's turn to take the cleaver and knife to that other sad-looking duck on the counter. When it came time for Michaela to lop off the head, she handed me the cleaver. I'd love to say this was because she was squeamish about the whole thing, but actually she suspected I was disappointed over not beheading my own duck. (People, we're talking about professional obligation here.) At any rate, it looked easy enough. *Whack, whack, whack*—hmm, maybe I should've raised the cleaver a little higher or hammered down with a bit more force because I kept inflicting parallel gashes on this poor bird's neck without actually severing it. Madame Daubas said something to me that I think meant: "Hit it harder and not in a different place each time." *Whack, whack, whack, whack*—OK, it wasn't pretty, but I got the job done. The room offered only enough counter space for one, so each of us had to stand around and watch the designated chopper. After Michaela was through, Madame Daubas brought out Dany's two ducks (he and Isabelle each had ordered a pair), and he put us to shame with his powerhouse cleaver work—one *whack* and out—and expert ripping and slicing.

"You've done this before," I said to Dany, who spoke basic English.

"No," he replied with a shrug.

When he pulled up the neck skin on one of his birds, several stray kernels of corn fell onto the table. Slicing open the abdomen produced a torrent of more kernels, which all but oozed out of the carcass. After Dany removed the foie, it sat on the counter with a single corn kernel perched atop it. Because the gizzard is considered a delicacy, one of our jobs was to cut each one open, turn it inside out like a halved tennis ball and scrape out the bright yellow gravel and muck that had collected in there. Dany's bird's gizzard was filled with, yes, more corn. I have to be honest here: Seeing the ducks' heads chopped off, intestines ripped out and hugely enlarged livers removed didn't particularly faze me, but all of that undigested food spilling out of various parts of this bird grossed me out; the duck had become a corn piñata. This one's liver, no surprise, turned out to be the largest of the bunch: a full 700 grams (a bit more than one and a half pounds, which actually isn't huge by American standards), with the smaller lobe almost equal in size to the larger one.

All of the meat went into that big tray on the floor—the *magrets,* legs, wings, necks and backs. The skin and fat were tossed into another tray. The only parts that wound up in the garbage can were the intestines and head. Myriam liberally sprinkled salt over the meat to cure it overnight; the following morning we would prepare and jar our confits. Now we had to cut up our foies.

The first task was to cut away the frightening fluorescence, as each liver had a sizable bile blotch, sometimes deceptively located; you'd think yours was clean, but then you'd separate the lobes to discover lemon-lime Kool-Aid stains on both inner surfaces. Slicing off the discolored areas made the foies far less pretty, as did deveining the livers, which Myriam Daubas said wasn't strictly necessary. But Dany, for one, was determined to remove the veins, and Michaela and I decided we'd also rather not bite into bloody dental floss either. And, yes, the veins were fairly bloody; some of them would squirt little red drops when we cut into them. When we got as many as we could without completely mangling the livers, our hostess brought out 200-gram jars and we smushed our foies into them and sprinkled them with salt and pepper. Michaela and I each filled four, with an additional one devoted to aiguillettes (strips of back meat) rolled with excess foie chunks like pigs in a blanket. These jars would be heated in the autoclave to seal them and to cook the foies enough that they could be stored almost indefinitely. *Voilà.*

With no more preparations required till the following morning, we had some time to visit. Myriam had begun renting out rooms of her farmhouse four years earlier. Most of her business came during the area's summer festivals, such as for Armagnac and country music (!). But after two years, she desired more steady year-round income, so she started offering "Foie Gras Weekends." Dany was a prime example of the target clientele—a skilled cook who lived in a city and thus had little contact with farm animals. He liked the idea of picking up a whole duck, taking it to his aunt (who lived nearby) and preparing foie gras for her. He also had never witnessed gavage.

In contrast, Michaela and I were as atypical as Myriam's clientele got, because, she told us, we were the first Americans ever to visit the farm. That explained some of the curious, though not unfriendly, looks we got from Myriam's 75-year-old father, Claude Fieux, who also lived in the house. A laconic man with a farm-weathered face and a cauliflower ear (he'd been a boxer years earlier), he spoke quickly with an accent that had an almost Slavic mumbled quality. Myriam's mom had left him after many years of marriage, and Myriam's husband was gone, too, so, she said, she and her father now had something in common. Claude regularly drove Myriam's 17-year-old son Armand to motocross competitions. (She also had a 20-year-old daughter who no longer lived at home.) Myriam's father ran much of the farm, which also raised chickens in groups of 4,000 in four barns and adjacent outdoor areas. While showing us the various barns, he prevented the family border collie from swallowing a chicken whole.

In the afternoon Myriam arranged for Michaela, Isabelle, Dany and me to visit a nearby farm that boasted its very own foie gras museum. Denise Berna, who ran La Ferme du Courdou with her husband William until his recent death, opened Le Petit Musée du Foie Gras 11 years earlier. It's a large woody room off to the side of her farm's store, where she sells her own foie gras and other duck products plus regional specialties such as apricot and peach aperitifs. The museum features placards recounting the history of foie gras, reproductions of ancient renderings of Egyptians feeding ducks with honey-covered figs, and information about how, for instance, foie gras is actually good for your heart because heart attacks in this region are two to five times less frequent than in Anglo-Saxon countries (thus echoing Didier Durand's much-ridiculed testimony in Chicago). One panel celebrates that southwest France had become the world leader in foie gras production: "*Au sommet de la Gloire gastronomique ce joyau de la nature.*" ("At the summit of gastronomic glory, this jewel of nature.") Among the museum's artifacts were pointy bones and wooden sticks formerly used to push the corn down the feeding tube; there was a photo of Denise Berna's grandmother holding one of these sticks. Also on display was a red metal funnel and built-in auger with an eight-inch pipe protruding from it; this is what the owner's mother used. Pass through a couple of doors, and you saw the end of the historical line: current gavage at La Ferme du Courdou.

In many ways, the farm's feeding techniques still would be considered old-fashioned. Eight pens, each holding about 10 ducks, were raised off the ground, with metal grates on the bottom so the duck feces could splat straight onto the concrete floor. The room was suf-fused with natural light thanks to a large horizontal opening that spanned the width of the long exterior wall, giving the ducks a view of the adjacent lush farmland. On the floor was a large pot of slightly cooked corn kernels. The funnel was suspended from a pulley that ran the length of the pens, and the feeder would sit inside each pen and scoop large cups of the corn into the funnel, the auger turning and sending it down the tube. These ducks were on day 12 of their 15-day gavage, and you could see their crops bulging downward as they filled up with corn, all while the feeder kept adding cupfuls into the funnel. But after the tube was removed, the birds showed no obvious signs of pain or distress, although they didn't appear to enjoy the feedings. As the feeder proceeded from duck to duck, pen to pen, a yellow Labrador retriever ventured under the pens to lap up a snack of fallen corn kernels and duck shit.

Memo to self: Don't kiss farm dogs.

"It's a lot of work this way," the feeder said as he worked. Indi-vidual cages would go faster, but the farm kept the ducks in group pens "because it's traditional. We don't want to expand. We want to remain traditional because the ducks are stressed less this way." In fact, La Ferme du Courdou had signed a charter as a farm recognized for feeding ducks the traditional way.

Soon Madame Berna showed us the rest of the modest facilities, including the small slaughterhouse in an appropriately equipped white room and the decades-old autoclave that shared the space. As we bid our hostess *adieu,* I asked Dany what he thought of his first gavage. "I observed the animals before and after, and I do not see the difference," he said in careful English. "The animal after the feeding seems just like the animal before. So it doesn't seem so bad."

Back at the Daubas home, Myriam was getting ready to conduct her own ducks' evening feeding. Her operation was even smaller than that of La Ferme du Courdou. She didn't grow the ducks, and she lacked her own slaughtering facility. Her primary job was to fat-ten those 48 gray-and-white Barbary ducks, hatched and raised on a nearby farm. She'd feed them for 16 days, take them to a nearby slaughterhouse, kill them and bring back the carcasses for process-ing and sale. Her gavage took place in a windowless garage-like room illuminated by a single exposed light bulb on one wall and permeated with that telltale gamey smell of duck droppings and mustiness. Two rows of six cages ran down the room's center, with a long water trough between them. These were cages, mind you, not pens, with five ducks occupying most of them, though one contained two weak birds that Myriam had separated from the others. These ducks had a lot less room to maneuver than those in the Courdou pens; when they flapped their wings, they swatted their neighbors. And there was much wild flapping going on as Myriam sat down outside each cage, reached in and grabbed a struggling duck by the neck, pulled his head between the cage's bars and lowered a clamp to hold the head in place. Then came the tube, which looked to be about 10 inches long, through which the birds were fed whole corn kernels.

Claude had built these cages in 1976, and he also devised the system of clamping down the duck's head during the feedings. The beak pointed more horizontally than vertically in this method. These birds were in their sixth day of gavage, with 10 to go. Leaving Isabelle and Dany near the doorway, Michaela and I ventured farther inside the dark, dank room, and Myriam beckoned me to come over and help. A clamped-down duck had a feeding tube in place, and Myriam had me massage the bird's neck to help keep things moving. I could feel the kernels making their way down the warm throat. The duck made little noise but flapped occasionally, and as Myriam talked, he remained on the pipe. His distress level didn't increase over time. He wasn't choking. He didn't appear to be having the time of his life either. Isabelle pointed out that male ducks lack voice boxes, hence their relatively quiet, raspy brand of quacking. By way of demonstration, Myriam went to another cage and pulled out a female duck that accidentally had been delivered with the males; it delivered a crisp *quack quack*.

Each feeding took several seconds, and the process of releasing one duck and grabbing another in the same cage looked to be a tumultuous one, with much flapping and darting around as Myriam tried to get hold of a bird she had yet to feed. This was the least peaceful of the gavage sessions I'd witnessed so far, and it gave me pause.

When Myriam was done feeding her ducks, she fed us. As at the Dubois farm, dinner was a homey affair with the hosts eating and drinking with the guests. I wasn't particularly craving foie gras at this point, but, you know, too bad. We started with a parfait (lighter than pâté) of duck foie gras on toast, then moved on to a pan-fried foie gras with a fig sauce that was thick and sweet. When you order hot foie gras in a U.S. restaurant, you're usually served a silver-dollar-sized slice. Here, Myriam Daubas was doling out servings the size of chicken cutlets. I hoped my arteries would forgive me this decadence. That wasn't even the main course. Myriam brought out another big tray, this one with sizable slices of steak-like *magret* done medium rare with pasta and mushrooms. Dessert was something that looked like more foie but was, in fact, crème caramel.

It's a wonder I remember any of this given the 10 bottles that were opened over the course of the meal. These included white and red *floc* (lightly fortified, chilled aperitifs), some unidentified red liqueur derived from cognac, red and white table wines, and a dessert-accompanying concoction made by pouring an unaged, 40-percent-alcohol Armagnac into a saucepan, dumping in a handful of sugar cubes and setting the liquid ablaze until the alcohol burned off, which took about 15 minutes. We must've made an impression on our hosts as the first American visitors or something, because after we downed this warm, sweet drink, Myriam's father reached into the dining room's aged wooden cabinet and pulled out a brown bottle draped with cobwebs: an 1893 Armagnac made by his great-grandfather and probably kept in that same cabinet ever since. He poured us each a bit, and it was like really smooth lighter fluid filling your mouth and throat with liquid flames. Then he pulled out another bottle: a 1945 Armagnac made by a neighbor. Before the 1893 stuff, this probably would have blown my head off, but now it seemed rather mellow and caramel-like.

The next morning we were back in our white lab coats and boots to make the confit. Myriam's hair was up in a bun, she wore a nose stud in the shape of a four-cornered star, and she had on a white Irish pub T-shirt and rubber slippers with roses painted on them. She turned on the gas burner beneath an oversized aluminum pot on the floor, and we chopped up the fat and skin into bite-sized pieces and tossed them into the pot. As it all melted, little bits of meat and skin rose to the top; I was assigned the job of skimming these pieces from the surface using a large slotted spoon and setting them aside; I was panning for *fritons,* which with a dash of salt and pepper made for a tasty if not at all nutritious snack. When the fat vat was clear and particle free, in went the breasts, legs, wings, necks, backs and other stray parts. *Magrets* now generally are considered too high grade to be made into confit, but for those of us who lacked the option of transporting raw meat, this was our only choice. We eventually packed the cooked meat in large glass jars and poured melted fat up to the brim. Myriam still had to heat all of the jars in the autoclave, but in the meantime she set us up to visit another farm down the road—this one, at our request, one that used individual cages. Finally, we'd be seeing an industrial farm, the kind of place where the vast majority of French foie gras ducks are fed.

Jean Luc's operation wasn't large as far as such farms go, with 705 ducks in gavage at one time. (He asked that his last name not be used.) The bigger farms, such as ones that supply France's largest producer, Rougié, may have 1,000 to 2,000 ducks being fed at one time. But Jean Luc fit the industrial model all the same. He wasn't raising birds. He wasn't slaughtering them. He wasn't producing his own brand of foie gras or other products. He just was fattening one group of ducks, then another, then another. He'd take custody of his 700-plus ducks when they were 12 weeks old, and 13 days later a truck would pick them up for a trip to the slaughterhouse. (Jean Luc said some unscrupulous farms try to speed the process to eight days.) A cooperative used his livers and other duck parts to create products marketed under various labels, including supermarket house brands. He could not point at any single jar of foie gras and say definitively: "That came from my ducks."

Each duck sat in a box-like cage just bigger than the dimensions of its body, with its head sticking out of the top. These birds were lined up in three double rows that ran the length of the long barn, with water troughs in front of them. Four fans were mounted at regular intervals in each row, and bigger fans at the far wall blew cool air through the room. The ducks stood on metal grates, and the droppings fell into a concrete trench. The barn had surprisingly little odor, but before anyone claims that the owner must have cleaned up and deodorized beforehand, I'll note that if he were trying to provide the so-called white-glove tour, he might have removed the six or seven dead ducks from their cages. You couldn't help but notice that the second cage from the entrance had its lid popped open with a lifeless duck lying beneath it; other similarly popped lids throughout the barn indicated the same. Affixed to the front end of one of the rows was a red funnel into which another dead duck had been stuck headfirst.

These canard corpses were no big deal to Jean Luc, a somewhat heavyset, friendly faced man in his mid-40s wearing a Christmasy sweater with a zippered collar. He said 1 to 2 percent of the ducks die in gavage, which he considered a low mortality rate, and given that the ducks currently in the barn were at the tail end of their feeding period—a truck would be coming by at 3 a.m. to take them to the nearby town of Vic-Fezensac for slaughter—these deaths were not surprising. In Jean Luc's mind, a delicate balance must be struck. The foies were sold by the gram, but he didn't want them to get too big because "if the liver weighs too much, the mortality rate goes up." But at the same time, if he had no dead ducks, he'd feel like he was doing something wrong. "If they reach zero percent mortality, that's a bad sign because that means the average livers will be small." He likened the ducks to professional athletes who test their physical capacities, though athletes of the human variety generally choose to undergo such tests. "Force-feeding is pushing the animal to its limits," Jean Luc said, "so for some ducks who are more fragile, it can be very difficult."

Jean Luc came by his expertise naturally. His mother and grandmother fed birds for foie gras, as did just about everyone else around them; they'd sell the livers for the holidays and keep the meat. Jean Luc opened his own operation in 1994. Keeping the ducks in the traditional way—that is, in group pens or cages—was "more in line with my character. I'd rather do it traditionally like Myriam. But this is more economical. To do it on this scale, you have to optimize, and the solution is the individual cages. Demand has exploded, and production has exploded."

The key advantage of the individual cages was that the feeder didn't have to do any work to get hold of the duck's head. It was sticking up out of the cage with nowhere to go, so he could just zip down the rows feeding one duck after the other through the pneumatic tube. This setup enabled Jean Luc to maintain a large operation while keeping his overhead relatively low. Until she hurt her arm recently, his wife was able to do all of the gavage herself, thus keeping the work and compensation in the family. "I decided to force-feed so many ducks so my wife could have a salary instead of looking somewhere else for work," Jean Luc said. His operation was at capacity because, he said, if he added any more ducks, he'd have to hire another feeder.

As he spoke, several of the ducks behind him were panting hard. They certainly didn't appear to be relaxed. "It's natural they do it a little more before the end of gavage because they're working harder, and this is the last day before slaughter," he said. Some farm visitors were more bothered by this scene than others, he noted, so he'd tell those who didn't like what they saw: "If they aren't treated well, they don't create a good foie. I'm much more shocked when I go to the cities and see people sleeping in boxes."

As Dany drove us away, I asked him what he thought of the individual cages. "Not so bad," he answered, and promptly stranded his Lexus sedan in a dirt field.

OK, that last detail isn't particularly relevant, but, man, sometimes people would rather believe a machine than their own eyes. His GPS Dude was telling him to turn left even though a cursory glance revealed just a couple of tractor marks disappearing into the distance. Yet he made the turn and ambled on until a large rock halted his progress. We all got out, and Michaela hauled the rock away while I jogged ahead to confirm that only increasingly rough terrain lay before us. Yet he resumed moving his Lexus forward as I ran toward him, palms up, shouting, "There's! No! Road! There!" Mind you, I'm not trying to draw any parallels between his trust in satellite guidance systems and his trust in the industrial system of force-feeding ducks. Then again, I wasn't nearly as comfortable with the individual cages as he was.

Back at the Daubas farm, we wiped off the fat that had seeped out of our foie and confit jars during cooking, then packed them up. This was some heavy-duty—and just plain heavy—duck product. (Weeks later I tried the foie gras at home. It was flavorful and my guests enjoyed it, but I'm guessing that the Daubas autoclave got pretty hot, because when I opened the jar there was more fat than liver, and the foie itself was pretty dense.) Myriam gave us each an honest-to-goodness diploma, as created by Gers's tourism department. It read in large type: "*Diplome d'initiation à la cuisine du Foie Gras du Gers.*" And then slightly smaller: "*Décerné à Mark CARO Par Loisirs Accueil Gers pour ses compétences mises en évidence lors de son séjour du 12 au 13 novembre 2007.*" Madame Daubas signed it, "*Fait à St Arailles chez Myriam DAUBAS.*"

I was told the translation is "Awarded to Mark Caro by Gers Tourism for the proficiency he showed during his stay of November 12 to 13, 2007." See, and I thought it said: "Look out, world. This guy is now qualified to chop up his own duck, yank out his own foie gras and eat lots and lots of the stuff without grabbing at his chest, 1893 Armagnac optional."

16.

Conveyor Belt Livers

"This is not very poetic."

In two different cities at two different French restaurants, I asked for a translation for one of the menu items, and the servers—a bubbly young woman the first time, a businesslike man the second—gave the exact same reply: "Venison. [Smile] You know, Bambi." Servers in the United States would make that joke at their own peril. *You expect us to eat Bambi?!?* Americans don't want to think about eating deer, period, never mind an adorable little cartoon one. At least there's nothing cute about the word "venison."

This fear of people making the connection between an animal and the food simply doesn't exist in France. A print ad for Rougié shows a smiling, white-jacketed waiter formally presenting a white porcelain terrine on a tray to a goose, who looks rather noncommittal about the whole exchange. The terrine presumably contains foie gras, meaning that the waiter is offering the goose the fattened liver of one of its brethren. Smart-ass Americans like myself can't help but note the irony of such an image, but it's unlikely many French people give it a second thought. Foie gras is made from geese, so there's a goose in the ad. *Voilà.* Forget about the pairing of Sauternes and foie gras; in France you're more likely to see the dish, and the farms that produce them, matched with whimsical images of the birds themselves. The road sign for La Ferme du Courdou (and its little foie gras museum) features a cartoon duck playing saxophone beside the large-print words "Foies Gras" and "Confits." The *chambres d'hôtes* sign for Myriam Daubas's farm and store also touts "Foie Gras," "Confits" and "*Gavage Traditionnel*" while a cartoon white duck in a black bow tie and formalwear happily gestures to the words "*Vente à la Ferme.*" Then there are those three large cut-out geese standing on the Dubois house's front lawn like a year-round Christmas display.

The small medieval town of Sarlat-la-Canéda, in the southwestern region known as the Black Périgord, is a beautifully preserved representation of 14th-century France; you can feel the rich, tumultuous history seeping out of the stone buildings and streets. But as you look around, you might conclude that the place is one big waterfowl appreciation enclave. Storefront after storefront is packed with stuffed geese and ducks; ceramic geese and ducks; paintings of geese and ducks; aprons, dish towels and linens featuring geese and ducks; reproductions of vintage ads featuring geese and ducks; and goose and duck key chains, stemware and tumblers, plates and trays, and, of course, terrines and other serving dishes meant for preparing and presenting geese and ducks. In a small plaza at the town's center stand three bronze life-size geese donated by Rougié in 1875, the year it was founded. If you haven't had a photo of yourself taken with these geese, you haven't really visited Sarlat. Perhaps the only items that outnumber these goose and duck images in Sarlat are jars, cans and other packages of foie gras itself. They fill the shelves and window cases of the town's plentiful souvenir shops and gourmet stores, and the restaurants invariably tout their foie gras specials on placards outside the front door. The town may not offer foie gras rides, and there are no feathery-costumed folks with bulging abdomens exchanging high fives with kids, but with good reason Michaela nicknamed this place "Foie Gras Disneyland."

Sarlat is anchored by Rougié, which produces 31 percent of France's foie gras. Rougié also is the only French company still exporting foie gras to the United States. Of course, Rougié's foie gras is marketed differently in the United States than in its home country. "When we want to advertise, we show animals in France," said Guy de Saint Laurent, Rougié's commercial export manager. "In America, my American manager said, 'No, don't show animals.' Because in America it's not good that people realize that what they have on their plate is coming from the farm." This point is more than an annoyance or source of amusement for Saint Laurent. He's convinced that the way to clear up foie gras's bad reputation in the United States is to show people how it's actually produced (without, that is, getting too graphic). That strategy isn't likely to work if Americans don't even want to acknowledge that the stuff comes from actual animals.

The personable, articulate, camera-ready Saint Laurent bore some resemblance to a younger Dan Quayle but with far more life behind his eyes. As the director of Rougié's sizable export business, Saint Laurent was well aware of the information wars being fought, and he felt it was his job to bolster his industry's defense and offense. After viewing the Al Gore documentary on global warming, *An Inconvenient Truth*, he had an epiphany:

"I have to become the foie gras Al Gore."

With Saint Laurent taking the lead, Rougié initiated creating a documentary on the subject and hooked up with a French production company. But ultimately that company opted to move ahead without Rougié's funding so that the documentary could maintain its independence. Thus Saint Laurent's visions of Al Gore–like glory would have to wait. (Industry officials did, however, manage to have the documentary delayed so it could be recut to deemphasize the anti-foie viewpoint.) Still, the Rougié executive remained an upbeat foie gras ambassador. When we arrived at the company's Sarlat plant, he immediately supplied us with white lab jackets, hairnets and blue shoe coverings so we could take a tour of the sizable modern factory that sits about a mile from the medieval center of town. First stop was the test kitchen, a large, antiseptic room (note: pretty much every room and hallway in this building is antiseptic, so keep that adjective on mental file, and I won't repeat it again) where workers in chefs' caps toiled at two long tables.

The lead chef, named Gilles, sprinkled sugar atop the tan, custard-like contents of two shallow, round porcelain dishes and blow-torched the surfaces to caramelize them. "He's now working on a crème brûlée foie gras," Saint Laurent explained, then asked us to taste it. Made from foie gras *bloc* (a diluted product) mixed with cream and a drop of vanilla, this mild custard was more creamy and sweet than livery. I'm one of those strange people who never much liked crème brûlée—it's too rich and buttery for my taste—but I would assume if you enjoy the original, you'd probably be OK with this variation. Plenty of chefs have attempted foie gras crème brûlée previously; the novelty here lay in its mass production.

That dish was basically an appetizer to the more intriguing taste treat now laid out in two thick, trapezoidal slices: yuzu foie gras. Yuzu is a Japanese citrus fruit that lies somewhere near the intersection of orange, lemon and grapefruit. It's fragrant with a distinct flavor that pops. When Saint Laurent had been in Japan a couple of weeks earlier, he'd picked up two variations of the fruit to bring back to Sarlat: One consisted of thick dried threads; the other had been ground to a powder. He thought that the ever-expanding Japanese market might go for a yuzu foie gras, so he asked his chefs, who have some experience in mixing unusual flavors with the fatty livers, to play around. Now Gilles had prepared two foie gras *mi-cuit* terrines, one incorporating the yuzu threads, the other the powder. Before trying it, Saint Laurent said he wasn't sure whether he'd ultimately sell a yuzu foie gras because the fruit was an expensive product being added to what already was an expensive product, so the resultant price would be a concern. Then again, he noted, Rougié and other companies already sold foie gras with truffles, and yuzu "can't be more expensive than the truffles anyway, so it should be OK." He dug in, as did we.

"It's very interesting," Michaela said, using "interesting" to mean "interesting" and not the common American euphemism for "Thank you. Now please look that way while I spit this into my napkin." It was a palate pleaser, and why not? Foie gras pairs well with assertive, slightly tart fruit, and this had a citrusy punch, the yuzu threads and occasional chunkier pieces providing a more dynamic contrast than the powdered stuff, which pretty much got lost in the liver. No foie gras purist would buy a terrine blended with exotic dried fruit rather than the straight stuff (perhaps seasoned with salt and pepper), but as something to eat on a thin slice of toast, sure, this worked.

This picture of chefs toiling over refined foie gras preparations in a large industrial kitchen dovetailed nicely with the image of Rougié that Saint Laurent was presenting. Rougié is a factory in terms of scale, but what actually goes on there is, in his view, hand-crafted, traditional work. At the Dubois farm, Danie and Gilles deveined the livers by hand at a table. Here, a large metal tank filled with fat livers sat at the mouth of an assembly line, and a middle-aged woman in a lab coat and hairnet removed them one by one and placed them onto a conveyor belt. Five other similarly clad women stood alongside the belt and pulled out the veins as the foies slowly passed by. If someone accidentally sped up that conveyor belt, an *I Love Lucy* episode would break out. "This is not very poetic," Saint Laurent acknowledged.

The last woman in the line took the livers and placed them into a white plastic bin that, when full, was sent farther along the conveyor belt. The livers passed under a salt-sprinkling machine and eventually reached a man who scooped a ladle full of Armagnac atop them. The conveyor belt then carried the bin through a gap in the wall into another room, where the livers were stuffed into jars and a machine pressed the lids into place. Other livers were being marinated in champagne; later pepper would be added, and the liver pieces would be cooked in cans in giant autoclaves.

Elsewhere, we came across a huge square metal tub filled with a frothy tan mixture that resembled a café au lait converted to pudding. This was *bloc,* an emulsion of the liver and water (and, in Rougié's case, port) to create a diluted, more spreadable product. "Americans, they like to spread, so the *bloc* is nicer for them, and the price is cheaper," Saint Laurent said. This product looked far removed from those assembly-line livers from which Lucy and Ethel had been yanking the veins. Rougié typically sells most of its *bloc* in various-sized tins, but it has found that consumers appreciate other serving options. Hence a machine squirted the whipped-up goo into the two shallow side-by-side circles to create ready-made plastic-encased slices.

There were many other rooms. One held 10 enormous drums for preparing confit. In another, decades-old machines slapped Rougié labels around *bloc* tins. The intensely fragrant spice room held 50 kinds of pepper in huge plastic containers, with the woman in charge diligently typing at a computer. The recipes for Rougié's products may vary from market to market. "For Japan we put in less salt," Saint Laurent said. "They don't like salt."

A cavernous warehouse boasted row upon row of tall shelves stocked with boxes of cans and jars. This may very well be the world's most concentrated accumulation of fatty bird livers. Saint Laurent explained that the large warehouse was necessary because foie gras must be produced year-round to cover the sales spike of November and December, which we were just approaching. Nearby in the shipping room, boxes were being labeled and packed for 120 countries. Rougié's foie gras was sold under several different names in France (including the supermarket brands Montfort and Bizac) and elsewhere, and was exported to such unlikely locales as Kuwait.

The Kuwaiti product is certified halal, meaning that it has been produced in accordance with Islamic law. Labeyrie, another of France's large foie producers, wound up in an Internet-fanned firestorm in 2007 when French nationalists loudly condemned the company for its halal foie gras. The complaint was that by paying the required certification fee to a French mosque, Labeyrie was funding Islamic worship and thus—as post-9/11 logic went—terrorism. (Companies pay commissions to rabbis for kosher certification as well.) Labeyrie introduced its halal foie gras in 2006, but by the end of December 2007, after widely publicized protests and boycott threats, the company had abandoned the product.

This controversy underscored the charged emotions generated by foie gras in France; after all, it's not like this was the first French item ever to be certified halal. "Foie gras is a very emotional and sensitive product," Saint Laurent said, "and the people who are these right extremists are very traditional people, and for them foie gras is only French." Still, he chalked up most of the controversy to the Internet's incendiary power. "Most of the other companies are doing halal for more than 20 years. Nobody complained."

At Rougié, an inspector registered by the mosque would come to witness the birds' slaughter to ensure that it was done according to Islamic law, "which is quite tough for the animal," Saint Laurent said. That is, instead of being electrically stunned and then killed with a thin knife to the temple, as was the fate of other Rougié ducks and geese, these birds were slaughtered with a knife to the throat and no stunning. (Kosher law also prohibits stunning.) What's more, at the moment of death, "the eyes have to watch Mecca," Saint Laurent said. "The eyes of the duck or eyes of the goose—you have to turn the animal the right way." He shrugged. "But anyway we have no choice. If we want to make it halal, we have to make it this way."

"Do many people in Kuwait eat foie gras?" I asked.

"No."

When our factory tour ended, Saint Laurent took us into the attached retail shop. In a refrigerator case sat *mi-cuit* terrines of duck foie gras combined with such flavors as gingerbread, grapefruit, tea aspic and ginger, and green fava beans and summer savory. The freezer case contained whole, deveined, vacuum-packed livers as well as zipper-locked bags filled with frozen lobe slices that you could remove for individual servings; they looked like thick-cut country fries. The shop also sold tubs of foie gras ice cream, which, of course, we had to sample. Made with sugar, water and foie gras *bloc,* it looked like coffee ice cream, but the texture was thick, creamy, veering almost into frozen butter territory. It was better than I expected. The flavor was distinct (more so than the foie gras crème brûlée), and it lingered nicely on the palate as the rich cream melted slowly in your mouth. Mind you, I'm not sure I'd want a huge scoop on a waffle cone, and I wouldn't douse it with hot fudge, but as far as novelty foods went, this certainly had more reason to exist than, say, foie gras cotton candy.

Saint Laurent wanted to see the foie gras markets continue to grow, of course, but promotion wasn't simply a matter of more, more, more. A delicate balancing act was at work as the industry tried to make the product more popular without sacrificing any of its prestige. Despite the bans and negative publicity, foie gras was being eaten by more people than at any previous time, particularly in Rougié's home country. French consumption, which dwarfed any other country's, had doubled over the past two decades. In 1991 France consumed about 9,000 metric tons, and in 2007 that figure exceeded 18,000 metric tons. Production was up by an even greater percentage. After France, Saint Laurent said, Spain consumed the most foie gras: less than 3,000 metric tons annually. The United States and Canada together consumed about 700 metric tons annually. A couple of decades' worth of declining foie gras prices had boosted sales, though dramatic jumps in corn costs were nudging the prices back upward.

The number of foie gras ducks processed in France, 35 million in 2007, was increasing by about 5 percent every year, Saint Laurent said, but sometimes the industry slowed down production. The goal of such limits was to prevent foie gras from being overproduced—like salmon, Saint Laurent said—and to keep the delicacy on the path of a certain other successful French prestige item. "We are very close to champagne, because champagne is still luxurious, but it's still sold anywhere: restaurants, supermarkets, delicatessen, with a very nice image."

Champagne, however, had the added advantage of not being tied to animal production and controversial feeding practices. Also handicapping Rougié: Many people equate mass production with "industrial," which they see as antithetical to foie gras's artisanal roots—even as, Saint Laurent pointed out, no one seems to mind that Veuve Clicquot is the world's largest champagne producer. The industrial/artisanal divide comes up often in France; it's not unusual for someone to say they're fine with the old-fashioned foie gras, but the *industrial* . . . ugh. Artisanal implies small, traditional, personal: grandma on the farm with her ducks or geese. Industrial is considered big, modern, dehumanizing: machines transforming animals into product.

Saint Laurent was aware of the image problem and had a simple explanation: "In France we all have a cousin who is a farmer. In my family there are farmers. In *his* family there are farmers. And we still have an image of agriculture, of the food coming from this farm. But we still go to supermarkets to buy and eat products produced by the agro-food industry." In other words, people don't think twice about loading up at the grocery store, but foie gras has remained inextricably linked to tradition and the family farm. "They have difficulty accepting that with a company like Rougié, the product is a live product coming from a farm but produced in big quantities."

In fact, although Rougié produces more foie gras than any other company, not one of its farms is nearly as big and populous as Hudson Valley Foie Gras. Rougié's ducks come from 800 farms in France, mostly in the southwest and mid-Atlantic region. These farms, contracted to the company (in addition to those that breed and grow the birds), might have a couple thousand ducks in gavage at one time, compared to the 20,000 at Hudson Valley. So does that mean Rougié is actually less industrial than Hudson Valley Foie Gras? That's a matter of definition, but as the term generally is defined in France, no. Rougié is textbook French industrial, because the ducks are being fed in one place, slaughtered in another and processed in another. The break from the artisanal lies in this division of labor—as well as the uniform conditions under which the company's ducks are raised and fed throughout Rougié's roster of farms, including confinement in individual cages and feedings via machines that send corn mush down their gullets.

So Jean Luc's farm was industrial because its sole job was to force-feed ducks before they were killed and processed elsewhere—and he boosted the speed of those feedings by keeping the ducks in individual cages and using a pneumatic feeding machine. Hudson Valley Foie Gras, in contrast, was raising its ducks from hatchlings, keeping them in group pens during gavage, hand-feeding them with funnels and augers, and killing and processing them to create their own labeled products. In the French view, Hudson Valley Foie Gras's "vertical integration" approximated a super-sized version of a traditional farm.

To Saint Laurent, the distinction also comes down to distribution. A traditional farm may sell to visitors and deliver its products to local markets, but it's not in the export business. Once you enter that business, you can't help but become industrial, because "if you start to export to America or Japan, the sanitary inspectors ask you to paint your walls in white because it's hygienic," Saint Laurent said. "You have to wear white stuff on your head everywhere, and you look like a factory."

To others, however, the difference between artisanal and industrial involves more than aesthetics, cultural perceptions, corporate structure and distribution. When a small family farmer such as Danie Dubois complains about the mass production of foie gras ducks, she's talking about a process that values efficiency and uniformity over individualized attention to the birds. Gilles Dubois feels each goose's abdomen to determine whether it is ready for processing, and the slaughter is staggered over several days, but the big farms clear out the gavage cages all at once; a feeder would have a tough time getting his hand into one of those cramped cages and under the duck's belly in the first place. For those hundreds of duck farms that it contracts for gavage, Rougié lays down a regimented set of standards across the board. The birds are kept in individual cages and are fed specified amounts of food via specified machinery over 12 days. In the end the livers are expected to weigh an average of 550 grams (about 1.21 pounds, smaller than the American standard and much smaller the Hudson Valley's two-pounders).

After the European Union's 1998 report singled out the individual cages in its criticism of industrial production, the French agriculture minister proposed that farms cease installing such cages as of 2005 and using them as of 2010. CIFOG negotiated to delay the transition for an additional five years, meaning that individual cage installations must stop in 2010, and they can't be used after 2015. When Michaela and I spoke to CIFOG president Jean Schwebel, he stressed that the industry agreed to this ban willingly, based on a government recommendation rather than a requirement, and the delay was necessary because it "will change fundamentally the conditions of production." Meanwhile, individual cages still were being built on foie gras farms despite the widespread criticism. Given how many other European countries already have moved against foie gras, Robert Dantzer, one of the EU report's co-authors, characterized the French industry's slow response to the panel's recommendations as "suicidal."

Saint Laurent chalked up the individual cage ban to "anthropomorphism," saying, "Activists always compare animals to humans. You need space. An animal needs space also. But for the last two weeks of its life, the ducks don't feel bad in the cage."

To Antoine Comiti, France's leading anti-foie-gras activist as founder of the Bordeaux-based group Stop Gavage, the increasing dominance of industrial production may ultimately work to his cause's advantage. He said he encounters basically three types of people in his country: those who say they don't eat foie gras; those who say, "Yes, we think industrial is awful, but artisan foie gras is fine, and the birds are treated well"; and the largest group "who don't know much about the reality of foie gras production and are angry that you want to prevent someone from eating something. I think the biggest obstacle is on the cultural level: People don't want to be told what to eat." Where Comiti saw the most potential for change lay in the same area that concerned Danie Dubois: "Little farms are disappearing, and in a few years it will be 98 percent industrial operations. I don't think people will have this kind of bind to production as they used to. This image of foie gras as a traditional artisan product will little by little disappear. It's not like in the past people are producing foie gras because their fathers and mothers were producing foie gras."

Ariane Daguin, who's otherwise ideologically far removed from Comiti, nonetheless agreed with him on one point: "In France you have two very different things. You have the industrial stuff that is truly, really horrible, and I'm afraid is going to kill the industry. And then you have the real small artisanal people who are trying their best and who are making it at a high price and selling it exclusively to restaurants who really want top quality. The industrial way of doing it in France right now is horrible. It's individual cages. It's 12 days of gavage feeding. The taste is not the same anymore." Michel Guérard wasn't prepared to make the same distinction. "There are small producers who don't do it well," he said, "and you have industrials who do it very well."

In Comiti's view, French foie gras will go almost fully industrial, people don't like industrial, and that'll make it easier to push for bans on individual or group battery cages—plus the pneumatic or hydraulic force-feeding machines—while continuing to allow the artisan pens and manual feeding methods. "In reality if you achieve that, you have stopped most of foie gras production, and it would raise prices quite a bit," Comiti said. "Once you've decreased the economic power of the industry, it's much easier to secure a complete ban later on. So I think it will happen in two steps—because nobody supports industrial production."

Saint Laurent was dismissive of Comiti and the prospect of France ever abolishing foie gras. The anti-foie attitude, the Rougié executive said, pretty much had been confined to North America and northern European countries "where the vegetarians have a kind of power." (To André Daguin, what distinguished the foie-banning northern European countries was "they don't care at all. They have no taste.") Saint Laurent found Israel's ban far more surprising given the dish's Jewish roots. His theory was similar to Izzy's: that the producers were isolated and never got around to mobilizing against the threat. Asian countries, in contrast, consume meat with no guilt, and he considered France safe for similar reasons. "If you said to a French person that you are vegetarian, the response would be 'Are you sick? Is something wrong?' It's not serious." As for Comiti, who is in his early 40s and designs health-care software in Bordeaux, Saint Laurent questioned his expertise and agenda. "Comiti is an anti-specieist. He puts the animal at the same level as a human being. It's very California in a way. His real target is to ask that we respect animals like human beings, that we don't kill anyone, and gavage is one of the first, easy targets."

Comiti denied that he equates the lives of animals and humans— or, for that matter, humans and other humans; the death of a child, for instance, was sadder than the death of an old person. The point was that "suffering is suffering, whoever is experiencing it. In the Stop Gavage campaign, we don't claim that an animal life equals a human life or that the suffering is equal. We're just saying it's so much suffering and so many lives for so little." Comiti wrote a 270-page book condemning foie gras and refuting Daniel Guéméne's research on the subject, yet the tone of Stop Gavage's campaign is a marked contrast to those of fellow American and British animal-welfare groups. For one—and this may simply be a byproduct of battling foie gras in its home country—Comiti is modest about his group's achievements thus far. "We obviously haven't succeeded in decreasing the consumption," he said, citing recent figures that showed 2007's French consumption to be up just barely over previous peak years of 2003 and 2005. "Maybe we succeeded in stopping a rise. People know how foie gras is produced today who didn't know five years ago. We've succeeded in giving many people a realistic picture of what foie gras production is."

Stop Gavage may try to educate the public, but unlike so many other groups, it wasn't concentrating its efforts on the consumer end by organizing boycotts or picketing restaurants and stores. Rather, the group operated mostly in the political realm. The "manifesto" on its Web site "asks" that: (1) the force-feeders stop force-feeding ("The fact that they do not intend to be cruel to these animals does not reduce the suffering they cause," the statement diplomatically puts it); (2) those who profit from foie gras stop doing so; (3) scientists and veterinarians denounce foie gras production methods; (4) judges deem foie gras production illegal on the basis of laws "limiting the suffering that can be inflicted on a sentient being"; and (5) politicians "legislate to ban this practice forever." The manifesto also poses the question: "How on earth can you say that a barbaric custom, consisting of sticking a funnel or a pneumatic pump down the throat of a caged animal, is a tradition of high culture?"

Effecting such changes in France may be a long shot, yet Comiti wasn't particularly concerned with pragmatism and little victories. When someone argued that the animal-rights folks wanted to ban foie gras today and hamburgers tomorrow, Comiti thought the response should be "Yes!" even though many more people would be willing to say good-bye to fatty duck livers than Big Macs. "It's not true to say that foie gras production is 100 times worse than chicken or pork production," Comiti said. "We're not campaigning saying that foie gras is the worst meat production. In the U.S. some activists are using this argument, trying not to make the link between foie gras and meat. But I don't think there is one activist against foie gras who is not in fact also against meat." In other words, be honest, and when foie gras defenders point out the problems with general meat production, activists "should take the opportunity that the opposition is offering and debate meat in general."

The hitch in this strategy is that many animal advocates consider foie gras to be a winnable battle while realizing that most folks aren't ready to make the leap to vegetarianism. The popular sentiment has been to get rid of this one especially vivid, objectionable practice first, then deal with everything else. Comiti was taking a much longer view, arguing that this was a campaign to be waged over decades, not months. "I don't think we will have foie gras banned in France if we don't have people questioning the legitimacy of meat and how it is produced today," he said. "You can argue that if you ban foie gras because the animals are badly treated, you should ban other intensive meat production as well. I have absolutely no hope to see any country ban meat during my lifetime, but I think it's a legitimate objective with very sound arguments to make. The first steps toward it are expressing this plainly and explaining why."

In December 1998, the USDA lifted its ban on importing fresh poultry from France. That was the good news. Soon came the bad: A mere seven months later, the United States imposed 100-percent tariffs on various European goods in retaliation for the European Union's decade-long ban against U.S. beef treated with growth hormones. Specifically targeted were such French luxury items as Roquefort cheese, truffles, mustard, shallots and foie gras. This volley in the trade wars did no favors to Rougié or its fellow French producers, as other forces were driving up the costs of doing business in the United States as well. As Saint Laurent explained, the USDA requires that foie gras for the American market be cooked in separate machines at higher temperatures for longer periods of time than the European product. The foie gras also must have U.S.-specific labels and recipes and be available for USDA inspection at all times. The labor costs were greater for U.S.-bound livers, and so were those for transportation and warehousing. No wonder French foie gras *bloc* often was pricier in the United States than the undiluted liver in France.

Jean Schwebel, the CIFOG president and owner of the 200-plus-year-old Strasbourg producer Edouard Artzner, said that in the mid to late 1990s, 15 French companies were exporting foie gras to the United States, even without the fresh stuff allowed. But with all of the added costs and requirements, French producers abandoned the U.S. market—except for Rougié. Saint Laurent said his company was the only one with the will and available capital to make all of the factory upgrades and to deal with the tariffs. The proactive U.S. strategy paid off as Rougié and its Canadian-based subsidiary Palmex chipped away at Hudson Valley's market share.

Saint Laurent lamented that he couldn't make even greater inroads in the United States, the country where, in his mind, the anti-foie-gras movement was most dangerous. A typical tug of war was going on: Rougié was selling more foie gras than ever but was having a harder time getting shops to stock it because the owner invariably would be bombarded with letters and e-mails—usually from the same few people, Saint Laurent contended. "So it's more and more popular in food service and delicatessens, but it's more and more difficult to promote it." I told him that when I wrote in the *Chicago Tribune*'s Sunday magazine about Chicago chef Graham Elliot Bowles competing on *Iron Chef America,* the Food Network dictated that he couldn't request foie gras as an ingredient because it's too controversial. Saint Laurent sighed. "The only problem for us is when we can't promote foie gras, like this *Iron Chef* situation," he said. "It's a pity, because a lot of people do not know this product, and if we could promote it, like making a foie gras week in Chicago in every restaurant or *Iron Chef* making foie gras, we could do much more." At that point a foie gras week in Chicago certainly wasn't going to happen.

To Saint Laurent, the solution lay in education, transparency, letting people see what foie gras production was all about. "For many, many years, the foie gras people didn't communicate about the feeding, never, because they say it's not the poetic part of the production," he said. "When you make food products, you don't show all the parts of production. But I think now the citizens are losing the knowledge between the beginning and the end of the plate, and there is a big gap between the farm and the plate. It's a long way, but I think the only way is to show and to explain. It's not too late."

After lunch in town, Saint Laurent took us to a nearby farm so we could observe the gavage there. This was the sixth French foie gras farm that Michaela and I had visited, and once again it presented a different picture from the others. Like the Dubois farm, La Ferme de Turnac raised geese. When we arrived a flock of about 40 of them— tall, elegant, regal and gray and white—wandered in sync over the hilly countryside. This cluster of males wasn't bound for gavage; they stuck around for reproduction purposes. "Look how beautiful they are," Saint Laurent cooed. "Happy ones. Happy job."

The farm kept about 1,200 geese, 180 in the dark gavage barn, where one window was mounted at the end of the room, with no light bulbs. Instead of residing in pens like the Dubois geese, these birds were grouped by three in smaller cages where they stood on metal grates, and their heads cleared the wooden slats laid across the top. The birds weren't so cramped that they couldn't switch places or flap their wings, but they had far less personal space than the geese in pens. These geese were relatively quiet—as were some ducks being kept, also three to a cage, in an adjacent room—but there was a constant percussive splatting sound that I eventually realized was liquid shit hitting the concrete floor. I looked around: no farm dogs.

When feeding time came, the proprietor reached into an opening at the front of a cage, took hold of a bird by the neck matter-of-factly, pulled the head out and lowered a body-molded metal clamp over the rest of the goose to keep it in place. The feeder was using a 30-year-old machine in which the cooked corn kernels were kept in an oversized yellow container attached to a funnel; it made a grinding, rattling sound as it deposited the corn into the goose while the man massaged the bird's crop to keep the food moving down. He gestured for me to help out. As I gently rubbed the bird, I could feel the corn under the soft feathers and baggy warm skin. No wonder people made pillows out of this stuff. The goose's eyes remained wide open and fixed, which I acknowledge is probably par for the course given that I've never seen a squinting bird. The feeding took more than a few seconds, the man releasing the corn a little at a time, and the goose didn't move much or struggle, not that it could all clamped down like that. I couldn't see how all of the geese could get fed at this rate. Sure enough, the proprietor pointed to another newer machine down the row that he said he actually uses to feed the geese a paste combined with whole kernels. He pulled out this old relic only for demonstrations to visitors. OK, then.

Likewise, this whole trip, it turned out, wasn't indicative of the methods used by Rougié-contracted goose farms because La Ferme de Turnac wasn't a supplier for the Sarlat-based producer. Saint Laurent had just brought us here because it was close, nice and visitor friendly, at least as long as you didn't mind the sight of geese clustered in small cages while their discharge goes *splat splat splat*. "One of the reasons you don't have the problems here in France is you have so many French tourists who visit the farms," Saint Laurent said. "The tourists come to see the gavage. It's kind of an attraction." Of course, Saint Laurent hadn't actually shown us Rougié's foie gras production (which, to be fair, was not nearby).

As we returned to his office, he insisted that the industry had to do a better job of showing rather than telling. "The only way to reverse the negative publicity, which I hope is not too late, is to explain by image," he said. "I will show you the Web site we did. I have a very nice image of a big goose who is swallowing a fish, which is very amazing, to show that these animals are different from human beings, to feed is nothing wrong, and just to explain." He called up the Web site on his computer and showed us a series of industry-produced short videos. They featured pleasant acoustic-guitar strumming, bucolic imagery (including a couple of fellows holding and petting ducks in the great outdoors) and smooth-voiced narrators delivering the standard talking points about how foie gras is a natural, historical and traditional product that requires nice treatment of the birds. We never actually saw a goose swallowing a fish, and there also was no footage of gavage, just an animated diagram like you might see in an educational film. *This* was the industry's best counterpunch to those gag-inducing images of bloody corpses, pipes plunging down trembling ducks' throats and the classic "Rat Munching on Ducks' Bloody Ass Wounds"?

Where was Al Gore when you needed him?

17.

Look for the Humane Label

"It was a clean fat."

By the time I returned from France, I thought I'd be armed with definitive answers along the lines of: This is right. This is wrong. But real life stubbornly appeared more nuanced than that. Could I look at the Duboises' lifestyle and say, "No, that shouldn't be allowed"? The geese lived relatively long for meat birds, their care couldn't have been more individualized, and they appeared calm up to the end. How I might have felt about watching these beautiful birds get their throats slit was beside the point in this context. Slaughter happens. As far as my comfort level was concerned, the industrialized farm was at the opposite end of the Dubois farm, though the *ducks'* comfort level would have been more relevant to know.

Meanwhile, eating Danie Dubois's home-cooked marvels, Michel Guérard's sumptuous creations and Emile Jung's classic preparations at his gastronomy palace Au Crocodile in Strasbourg made me further appreciate the artistry that this product has inspired, as well as what's at stake from a culinary viewpoint. One argument that never has flown with me is that foie gras should be easy to ban because it's an unnecessary, decadent luxury. I appreciate the slippery-slope arguments about such distinctions, but I object on more basic grounds: Food isn't just fuel. It's a source of pleasure, and if some people love foie gras the way others love chicken nuggets, who are we to say one dish is frivolous while the other is acceptable? At the same time, the fact that some chefs can prepare fantastic foie gras dishes has no bearing on whether the birds are treated humanely.

There is, however, some precedent in linking animal treatment with culinary appreciation, as Efrain Cuevas attempted to do. Various cultures have stressed paying respect to the animals they're eating, and many chefs express satisfaction over being able to serve almost every part of, say, a pig or a lamb so none of it is being taken for granted. So if foie gras has grown less exceptional over the years, does that make the birds' treatment seem more callous? One of Charlie Trotter's initial complaints to me was that foie gras had become a culinary cliché. "Do you know how easy it is to serve it up with tropical fruits and different little accents and sweet-and-sour notes and things like that?" he asked. "People are gushing. That's child's play. That's the least of what gastronomy is, and I just think as time goes on, we have to be more morally judicious than we've been."

Paul Virant, chef of a highly regarded locally driven restaurant in Chicago's western suburbs called Vie, also expressed reservations over how commonplace this product had become. "It should be kind of a special treat," he said. "There was a time when Hudson Valley really grew, and everybody had it. The neighborhood joint, you get a beer and piece of foie gras. And I don't think a lot of that stuff was prepared with the kind of integrity it should be." If Virant served foie gras, he wanted it to have such integrity, not just in his creative yet traditional preparations but also in its sourcing. He had nothing against Hudson Valley or Sonoma, he said, but when the Chicago ban went into effect, he wanted to make sure he was buying from the farm that made him the most comfortable. Soon Vie became the only Chicago-area restaurant to carry foie gras from a small Minnesota farm called Au Bon Canard, which was producing a mere 60 to 70 ducks a week. I didn't even know about this farm when I began my foie journey, in part because it distributes its very limited supplies almost exclusively in Minnesota. It's more expensive than other U.S. foie gras, but Virant preferred its "hand-crafted, artisanal" approach as well as the product itself. "It's a little richer," he said. "I think it has a little bit more complexity and depth of flavor than the Hudson

Valley does. It could be a bit of a psychological thing too, though. You taste that integrity that's put into how it's raised, how the ducks are treated."

I felt compelled to check whether I could detect the integrity in Virant's foie gras, so I dined at Vie. Whatever I was tasting, it was awfully good—a perfectly seared slice of foie gras atop a pistachio macaroon accompanied by Sicilian pistachios, pickled peaches and blackberry and peach preserves. Would I have known the foie gras came from a small farm if I hadn't been informed previously? Maybe not. But I had no complaints.

Now I wanted to see Au Bon Canard for myself. The farm was located in Minnesota's southeast corner in the small town of Caledonia, a five-hour drive from Chicago, so I hit the highway on an April day in which the temperature started in the mid-70s before free-falling in the late afternoon. When I arrived, owner/farmer Christian Gasset was there with his two dogs and fluffy orange cat while his wife, Liz Gibson-Gasset, who runs a small library when she's not helping out on the farm, was out. A rugged guy in his mid-40s who stands six-foot-two with spiky gray hair, Christian grew up in southwestern France so of course he had relatives who were foie gras farmers. He was a logger in the Congo when he met Liz, an Omaha native who was in the Peace Corps, and after he attended foie gras school in Périgord, the couple eventually decided to settle in Minnesota, where she had attended college. The farm he found was 60 acres of bluff country—hilly, panoramic and more than a little reminiscent of Périgord's rolling countryside. Au Bon Canard, which produced its first foie gras in early 2004, was basically a small French artisan farm, complete with equipment shipped from France, plopped down in the Midwest.

This was two-person operation (with some help on slaughter and processing days), and Christian did just about all of the farming. He gets the Mulards as day-old ducklings (350 delivered every five or six weeks from Grimaud) and is with them as they move from the incubation barn to the outdoor growing areas to the gavage barn to slaughter, which he performs himself. He thinks the ducks are less stressed dealing with the same person the whole time. "You have to have happy ducks to get a nice product in the end," he said in his deep, French-accented voice. "If they are stressed, they're not going to cooperate all the way." Each shipment is divided into five groups of 70 that are placed among the farm's eight fenced-off fields (with barn access in wintertime). The lucky group gets the field with the pond, but the land is so hilly that a significant rainfall, like one that hit the day before I arrived, creates puddles and mud streams from which the ducks can sip and pluck worms.

Christian staggers each group's entry into the force-feeding barn on a weekly basis, so the first batch will move into gavage at 12 weeks, the next at 13 weeks, and so on till the fifth group begins at 16 weeks old. This gavage barn is especially bright and open. Four square windows line the long wall below which the pens are lined up in a single row, and large doors on either end often are kept open, offering more sunlight and views of neighboring farms. Decorating the walls are nature-scene paintings, most of which Liz picked up at garage sales just in case the ducks enjoy pastoral art. This is as homey as force-feeding barns get. Each group from the outside is placed into four long, large pens, 16 or 17 apiece. I arrived on a Friday afternoon, and the four pens on the right contained ducks in their 12th day of gavage, and the four on the left housed ducks that had arrived in the barn on Monday. Slaughter day would be the following Tuesday for the ones on the right.

There were some instructive differences between the two groups of ducks. The ones that had been in gavage longer were less skittish. When I walked up the aisle the first time, they moved toward the rear of their pens, but as I stood there, they gradually spread out as before and soon were paying little attention to me, some of them standing right by the front rail. The newer-to-gavage ones on the left moved farther from me and stayed there. The two groups' reactions to Christian were similar; the fatter ducks showed less avoidance, just as at Hudson Valley the veteran gavage ducks resisted human hands less than the birds a couple of days into the feedings.

Many of the fatter ducks on the right also were panting while none on the left were. This was yet another indication that the fattening process triggers the panting. But here's the interesting part: When Christian first showed me the barn and I noticed the panting ducks, a wall thermometer read 60 degrees. He wasn't due to feed them for another hour (the twice-dailies took place around 7 a.m. and 7 p.m.), so we left, and when we returned, the temperature had dropped to 48 degrees. Now none of the ducks were panting—a clear sign (to me anyway) that the panting was directly related to heat processing, as Guillermo Gonzalez and scientists supporting his viewpoint had contended. To Christian and Liz, the panting didn't appear to be a big deal anyway. "If they are panting, if they're hot, if they're a little uncomfortable, there's a big difference between that and being tortured," Liz said. "I wouldn't want to eat meat that was tortured. In fact, I don't like to eat meat that I don't know where it was raised and who took care of it." Acknowledging that heat is an issue for ducks, Au Bon Canard stops producing foie gras from mid-May till September every year.

"Hey, guys," Christian repeatedly greeted the birds as he carried plastic buckets filled with freshly kettle-cooked whole corn kernels into the barn. They didn't respond. He used a funnel-and-auger rig not unlike the one used at Hudson Valley, and the process was similar, too, with Christian sitting in the pens and feeding the ducks one by one for eight to 10 seconds per bird. Was this a peaceful, happy process? Not this night it wasn't. The wind outside was whipping up fiercely, and the ducks were spooked, which, Christian said, was the reason there was so much struggling and wild flapping going on. "On these windy nights, they're crazy," he said. I returned for the feeding the following morning, and the birds were less agitated, though they still resisted somewhat—not because of the tube, Christian said, but because they're not accustomed to being grabbed. "They are not pets."

Of the 130 ducks in gavage, one had a noticeable leg injury; it limped away from Christian after its feeding. No, it would not receive veterinary care. Christian felt its crop and abdomen and determined that it was digesting fine and looked otherwise healthy. It would go to slaughter as scheduled in a few days.

Au Bon Canard produces about 2,500 ducks a year. Ariane Daguin called Christian about distributing his product, but he and Liz were selling everything anyway without the middleman. He said Thomas Keller asked whether the farm could provide 50 pounds of foie gras a week to the French Laundry in Napa Valley and Per Se in Manhattan, two of the country's finest restaurants. Christian said no because then he wouldn't have had enough livers to supply his other customers, and he didn't want to boost his production. He also didn't like the idea of shipping meat all over the country; he appreciated that his customers were primarily in Minnesota.

Christian told me Au Bon Canard did $135,000 in sales in 2007, for about a $45,000 profit. "We are working all the time," he said. "It's a way of living. I enjoy what I'm doing. It's not all about money."

The Gassets' operation certainly felt different from Hudson Valley and Sonoma, but in all three places you had a feeder and a duck sharing eight-second intervals with a tube down the bird's throat. You might prefer the small to the big and appreciate the farmer/owner personally handling each duck, but as long as the birds were being fed with a tube, the animal advocates' concerns didn't waver. The question that continued to linger over the debate was this: Isn't there a way to produce foie gras without the force-feeding? Attempts had been made over the years.

In his seven-and-a-half-year window before the California ban kicked in, Guillermo Gonzalez maintained that his animal husbandry practices were noninjurious, but in the meantime he investigated alternative feeding methods. He worked with a scientist at California Polytechnic State University who theorized that certain natural ingredients in the feed formula might impel the ducks to overeat naturally, but the experiments' results were negative. In the late 1980s, INRA, the French agriculture department, had funded a study to determine whether the birds' brains could be manipulated to cut off their ability to realize they were satiated, thus prompting them to gorge themselves. "But everybody knows that geese and ducks have not a big brain," André Daguin said with a laugh. "And the area is so small that if you destroy this area, you destroy always something—suddenly they can't walk. It didn't work. It was dangerous, very expensive, and we stopped." It's not like many animal advocates would have considered birds with surgically manipulated brains a sound ethical alternative anyway.

Some chefs and companies tried offering "faux gras" as a happy substitute. No longer able to serve the real stuff at Tru, Rick Tramonto put a $16 Faux Gras on the menu, made from sautéed chicken livers and rendered pork fat, wrapped in a gel flavored with sauternes, dusted with cocoa (to mimic vein patterns) and sprinkled with sea salt. (He created the dish with Laurent Gras, a celebrated chef then spending time in the Tru kitchen.) It was creamier than actual foie gras, but *Tribune* critic Phil Vettel wrote that "the deep and rich flavor is spot on, right down to the almost-metallic aftertaste." At Spiaggia, Chicago's finest Italian restaurant, chef Tony Mantuano offered *Terrina de Fagato Grasso Vegetariano* ("vegetarian foie-gras terrine"), a bright yellow combination of garbanzo beans, caramelized onions, *vin santo* and butter, accompanied by sliced figs slices and a drizzle of balsamic vinegar. It was rich, loose, buttery and—no surprise— lacking in any hint of liver. In late 2007, the British supermarket chain Waitrose launched a product called Faux Gras, which blended the livers of free-range geese and ducks with goose or duck fat to create creamy pâtés sold in tins.

The desire for a non-force-fed version of foie gras was so strong that when a Spanish farmer named Eduardo Sousa came out with a line of "ethical foie gras," he couldn't produce close to enough to satisfy consumer appetites. Those who have been there say Sousa has a scenic spread in rural Spain where his geese enjoy a never-ending buffet of figs, olives and other natural offerings of the land, as well as grain he provides for them. By the time he finally slaughters these geese, their livers have plumped up on their own—maybe not up to the French standard but large enough that he was calling his product "ethical foie gras." When the Patería de Sousa won the Coup de Coeur award for innovation at the Paris International Food Salon (a trade show) in October 2006, the French foie gras community was aghast. This wasn't real foie gras, charged the traditionalists, including André and Ariane Daguin and Guy de Saint Laurent. He *couldn't* have produced sufficiently fatty livers while letting the geese voluntarily feed themselves; thousands of years of history indicated this couldn't be done. That Sousa sold no fresh lobes, just products in jars and cans, only fed the skepticism. On the other side, animal-rights groups seized on Sousa's products as proof that the traditional means of making foie gras could be replaced. HSUS cited Patería de Sousa in one of its lawsuits to declare, "The process of force feeding is completely unnecessary for the production of foie gras."

Some restaurants and stores certainly welcomed the opportunity to serve a foie gras they considered humane. "It was actually our best-selling dish when it was on because people loved the whole ethical concept of it," said John Hudgell, owner of Cambridge's Alimentum, the first U.K. restaurant to carry Sousa's product. "I need to get some more; the demand is outstripping the supply." The London department store Selfridges pledged to stock the Spanish "welfare-friendly foie gras" and incurred public wrath—including a scolding by the duke and duchess of Hamilton—when it failed to do so while still offering the traditional version. "The weather remained too warm, and the birds intuitively did not prepare for migration," Selfridges chief executive Paul Kelly wrote to the duchess of Hamilton in April 2008. "Hence, the farmer has not been able to supply us."

Supply turned out to be a significant issue. Now that the prospect of non-force-fed foie gras had been publicized, everybody wanted it—and just about no one had it. Even Hudgell, the restaurateur whose endorsement of Patería de Sousa in the British press and food publications helped fuel international demand, couldn't get anything beyond his initial shipment despite assurances to the contrary. After more than a year of waiting, he'd become disillusioned. "He promises the world and delivers nothing, which is all very frustrating," Hudgell said of Sousa when I spoke to him again. "He doesn't return calls. He doesn't return e-mails. He loves the limelight, but he just doesn't deliver." (Sousa couldn't be reached for this book either.)

Hudgell even had come to wonder about Sousa's claims for his product. When the British restaurateur had visited the farm, he'd seen only about 30 geese, so, really, he was taking the producer's word for just about everything. Still, to Hudgell, the larger, more important point was this: "I can't understand why there aren't other people out there who are rearing geese and producing natural foie gras. The market would be so huge." Of course, the skeptics' simple answer was it can't be done.

In the United States, Dan Barber, chef of Blue Hill at Stone Barns, shared Hudgell's thinking. He returned from a visit to Sousa's farm not only raving about its product but also hoping to emulate the Spaniard's natural way of raising and fattening geese in the United States. The Stone Barns Center for Food and Agriculture is a nonprofit, sustainable farm located near Tarrytown, New York (about 30 miles north of New York City), on grounds donated by the Rockefeller estate. The independently operated Blue Hill is contracted to obtain the bulk of its meat and produce from the farm. You could walk down to see the black Berkshire pigs, lambs and cows hanging out in their barns or roaming the hilly fields; you could stroll through the greenhouse and admire the great variety of lettuces and other vegetables being grown; and then you could dine in the restaurant and enjoy products that couldn't be fresher or more local. School groups and other visitors constantly tour the farm to see what organic, sustainable farming looks like. In a way the idyllic setting is reminiscent of Farm Sanctuary in Watkins Glen but with a key distinction: Eventually all of these animals will be eaten. The farm faced a bit of a dilemma early on in deciding what to do about Boris, a five-and-a-half-year-old, 900-pound boar that had become something of a fixture there. Boris had grown too big for breeding, and the farm mangers didn't like the message of a large wild pig with no purpose serving as an unofficial mascot. This was a viable farm, not a petting zoo. Boris became charcuterie and other dishes at the restaurant and a food bank.

Barber is one of the country's highest-regarded young chefs (he was a finalist for the James Beard Foundation's 2008 Outstanding Chef Award), and the foremost issue to him was flavor, which he thought the Sousa liver had in spades. "It's far and away the best I've ever had," he told me.

"Better than your standard foie gras?" I asked.

"Oh, yeah. It doesn't compare," he said. "It was rich without being coating in your mouth. It was a clean fat. What you're tasting really is the liver as opposed to the corn products. That's revelatory because in that sense, when you're tasting just the fat, you're really tasting the nearly 100-percent corn diet, and the variances in the flavor are pretty flat." In contrast, he continued, the Patería de Sousa liver didn't need to be offset by traditional sweet or vinegary complements because the geese's varied diet already had built such flavor complexity into the organ.

All that said, though, Barber acknowledged that Sousa's product wasn't necessarily a substitute for standard foie gras. For one, eating a precooked, preserved liver is different from searing or making a terrine out of the raw stuff. "I'm pretty sure that if I had roasted Eduardo's foie gras, I would have been disappointed," Barber said. But to Barber, this wasn't an either-or equation; he was encouraged and inspired that a farmer was coming up with a new method of producing something that's delicious and ethically sound. "Is there a way to solve this unending quest for good flavor with good ecology, with good ecological decisions?" he asked. "It seemed to me like this was the kind of guy with a red-hot-button issue like foie gras that did both."

Barber told me he had brought some of Sousa's jarred foie gras back from Spain, and he invited me to have a taste. I wasn't going to say no. To contribute something from my end, I ordered Barber a two-pound package of Grade 1 Natural Fatty Goose Liver from Schiltz Goose Farm, the same South Dakota farm that Guillermo Gonzalez had visited decades earlier in his quest for foie gras knowledge. The Schiltz operators had noticed that the older geese that it processed later in the year had livers that were fattier and almost three times larger than the norm, so given the furor over foie gras, they decided to market them separately. The retail price was $56 for two pounds, a bit less than one would pay for fresh foie gras. These geese had been grain fed rather than living off the land, but still, could this be the U.S. answer to Sousa?

I flew out to New York in April 2008, and Barber arranged a taste test as part of a mind-blowing meal at Stone Barns. On the plate was some of Sousa's product straight from the jar, which was labeled "Spanish ethical foie gras (without mistreatment)," and a seared slice of the Schiltz liver. This was an apples-and-oranges comparison, but there was no question which was more enjoyable. The Sousa was indeed meatier than the preserved foie gras I'd sampled in France; it most resembled the foie gras I'd prepared at the Daubas farm in which the bulk of the fat had been cooked out of it. The Sousa liver wasn't particularly rich or fatty, it was more dense than buttery, and it had a more pronounced liver flavor than the more delicate foie. For a jarred product, this was tasty—and I imagined I could detect the figs and olives, though I wouldn't swear to it. I doubted, however, that fans of a *mi-cuit* foie gras preparation would find this an adequate substitute. The Schiltz liver, in contrast, was closer to liver-liver than foie gras liver in its taste and texture. It was intense to the point of harsh, with an unpleasant metallic quality. Maybe something in its freezing or shipping had affected its flavor, but as it was this product had not justified its inclusion in the foie gras discussion.

Barber was so excited about his Sousa visit that he'd arranged a collaboration with the Stone Barns farmers. In the next week, the farm would receive 100 geese that it would raise mostly to sell as meat to the public or the restaurant. But come fall, Barber would assume the care of 40 of these birds and would try to feed them naturally in a Sousa-inspired way. Of course, the Tarrytown farm lacked figs and olives growing everywhere, so Barber would have to improvise. When we spoke over the summer, he envisioned cooking sweet carrots for his geese or maybe giving them overripe fruit in addition to the grass and perhaps grain that they would eat. "I don't know what a good substitute for figs and some of that other stuff is," he said. "I'm trying to figure that out, but it's got to be economical and from our farm or around us."

Barber was aware that he was improvising—and he had to learn the best ways to cook goose as well. He didn't see himself as threatening Hudson Valley; he just appreciated the challenge of approaching foie gras in new, ethically and environmentally sound ways. The spike in corn prices alone was enough to make the chef think that alternative feeding strategies were worth exploring. "What I understand is there's a different way to think about a difficult situation," he said, "and the way to answer the challenge just might be to think that there's an ecological solution to what we want."

Regardless of whether Barber's experiment yielded fantastic goose livers, a farm such as Hudson Valley wasn't about to let loose its hundreds of thousands of ducks so they could fatten themselves naturally. As Michael Ginor told Nick Cooney, there was no way that would work from a practical or financial standpoint. After 5,000 years that's not what foie gras would become.

So what I wanted was a final assessment of foie gras as it exists. Is it cruel? Humane? Somewhere in between? Part of the challenge all along had been to find anyone who could offer knowledgeable insights without being accused of partiality by either side. Wasn't there any so-called expert who was universally revered?

Actually . . . yes. Colorado-based animal scientist Temple Grandin has credentials like no other. An autistic woman now in her early 60s, Grandin is considered a groundbreaker in her work to relieve animal distress. The author of such bestsellers as *Animals in Translation: Using the Mysteries of Autism to Decode Animal Behavior* (2004) and *Thinking in Pictures: And Other Reports from My Life with Autism* (1995), the Colorado State University associate professor has conducted extensive research into how various animals process fear, pain and suffering. But her impact goes far beyond the theoretical: In redesigning companies' livestock handling systems and slaughterhouses to reduce cattle stress while increasing efficiency, she is considered a revolutionary.

For her efforts she received PETA's 2004 Proggy (for "progress") Award in the Visionary category. Yes, the same PETA that stridently tolerates zero consumption of animal flesh was lauding someone who designs slaughterhouses for the meat industry. "Dr. Grandin's improvements to animal-handling systems found in slaughterhouses have decreased the amount of fear and pain that animals experience in their final hours, and she is widely considered the world's leading expert on the welfare of cattle and pigs," PETA noted approvingly. Even PETA provocateur and founder Ingrid Newkirk acknowledged to Michael Specter in the *New Yorker*: "Temple Grandin has done more to reduce suffering in the world than any other person who has ever lived."

True, she specializes in larger animals than waterfowl, but still, I thought, if anyone could offer a universally accepted diagnosis on the welfare of foie gras ducks, it would be Grandin. Then I spoke to Michael Ginor, and he dropped this bombshell: Hudson Valley Foie Gras already had asked Grandin to assess the way it handles its ducks. Wow. If Grandin declared the treatment of foie gras ducks to be humane, this small industry would gain an unassailable ally. On the flip side, if she condemned the force-feeding of ducks, the producers would have to admit that the arguments against their industry amounted to more than militant vegans picking on the little guys. Ginor asked me to hold off for a few weeks before calling her. So I waited, then left her a message.

She called me right back (which I really appreciated, by the way), and I asked her what she'd thought of the farm, and . . . trumpets, please . . . big buildup . . . la la la la la . . . she never went to Hudson Valley Foie Gras. It turned out she couldn't make the trip, so she recommended instead that the company call one of her colleagues, Erika L. Voogd, an independent consultant based in West Chicago. (Ginor, who is based in Long Island rather than on the farm, didn't know this when we spoke.) Voogd visited Hudson Valley, spent much time observing the ducks and offered an overall assessment. Citing confidentiality with her client, Voogd wouldn't discuss her findings with me, but Grandin and the folks at Hudson Valley outlined her main points. Her biggest concern apparently was that the farm had to adjust the pH levels in the ducks' bedding in the barns where they lived before the force-feeding period began. Their feet and legs had sores, and this was a problem.

Other aspects of the ducks' conditions required attention as well, such as the voltage of the slaughterhouse stunner, but nowhere in her report did she mention the force-feedings. Izzy Yanay wasn't surprised—but then again he was. "I know what I know, he said, "but I thought that she's going to have a problem with the feeding from the point of view of the ducks. Even though I *know* it doesn't bother them, I was a little bit relieved." Hudson Valley began adjusting the ducks' bedding while setting its sights on the best-case scenario of Voogd's visits: her eventually giving the farm an audit and, if it passed, declaring it to be "humane." Already Rick Bishop had begun work on improving Hudson Valley Foie Gras's public image. For one, the egg industry and others had demonstrated the power of the label "cage free," yet Hudson Valley had done nothing to get the word out that its ducks were not in cages. So in early 2008, Hudson Valley's products began carrying a "cage free" label, and company literature also touted the product as "America's Foie Gras," the redundant "100% All Natural" and "The Humane Choice," with Hudson Valley identifying itself as "The premier source of foie gras in America produced by artisanal farmers using humane and sustainable farming methods."

I still wanted to look at those ducks one last time. Seeking expert advice to prepare for my return trip to Hudson Valley, I asked Holly Cheever how I could tell whether I was getting the "white glove" tour. She previously had complained that upon her third trip to Hudson Valley, the farm had become expert at covering up the kind of problems she saw on her first two visits. She told me I was likely to see just one or two feeders working exceptionally slowly rather than a full battalion of workers "jamming" the tubes rapidly. She also was convinced that the ducks typically identified as being in their third or fourth week of gavage actually were in their second week, when they weren't showing many symptoms of distress. "If you see nothing but very pretty birds with nice intact feathers, those are going to be birds that are probably typically two-and-a-half weeks or less," she said. In addition, I should look for leg fractures, wounds and sores as well as strange behavior due to neurological problems, though she doubted I'd see any of those symptoms because those ducks no doubt would have been removed beforehand. "I think what Izzy does is try to make sure that any animal you see is going to be pretty free of blemishes and free of pathological behaviors, attitudes, movements, etc.," she said. I probably would see panting, however.

When I spoke with Grandin, I asked what she would look for at the farm. For one, she said, the basics must be in place. "The feathers better be in good condition. They don't have sores on their feet. They're free to walk around." Individual cages, as used in France and Canada, would be "totally unacceptable." Panting also might be a problem. "If the birds are panting, you've pushed the force-feeding too far," she said. "You should stop before they get to the panting stage. It gets into this whole thing of overloading the biology to the point where the biology is starting to fall apart." Likewise, the ducks shouldn't be struggling to walk. "Hobbling is not OK," she said, though she acknowledged that every farm is going to have some lame animals. "It's a matter of how many. There's no way that the lame animals can be zero. One percent probably would be acceptable, but 10 percent is not acceptable."

Whether the ducks could go outside was not a particular concern for Grandin. "That's a separate issue from the foie gras, because that issue comes up with lots of other animals, too." But the air in those barns must be relatively clean and well circulated. "Overpowering ammonia, that's not acceptable, I don't care what species you've got in the house." At the same time, though, "you're going to have some gamey duck smell. You can't get rid of the barnyard totally."

"OK," I said, "but is making a bird's liver grow to 10 times its normal size inherently cruel?"

"It's unnatural to make the liver grow that big, but it doesn't cause a welfare problem as long as the birds are walking around, the birds are not hyperventilating, they're not so weak they can barely move," Grandin said. "Look at what we've got with the dairy cow. She gives 10 times more milk than a beef cow does. But there's a point where the whole animal starts to have all kinds of problems, like some of these ducks that I saw within this awful place in France in these small cages—they would force them to the point where the ducks could barely even lift their heads up. That's just hideous . . .

"Foie gras is not the sort of thing that I'm going to encourage. You're not going to find me an active supporter of this. But on the other hand, I'm not going to go after it either unless they're doing stuff like forcing them to the point where they become lame and they can't hardly move, they're panting, they're in ammonia-infested buildings, they've all got foot lesions, you walk in the pen, and the birds are trying to climb up the wall on the other side."

Basically, Grandin said, there was one simple way to measure whether foie gras production is cruel—and it was basically the same method in which Izzy had said this matter should be assessed: Watch the ducks. "Look at their behavior," she said. "Do they approach the feeder, or do they try to run away? If they actively avoid, then that may be torture." Voogd, she noted, didn't make a determination on this point. "What I would like to do if I had been there, I would have asked the feeder to just stand, and I want to see if the geese or the ducks come up to him," she said. "I would give them a chance to approach rather than just going in and grabbing them."

"But what if they're somewhere in the middle," I asked, "not scrambling to get away but not approaching the feeder either, appearing more indifferent than eager or horrified?"

The key, she replied, was active avoidance. The ducks wouldn't have been conditioned to accept the force-feeding passively—"let's say you shocked them; they would actively avoid"—so if the birds are feeling distress, they will unambiguously move away from the feeder.

I asked Grandin whether she would accompany me to Hudson Valley Foie Gras so she could conduct such an experiment, but she said no. Repeatedly. But she also said she didn't need to be there; I could make these observations as easily as she could.

Well . . . OK.

I returned to Hudson Valley on a spring morning, and Izzy again pledged to show me whatever I wanted to see. We started right away in the "hand-feeding" barns, and the first thing I noticed was that the air was cool and ducky without any ammonia smell. The second thing I noticed was that five feeders were working in the long rows of pens on the second floor, and several more were feeding the ducks downstairs, so I seemed to be witnessing business as usual. Having seen feedings on about 10 farms by that point, I also didn't notice them working any slower or more delicately than anywhere else. They were taking the duck, lowering the tube down its esophagus, scooping in the feed and releasing the duck. If the birds found this traumatic, they still weren't showing it. Their feathers for the most part looked like feathers.

Izzy asked his foreman in Spanish how long the ducks had been in gavage, and the answer was 22 and 24 days for the ones on the right and 15 days for those on the left. I watched the 22-day birds getting fed, and I paid special attention to the ducks' reactions as the feeder stepped into the pen. Did they crowd around him with their beaks open? No. Did they climb over each other on tattered wings to get away? No. Upon his appearance, they huddled in the corner and looked away, resisting the catch without getting wild. "They don't love it to be caught," Izzy said, "but it's not in any way causing them panic." When we walked up the rows, most of the ducks ignored us. A bunch of them were panting, which if nothing else suggested that these birds were, in fact, far along in the feeding process. "It's hot," Izzy said.

"It feels cool to me," I said, though it probably was close to the same temperature as when the ducks were panting at Au Bon Canard.

"They're covered in down," Izzy said. "If you come like a month ago, you won't see panting at all."

Downstairs were ducks that had been in gavage for only three days, and they were more aversive to us and their feeders, clustering in the backs of the pens. "You see?" Izzy said. "That's panic."

Back upstairs, Izzy was ready to move on, but I wandered all the way to the rear of the barn. This was an experimental area, Izzy told me, where Marcus Henley was attempting to feed the ducks over 23 days instead of 28. These birds were near the end, and their feathers looked a little more ragged and wet. A dead one lay in one pen. I saw another duck that couldn't walk. These were unpleasant sights, though these few distressed or dead ducks represented a small percentage of the population back here. "I don't know what the story of this experiment is," Izzy said.

Overall, Izzy was feeling encouraged. The Humane Society's lawsuit over Hudson Valley selling adulterated food had been dismissed (though HSUS was appealing), as had been the one objecting to Hudson Valley's development grant from the state. What especially surprised him was that in March 2008, the Maryland legislature shot down a proposed ban of the sale and production of foie gras even though 13 senators and 41 house members had co-sponsored the respective bills. Maryland didn't boast a terribly strong gourmet food scene, and Izzy had a feeling of foreboding as he traveled down there for yet another round of government hearings. Yet the Restaurant Association of Maryland had led a tour of Hudson Valley Foie Gras, food professionals and veterinarians spoke out against the bill, and the senate bill's chief sponsor, Joan Carter Conway, backed away, saying, "I have heard additional information about the foie gras process that has caused me to change my mind." The ban died.

Izzy may not have reverted to his old happy-go-lucky self, but he had visions of his farm officially being declared humane by an animal-treatment specialist, although the process might take years. "With this audit we will be able to tell the animal rights people, 'Look, go someplace where you're needed, because here, the ducks don't need you. The ducks here are fine. They are not in any way disturbed, and what you say about hand-feeding being inhumane is simply not true.'"

Guillermo Gonzalez at Sonoma Foie Gras wasn't feeling too bad either. Business had rebounded to the extent that he sold 70,000 ducks' worth of his Artisan Foie Gras in 2007, close to the peak level of 2005. Plus, his lawsuit against Whole Foods had withstood all court challenges and now had a trial date: April 28, 2008. It promised to be an epic battle: a prominent producer of the world's most controversial food item against the nation's most powerful natural-food chain. Whose ethics would reign supreme?

On April 27, Whole Foods and Sonoma settled, with terms to be kept strictly confidential.

Izzy and Guillermo hoped the California legislature might revisit its foie gras ban somewhere down the line. In the meantime, there was unfinished business in Chicago.

18.

Chicago Redux

"Thank you, Alderman Joe 'Foie Gras' Moore."

A woman stood outside Chicago's City Hall on the morning of May 23, 2007, alongside a large placard showing a bloody, dead duck with the caption: "The brutality of force-feeding." Most people breezed by on their way to work amid this congested cluster of government buildings, but a few paused, such as a paunchy middle-aged guy who did not look part of the white-collar crowd. The woman told him what she was protesting, and he said, "Is that the liver? I never eat that. I eat chicken liver."

Inside the building and outside the second-floor elevators, the scene was more raucous. Mayor Richard M. Daley previously had hinted that the city council might try to repeal its foie gras ban at that morning's meeting, so the animal-rights crowd mobilized. The Humane Society of the United States took out full-page ads in the *Tribune* and *Sun-Times* reinforcing its appreciation of the ban that the city council had passed 13 months earlier and instructing readers: "Tell your alderman that repealing this humane law would be just as tough to swallow as the cruel force-feeding of birds." The Humane Society and Farm Sanctuary also enlisted animal experts and other sympathetic professionals to send new letters to city hall backing the ban, and PETA designed a new poster that, in typically sensational form, appealed to the public's tendency to imagine themselves as the ducks: It depicts a woman—Miss United Kingdom, in fact—in a black dress tied to a restaurant chair with a plate of what appears to be foie gras in front of her. She's looking terrified toward the waiter whose gloved right hand is holding her jaw open while his gloved left hand clutches a yellow-food-filled funnel with a fat tube sticking down her throat, yellow gunk overflowing from her open, blood-dripping mouth. "Get a Taste for Foie Gras," blares the bold type while a smaller message asks viewers to call the 311 city services number "to urge your alderman to keep this cruel product *banned* in Chicago."

Meanwhile, local activists posted online "meetup" notices to promote a strong turnout at the "demo and press conference" before the meeting, and their efforts paid off. A few dozen protesters plus several TV news crews crowded the second-floor hallway where, against the wall opposite the doors leading to the council chamber, a lectern was flanked by posters and protesters clutching signs with slogans such as "Ducks lie in vomit 24 hours a day," "DALEY WANTS TO FIX IT SO ELITE PALS CAN HAVE THEIR TASTE OF TORTURE," "Foie Gras. How much cruelty can you swallow?" and "DALEY'S SLOGAN FOR OLYMPICS: CHICAGO ♥ TORTURE." The accompanying imagery was your standard array of grisly duck photos plus cartoon caricatures of, for example, Mayor Daley stuffing tubes down the throats of obese rich donors with the caption, "FANCY FEAST FOR FAT CATS." From the lectern, the Humane Society's Paul Shapiro lambasted those who had deemed the city's foie gras ban a waste of time and resources: "More than a year later, it is Mayor Daley who refuses to let the issue go, and he keeps revisiting it over and over and over in an effort to bring animal cruelty back to Chicago." Alderman Joe Moore hit his usual populist notes hard, characterizing the repeal efforts as being at the behest of "the very few elite people who are able to spend $20 to $25 for an appetizer at a fancy French restaurant . . . the fat cats that want to satisfy their palates with an appetite for inhumanity and cruelty."

Standing out amid the receptive crowd was Didier Durand of Cyrano's Bistrot in his chef's whites, tall toque and that oh-so-French pencil-thin mustache. He was silently holding up an index card on which he had scribbled in pencil: "I love foie gras." After the speeches ended, a local TV crew interviewed Durand, and activists bunched up behind him, held up a poster of a particularly gross-looking liver, and chanted, "Stop the insanity! Cruelty isn't a delicacy!" and "Stop the torture! Stop the pain! Foie gras is to blame!" and "Foie gras is obscene! Foie gras is obscene! Broken beaks and force-feeding!"

As Moore walked toward the chambers, I asked him whether the council really was going to vote on a repeal this morning. "No," he said. He was correct.

The prospect of a repeal had been floating around since the month after the ban took effect. Two of the city's most veteran aldermen, Burt Natarus and Bernard Stone, introduced the rollback legislation in September 2006 with the mayor's approval; in fact, they proposed it the same day that the mayor issued his first veto since taking office in 1989, of another Moore-sponsored ordinance, one that would have required big-box stores such as Wal-Mart to pay employees a "living wage" rather than the lower minimum wage required of any other business. The living-wage ordinance *was* an issue in which Daley had much invested—he wanted those chain megastores in the city—and as he took a stand against an increasingly combative council, he bashed them harder on foie gras as well. Days before the repeal effort was announced, he came up with yet another way to apply the word "silliest" to the ban, saying: "I think that was one of the silliest, silliest decisions anyone made, to outlaw foie gras." The mayor also told reporters he planned to "take care of" the ordinance, a statement that took on more weight given that his former chief of staff, Sheila O'Grady, had just become president of the Illinois Restaurant Association.

The two aldermen, however, denied that the mayor had prompted them to sponsor the repeal. Natarus was quoted as saying he'd changed his mind about foie gras since the ban's passage, noting he'd spoken to restaurant people, their customers and animal-welfare people, "and they really don't think it is that much of a problem." Stone's main issue was the ridicule he felt Chicago was enduring because of the ban. Stone said someone in Houston "told me what a laughingstock it is in Houston," and that person's sister in Albany, New York, said "we are a laughingstock in Albany." If that person had an uncle in Wichita, he no doubt would've said Chicago was a laughingstock there, too. Of course, the mayor's continued public deriding of the council didn't help. "He made us look like a bunch of silly asses," Stone told a local TV station.

The repeal legislation's introduction spurred new, intense efforts to lobby aldermen and the public. Moore held a City Hall news conference where he name-checked St. Francis of Assisi and St. Philip Neri and quoted Mahatma Gandhi and the prophet Muhammad. Sharing the podium with Moore were a rabbi and a priest who also praised the ban, as well as Holly Cheever, back again to "thank Chicago for passing such an enlightened ordinance, which far from being a source of shame across the country really should be a badge of courage." Meanwhile, the foie gras supporters flew in Hudson Valley defender Lawrence Bartholf and French researcher Daniel Guémené to meet with aldermen and local chefs and restaurant owners at a scenic Navy Pier restaurant. After hearing the pair discuss studies showing that the ducks do not suffer, Alderman Shirley Coleman, who had been so wowed by Loretta Swit's testimony before she voted for the ban, sounded a new tune. "It opened my eyes," she told the *Tribune.* "I'm really searching for the right side of the moral and the ethical. We are trying to be a global city. I'm not sure it's my job to tell restaurants what they can or cannot sell."

Shortly after Stone and Natarus filed their repeal ordinance, Alderman Ed Burke, the council's most powerful and longest-serving member, wrote a letter to a Massachusetts animal-protection group's leader who had praised the city's foie gras ban. Burke wrote:

> Some aldermen have announced that they will attempt to roll back the ban on foie gras. I strongly supported passage of this measure in the past and I plan to continue to fight against its repeal in the future.
>
> The unethical treatment of animals should be completely distasteful to anyone who stops to consider the horrible process by which this so-called delicacy is produced. The City Council would do itself a great disservice by reversing this humane and progressive decision. Despite the pressure that is coming from the restaurant industry and some of my colleagues, I believe that this law should be left on the books and properly enforced by city inspectors.

Burke, you may recall, also is the alderman who congratulated Moore from the council floor immediately after the foie gras ban was passed into the omnibus. As chairman of the powerful Finance Committee—and a veteran of almost 40 years in the council—Burke wields more clout than anyone apart from the mayor, and the two work closely together. So if Daley was publicly pushing a repeal, one might have expected Burke to follow suit. But then again the mayor had been complaining about the ordinance even when he was taking no action to halt it. At any rate, Burke felt comfortable pledging his support to the ban.

The repeal measure went back into Ed Smith's Health Committee, but Smith wanted nothing to do with it. He'd moved the foie gras ban from his committee in the first place and gotten it passed through the full council. That was his job. "I don't think we ought to be in the habit of coming to the floor and dismantling everything that has taken place in committee," he told me. "That's bad government. It really is. It shows in the first place that you weren't on your p's and q's, and you weren't there when you should have been there." Smith never scheduled a hearing on the repeal ordinance, so it just sat there.

Finally in May 2007, one alderman pulled an obscure parliamentary move to free the legislation from Smith's clutches. That alderman was, yes, Burke. He posted a notice that he intended to "discharge" the ordinance from the Health Committee so the full council could vote on it. An incensed Smith wrote a letter to his fellow aldermen threatening to resign his Health Committee chairmanship and membership in all other committees if they repealed the foie gras ban. "My manhood, my integrity is at stake," he declared to reporters. When I spoke with him later, he complained, "Why would you want to do that to me? Ordinances haven't been taken out of anyone else's committee over the years that I have read about. It had never been done to anyone else, so why do you want to do this to me?" Yes, he took this personally.

Burke told me later that he moved to discharge the ordinance from Smith's committee because committee chairmen are supposed to schedule hearings on new ordinances, period. "If the rules are to be the rules, then they have to be followed," Burke said matter-of-factly. But he ultimately did not bring the matter to a vote. The city council session ended with the foie gras ban still on the books.

By this time the city's 2007 aldermanic elections had taken place, and repeal cosponsor Burt Natarus had gone down to defeat (though not because of foie gras), as had Shirley Coleman. Joe Moore, meanwhile, couldn't muster a majority against three opponents and faced a tough run-off against banking executive Don Gordon. It was a tight, tense race, with the restaurant crowd cheering on Gordon, who characterized the incumbent as someone who spent too much energy on issues other than improving his constituents' lives. "We don't have stores to shop at here, we still have crime problems, our affordable housing is disappearing, and this guy is introducing legislation for ducks," Gordon complained to the *Tribune*. Moore's official city council biography on his Web site offered more than 1,200 words' worth of legislative and public-service accomplishments, but two words that did not appear were "foie" and "gras."

Moore beat Gordon in the run-off by 251 votes.

In the next legislative session, Bernard Stone introduced another repeal ordinance, as did Tom Tunney, the alderman who said he'd intended to vote against the ban the first time but missed his chance. First elected in 2003, Tunney was a relative newcomer to the council, and he made headlines as the first openly gay alderman, but more relevant to this issue, he also was the successful owner of Ann Sather, a beloved Swedish-themed breakfast-and-lunch restaurant chain anchored in the upscale Lakeview neighborhood that he now represented. Tunney was sympathetic to his fellow restaurateurs' concerns, and he was working closely with the Illinois Restaurant Association to strategize the introduction of his ordinance.

Burke assisted Tunney by moving the repeal measure into the Committee on Committees, Rules and Ethics (more commonly known as the Rules Committee), the place where ordinances go when there's a turf war regarding how it should be handled—the dispute here being that Smith had refused to call a Health Committee hearing on the previous incarnation. This committee included the whole of the council membership, and its chairman was Alderman Richard Mell, who had complained about the ban's lack of a roll-call vote. He wouldn't be scheduling a hearing on this ordinance either, but for a different reason than Smith. The one relevant point about all of this maneuvering was that Tunney's repeal had found a safe place to park.

By this point about a dozen restaurants in town still were serving the delicacy either on a by-request basis or through the "it's free" ruse. Still, most restaurants that had been serving foie gras before the ban no longer were. European Imports, the city's largest distributor of gourmet foods, was supplying foie to a few individual Chicago chefs but otherwise had quit selling it in the city. Tim Doyle, in charge of meat and game at European, estimated that his company lost $500,000 in foie gras sales in Chicago in 2007. Most restaurants did not wish to risk citations and fines, no matter how sporadically the ban actually was being enforced. The city still occasionally fielded and responded to complaints about foie-serving restaurants. Health inspectors visited Durand's Cyrano's Bistrot looking for the contraband ingredient but instead found cockroaches and shut down the restaurant for a week. Construction had been taking place on Cyrano's block for months, but Durand had his own theory on why he failed that inspection: "I think PETA planted them. I never had roaches in 12 years."

In late March 2008, I visited Ed Burke in his aldermanic office trying to get a read on the proposed repeal that had been gathering dust for months. If Alderman Tunney and his allies pushed it at the April meeting, would he support it?

"It doesn't seem to have any real legs to get it repealed, does it?" Burke said. "Has the restaurant association done anything? They have not been lobbying the issue. Nobody has talked to me about this except you in months."

"What is your gut feeling on this?" I asked.

"Right now I'd say it's just going to stay in the books. It's not enforced. It's not like there is any foie gras police out there sneaking around restaurants to see if people are serving it."

Chef Durand had a different gut feeling; he was so convinced that the ban would be repealed at that April meeting that he made some unusual preparations for the photo opportunities that inevitably would follow. When the council wound up taking no action yet again, he e-mailed me: "That blew my mind! I was so sure! I had my live pet duck 'Nicolas' (after Nicolas Sarkozy) in my Truck!!!"

No one was standing outside City Hall on the morning of May 14, 2008, with any placards showing bloody dead ducks. In the lobby by the second-floor elevators, no lectern had been set up. No activists were hoisting posters or chanting slogans. No officials from the Humane Society of the United States, Farm Sanctuary or People for the Ethical Treatment of Animals were present. All was quiet. It was a routine morning of a routine city council meeting.

But something was afoot. Two days earlier Alderman Tunney had posted a letter on the council's hallway bulletin board that read:

To Whom It May Concern:

Pursuant to Rule 41 of the City Council Rules of Order, I hereby give notice that at the City Council meeting to be held on May 14, 2008, I intend to move to discharge the Committee on Committees, Rules and Ethics from further consideration of an ordinance repealing Chapter 7-39 of the Municipal Code, which ordinance was referred to and is pending in that Committee, and further intend to place that ordinance for immediate consideration by the City Council by calling for a vote thereon, under the heading of Miscellaneous Business.

You had to be paying attention to know that chapter 7-39 of the Municipal Code was the city's foie gras ban.

Tunney's and the Illinois Restaurant Association's strategy all along was to push this repeal quietly and to bring it up when the votes were there and the council wasn't tackling any big, emotionally charged issues. The fall's budget battles were a bad time. That April meeting *had* been a strong possibility, but the city was reeling from a string of child murders on the South and West Sides, and the council risked further ridicule if they juxtaposed duck livers with those headlines. In May, however, the coast seemed relatively clear.

The May 14 council meeting began, as many do, with a series of resolutions honoring Chicagoans who had done good. The Miscellaneous Business part of the meeting, where Tunney had announced his intentions to call for the ban's repeal, wouldn't take place until after all of these resolutions had passed and the 19 council committee chairmen had presented their reports. The special resolutions alone took more than two hours, with council members grabbing doughnuts in the back room, speaking on their cell phones and hobnobbing. Even the mayor was going back and forth amid the speechifying, as was Joe Moore.

The foie gras ban's champion projected a casual cheerfulness as he chatted with colleagues and reporters. As Moore passed by the press table, I asked him whether the ban was getting repealed this day, and he shook his head and said, "I've got a trick or two up my sleeve, so we'll see what happens." Then he winked. A bit later, he and Daley chatted briefly in the doorway and again in the back room, the alderman towering over the mayor in every way but stature.

"What did he say?" one reporter asked Moore as he reemerged.

"He hates ducks," Moore quipped. "Just kidding." (Actually they were discussing another of those Moore ordinances that drove the mayor nuts: a resolution formally opposing a U.S. invasion of Iran. Daley got his way; the aldermen tabled it till a future meeting.)

As the meeting progressed, Moore worked the chamber floor, seating himself beside one colleague after another and talking extensively. Tunney also was making the rounds. At times the two aldermen were one row apart, pitching away. In the back room, someone on the restaurant association side confidently stated that none of this activity would matter. Moore ultimately would stand up and give a speech opposing the repeal. Another of the ban's supporters might do the same. But it wouldn't make a difference. The repeal had the votes.

Nevertheless, the aldermen and behind-the-scenes folks carried on many an intense powwow in the back room, phrases like "But state law says . . ." wafting out of hushed conversations. Back on the floor, the committee chairmen were dutifully presenting their reports, thus chewing up another hour and change. Usually by this point, the mayor would have departed to a nearby meeting room with a cluster of reporters in tow to offer a briefing and to field questions before he took off. Today, however, he was sticking around, and everyone knew why. He killed time in the back bantering with doughnut-munching reporters.

By the time the meeting hit the three-hour-and-50-minute mark, however, the reporters were back at their tables set off to stage left, the TV folks were poised by their cameras, the aldermen had returned to their designated seats, and the mayor was in his raised chair facing them all and calling for Miscellaneous Business. The room fell silent.

Tunney stood, and, sounding like he was reciting a script that he had nervously memorized, moved "to discharge the Committee on Committees, Rules and Ethics from further consideration of an article repealing chapter seven dash 39, foie gras ban." Tunney asked whether that committee's chairman, Richard Mell, had any objection, and Mell responded no—and also that he wasn't concerned that the ordinance's removal from his committee might set a dangerous precedent because it was being done with his approval. In other words, his manhood wasn't threatened. Tunney then called for a roll-call vote on his first motion.

"Clerk, call the roll," the mayor said.

"Mr. President?" Moore, now standing, addressed the mayor. "Thank you, Mr. President. Ladies and gentlemen of the council, this is nearly unprecedented, certainly in the time that *I've* been in the city council, that any chairman—"

"The chair recognizes Alderman Stone," the mayor cut in with a bang of his gavel, referring to Bernard Stone, who, as 50th Ward alderman, was standing directly to Moore's left.

"This vote as a motion is not debatable," Stone said matter-of-factly.

Daley banged his gavel again. "So moved," he said. "Clerk, call the roll."

"Mr. President?" Moore interjected.

"Clerk, call the roll," Daley repeated without pause.

The clerk started calling the names of the 50 council members, 49 of whom were present, in their ward's numerical order.

"Alderman Flores."

"Yes."

"Alderman Fioretti."

"Aye."

"Alderman Dowell."

"Aye."

"Alderman Preckwinkle."

"No."

It went on like that to the tune of 38 in favor, five opposed and six who sat on their hands.

"Motion is carried," Daley said. "Chair recognizes Alderman Tunney." He banged the gavel.

"Thank you, Mr. President," Tunney said.

"Mr. President?" Moore interrupted.

"The matter now being before the council, I call for a roll-call vote—," Tunney continued.

"Mr. President!"

"—on the ordinance to repeal the foie gras ban."

Moore persisted: "Mr. President, Alderman Muñoz and I move to defer and publish."

This apparently was the trick that Moore had up his sleeve. "Defer and publish" is a parliamentary maneuver in which a minimum of two aldermen can move to have a vote postponed until the following meeting. Give the ban a stay of execution, mobilize the animal-rights folks to flood the aldermen's offices with letters and e-mails, and who knew what might happen?

"The chair recognizes Alderman Burke," Daley said and banged his gavel.

"The motion to defer and publish, in my humble opinion, is created by state law and permits only a report of a committee to be deferred," Burke said. Because this ordinance wasn't being reported out of a committee, Moore's motion wasn't valid.

"That is correct," Daley said and banged his gavel.

"Mr. President, I appeal the ruling of the chair?" Moore asked.

Daley gave him an "Are you crazy?" look. The mayor *was* the chair. "The ruling of the chair is sustained," he stated, and as Moore kept talking, he continued, "All those in favor say 'Aye.'"

The room erupted in one loud "AYE!"

"ROLL CALL!" one alderman shouted with a little extra relish.

"The chair recognizes Alderman Tunney," Daley said.

Moore remained standing. "I'd like to state the basis of my appeal of the ruling," he said.

"The chair recognizes Alderman Tunney."

"The matter now being before the council," Tunney repeated from before, "I call for a roll-call vote on the ordinance to repeal the foie gras ban."

Moore continued trying to be recognized but was instead getting ignored. "Mr. President, on the merits?" he tried again.

"Clerk, call the roll," Daley directed, his arms crossed, his look stern.

"On the merits, Mr. President!" Moore shouted.

"Clerk, call the roll."

"Alderman Flores."

"Yes."

"Alderman Fioretti."

"Aye."

"Alderman Dowell."

"Aye."

"Mr. President," Moore implored, his face turning red, his voice rising in volume and pitch, "I would respectfully ask that you respect the members of this council—"

"Alderman Preckwinkle."

"No."

"—and allow us to debate the ordinance itself!"

"Alderman Hairston."

(No response.)

"Mr. President!" Moore kept shouting.

"Alderman Lyle."

"Aye."

"I think we are entitled to a debate on the ordinance that we are being asked to consider!" bristled Moore.

"Alderman Jackson."

(No response.)

"Mr. President!"

"Alderman Harris."

"Aye."

"Alderman Beale."

"Aye."

"Alderman Pope."

"Aye."

Moore finally stopped trying to shout over the vote. He just stood there like a captain stubbornly clutching the wheel of a sinking ship. He was drowning in ayes.

"Alderman Balcer."

"Aye."

"Alderman Cardenas."

"Aye."

Eventually, the clerk reached the 49th Ward representative. "Alderman Moore."

Pause.

"NO," Moore announced irritably, prompting titters in the chamber.

"Alderman Stone."

"Aye."

That was it. "There are 37 yeas, six nays, the ordinance is passed," Daley said sleepily. There was no applause or reaction.

As the mayor attempted to proceed with some procedural business, Moore called out, "Mr. President!"

"Date of next meeting—," Daley said.

"Mr. President!"

"Date of next meeting—"

"Mr. President!"

Daley paused, then said simply, "Alderman Moore."

"Thank you, Mr. President. Under miscellaneous business that we just—note for the record that where today it could happen to me, tomorrow it could happen to you," Moore said, looking around at the room of aldermen who had just silently witnessed him getting squashed like a bug. He added in an exasperated voice, "All we were asking for was *a simple debate on the issue.* Thank you, Mr. President."

"Thank you—," the mayor began.

"A Simple. Public. Debate."

Deliberately, dryly, Mayor Daley responded, "Thank you, Alderman Joe 'Foie Gras' Moore."

He banged his gavel. After eight heated minutes at the tail end of a four-hour city council meeting, Foie Gras Prohibition was over.

• • •

In the back room minutes later, the TV, radio and print reporters stood with their cameras and recorders waiting for Moore to take his usual spot before the microphones. "Why's everybody here?" Moore asked mock jovially as he approached the group. "You guys let me talk? You'll let me talk?"

"We'll let you talk," one reporter said. "We'll give you a hearing."

"Alderman, what just happened to you?" asked another.

"Even in the ugliest days of one-man rule, members of the city council still had the opportunity to debate the issues, to state their case," he said. "And quite frankly for the mayor to fail to recognize me to debate the merits of this issue was the height of arrogance. I thought we were in a democratic society here, and I thought the city council still had some semblance of democracy, but apparently today it doesn't."

While Moore complained that his fellow aldermen had ceded to the mayor what little power they had left, an official shouted from the room's entrance that Mayor Daley's news conference was about to begin. Yes, the mayor was trumping Moore once again. Most of the reporters peeled off, leaving Moore railing about the "kangaroo legislative session" to a few stragglers.

The mayor went on at length about the meeting's various innocuous resolutions before *Sun-Times* veteran City Hall reporter Fran Spielman asked, "Why did you ram through the foie gras ban?" She sounded pissed.

"Well, we didn't," the mayor said calmly. "There's been extensive, extensive, extensive debate on this . . . All the aldermen knew about the debate. They knew about the decision. They knew how they were going to vote. It's as simple as that."

"Alderman Moore seemed to feel he was being muzzled," chipped in a television reporter. "He called it one-man rule."

"No, it wasn't," Daley said. "Just look how they all voted."

"What was the downside to allowing debate today?" another TV reporter asked.

"We had all debated. We had so much debate on this. This has been going on forever. Everybody knew how they were going to vote. No one really objected. Not one other person stood up and objected. Everybody knew."

In the mayor's view, the council had made a mistake two years earlier. Now "they corrected it, simple as that." The unspoken message was this: The aldermen had defied the mayor's will and had made fools of themselves and the city. Now they had come back to papa, and natural order was restored.

Meanwhile, by refusing to let Moore speak—something the restaurant folks did *not* anticipate—the mayor gave Tunney and his restaurateur supporters some political cover. The anti-ban lobbying effort had been spearheaded by the Illinois Restaurant Association, not the mayor's office, but Mayor Daley had put himself in the position to take the heat for the ban's repeal. He could take it.

At his news conference, the mayor talked about the restaurant industry's importance in the city and the absurdities that ensued because restaurants—and restaurants only—were being barred from selling foie gras. "I mean, you could buy it in retail," he said. "You can bring it with you. They can't sell it to you. They can put it on your salad and increase your salad by $20. They can put it on a piece of toast and charge you $10 for a piece of toast. Does that make sense?" His voice grew quiet, like he was trying to impart a lesson to a grandchild. "I mean, this is what government should be doing? Telling you what you should be putting on toast?"

Izzy Yanay felt vindicated: The aldermen obviously had realized that foie gras production doesn't abuse ducks and that the council shouldn't have gotten involved in this issue in the first place. Now the animal groups no longer could point to Chicago in their literature and campaigns. "They have used this 'win' as a tool that a civilized city like Chicago has resorted to ban foie gras," Izzy said, "and now the truth is coming out, and justice is prevailing." He hoped the foie gras producers could ride their newfound momentum to push California to repeal its 2012 foie gras ban.

The animal-rights advocates felt blindsided. Although Tunney had informed Moore and Ed Smith of his intentions a month ahead of time—and although he had posted notice of the repeal ordinance on prominent council billboards 48 hours before the meeting—Moore didn't round up the usual activists. Officials at the Humane Society, Farm Sanctuary and PETA didn't know the repeal was on the agenda until the *Tribune* posted an online story the night before the meeting. Moore said he didn't give his animal-loving allies more advance notice because the repeal had been pending for so long that "I got lulled into a false sense of security." Some on the restaurant association side speculated that he'd kept his mouth shut because he knew he didn't have the votes and wanted to spare himself the embarrassment.

"Chicago politics is a messy thing. I have no idea why we were not informed earlier," Baur said, noting that if Farm Sanctuary had been given advance notice, "we would have gotten a ground game going. We would have taken it to the people. We would have raised the issue, created a public awareness about it, and I think in doing so, the mayor would have been less likely to push forward, and Tunney would have as well." PETA made a last-ditch effort to ask members to e-mail, call or fax their aldermen the morning of the meeting, "but it apparently wasn't enough time to get the message to them," PETA spokeswoman Lindsay Rajt said. "This was truly the industry's dirty political maneuvering at its worst."

Instead of another City Hall rally before the meeting, any demonstrations would have to take place after the fact, like a candlelight vigil for the ducks organized by a local group called Mercy for Animals. It was set for 7 p.m. that Friday in front of City Hall, never mind that at that time on a Friday hardly anyone is around City Hall, and it's not even dark out. Still, about 80 protesters showed up wielding candles and the usual posters of living and dead ducks in individual cages. Eventually, angrier protesters showed up outside Tunney's Ann Sather restaurant, more to punish him than to effect any change, given that the restaurant doesn't serve foie gras and Tunney wasn't about to sponsor a repeal of the repeal. The animal-rights groups faced a tough decision: whether to continue fighting in Chicago or to direct their efforts elsewhere. After all, Mayor Daley wasn't going anywhere. "He's a pretty influential voice in Chicago, and that's a problem for us right now," Baur admitted. "This is going to be a long game now."

Tunney was surprised that the mayor had silenced Moore so dramatically ("I would have cut him off at some point, but I think the idea of having no discussion was a little abrupt"), but he found symmetry in the fact that aldermen hadn't discussed the issue on the floor when the ban originally was passed. "That's why so many of them didn't have any problem repealing." He also imagined how everything might have played out if he'd put the repeal ordinance through the typical drawn-out process: The Rules Committee would pass it, the opponents would "create a storm" and demonstrate on the council floor, Moore and another alderman would move to postpone the vote, "so we'd be discussing it all summer. A number of my colleagues felt we don't want to discuss this to begin with, we *certainly* don't want to be discussing this all summer, and so I think that was enough encouragement for them to do it the extraordinary way we did it."

Moore had heard the suggestion that speedy repeal was payback for the discussion-free way the ban had passed, and he called it "such a bunch of hooey." After all, no one actively prevented anyone from speaking the first time. Baur agreed, though I asked him whether his side wouldn't have had a stronger case if the ban *had* been fully debated the first time. "It's true," Baur acknowledged. "If there was a debate on the council floor at that time and it passed, then we would have been in a stronger position later on to say, 'Look, if there was an open debate again, the repeal would fail.'"

Paul Shapiro just sounded depressed after the meeting. "The reality is this is a popular ordinance that protected animals from cruelty that should not have been repealed," he said from his Washington, D.C., office. "The council flip-flopped when it comes to animal cruelty and it shouldn't have." But in reality the council *didn't* flip-flop on animal cruelty. It never took a principled stand on animal cruelty in the first place; otherwise the tally wouldn't have swung so dramatically from 48 to one for the ban to 37 to six (plus abstentions) against. Danny Solis, who supported the ban the first time, voted for the repeal. So did Ed Burke. What changed? "Apparently, the mayor decided it was time, and that was it," Burke told me.

The senior alderman also blamed the ban's advocates for going "AWOL" while Tunney was lobbying his colleagues (apparently whoever lobbies last laughs last), but ultimately Burke considered the ban a failed law because it was barely enforced by the city's Health Department (which reports to the mayor) and ignored by many restaurants. "It might have been well intentioned, but it didn't have any effect," Burke said. "So once you realize it has no effect, do you go ahead and continue a failed strategy or do you end this embarrassment?" Still, Burke made sure to throw the ban's defeated sponsor another daisy: "I think it got a lot of public attention, so to that extent I think Joe Moore accomplished something."

And what did the city council learn? All of the time that the city was in the spotlight over foie gras, that Chicago was the one place where selling foie gras in restaurants was illegal, none of the aldermen actually went to see firsthand how this product is produced despite invitations to do so. Granted, if legislators took out-of-state field trips for every controversial issue that crossed their desks, they'd never be around to take care of business. Nevertheless, they weren't all that curious about the welfare of force-fed ducks even if those ducks were the basis of the groundbreaking legislation. None of the aldermen's constituents had webbed feet, after all, though some constituents served or ate such creatures. So the council spent 20 seconds passing the foie gras ban in 2006 and eight minutes repealing it in 2008 without one minute of true public debate. The bulk of the aldermen initially banned foie gras because they weren't paying attention, or they didn't think their constituents would care one way or another, *they* certainly didn't care, and so they figured they'd do Joe Moore a favor and maybe get some payback down the line. The aldermen repealed that very same ban because they thought people were laughing at them—and their all-powerful mayor was laughing the loudest. What they learned was that they'd inadvertently opened a can of worms, and they wanted it shut.

"This is really a good Political Science 101 example of how government really works, that a loud, vocal minority can oftentimes set the agenda," a cooled-down Joe Moore told me a week after the repeal, adding with a laugh: "I leave it to everyone's predisposition to say which side is the vocal minority. I think what you had are two relatively small groups who care passionately about the issue, and one held sway initially, and the other one held sway subsequently."

"I don't think most of the council members know any more about the ducks now than they did in the first place," I responded.

"To a large degree, that's probably true, yeah."

But everyone in the city now knew about foie gras, and suddenly they could order it just about everywhere, even though the repeal

wasn't scheduled to go into effect until June 11. If the city wasn't enforcing the ban before, it certainly wasn't going to now, so foie gras
immediately returned to menus minus the euphemisms. Tsonton
gave Copperblue's appetizer the new mouthful of a name: "'Freedom
of Choice' Foie Gras Terrine 'Thank You Mayor Daley & Alderman
Tunney' Wildflower Honeyed–Sweet Pea Jam, Toasted Yellow Mustard Seed Vinaigrette." At Cyrano's the menu read simply: "Duck
Foie Gras, Tonight's Preparation." With a typical mixture of enthusiasm and zaniness, Didier Durand reacted to the repeal's passage by
declaring, "We're going to paint the town with foie gras!" As he'd anticipated, the TV and print reporters came calling, and he conducted
his interviews with Nicolas, a green-necked mallard, at his side. (I
stopped by Cyrano's at the end of the day, and Nicolas was once again
in his cage in the rear of Durand's van, though the chef brought him
out and petted his head.) A large photo of the happy chef and his bird
was splashed across the morning papers.

Soon Durand was declaring June 11 to be "Culinary Freedom Day"
in a news release in which he wrote: "I want to commend all the Duck-
easies who have joined me 'in resistance' serving the unauthorized
liver hidden under lettuces!" The release also noted: "After this experience, Didier says, you never know what is next (another food ban?) so
he is warning all frogs to get their legs out of the way (in case Alderman Joe Moore is whipping up something 'Unfrenchy' again)."

Yes, Didier was gearing up for the frog leg wars.

My wife and I were joining three other couples for dinner in Chicago
the weekend after the city repealed the ban, so I suggested we try
somewhere known for serving foie gras just to see whether it was on
the menu. (My friends have kindly indulged me as I've done such research.) We wound up at the intimate Sweets & Savories on the North
Side, and, sure enough, of the 15 appetizers and entrées on the menu,
three boasted foie gras: a seared Hudson Valley slice with brûléed ba-
nana and chocolate sauce, a foie gras risotto that accompanied grilled
scallops, and the restaurant's signature American Kobe beef burger
with foie gras pâté and truffled mayonnaise. That burger is the dish
that Peter Sagal had immortalized in *Saveur,* so I felt duty-bound to
get it and also to share the choco-banana foie appetizer (it worked),

and when one of my friends ordered the duck-fat *frites* for the table, I couldn't help but grab a fistful. I felt like one of those French court gluttons exploring the phrase "rich as sin."

It occurred to me that I was being quite stupid, because I had a physical exam scheduled for the following morning, and I no doubt was blowing my cholesterol levels to hell with this fat bomb of a dinner. (Did I also mention the sticky toffee bread pudding with ice cream for dessert?) Truth be told, my diet had become decidedly less healthy since I'd begun my immersion into the world of foie gras. I had been intent on exploring both sides of the issue fully, but the fact was that when I explored the culinary side, I tended to eat a lot more than when I explored the animal-ethics side. Well, if I was going to deal with the consequences of foie gras, I couldn't sweat one medical exam. Besides, Didier had testified before the city council that southwest France has some of the world's lowest cholesterol levels due to the high intake of foie gras and duck fat, and I'd read pretty much the same thing in that little French foie gras museum. So, really, I should have been specimen of perfect health.

The physical went fine. My blood pressure was OK. My weight was up a bit, but I knew that, and the doctor wasn't concerned because I seemed to be getting adequate exercise. I even was half an inch taller, which I found weird, but I'll take it. "You're one of the few patients who I can't tell to do anything differently," Dr. Levine told me cheerfully. His office would call me the following day with the blood work results.

When the phone rang the next afternoon, Dr. Levine himself was at the other end, and his tone was markedly changed. He took a deep breath. My cholesterol had jumped almost 60 points, from a healthy 185 to an artery-clogging 242. "Normally I'd prescribe Lipitor for this," he said. But given what I'd told him about my recent indulgences, he said he'd retest me in three months. Meanwhile, now he *did* have something to tell me to do differently:

"You're done eating foie gras."

I didn't argue.

Epilogue

"Oh, come on!"

In Philadelphia, Hugs for Puppies bit the dust—the name, that is.

Nick Cooney finally decided that his group's cute novelty tag had run its course, so in April 2008 he redubbed the organization the Humane League of Philadelphia. "It's something I've been wanting do to for quite some time," Cooney said. "We are a professional organization and wanted to have a name that reflected that." The Humane League Web site depicts an open-beaked yellow chick looking at the viewer beneath the words "Every animal has a voice."

The summer of 2008 turned out to be far more peaceful than the previous year for Cooney and Philadelphia's restaurants. Cooney still led some anti-foie demonstrations, branching out to the suburbs, and he was able to add a few more names to his not-serving-it list, which now exceeded 50. He also discovered at least one "back-sliding" restaurant and resumed demonstrations until it once again quit serving the dish. In the fall of 2008, he was considering going after Olivier Desaintmartin's Caribou Café for including foie gras in his "duck liver pâté," which, you may recall, the chef had admitted he'd been doing all along.

But foie gras no longer was Cooney's number one concern. He was directing greater energies toward the problem that he'd always considered tops on the animal-cruelty chart: battery cages for egg-laying hens. His aim was to convince five local colleges and institutions—the largest among them the University of Pennsylvania—to switch to cage-free egg purchases. His tactics were "significantly different" from how he engaged in the foie gras battle. Stand in front of a restaurant and make a lot of noise, and you can seriously affect business, but, he said, "it's certainly not the same for a dining services at a university." Instead, the Humane League had sought low-key meetings with campus officials, faculty members and student groups to rally support.

Still, Cooney said he hadn't abandoned the foie gras fight. His group would mobilize if Councilman Jack Kelly ever pushed forward his proposed ban (which had yet to happen as of late 2008). And if the city council never took action, Cooney said, he'd consider pushing a voter referendum—because by this point Cooney had become convinced that the only chance for resolution involved legislation. "That certainly would be nice, to have some closure."

As for the efficacy of continued demonstrations, he said, "most of the restaurants that served foie gras have made a decision one way or another, and at this point I don't think they're going to change." So the Humane League didn't bother returning to Le Bec-Fin or the London Grill, although the group's ACLU lawyers continued challenging the restrictiveness of the London Grill's injunction, due to expire in late 2008.

What Cooney didn't know was that the London Grill had removed foie gras from its menu over the summer anyway. "We just couldn't afford it," sighed Terry McNally. "It's hard to push foie gras in these times." With the economy so weak, many restaurants were struggling, so the London Grill lowered prices across the board. Terry and ex-husband/chef Michael McNally were able to make the hanger steak more affordable by taking away the accompanying foie gras–green peppercorn butter. Still, she said, the London Grill hadn't banned foie gras. "I'm looking forward to bringing it back in the winter."

At Hudson Valley Foie Gras, the experiment worked. For its first 28 years, the farm kept the ducks in gavage for 28 days, but in the second half of 2008, it was transitioning the birds into 21-day force-feeding periods. Izzy Yanay said the feedings remained three times daily, the food itself was unchanged, and the ducks ultimately ate a little less than over the 28-day feedings. The biggest difference? "The pacing," he said. "That's basically it."

The other big difference would be to the company's bottom line.

The resultant livers were "slightly smaller," Izzy said, but that was no big deal because "if you don't pay for another week, you save much more money than what you'd get from that shading of the liver that you lose." What's more, the farm had been trying out the abbreviated feeding schedules over the summer, when the heat typically triggers more duck deaths, but Izzy said the mortality rate actually dropped to 1.8 percent (from its usual 3 percent or so). Losing fewer birds was good for business, and it certainly couldn't hurt Hudson Valley's efforts to be recognized as a humane product.

The farm was still trying to clear up those sores on the ducks' feet, and Izzy remained hopeful that down the line Hudson Valley Foie Gras could be officially deemed humane. In the meantime, the company's "cage free" campaign was getting out the message that the farm's ducks didn't live in the cramped conditions frequently shown in animal-rights literature and videos. These efforts were having some impact; even someone from Wolfgang Puck's Spago had given the product a second look, though Puck ultimately stuck with his no-foie policy. In Chicago, Michael Tsonton's Copperblue changed the name of its foie appetizer once again to Hudson Valley Farm "Cage Free" Foie Gras Terrine.

Tsonton, by the way, said he had been fielding even more orders for foie gras now than before the Chicago ban "because more people know about it." Had he received any protests for serving the dish since the ban was reversed? "Not at all," he said. "Zero." Tim Doyle at European Imports said his foie gras sales in Chicago nonetheless were down about 30 percent compared to the pre-ban days, though he blamed the economy and restaurants' overall struggles.

Chicago didn't go down the path of Philadelphia and other cities where activists demonstrated against restaurants to force foie gras's removal. After the respective joy, relief and fury (depending on one's position) over the city council's repeal of its ban, the issue all but disappeared in Chicago. People seemed sick of even talking about it.

But just as the nation's third largest city was closing the book on its foie gras war, the nation's biggest one was writing another chapter. Fresh from his announcement that he was running for mayor of New York City, Councilman Tony Avella proposed on June 11, 2008, a city ordinance supporting a pending state senate bill that would prohibit the force-feeding of birds to enlarge their livers (without actually banning foie gras's sale). That same day, the mayoral candidate appeared on WNYC's *The Brian Lehrer Show* to debate his bill's merits with Michael Ginor of Hudson Valley Foie Gras.

Here are some choice snippets:

AVELLA: You're literally blowing food into the stomach in order to artificially enlarge the liver. I mean, this is extremely painful to the animal and really is animal cruelty. The industry should be ashamed of itself.

GINOR: The councilman has mentioned that the process is painful, and he mentioned there's food that is blown through a huge tube. Unfortunately none of those words are accurate whatsoever in describing the process.

AVELLA: They push the metal pipe down into the animal's stomach, and they literally, through compressed air, force huge amounts of food into the duck's stomach.

GINOR: Every single thing that Mr. Avella just said is factually, completely incorrect, false, and I would welcome him to visit the farm one day. I just wish that before people go out and try to make such drastic economic changes and take the livelihood of 200 employees in a New York state company, that they would at least do the minimal, the minimal research before just jumping on a bandwagon.

AVELLA: The truth is, they are doing this inhumane cruelty to the animal. Let them feed the animals normally. Let them feed as though they would on their own. And if they could still do foie gras under that circumstance, fine.

GINOR: It's very, very difficult to have an intelligent discussion with someone who knows so little about the subject.

AVELLA: Oh, come on!

Avella made his announcement the same week that one of the sponsors of the state bill, Assemblyman Michael Benjamin, withdrew his support for the ban. He told Bloomberg News that after visiting Hudson Valley Foie Gras, he no longer thought its feeding methods were inhumane. "I had a change of heart," he said. The ensuing months saw no further action on either the city or state measure.

Meanwhile, Ariane Daguin and the domestic foie gras producers were hoping to convince California to repeal its 2012 ban. But that state already was facing a large animal-related vote on the November 2008 ballot: Proposition 2, the Standards for Confining Farm Animals initiative to prohibit veal crates, sow gestation crates and hen battery cages. Paul Shapiro and the Humane Society of the United States had spearheaded that measure, seen as a potential landmark in the battle against factory farming, and that's where the animal-rights movement's energies were being channeled. A revival of the foie gras fight in California would have to wait. (Yes, Prop 2 passed.)

So Guillermo Gonzalez continued making his Artisan Foie Gras—he estimated producing 60,000 to 70,000 ducks by the end of 2008—while investigating the possibility of starting another business completely unrelated to animal agriculture. "I am really tired of being in a niche and controversial activity," he said. "I'm proud of it. I know exactly what I'm doing. I'm completely at ease and at peace with myself, but it's not pleasant to live a life when people are picking on you and bullying you all the time."

He said he didn't plan on closing his business before 2012, but he also wasn't going to continue to fight without much broader industry support. "I am not going to stand alone," he said. "I came to the States to pursue a better life, the American dream, through hard work, and now Americans are trying to take it away from me. That's the reality."

When I spoke with Charlie Trotter in early fall 2008, he sounded amazed that I (or anyone else) was still talking about foie gras. Toward the beginning of the decade he'd quietly dropped one ingredient from his repertoire. Now he continued to be associated with that ingredient and a whole lot of turmoil. He hadn't budged from his original assessment of how the delicacy is produced, but he had other things on his plate. After all, said Trotter, "I'm just a simple guy trying to make a living."

My three months between blood tests were up, and I returned to Dr. Levine's office, rolled up my sleeve and looked the other way as the needle went in. I hadn't touched foie gras over that time. I'd also mostly laid off ice cream, French fries, cheese and rich desserts while eating a lot more oatmeal and high-fiber bread.

The verdict?

"Better," he said over the phone the next day.

My overall cholesterol level was back down to 200—still borderline high and 15 points above where it used to be, but I was relieved that I'd shed 42 points in three months. Plus, the bulk of that drop was in "bad" cholesterol, which went from 172 to 138. I still had much room for improvement, but I had emerged from code red. Moderation could once again be my guide, and whether to eat foie gras was no longer strictly a medical question. It was up to me to decide.

Sources

The bulk of this book was researched through interviews with the players involved, in person when possible. I also benefited from video and audio recordings of governmental hearings, as well as, for instance, Terry McNally's camcorder chronicling of protests outside the London Grill. In addition, I viewed much footage shot on foie gras farms, edited and unedited, plus various TV news reports on the controversy, some of which can be found online as videos or printed transcriptions.

The edited videos I watched included:

Delicacy of Despair, GourmetCruelty.com
Foie Gras: Culinary Cruelty, Farm Sanctuary
*The Foie Gras Assembly Line: Exposing Cruelty Inside Elevages Perigord,
    Canada's Largest Foie Gras Producer*, Farm Sanctuary
Inside Sonoma Foie Gras, StopForceFeeding.com
Victims of Indulgence, People for the Ethical Treatment of Animals
The 2005 PETA video narrated by Roger Moore (no title as far as I
    can tell)
Assorted short French industry videos from www.foiegras-factsand
    truth.com

By the way, if you'd like to watch Jeremy Clarkson and André and Ariane Daguin eating ortolan, you can do so by finding the appropriate 2002 clip of *Jeremy Clarkson Meets the Neighbours* on YouTube.

Some accounts of events and arguments were aided by court documents such as the Israeli Supreme Court's 2003 decision in the case of "Noah" vs. The Attorney General (and others); copies of Humane Society of the United States lawsuits against Hudson Valley Foie Gras; a New York State Department of Environmental Conservation report regarding violations by Hudson Valley Foie Gras; a transcription of the July 12, 2007, hearing on London Grill's injunction request against Hugs for Puppies; restraining orders filed against Nick Cooney and other activists in cases involving Huntingdon Life Sciences; and filings in Sonoma Foie Gras's lawsuit against Whole Foods Market.

Early in the process, I signed up for Google Alerts regarding foie gras, little suspecting the avalanche of news stories and updates that would wind up in my inbox daily. Thanks to the Internet, I was able to access an international array of newspaper stories and Web reports and opinion pieces about foie gras. Over the course of my research, I printed out a few file drawers' worth of such reports, which are too numerous to mention here. In particular, though, I'd like to acknowledge coverage in the *Philadelphia Inquirer* (particularly by Michael Klein) and *Philadelphia Daily News* (with several columns by Stu Bykofsky), Peter Sagal's "Let Them Eat Pâté" in the October 2007 issue of *Saveur*, Michael Specter's illuminating *New Yorker* profile of PETA founder Ingrid Newkirk ("The Extremist: The woman behind the most successful radical group in America," Apr. 14, 2003) and the dozens of stories that the *Chicago Tribune* and *Sun-Times* contributed to the foie gras record. My own reporting for the *Tribune* on this issue included "Liver and let live" (March 29, 2005), "Trotter won't turn down heat in foie gras flap" (April 7, 2005), "Although Charlie Trotter had visited foie gras farms . . ." (October 5, 2005), "Foie Gras Finale?" (with Phil Vettel, August 10, 2006), "Lovers of liver may taste victory after all" (with Gary Washburn, September 12, 2006), "The search for foie gras proves foggy" (September 21, 2006), "'Gentlemen, start your ranges'" (February 11, 2007) and "Daley special: Foie gras back on the menu" (with Dan Mihalopoulos, May 15, 2008). The news items in the "Dispatches" sections came from various sources, including the *Seattle Post-Intelligencer, China View, Austin American-Statesman,* CTV, Salt Lake

City's *Deseret Morning News,* Caterersearch, *The Oregonian,* Drinks Media Wire, London's *Daily Mail* and wire-service reports.

The historical passages of the second chapter ("Animals vs. Appetites") made use of several books that trace foie gras back to its ancient roots. Of particular help was Michael A. Ginor's *Foie Gras: A Passion* (Wiley, 1999), which provides the most comprehensive English-language overview that I've found, and Silvano Serventi's *Le Foie Gras* (Flammarion, 2005), which would have been useless to me without Michaela DeSoucey's French translation work. Her own as-yet-unpublished account of foie gras's history also was helpful.

Other books that informed this work:

Katherine Alford, *Caviar, Truffles, and Foie Gras* (Chronicle Books, 2001)

Gene Baur, *Farm Sanctuary* (Touchstone, 2008)

Henri Combret, *Foie Gras Tentations* (Editions Henri Combret, 2004)

Curnonsky, *Larousse Traditional French Cooking* (Doubleday, 1989)

André Daguin and Anne de Ravel, *Foie Gras, Magret, and Other Good Food from Gascony* (Random House, 1988)

Ariane Daguin, George Faison, and Joanna Pruess, *D'Artagnan's Glorious Game Cookbook* (Little, Brown, 1999)

Alan Davidson (Tom Jaine, ed.), *The Oxford Companion to Food,* 2nd ed. (Oxford University Press, 1999/2006)

André Dominé (ed.), *Culinaria France* (Könemann, 2004)

Thomas Hardy, *Jude the Obscure* (numerous publishers, 1895)

Tankred Koch (ed. and trans. from German by Bernard H. Skold and Louis DeVries), *Anatomy of the Chicken and Domestic Birds* (The Iowa State University Press, 1973)

Jenifer Harvey Lang (ed.), *Larousse Gastronomique: The New American Edition of the World's Greatest Culinary Encyclopedia* (Crown, 1988)

Stephen Mennell, *All Manners of Food: Eating and Taste in England and France from the Middle Ages to the Present* (University of Illinois Press, 1996)

Michael Pollan, *The Omnivore's Dilemma* (The Penguin Press, 2006)

Waverly Root, *The Food of France* (Vintage, 1958)

Eric Schlosser, *Fast Food Nation* (Houghton Mifflin, 2001)

Matthew Scully, *Dominion* (St. Martin's Griffin, 2002)

Peter Singer, *Animal Liberation* (Ecco, 1975/2002)

Peter Singer and Jim Mason, *The Ethics of What We Eat* (Rodale, 2006)

Keith Thomas, *Man and the Natural World* (Pantheon, 1983)

Charlie Trotter, *Charlie Trotter's Meat & Game* (Ten Speed Press, 2001)

Paula Wolfert, *The Cooking of Southwest France* (Wiley, 2005)

In addition, I was able to access certain works online, such as those vivid recipes described in Giambattista della Porta's 16th century series *Magia Naturalis* and the 15th century French cookery book *The Vivendier* (translated by Terence Scully, Prospect Books, 1997). These and many more glimpses into the colorful worlds of medieval and Renaissance cuisine (for example, "*Coqz Heaumez*—A roast chicken, dressed in helmet, shield, and lance, rides upon a pig") can be found at the Web site for Gode Cookery (www.godecookery.com), particularly in the section dubbed "Incredible Foods, Solteties, and Entremets." Information about Richard Wiseman and the British Association for the Advancement of Science's humor study can be found at www.laughlab.co.uk. For Matthew Diffee's essay on why ducks are the funniest bird, go to this link to the Huffington Post: http://www.huffingtonpost.com/matthew-diffee/finally-i-have-an-opinio_b_36888.html.

For scientific, medical and technical information, I interviewed and reviewed the public testimony of numerous experts (such as adversarial veterinarians Holly Cheever and Lawrence W. Bartholf) and reviewed additional materials sent my way (such as duck necropsy reports). I spoke to representatives of the foie gras and greater poultry industries and also read an assortment of academic papers, studies and reports, among them:

Jean-Michel Faure, Daniel Guémené, Gérard Guy, "Is there avoidance of the force feeding procedure in ducks and geese?" INRA, EDP Sciences, 2001

D. Guémené and G. Guy, "The past, present and future of force-feeding and 'foie gras' production," *World's Poultry Science Journal*, 2004

Daniel Guémené, Gérard Guy, Jacques Servière and Jean-Michel Faure, "Force Feeding: An Examination of Available Scientific Evidence," 2006

G. B. Havenstein, P.R. Ferket and M. A. Qureshi, "Growth, Livability, and Feed Conversion of 1957 Versus 2001 Broilers When Fed Representative 1957 and 2001 Broiler Diets," *Poultry Science*, 2003

Alan Solomon, Tina Richey, Charles L. Murphy, Deborah T. Weiss, Jonathan S. Wall, Gunilla T. Westermark and Per Westermark, "Amyloidogenic potential of foie gras," Proceedings of the National Academy of Sciences of the United States of America, January 2007

Mariann Sullivan and David J. Wolfson, "What's Good for the Good . . . The Israeli Supreme Court, Foie Gras, and the Future of Farmed Animals in the United States," Law and Contemporary Problems, Duke Law School, 2007

Tiffany Prather and Dr. Frank Flanders, "Layer Hen House Production: Which Came First, the Chicken or the Egg?" Georgia Agriculture Education Curriculum

U.S. Poultry & Egg Association, "Poultry Industry Frequently Asked Questions"

"Welfare Aspects of the Production of Foie Gras in Ducks and Geese," Report of the Scientific Committee on Animal Health and Animal Welfare (for the European Union), adopted December 16, 1998

"The Welfare of Ducks and Geese in Foie Gras Production: A Summary of the Scientific and Empirical Evidence," A Farm Sanctuary Report

David Wolfson and Mariann Sullivan, "Foxes in the Henhouse: Animals, Agribusiness, and the Law: A Modern American Fable," *Animal Rights: Current Debates and New Directions,* edited by Cass R. Sunstein and Martha C. Nussbaum (Oxford University Press, 2004)

I was present for much of what I describe, and when there was no written, video or audio record available of certain events, I tried my best to piece together what happened from recollections and observations of those who were there. Reconstructing past events, whether ancient or recent, is an inexact science, and the portrayal of events here is inevitably a product of whom I did and didn't interview (or read or observe) as well as my own way of processing this information. I appreciate the vast resources made available for my research and take full responsibility for any mistakes that might become apparent to me only after this book is closed.

Acknowledgments

"Thanks."

My adventures in foie gras started on a spring day in 2005, when *Chicago Tribune* restaurant critic Phil Vettel suggested I write about Charlie Trotter's decision to quit serving the dish. I had little idea that this story would land on page 1, even less inkling that I'd wind up immersing myself in the culture, ethics and politics of fat livers. I'm grateful for Phil's generosity and ongoing support as well as that of other *Tribune* colleagues and friends, among them Scott Powers, Carmel Carrillo, Monica Eng, Charlie Storch, Ray Gibson, Gary Washburn, and Nancy Stone.

I couldn't have written this book without the cooperation of many chefs, activists, farmers and politicians who shared their time and knowledge without losing their patience with a writer who started off far from an expert on these topics. First on that list is Trotter, who shared his opinions in typically blunt, colorful fashion and didn't disappear when the heat was turned up. Rick Tramonto, Trotter's foil in this debate, was unfailingly gracious whether over the phone or in person. Other Chicago chefs providing much help and expertise included the ever-enthusiastic Didier Durand, who made a much-appreciated introduction to Michel Guérard; Jean Joho, who set me up with chefs in Strasbourg and Colmar; Michael Lachowicz, who demonstrated the art of preparing foie gras in his fine restaurant that shares his first name; Michael Tsonton, always candid in his advocacy against the Chicago ban; plus Paul Virant, Graham Elliot Bowles, Bill Kim, Carrie Nahabedian, Jean Banchet, Sarah Stegner, Grant Achatz,

"Hot" Doug Sohn, Efrain Cuevas and Turtle Soup founder Dave Thomas.

While we're in Chicago, let me also thank Alderman Joe Moore, who was consistently accessible and amiable, as well as Ed Burke, Ed Smith, Tom Tunney and other aldermen and lobbyists who took time to provide behind-the-headlines insights into the legislative battle. Thanks also to Rabbi Peter Knobel for his ever-wise perspective and to some folks at that rarely recognized but vital part of the gourmet food chain, the distributors: Tim Doyle at European Imports, Peter Andrews at Chicago Game & Gourmet and Nick Sahlas at Pasture to Plate.

Animal advocates often get painted with the broad brush of extremism, but even the most dedicated of vegans proved to be open and immensely helpful to this trying-to-be-ethical meat eater. At Farm Sanctuary, Gene Baur, Tricia Barry and Susie Coston spent hours with me at the Watkins Glen farm, and Baur and Barry also were quick to answer numerous queries that came up over an extended period of time. I'm also grateful to Norm Scott at Farm Sanctuary for supplying video and audio copies of key governmental hearings. Bryan Pease of the Animal Protection and Rescue League filled in numerous gaps with me over more than three years and provided many useful materials. Despite his reputation among some Philadelphia restaurateurs, Nick Cooney of the Humane League of Philadelphia (formerly Hugs for Puppies) was unfailingly respectful and willing to have his views challenged over a long afternoon in Philadelphia and many conversations beforehand and afterward.

Paul Shapiro and Jonathan Lovvorn at the Humane Society of the United States were generous with insights and documents, as were Paul's brother Ryan and Sarahjane Blum of GourmetCruelty.com. Thanks also to Ingrid Newkirk and Bruce Friedrich at People for the Ethical Treatment of Animals, veterinarian Holly Cheever, Chicago-based activist Jana Kohl and French activist Antoine Comiti. David Wolfson and Mariann Sullivan's writings do as comprehensive a job as I've seen of placing foie gras in the context of greater factory-farming and legal issues, and I particularly appreciated Wolfson's candor and intelligence in helping me weigh these matters. Throughout my interviews with all of these people, I played devil's advocate a fair amount, and they invariably responded with reason rather than defensiveness.

The same was true of the foie gras farmers, producers and promoters who let me into their world. Sonoma Foie Gras's Guillermo Gonzalez was the first farmer to host me, and he set a tone of openness that is far from the norm at your average factory farm. Hudson Valley Foie Gras's Izzy Yanay was patient, good humored and refreshingly unfiltered as he showed me around his farm on two separate trips, let me tag along on his excursion to Kohler, Wisconsin, and answered many phone calls. His partner, Michael Ginor, proved keen on digging into the ethical/philosophical issues while sharing time with me in Chicago and Philadelphia, and also in Great Neck, New York. Marcus Henley, Rick Bishop and veterinarian Lawrence Bartholf also provided great assistance. I'm grateful as well to Christian Gasset and Liz Gibson-Gasset, who made me feel at home at their small southeastern Minnesota farm, Au Bon Canard.

D'Artagnan owner Ariane Daguin proved an invaluable resource with her encyclopedic knowledge of the business and the culinary and cultural angles of foie gras. Many chefs could have learned much from the cooking demonstration she gave me in the D'Artagnan kitchen. Thanks also to Dan Barber and Irene Hamburger at Stone Barns, Anthony Bourdain, Laurent Manrique, Daniel Guéméne, Robert Dantzer, Ed Schiltz, Temple Grandin, culinary historian Cathy Kaufman and Israeli Supreme Court justices Asher Grunis, Tova Strasberg-Cohen and Eliezer Rivlin.

In Philadelphia, I owe a big shout-out to the London Grill gang, particularly the hospitable and spirited Terry McNally, Michael McNally and Jenny Holcomb. Thanks also to Stu Bykofsky at the *Philadelphia Daily News*, Councilman Jack Kelly, Emilio Mignucci of DiBruno Bros. grocery and Philadelphia chefs Georges Perrier, David Ansill, Olivier Desaintmartin, Jose Garces and Douglas Rodriguez.

In France, I'm indebted to two families that, although they may routinely open their homes and farms to tourists, nonetheless far exceeded their duties in filling me with knowledge and sustenance: Danie, Guy and Gilles Dubois; and Myriam Daubas and her father, Claude Fieux. Michel and Christine Guérard couldn't have been more charming or gracious at their resort, Les Prés d'Eugénie, and

Michel happily fielded questions before preparing his ultimate foie gras menu. Special thanks also to André Daguin for welcoming me into his Auch home; Guy de Saint Laurent for providing a comprehensive tour of Rougie, complete with tastings; chefs Emile Jung at Au Crocodile in Strasbourg and Jean Yves Schillinger in Colmar for sharing their culinary talents and insights; French foie gras industry leader (and owner of the Strasbourg company Edouard Artzner) Jean Schwebel for taking a long meeting on a Saturday morning; and documentarian Jimmy Leipold for swapping insights as we traveled sometimes-parallel paths.

Closer to home, I'm blessed with a wonderful network of friends and family members who have offered consistent support, encouragement and constructive criticism. Jimmy Guterman and Stuart Shea are lifelong friends who read everything promptly and provided invaluable feedback. Jim Powers and Lou Carlozo gave me numerous boosts throughout this process, as did the rest of the Hungerdungers writers' group: James Finn Garner, Jonathan Eig and Pat Byrnes. Thanks also to Alec Harris and Carollina Song, Ruth Masters and Loren Williams, Jennifer Atkins and Alvaro Donado, Peter Canellos, Charlie Gofen, Ellen Flax, David Frankel and two writers who inspired me to get going: Stefan Fatsis and Robert Kurson. William and Joan Caro, Judy and James Dixon, and my brother, David, were much-appreciated cheerleaders. My late mother, Ruth Caro, continued to inspire me as my first writing role model and most nurturing fan.

I can't imagine how this book might have come out if I hadn't crossed paths with Michaela DeSoucey at a food conference in Chicago. She too was writing a foie gras book—her sociology Ph.D. dissertation at Northwestern University—and we quickly realized that as the two most foie-obsessed writers in Chicago (if not the country), we'd benefit greatly by working together. My France trip, as planned and executed, would have been an impossibility without her translating abilities and overall France know-how, and throughout the process she was a most energetic, curious, well-informed colleague. I also doubt I could've finished this book if not for the stalwart efforts of Northwestern journalism undergrads Perry Gattegno, Mindy Yahr and Sarah Tompkins, who transcribed many hours of interviews while serving as enthusiastic, intelligent sounding boards.

Various coffee houses gave me an office away from home when I needed a change of scenery, and in particular I'd like to raise my cup to Peet's Coffee and Tea in Evanston, where the baristas pull a terrific traditional cappuccino and are very nice.

I've known Robert Shepard since I was a green up-and-comer at the *Daily Pennsylvanian* (at the University of Pennsylvania), and he was already the distinguished news editor emeritus. He's a supremely smart, dedicated word person and a warm, caring friend—qualities I wouldn't necessarily have associated with an agent. Thanks, Robert, for taking me on, encouraging me to tackle this project and allowing my writing to benefit from your excellent eye and mind.

I'm also grateful that Robert found Denise Roy at Simon & Schuster. While others were asking me, "You're writing a book about *what?* An *entire book?*" she clicked onto my wavelength from the start. She was always positive without sacrificing candor, and she sweated the details. I couldn't have asked for more from her or the rest of the S&S team.

Finally, I must bow down to my wife, Mary Dixon, and two daughters, Ruth and Madeline, who kept the boat afloat while daddy was getting bogged down in duck livers and deadlines. Thanks, honey, for reading me better than anyone. Thanks, girls, for telling my duck jokes better than I do. Thanks, all of you, for keeping it together and keeping me together. I'll make dinner tonight.

Speaking of dinner, I'd be remiss if I didn't also thank a huge, perpetually taken-for-granted population: the billions of animals that feed most of us. Without them, the world food system wouldn't exist in its current form. How much this is a positive or negative thing, I leave to you.

Index

About the Author

Mark **Caro** is a longtime *Chicago Tribune* reporter whose writing on the foie gras controversy received honors from the James Beard Foundation and the Association of Food Journalists. He lives in the Chicago area with his wife and two daughters.